Via Veneto

Piazza di Spagna

Piazza della Rotonda

Quirinal

⑬

⑧

⑩

Esquiline

⑨

Capitol

Forum

⑪

Palatine

⑫

Lateran

⑭

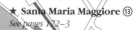

Caracalla

Aventine

Santa Maria in Trastevere ⑤

EYEWITNESS TRAVEL GUIDES

ROME

LONDON, NEW YORK,
MELBOURNE, MUNICH AND DELHI
www.dk.com

PROJECT EDITOR Fiona Wild
ART EDITOR Annette Jacobs
EDITORS Ferdie McDonald, Mark Ronan, Anna Streiffert
DESIGNER Lisa Kosky
DESIGN ASSISTANT Marisa Renzullo
PICTURE RESEARCH Catherine O'Rourke
RESEARCH IN ROME Sam Cole
DTP EDITOR Siri Lowe

MAIN CONTRIBUTORS
Olivia Ercoli, Ros Belford, Roberta Mitchell

PHOTOGRAPHERS
John Heseltine, Mike Dunning, Kim Sayer

ILLUSTRATORS
Studio Illibill, Kevin Jones Associates,
Martin Woodward, Robbie Polley

This book was produced with the assistance of
Websters International Publishers.

Reproduced by Colourscan, Singapore
Printed and bound by South China Printing Co. Ltd., China

First published in Great Britain in 1993
by Dorling Kindersley Limited
80 Strand, London WC2R 0RL
Reprinted with revisions 2001, 2002, 2003, 2004, 2005

FLOORS ARE REFERRED TO THROUGHOUT IN
ACCORDANCE WITH EUROPEAN USAGE; IE THE "FIRST FLOOR"
IS THE FLOOR ABOVE GROUND LEVEL.

**The information in this Dorling Kindersley
Travel Guide is checked annually.**
Every effort has been made to ensure that this book is as up-to-
date as possible at the time of going to press. Some details,
however, such as telephone numbers, opening hours, prices,
gallery hanging arrangements and travel information, are liable
to change. The publishers cannot accept responsibility for
any consequences arising from the use of this book, nor for
any material on third party websites, and cannot guarantee
that any website address in this book will be a suitable source
of travel information. We value the views and suggestions of
our readers very highly. Please write to: Publisher,
DK Eyewitness Travel Guides, Dorling Kindersley,
80 Strand, London WC2R 0RL, Great Britain.

CONTENTS

HOW TO USE
THIS GUIDE 6

Colosseum

INTRODUCING
ROME

Moses by Michelangelo in
San Pietro in Vincoli

The basilica of St Peter's in the Vatican City

HOW TO USE THIS GUIDE

THIS EYEWITNESS TRAVEL GUIDE helps you get the most from your stay in Rome with the minimum of practical difficulty. The opening section, *Introducing Rome*, locates the city geographically, sets modern Rome in its historical context and explains how Roman life changes through the year. *Rome at a Glance* is an overview of the city's attractions. The main sightseeing section, *Rome Area by Area*, starts on page 62. It describes all the important sights with maps, photographs and detailed illustrations. In addition, six planned walks take you to parts of Rome you might otherwise miss.

Carefully researched tips for hotels, shops and markets, restaurants and cafés, sports and entertainment are found in *Travellers' Needs*, and the *Survival Guide* has advice on everything from posting a letter to catching the Metro.

ROME AREA BY AREA

The chapters covering the 16 central sightseeing areas are indicated by colour-coded bars. Each chapter opens with a portrait of the area and a list of the sights to be covered. These are located by numbers on an *Area Map*. This is followed by a large-scale *Street-by-Street Map* focusing on the most interesting part of the area. The main body of the chapter consists of detailed descriptions of all the sights. Finding your way about the chapter is made simple by a consistent numbering system used throughout for the sights. This refers to the order in which they are described in the chapter.

Sights at a Glance lists the sights in the area by category: Churches and Temples, Museums and Galleries, Historic Streets and Piazzas, Historic Buildings, Arches and Gates, Columns, Obelisks and Statues, Fountains, Ancient Sites and Parks and Gardens.

The area covered in greater detail on the *Street-by-Street Map* is shaded red.

Numbered circles pinpoint all the listed sights on the *Area Map*. Palazzo Doria Pamphilj, for example, is **6**.

1 Area Map

For easy reference, the sights in each area are numbered and located on a map of the area. To help the visitor, the map also shows Metro stations and parking areas.

Photographs of distinctive details of buildings help you to identify the sights.

Colour-coding on each page makes the area easy to find in the book.

PIAZZA DELLA ROTONDA

SIGHTS AT A GLANCE

2 Street-by-Street Map

This gives a bird's-eye view of the heart of each sightseeing area. To help you locate and identify important sights as you walk around, these are picked out in stronger colour.

A locator map shows you exactly where you are in relation to surrounding areas. The area shown in the *Street-by-Street Map* is marked in red.

Palazzo Doria Pamphilj 6 is shown on this map as well.

A suggested route for a walk takes in the most interesting and attractive streets in the area.

Stars indicate the sights that no visitor should miss.

Travel tips help you to reach the area quickly.

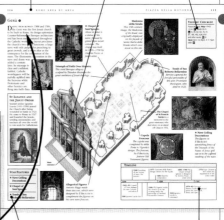

ROME AT A GLANCE

Each map in this section covers a specific theme: *Churches and Temples, Museums and Galleries, Fountains and Obelisks, Celebrated Visitors and Residents.* The top sights are shown on the map; other sights are described on the following two pages.

Each sightseeing area is colour-coded.

The theme is explored in greater detail on the two pages following the map.

3 Detailed Information on Each Sight

All the important sights in each area are described individually. They are listed in order, following the numbering on the Area Map. Practical information is also provided.

4 Rome's Major Sights

These are given two or more full pages in the sightseeing area in which they are found. Historic buildings are dissected to reveal their interiors, and museums and galleries have colour-coded floorplans to help you find important exhibits.

PRACTICAL INFORMATION

Each entry provides all the information needed to visit the sight. A key to the symbols used is inside the back cover.

Map reference to *Street Finder* at back of book

Sight number

Telephone number

Address

Palazzo Doria Pamphilj ❻

Piazza del Collegio Romano 2.
Map 5 A4 & 12 E3. **☎** 06-679 73 23.
🚍 64, 81, 85, 117, 119, 492 and many other routes. **Open** 10am–5pm Fri–Wed.
Closed 25 Dec, 1 Jan, 1 May, 15 Aug.
Adm charge. **♿** limited. **📷** compulsory for private apartments. **🅿**

Opening hours

Useful bus routes

Services and facilities available

The Visitors' Checklist provides the practical information you will need to plan your visit.

The façade of each major sight is shown to help you spot it quickly.

Stars indicate the most interesting architectural details of the building, and the most important works of art or exhibits on view inside

A timeline charts the key events in the history of the building.

Putting Rome on the Map

Sᴵɴᴄᴇ ɪᴛs ꜰᴏᴜɴᴅᴀᴛɪᴏɴ over 2,700 years ago on seven hills near the banks of the River Tiber, Rome has grown into a city of three million people covering 1,500 sq km (580 sq miles) of central Italy. Within this area is the independent Vatican City State. Rome was made capital of the newly united Italy in 1870. It is about 28 km (17 miles) from the sea and has good rail and road links to many other historic Italian towns and cities.

Key

☐ Rome and Environs

— Main railway

✈ Airport

═ Motorway

═ A Road

| 0 kilometres | 50 |
| 0 miles | 25 |

Pisa

Arno

Livorno

Firenze (Florence)

Siena   *326*

Arezz

Isola d'Elba

Lago di Bolsena

Vite

Tarqu

Civitavecchia ●

(Vatican City) Ci

Aerial view looking north over Isola Tiberina

M A R

T I R R E

(TYRRHENIAN S

EUROPE   NORWAY   SWEDEN   FINLAND   ESTONIA   RUSSIAN FED.   LATVIA   LITHUANIA   DENMARK   RUSSIAN FED.   BELORUSSIA   REPUBLIC OF IRELAND   UNITED KINGDOM   NETHERLANDS   POLAND   BELGIUM   GERMANY   LUXEMBOURG   CZECH REPUBLIC   UKRAINE   FRANCE   SLOVAKIA   SWITZERLAND   AUSTRIA   HUNGARY   SLOVENIA   CROATIA   ROMANIA   ITALY   BOSNIA AND HERZEGOVINA   SERBIA & MONTENEGRO   BULGARIA   Rome   ALBANIA   PORTUGAL   SPAIN   GREECE   ALGERIA   TUNISIA

Europe

Rome is in southern Europe, on the same line of latitude as New York. It has two airports and is about 3 hours' flying time from London. Rome is also linked to the rest of Europe by road and rail. It is about 15 hours from Paris by train. It is also at the centre of Italy's main road network, parts of which follow the routes of ancient Roman roads.

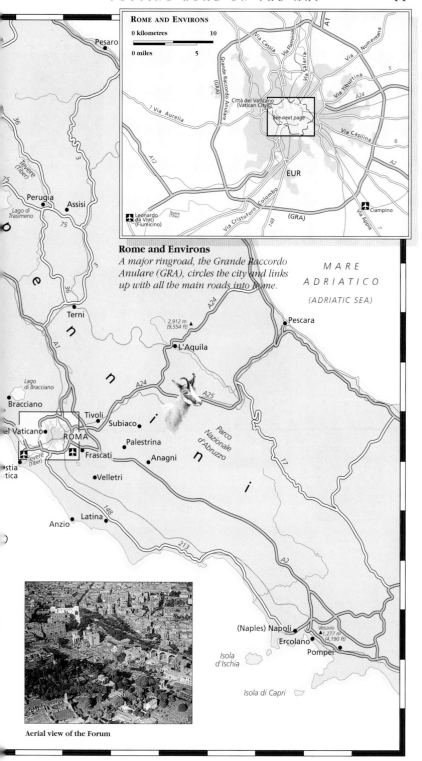

Rome and Environs

*A major ringroad, the Grande Raccordo
Anulare (GRA), circles the city and links
up with all the main roads into Rome.*

ROME AND ENVIRONS

0 kilometres   10

0 miles   5

1 Via Aurelia

Grande Raccordo Anulare (GRA)

Via Cassia

Via Flaminia

A1

Via Nomentana

Via Salaria

Via Tiburtina

A24

Città del Vaticano
(Vatican City)

See next page

Via Casilina

A12

EUR

Ciampino

Via Cristoforo Colombo

Tevere
(Tiber)

(GRA)

Via Appia

148

Leonardo
da Vinci
(Fiumicino)

MARE
ADRIATICO

(ADRIATIC SEA)

Pesaro

Perugia

Assisi

Lago di
Trasimeno

Tevere
(Tiber)

36

75

3

A1

Terni

A24

2,912 m
(9,554 ft)

L'Aquila

Pescara

Lago
di Bracciano

Bracciano

A24

A25

Tivoli

Subiaco

el Vaticano

ROMA

Tevere
(Tiber)

Frascati

Palestrina

Anagni

Parco
Nazionale
d'Abruzzo

stia
tica

Velletri

17

148

Latina

Anzio

213

A2

(Naples) Napoli

Ercolano

Vesuvio
1,277 m
(4,190 ft)

Pompei

Isola
d'Ischia

Isola di Capri

Aerial view of the Forum

Central Rome

M OST OF THE SIGHTS described in this book lie within the old city wall in 16 areas shown on the map below. Each of the areas has its own chapter. If you are on a short visit, you may have to restrict yourself to just a few of the central areas: the Forum to see ancient Rome; the Capitol, Piazza della Rotonda and Piazza Navona for the historic centre of the city; Campo de' Fiori for its grand Renaissance palazzi; Piazza di Spagna for its reminders of the 18th-century Grand Tour and its smart modern shops; and the Vatican to see St Peter's and the centre of Roman Catholicism.

PAGES 128–41
Street Finder maps
4, 5

PAGES 222–49
Street Finder maps
3, 4

PAGES 116–27
Street Finder maps
4, 11, 12

PAGES 142–53
Street Finder maps
4, 8, 11, 12

0 metres   500
0 yards   500

Vatican

Piazza a Spagna

Piazza Navona

Piazza della Rotonda

T I B E R

Campo de' Fiori

Janiculum

Trastevere

PAGES 214–21
Street Finder maps
3, 4, 7, 11

PAGES 206–13
Street Finder maps
4, 7, 8, 11

PAGES 102–15
Street Finder maps
4, 5, 12

PAGES 198–205
Street Finder maps
7, 8, 12

PAGES 154–65
Street Finder maps 5, 6, 12

PAGES 250–55
Street Finder maps 5, 6

PAGES 64–75
Street Finder maps 5, 12

PAGES 166–75
Street Finder maps 5, 6

PAGES 76–95
Street Finder maps 5, 8, 9, 12

PAGES 96–101
Street Finder map 8

PAGES 188–97
Street Finder maps 8, 9

PAGES 176–87
Street Finder maps 6, 9, 10

Via Veneto

Quirinal

apitol

Forum

Palatine

ventine

Caracalla

Esquiline

Lateran

Rome's Early Development

ACCORDING TO THE HISTORIAN Livy, Romulus founded
Rome in 753 BC. Sometime later, realizing his tribe
was short of females, he invited the neighbouring
Sabines to a festival, and orchestrated the mass
abduction of their women. Although Livy's account is
pure legend, there is evidence that Rome was founded
around the middle of the 8th century BC, and that the
Romans and Sabines united shortly afterwards.
Historical evidence also gives some support to Livy's
claim that after Romulus's death Rome was ruled by a
series of kings, and that in the 7th century BC it was
conquered by the Etruscans and ruled by the Tarquin
family. Last of the dynasty was Tarquinius Superbus
(Tarquin the Proud). His despotic rule led to the
Etruscans being expelled and the founding of a
Republic run by two annually elected consuls.
The uprising was led by Lucius Junius Brutus, the
model of the stern, patriotic Roman Republican.

EXTENT OF THE CITY

▨ 750 BC   ☐ Today

Ceremonial trumpets

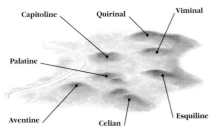

The Seven Hills of Rome
*By the 8th century BC, shepherds and
farmers lived on four of Rome's seven hills.
As the population grew, huts were built in the
marshy valley later occupied by the Forum.*

Capitoline   Quirinal   Viminal

Palatine

Aventine   Celian   Esquiline

Iron Age Hut
*Early settlers lived
in wattle and
daub huts.
Traces of their
foundations
have been
found on the
Palatine.*

Augur, digging
foundation

TEMPLE OF JUPITER
*This Renaissance painting by Perin del
Vaga shows Tarquinius Superbus
founding the Temple of Jupiter on the
Capitol, the sacred citadel of Rome.*

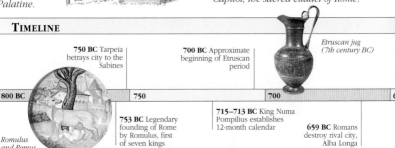

TIMELINE

800 BC	750	700	6

750 BC Tarpeia
betrays city to the
Sabines

700 BC Approximate
beginning of Etruscan
period

Etruscan jug
(7th century BC)

753 BC Legendary
founding of Rome
by Romulus, first
of seven kings

715–713 BC King Numa
Pompilius establishes
12-month calendar

659 BC Romans
destroy rival city,
Alba Longa

*Romulus
and Remus*

The Legend of the She-Wolf
The evil King of Alba threw his baby nephews, Romulus and Remus, into the Tiber but they were washed ashore, and suckled by a she-wolf.

Raven, guardian of the citadel

Apollo of Veio
Etruscan culture and religion were influenced by the Greeks. This 5th- or 6th-century statue of the Greek god Apollo comes from Veio, a powerful, wealthy Etruscan city.

King Tarquin, holding stone worshipped as a thunderbolt

The Legend of Aeneas
Some Roman legends make the Trojan hero Aeneas the grandfather of Romulus and Remus.

WHERE TO SEE ETRUSCAN ROME
The Cloaca Maxima sewer still functions, but there are few other traces of Etruscan Rome. Most finds come from Etruscan sites outside Rome like Tarquinia, with its tomb paintings of sumptuous banquets *(see p271)*, but there are major collections in the Villa Giulia *(pp262–3)* and Vatican Museums *(p238)*. The most famous object, however, is a bronze statue of the legendary she-wolf in the Capitoline Museums *(p73)*. The Antiquarium Forense *(p87)* displays objects from the necropolis which once occupied the site of the Roman Forum.

Funeral urns shaped like huts were used for cremation from the mid-8th century BC.

Etruscan jewellery, like this 7th-century BC gold filigree brooch, was lavish. Treasures of this kind have given the Etruscans a reputation for luxurious living.

578 BC Servius Tullius Etruscan King

600 BC Possible date of construction of Cloaca Maxima sewer

565 BC Traditional date of the Servian Wall around Rome's seven hills

Statue of Jupiter

510 BC Temple of Jupiter consecrated on the Capitoline hill

| 600 | 550 | 500 |

616 BC Tarquinius Priscus, first Etruscan king. Forum and Circus Maximus established

L J Brutus

534 BC King Servius murdered

509 BC L J Brutus expels Etruscans from Rome and founds the Republic

507 BC War against Etruscans. Horatius defends wooden bridge across Tiber

Kings, Consuls and Emperors

R OME HAD OVER 250 RULERS in the 1,200 years between its
foundation by Romulus and AD 476, when the last emperor
was deposed by the German warrior Odoacer. Romulus was the
first of seven kings, overthrown in 509 BC when Rome became a
Republic. Authority was held by two annually elected consuls, but
provision was made for the appointment of a dictator in times of
crisis. In 494 BC, the office of Tribune was set up to protect the
plebeians from injustice at the hands of their patrician rulers.
Roman democracy, however, was always cosmetic. It was
discarded completely
in 27 BC, when
absolute power
was placed in
the hands of
the emperor.

70–63 BC Pompey

107–87 BC
Marius is
consul
seven times

205 BC Scipio
Africanus

218 BC Quintus Fabius
Maximus

*Romulus, his twin Remus and
the she-wolf who suckled them*

456 BC Lucius
Quintus
Cincinnatus

c.753–715 BC
Romulus

800 BC	700	600	500	400	300	200	10●
SEVEN KINGS			**REPUBLIC**				
800 BC	700	600	500	400	300	200	10●

c.715–673 BC
Numa
Pompilius

396 BC Marcus
Furius Camillus

133 BC Tiberius Gracchus

c.673–641 BC
Tullus Hostilius

c.509 BC Lucius
Junius Brutus and
Horatius Pulvillus

122–121 BC
Gaius Gracchus

c.641–616 BC
Ancus Marcius

c.534–509 BC
Tarquinius Superbus

82–80 BC
Sulla

c.579–534 BC
Servius Tullius

63 BC
Cicero

616–579 BC
Tarquinius Priscus

60–50 BC Triumvirat●
of Julius Caesar
Pompey and Crassu●

45–44 BC Juli●
Caesar is sole ru●●

Tarquinius Priscus consulting an augur

*Julius Caesar,
whose rise to
power marked the
end of the
Roman Republic*

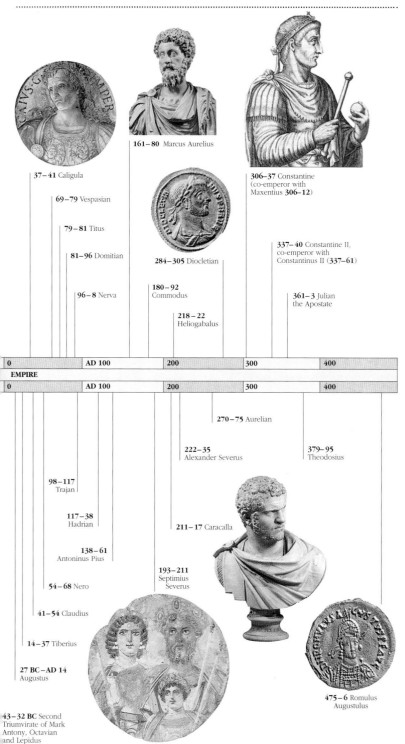

37–41 Caligula

161–80 Marcus Aurelius

306–37 Constantine
(co-emperor with
Maxentius **306–12**)

69–79 Vespasian

79–81 Titus

81–96 Domitian

284–305 Diocletian

337–40 Constantine II,
co-emperor with
Constantinus II (**337–61**)

96–8 Nerva

180–92
Commodus

361–3 Julian
the Apostate

218–22
Heliogabalus

| 0 | AD 100 | 200 | 300 | 400 |

EMPIRE

| 0 | AD 100 | 200 | 300 | 400 |

270–75 Aurelian

222–35
Alexander Severus

379–95
Theodosius

98–117
Trajan

117–38
Hadrian

211–17 Caracalla

138–61
Antoninus Pius

193–211
Septimius
Severus

54–68 Nero

41–54 Claudius

14–37 Tiberius

27 BC–AD 14
Augustus

475–6 Romulus
Augustulus

43–32 BC Second
Triumvirate of Mark
Antony, Octavian
and Lepidus

Septimius Severus and family

The Roman Republic

Bronze coin, showing Temple of Vesta (c.57 BC)

BY THE MID-2ND CENTURY BC, Rome controlled the west Mediterranean, policing and defending it with massive armies. The troops had more loyalty to the generals than to distant politicians, giving men like Marius, Sulla, Pompey and Caesar the muscle to seize political power. Meanwhile, peasants, whose land had been destroyed during the invasion of Hannibal in 219 BC, had flooded into Rome. They were followed by slaves and freedmen from conquered lands such as Greece, swelling the population to half a million. There was plenty of work for immigrants, constructing roads, aqueducts, markets and temples, financed by taxes on Rome's expanding trade.

EXTENT OF THE CITY

▨ *400 BC*   ☐ *Today*

Arch spanning road

The gradient of an aqueduct was about 1 in 1,000.

Cut stone blocks

Covered water channels

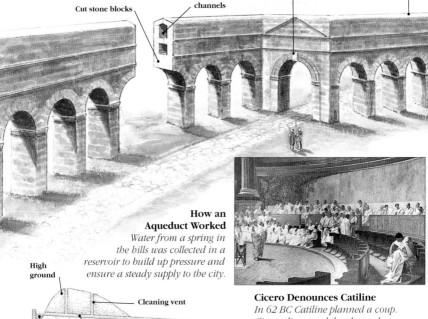

How an Aqueduct Worked
Water from a spring in the hills was collected in a reservoir to build up pressure and ensure a steady supply to the city.

High ground

Cleaning vent

Reservoir

Underground water channel

Arches carrying water across low ground

Cicero Denounces Catiline
In 62 BC Catiline planned a coup. Cicero discovered the plot and persuaded the Senate to condemn the conspirators to death.

TIMELINE

499 BC Battle against Latin tribes; Temple of Castor and Pollux built to commemorate the victory

396 BC Definitive victory over rival Etruscan city, Veio

380 BC Servian Wall rebuilt

Via Appia

312 BC Construction of Via Appia and Rome's first aqueduct, the Aqua Appia

500 BC	450 BC	400 BC	350 BC	300

Relief of Capitoline geese

390 BC Rome invaded by Celtic Gauls: quacking geese on Capitoline hill warn of impending attack

264–241 BC First Punic War (against Carthage)

THE HISTORY OF ROME

Roman Street
In the 1st century BC, most buildings in Rome were made from brick and concrete. Only a few public buildings used marble.

AQUEDUCT (2ND CENTURY BC)
Rome owed much of her prosperity to her skilled civil engineers. When the city's wells were no longer sufficient, aqueducts were built to bring water from surrounding hills. Some were over 80 km (50 miles) long.

Arches for maintaining a constant gradient over low-lying land

Temple of Juno
The ruins of this 197 BC temple are embedded in the church of San Nicola in Carcere (see p151). Romans consulted their gods before all important ventures.

Scipio Africanus
In 202 BC the Roman general Scipio defeated Hannibal. Rome replaced Carthage as master of the Mediterranean.

WHERE TO SEE REPUBLICAN ROME

This fresco depicting a gang of slaves building a wall can be seen at the Museo Nazionale Romano *(see p163).*

The Temple of Saturn, first built in 497 BC, now consists of eight majestic columns overlooking the Forum at the end of the Via Sacra *(see p83).*

Rome's loveliest Republican buildings are the two Temples of the Forum Boarium *(see p203).* Four more temples can be seen in the Area Sacra of Largo Argentina *(p150).* Most monuments from this period, however, lie underground. Only a few, like the Tomb of the Scipios *(p195),* have been excavated. One of the bridges leading to Tiber Island *(p153),* the Ponte Fabricio, dates from the 1st century BC and is still used by pedestrians.

Ponte Fabricio, built in 62 BC

250 BC	200 BC	150 BC	100 BC	

220 BC Via Flaminia built, linking Rome to the Adriatic coast

168 BC Victory in Macedonian War completes Roman conquest of Greece

133–120 BC Gracchi brothers killed for trying to introduce land reforms

51 BC Caesar conquers Gaul

218–202 BC Second Punic War; Scipio Africanus defeats Carthaginians

Hannibal

149–146 BC Third Punic War; Carthage destroyed

71 BC Spartacus's slave revolt crushed by Crassus and Pompey

60 BC Rome has three joint rulers: Pompey, Crassus and Caesar

Imperial Rome

IN 44 BC Caesar became dictator for life, only to be assassinated a month later. The result was 17 years of civil war, which ended only in 27 BC when Augustus became Rome's first emperor. The Empire expanded in fits and starts, but by the late 3rd century was so huge that Diocletian decided to share it between four emperors. Thanks to trade and taxes from its vast domains, Rome was the most magnificent city in the world, studded with the lavish buildings of emperors keen to advertise their civic munificence and military triumphs.

Statue of Bacchus, god of wine

EXTENT OF THE CITY
☐ *AD 250*   ☐ *Today*

Cross-vaulted ceiling with mosaic decoration

Natatio **(swimming pool)**

Apotheosis of Augustus
The first and perhaps the greatest Roman emperor, Augustus ruled for 27 years and was deified by the Senate after his death.

ROMA CAPVT MVNDI

The baths could hold up to 3,000 people. They met to gossip in the central *frigidarium* (cold room).

Area for exercise and gymnastics

The Roman Empire under Trajan
By the 2nd century AD, the Roman Empire stretched from Britain to Syria, and Rome was known as the Caput Mundi, *the head of the world.*

TIMELINE

49 BC Caesar crosses the Rubicon and takes Rome

27 Augustus becomes first emperor

Emperor Nero

64 Fire during Nero's rule destroys much of city

65 First persecution of Christians under Nero

72 Colosseum begun

50 BC	0	AD 50	100

44 Caesar becomes dictator for life, and is murdered by Brutus and Cassius

AD 42 St Peter the Apostle comes to Rome

13 Ara Pacis is erected to celebrate the peace Augustus has secured in the Empire

67 St Peter is crucified and St Paul executed in Rome

Statue of St Peter in San Paolo fuori le Mura

Roman Revelry
Banquets could last for up to 10 hours, with numerous courses, between which guests would retire to a small room to relax.

WHERE TO SEE IMPERIAL ROME

There are relics of Imperial Rome throughout the city centre, some hidden below churches and palazzi, others like the Forum (*see pp76–87*), the Palatine (*pp97–101*) and the Imperial Fora (*pp88–91*), fully excavated. The magnificence of the era, however, is best conveyed by the Pantheon (*pp110–11*) and the Colosseum (*pp92–5*).

BATHS OF DIOCLETIAN (AD 298)

Rome's public baths were not just places to keep clean. They also had bars, libraries, barbers' shops, brothels and sports facilities.

The Arch of Titus (*p87*), erected in the Forum in AD 81, commemorates Emperor Titus's Sack of Jerusalem in AD 70.

Tepidarium **(warm room)**

Virgil (70 –19 BC)
Virgil was Rome's greatest epic poet. His most famous work is the Aeneid, *the story of the Trojan hero Aeneas's journey to the future site of Rome.*

A relief of Mithras, a popular Persian god (3rd century AD), can be seen beneath the church of San Clemente (*pp186 –7*).

164–180 Plague rages in Roman Empire

212 Citizenship granted to virtually all inhabitants of the Empire

270 Aurelian Wall begun

Section of Aurelian Wall

150　　**200**　　**250**

125 Hadrian redesigns the Pantheon

216 Baths of Caracalla completed

247 Rome's Millennium is celebrated

284 Empire divided into West and East

Mosaic from the Baths of Caracalla

Early Christian Rome

Crucifixion in Santa Maria Antiqua

IN THE 1ST CENTURY AD, during the reign of Tiberius, a rebellious pacifist was crucified in a distant corner of the Empire. This was nothing unusual, but within a few years Jesus Christ and his teachings became notorious in Rome, his followers were perceived as a threat to public order, and many were executed. This was no deterrent, and the new religion spread through all levels of Roman society. When the Apostles Peter and Paul arrived in Rome there was already a small Christian community, and in spite of continued persecution by the state, Christianity flourished. In AD 313 the Emperor Constantine issued an edict granting freedom of worship to Christians, and soon after founded a shrine on the site of St Peter's tomb. This secured Rome's position as a centre of Christianity, but in the 5th century the political importance of Rome declined and the city fell to Goths and other invaders.

EXTENT OF THE CITY

▨ AD 395   ☐ Today

St Paul — **Youthful, beardless representation of Christ**

Santo Stefano Rotondo
This 17th-century engraving shows how a Roman temple (top) might have been transformed (above) into the 5th-century round church of Santo Stefano.

Classical-style border decorated with fruit

The Good Shepherd
The pagan image of a shepherd sacrificing a lamb became a Christian symbol.

4TH-CENTURY MOSAIC, SANTA COSTANZA
Beautiful mosaics, often with palm trees and other oriental motifs suggesting Jerusalem, helped spread the message of early Christianity.

TIMELINE

c.320 Building of first St Peter's

356 Legendary founding of Santa Maria Maggiore

Gold solidus of Theodosius

410 Rome sacked by Alaric's Goths

455 Rome sacked again by Vandals

300	350	400	450

312 Control of Empire won by Constantine after battle at Milvian Bridge

Battle of the Milvian Bridge

380 Emperor Theodosius makes Christianity the official religion of the Roman Empire

395 Division of the Empire between Ravenna and Constantinople

422 Founding of Santa Sabina

Epigraph of Peter and Paul
This is one of hundreds of early Christian graffiti housed in the Lapidary Gallery of the Vatican (see p237).

(see p237)

WHERE TO SEE EARLY CHRISTIAN ROME

There are traces of early Christianity all over Rome. Many ancient churches were built over early Christian meeting places and sites of martyrdoms: among them San Clemente *(see pp186–7)*, Santa Pudenziana *(p171)* and Santa Cecilia *(p211)*. Outside the walls of the old city are miles of underground catacombs *(pp265–6)*, many decorated with Christian frescoes, while the Vatican's Pio-Christian Museum *(p240)* has the best collection of early Christian art.

(see pp186–7), (p171) (p211). (pp265–6), (p240)

Crucifixion, Santa Sabina
This 5th-century panel on the door of Santa Sabina (see p204) is one of the earliest known representations of the Crucifixion. Interestingly, Christ's cross is not actually shown.

This statuette, carved out of bone, is embedded in the rock of the Catacombs of San Panfilo, just off the Via Salaria (**map** 2 F4).

St Peter receiving peace from the Saviour

Lambs symbolizing the Christian flock

Constantine's Cross
Constantine's vision of the True Cross during the Battle of the Milvian Bridge made him convert to Christianity.

The Cross of Justin, in the Treasury of St Peter's *(p232)*, was given to Rome by the Emperor Justin in AD 578.

---

475 Fall of Western Roman Empire; Byzantium becomes seat of Empire

A Byzantine image of St Paul

609 Pantheon is consecrated as a Christian church

500   **550**   **600**

496 Anastasius II is first pope to assume title *Pontifex Maximus*

590–604 Pope Gregory the Great strengthens the papacy

630 Sant'Agnese fuori le Mura is built in Roman Byzantine style

The Papacy

THE POPE is considered Christ's representative on earth, claiming his authority from St Peter, the first Bishop of Rome. Though some popes have been great thinkers and reformers, the role has rarely been purely spiritual. In the Middle Ages, many popes were involved in power struggles with the Holy Roman Emperor. Renaissance popes like Julius II and Leo X, the patrons of Raphael and Michelangelo, lived as luxuriously as any secular prince. The popes listed here include all those who exercised significant political or religious influence, up as far as the end of the Counter-Reformation, when the power of the papacy began to wane.

St Ludovic Kneels before Boniface VIII *by Simone Martini*

314–35 St Sylvester I

590–604 St Gregory the Great

Gregory the Great leading a procession to end the plague

955–64 John XII

1227–41 Gregory IX

222–30 St Urban I

496–8 Anastasius II

931–5 John XI

1216–27 Honorius III Savelli

217–22 St Callixtus I

891–6 Formosus

| 0 | 200 | 400 | 600 | 800 | 1000 | 1200 |

PAPACY BASED IN ROME

| 0 | 200 | 400 | 600 | 800 | 1000 | 1200 |

336 Mark

352–66 Liberius

579–90 Pelagius II

1032–44, 1047–8 Benedict IX

c.88–97 St Clement

608–15 St Boniface IV

1073–85 St Gregory VII

c.42–67 St Peter

731–41 St Gregory III

1099–1118 Paschal II

772–95 Adrian I

1130–43 Innocent II

1154–9 Adrian IV

847–55 St Leo IV

817–24 St Paschal I

1198–1216 Innocent III

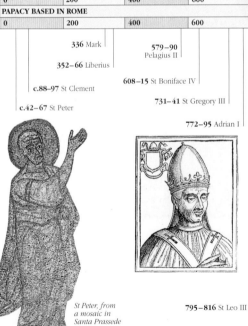

St Peter, from a mosaic in Santa Prassede (see p171)

795–816 St Leo III

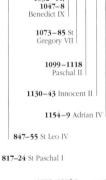

Innocent III's Vision of the Church, *from a fresco by Giotto*

Portrait of Gregory XIII
by Lavinia Fontana

1560–65 Pius IV Medici

1555–9 Paul IV

1523–34
Clement VII Medici

1513–21 Leo X Medici

1492–1503
Alexander
VI Borgia

1572–84 Gregory XIII Boncompagni

1670–76 Clement X Altieri

1667–9 Clement IX

1655–67
Alexander VII Chigi

1294–1303
Boniface VIII

1484–92
Innocent VIII Cybo

1471–84 Sixtus IV della Rovere

1464–71 Paul II Barbo

1605 Leo XI
Medici

1700–21 Clement XI

1458–64
Pius II Piccolomini

1300	1400	1500	1600	1700

AVIGNON	PAPACY AGAIN BASED IN ROME

1300	1400	1500	1600	1700

1417–31
Martin V Colonna

1644–55 Innocent X Pamphilj

1447–55
Nicholas V

1623–44 Urban VIII Barberini

1585–90
Sixtus V

Nicholas V Receiving a
Book, *illustration from a
contemporary manuscript*

1592–1605
Clement VIII
Aldobrandini

Urban VIII Approving a Building
Project *in the Vatican's Gallery
of Tapestries* (see p241)

1503–13 Julius II della Rovere

1605–21 Paul V
Borghese

Raphael's portrait of Julius II

1534–49 Paul III Farnese

Paul III Gives His Approval to
the Capuchin Order *by
Sebastiano Ricci*

Medieval Rome

Mosaic, San Clemente

Sᴜᴘᴘʟᴀɴᴛᴇᴅ ʙʏ ᴄᴏɴꜱᴛᴀɴᴛɪɴᴏᴘʟᴇ as capital of the Empire in the 4th century, Rome was reduced to a few thousand inhabitants by the early Middle Ages, its power just a memory. In the 8th and 9th centuries, the growing importance of the papacy revived the city and made it once more a centre of power. But continual conflicts between the pope and the Holy Roman Emperor soon weakened the papacy. The 10th, 11th and 12th centuries were among the bleakest in Roman history: violent invaders left Rome poverty-stricken and the constantly warring local barons tore apart what remained of the city. Despite this, the first Holy Year was declared in 1300 and thousands of pilgrims arrived in Rome. But by 1309 the papacy was forced to move to Avignon, leaving Rome to slide into further squalor and strife.

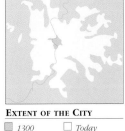

Eхтᴇɴᴛ ᴏꜰ ᴛʜᴇ Cɪᴛʏ

☐ *1300*　　　☐ *Today*

Charlemagne Crowned in St Peter's
On Christmas Day in 800, Charlemagne was made emperor of the Holy Roman Empire, a new Christian dominion to replace that of ancient Rome.

San Giovanni in Laterano

Aurelian Wall

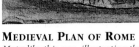

Trajan's Column

Column of Marcus Aurelius

Madonna and Child Mosaic
The Chapel of St Zeno (817–24) in the church of Santa Prassede (see p171) has some of the best examples of Byzantine mosaics in Rome.

MEDIEVAL PLAN OF ROME
Maps like this one, illustrating the principal features of the city, were produced for pilgrims, the tourists of the Middle Ages.

TIMELINE

725 King Ine of Wessex founds the first hostel for pilgrims in the Borgo	**852** The Vatican is fortified with walls following a raid by Saracens	*Emperor Otto I*	**961** King Otto the Great becomes first German Holy Roman Emperor
700	**800**	**900**	**100**
778 Charlemagne, King of the Franks, conquers Italy	**800** Charlemagne crowned emperor in St Peter's	**880–932** Rome is ruled by two women, Theodora and then her daughter, Marozia	

Stefaneschi Triptych *(1315) Giotto and his pupils painted this triptych for Cardinal Stefaneschi as an altarpiece for St Peter's. It is now in the Vatican Museums (see p240).*

WHERE TO SEE MEDIEVAL ROME

Among the most interesting churches of the period are San Clemente, with a fine apse mosaic and Cosmati floor *(see pp186–7)*, Santa Maria in Trastevere *(pp212–13)* and Santa Maria sopra Minerva, Rome's only Gothic church *(p108)*. Santa Cecilia in Trastevere *(p211)* has a Cavallini fresco, and there is fine Cosmati work in Santa Maria in Cosmedin *(p202)*.

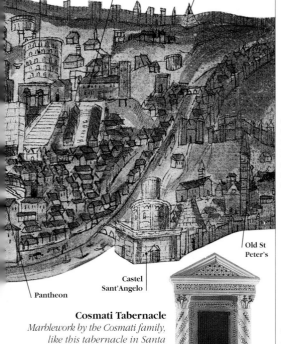

Colosseum — Capitol — Pyramid of Caius Cestius — Old St Peter's — Castel Sant'Angelo — Pantheon

Charlemagne's Dalmatic in the Treasury of St Peter's *(p232)* was supposedly worn by the Holy Roman Emperor at his coronation. In fact the richly embroidered vestment probably dates from the 14th century.

Cosmati Tabernacle
Marblework by the Cosmati family, like this tabernacle in Santa Sabina (see p204), decorates many of Rome's medieval churches.

Santa Sabina *(p204)* on the Aventine Hill has a medieval bell tower.

1084 Rome is attacked by Normans	**1108** San Clemente is rebuilt	**1200** Rome is an independent commune under Arnaldo di Brescia	**1309** Pope Clement V moves the papacy to Avignon — **1300** First Holy Year proclaimed by Pope Boniface VIII — **1348** Black Death strikes Rome

1100 — **1200** — **1300**

Mosaic façade, Santa Maria in Trastevere (pp212–13) — **1232** Cloister of San Giovanni in Laterano completed — **1140** Santa Maria in Trastevere is restored — *Cola di Rienzo* — **1347** Cola di Rienzo – an Italian patriot – tries to restore the Roman Republic

Renaissance Rome

POPE NICHOLAS V came to the throne in 1447 determined to make Rome a city fit for the papacy. Among his successors, men like Julius II and Leo X eagerly followed his lead, and the city's appearance was transformed. The Classical ideals of the Renaissance inspired artists, architects and craftsmen, such as Michelangelo, Bramante, Raphael and

Detail of Botticelli's *Youth of Moses* (1480s) Cellini, to build and decorate the churches and palaces of a newly confident Rome.

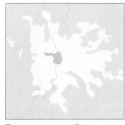

EXTENT OF THE CITY

▣ 1500   ☐ Today

School of Athens by Raphael
*In this fresco (see p243) Raphael
complimented many of his peers by
representing them as ancient Greek
philosophers. The building shown is
based on a design by Bramante.*

Hemispherical dome

Balustrade of small columns

Classical colonnade of 16 Doric columns

THE TEMPIETTO
*The Tempietto (1502) at
San Pietro in Montorio
(see p219) was one of
Bramante's first works
in Rome. A simple,
perfectly proportioned
miniature Classical
temple, it is a model of
High Renaissance
architecture.*

Cosmati-style mosaic floor

Palazzo Caprini
*Bramante's design had a strong influence on
later Renaissance palazzi. Parts of the building
survive in Palazzo dei Convertendi (see p227).*

TIMELINE

1377 Papacy returns to Rome from Avignon under Pope Gregory XI

1409–15 Papacy moves to Pisa

1452 Demolition of old St Peter's basilica begins

1444 Birth of Bramante

| 1350 | | 1400 | | 1450 |

1378–1417 The Great Schism, a division in the papacy in Avignon

1417 Pope Martin V ends the Great Schism in the papacy

*Pope Martin V,
reigned 1417–31*

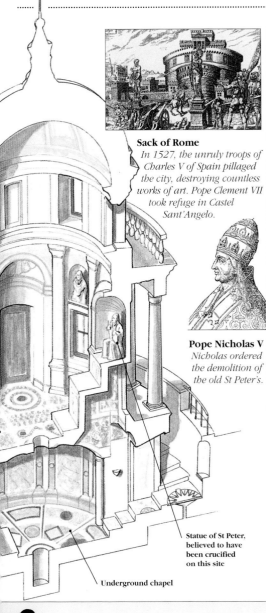

Sack of Rome
In 1527, the unruly troops of Charles V of Spain pillaged the city, destroying countless works of art. Pope Clement VII took refuge in Castel Sant'Angelo.

Pope Nicholas V
Nicholas ordered the demolition of the old St Peter's.

Statue of St Peter, believed to have been crucified on this site

Underground chapel

WHERE TO SEE RENAISSANCE ROME

The Campo de' Fiori area *(see pp142–53)* is full of grand Renaissance palazzi, especially along Via Giulia *(pp276–7)*. Across the river stands the delightful Villa Farnesina *(pp220–21)*. The most typical church of the period is Santa Maria del Popolo *(pp138–9)*, and the best collection of Renaissance art is in the Vatican Museums *(pp234–47)*. These include the Sistine Chapel *(pp244–7)* and the Raphael Rooms *(pp242–3)*.

The Madonna di Foligno by Raphael (1511–12) is one of the fine Renaissance paintings in the Vatican Pinacoteca *(p241)*.

The Pietà, commissioned for St Peter's in 1501, was one of Michelangelo's first sculptures executed in Rome *(p233)*.

1483 Birth of Raphael	**1486** Building of Palazzo della Cancelleria	**1519** Frescoes completed in Villa Farnesina	**1527** Troops of Emperor Charles V sack Rome

Emperor Charles V

1500   **1550**

1475 Birth of Michelangelo   **1506** Pope Julius II orders start of work on new St Peter's   **1508** Michelangelo begins painting the Sistine Chapel ceiling   *Cumaean Sibyl, Sistine Chapel*   **1547** Pope Paul III appoints Michelangelo architect of St Peter's

Baroque Rome

Baroque putto

BY THE 16TH CENTURY, the Catholic Church had become immensely rich – one of the chief criticisms of the Protestant reformers. The display of grandeur and extravagance by the papal court contrasted sharply with the poverty of the people, and wealthy Roman society was characterized by sumptuous luxury and a ceaseless round of entertainment. To make the Catholic faith more appealing than Protestantism, scores of churches were built and monuments and fountains were erected to glorify the Holy See. The finest architects in the ornate, dramatic style of the Baroque were Bernini and Borromini.

EXTENT OF THE CITY

| 1645 | Today |

Ceiling portraying heavenly scenes

Monument to Pope Alexander VII
This Bernini tomb in St Peter's (pp230–33) includes a skeleton brandishing an hour glass.

Gian Lorenzo Bernini *(1598–1680)*
The favourite artist of the papacy, Bernini transformed Rome with his churches, palaces, statues and fountains.

Holy Family fresco

Tapestry of Pope Urban VIII
Bernini's most devoted patron, Pope Urban VIII Barberini (1623–44), is shown here receiving the homage of the nations.

A marble rose marks the best place to stand to appreciate the illusion of space created by the artist.

TIMELINE

1568 The Jesuits build the Gesù, prototypical church of the early Baroque

Altar carving from the Gesù

1595 Annibale Carracci begins to fresco Palazzo Farnese

1624 Bernini's sculpture of *Apollo and Daphne*

1626 Work on St Peter's is completed

| 1550 | 1575 | 1600 | 1625 |

1571 Birth of Caravaggio

1585 Pope Sixtus V plans new streets

1600 Philosopher Giordano Bruno is burned at the stake for heresy

Galileo

1633 Galileo condemned to house arrest for heresy

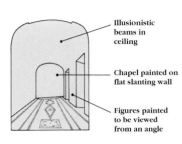

Illusionistic beams in ceiling

Chapel painted on flat slanting wall

Figures painted to be viewed from an angle

Queen Christina of Sweden
In a coup for Catholicism, Christina renounced Protestantism and abdicated her throne. In 1655 she moved to Rome, where she became the centre of a lively literary and scientific circle.

St Ignatius, founder of the Jesuits

Francesco Borromini
(1599–1667)
In the many churches he built in Rome, Borromini made use of revolutionary geometric forms.

POZZO CORRIDOR
The use of perspective to create an illusion of depth and space was a favourite Baroque device. Andrea Pozzo painted this illusionistic corridor in the 1680s in the Rooms of St Ignatius near the Gesù (see pp114–15).

San Carlo alle Quattro Fontane
One of Borromini's most influential designs was this tiny oval church (see p161) on the Quirinal hill.

1651 Bernini redesigns much of Piazza Navona

Bernini's Fontana dei Fiumi in Piazza Navona

1694 Palazzo di Montecitorio is completed

1735 Spanish Steps are designed

1732 Work starts on the Trevi Fountain

1650 | 1675 | 1700 | 1725

1657 Borromini completes Sant'Agnese in Agone

1656 Work starts on Bernini's colonnade for St Peter's Square

Bonnie Prince Charlie, pretender to the throne of England

1721 Bonnie Prince Charlie is born in Rome

1734 Clement XII makes Palazzo Nuovo world's first public museum

Understanding Rome's Architecture

Arch of Titus

THE ARCHITECTURE of Imperial Rome kept alive the Classical styles of ancient Greece, at the same time developing new, uniquely Roman forms based on the arch, the vault and the dome. The next important period was the 12th century, when many Romanesque churches were built. The Renaissance saw a return to Classical ideals, inspired by the example of Florence, but in the 17th century Rome found a style of its own again in the flamboyance of the Baroque.

The entablature above these columns has both straight and arched sections (Hadrian's Villa).

CLASSICAL ROME

Most Roman buildings were of concrete faced with brick, but from the 1st century BC, the Romans started to imitate earlier Greek models, using marble to decorate temples and other public buildings.

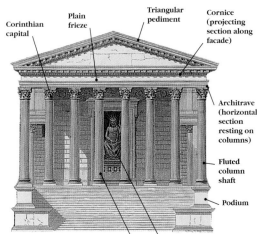

Corinthian capital

Plain frieze

Triangular pediment

Cornice (projecting section along facade)

Architrave (horizontal section resting on columns)

Fluted column shaft

Podium

Cella (inner sanctuary)

Colonnade enclosing portico

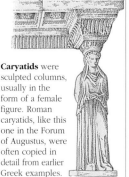

Caryatids were sculpted columns, usually in the form of a female figure. Roman caryatids, like this one in the Forum of Augustus, were often copied in detail from earlier Greek examples.

Roman temples were usually built on a raised dais or podium, to make them prominent. Many were fronted by a portico, a roofed porch with columns.

The orders of Classical architecture were building styles, each based on a different column design. The three major orders were borrowed by the Romans from the Greeks.

Doric order

Ionic order

Corinthian order

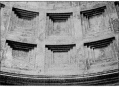

Aedicules were small shrines, framed by two pillars, usually containing a statue of a god.

Coffers were decorative sunken panels that reduced the weight of domed and vaulted ceilings.

EARLY CHRISTIAN AND MEDIEVAL ROME

The first Christian churches in Rome were based on the basilica: oblong, with three naves, each usually ending in an apse. From the 10th to the 13th centuries, most churches were built in the Romanesque style, which used the rounded arches of ancient Rome.

Basilicas in Rome have, in most cases, kept their original rectangular shape. The nave of San Giovanni in Laterano retains its 4th-century floorplan.

The triumphal arch divides the nave of a church from the apse. Here, in San Paolo fuori le Mura, it is decorated with mosaics.

RENAISSANCE AND BAROQUE ROME

Renaissance architecture (15th–16th centuries) drew its inspiration directly from Classical models. It revived the use of strict geometric proportions. The Baroque age (late 16th–17th centuries) broke many established rules, favouring grandiose decoration over pure Classical forms.

Putti were a popular decorative feature in the Baroque. A putto is a painting or a sculpture of a child like a Cupid or cherub.

A loggia is an open-sided gallery or arcade. It may be a separate structure or part of a building, as here at San Saba.

A tabernacle is used to house the Sacrament for the mass. This 13th-century Gothic wall tabernacle is in San Clemente.

A baldacchino is a canopy, supported on columns, rising over the main altar. This Baroque example is in St Peter's.

Rusticated masonry decorates the exterior of many Renaissance palazzi. It consists of massive blocks divided by deep joints.

COSMATESQUE SCULPTURE AND MOSAICS

The Cosmati family, active in Rome during the 12th and 13th centuries, have given their name to a particularly Roman style of decoration. They worked in marble, producing all kinds of fittings for churches, including cloisters, episcopal thrones, tombs, pulpits, fonts and candlesticks. These were often decorated with bands of colourful mosaic. They also left many fine floor mosaics, usually of white marble with an inlay of red and green porphyry. Ancient Roman columns were cut up to provide the materials. Several other families of stonemasons used a similar style, and their work is also described as Cosmatesque.

Cosmatesque floor, Santa Maria in Cosmedin

Rome during Unification

UNDER NAPOLEON, Italy had a brief taste of unity, but by 1815 it was once more divided into many small states and papal rule was restored in Rome. Over the next 50 years, patriots, led by Mazzini, Garibaldi and others, struggled to create an independent, unified Italy. In 1848 Rome was briefly declared a Republic, but Garibaldi's forces were driven out by French troops. The French continued to protect the pope, while the rest of Italy was united as a kingdom under Vittorio Emanuele of Savoy. In 1870, troops stormed the city, and Rome became capital of Italy.

Garibaldi in his distinctive red shirt

EXTENT OF THE CITY

☐ *1870*   ☐ *Today*

Allegory of Italy's Liberty
This patriotic poster from 1890 shows the king, his chief minister Cavour, Garibaldi and Mazzini. The woman in red represents Italy.

Vittorio Emanuele II
Vittorio Emanuele of Savoy became the first King of Italy in 1861.

Porta Pia

Tricoloured flag of the new Italian kingdom

Plumed hat of the Bersaglieri, crack troops from Savoy

ROYALISTS STORM PORTA PIA
On 20 September 1870, troops of the kingdom of Italy put an end to the papal domination of Rome. They breached the city walls near Porta Pia; the pope retreated and Rome was made the Italian capital.

TIMELINE

Napoleon Bonaparte

1751 Piranesi's *Views of Rome* revive interest in Classical ruins

1762 Trevi Fountain is completed

1797 Napoleon captures Rome

1799 Napoleon expelled from Italy by Austrians and Russians

1750

Piranesi etching of Trajan's Forum

1775

1792 Canova creates the Tomb of Pope Clement XIII, St Peter's

1800–1 Napoleon takes Italy again

1800

1807 Birth of Garibaldi

Garibaldi and Rome

The charismatic leader Giuseppe Garibaldi had taken much of Italy from foreign rule by 1860. Rome still remained a crucial problem. Here he declares "O Roma o morte" (Rome or Death).

Villa Paolina

Giuseppe Verdi

(1813–1901)
Verdi, the opera composer, supported unification and in 1861 became a member of Italy's first national parliament.

Breach in Aurelian Wall

A Freed City

This marble plaque was set up at Porta Pia to commemorate the liberation of Rome.

Victor Emmanuel Monument

A vast monument to Italy's first king (see p74) stands in Piazza Venezia.

· S·P·Q·R ·
VRBE · ITALIAE · VINDICATA
INCOLIS · FELICITER · AVCTIS
GEMINOS · FORNICES · CONDIDIT

1816 Work begins on Piazza del Popolo

Fountain in Piazza del Popolo

1848 Nationalist uprising in Rome. Pope flees and a Republic is formed

1860 Garibaldi and his 1,000 followers take Sicily and Naples

1870 Royalist troops take Rome, completing the unification of Italy

1825

1850

1820 Revolts throughout Italy

1821 English poet Keats dies in Piazza di Spagna

1849 Pope is restored to power, protected by a French garrison

Pope Pius IX

1861 Kingdom of Italy founded with capital in Turin

Modern Rome

World Cup
mania

THE FASCIST DICTATOR Mussolini dreamed of recreating the immensity, order and power of the old Roman Empire: "Rome", he said, "must appear wonderful to the whole world." He began to build a grandiose new complex, EUR, in the suburbs, and razed 15 churches and many medieval houses to create space for wide new roads. Fortunately most of the old centre has survived, leaving the city with one of Europe's most picturesque historic cores. To mark the Holy Year and the new millennium, many crumbling churches, buildings and monuments were given a thorough facelift.

EXTENT OF THE CITY

▢ *1960s*   ☐ *Today*

Mussolini's Plans for Rome
This propaganda poster reflects Mussolini's grandiose projects such as Via dei Fori Imperiali in the Forum area (see p76), and EUR (p267).

Pope John Paul II
Karol Wojtyla became Pope John Paul II in 1978, the first non-Italian pope since the 1520s. The Pope exerts a tremendous influence on the lives of the world's Catholics.

JUBILEE CELEBRATIONS
Jubilee Years are usually celebrated every quarter of a century. Millions of Catholics visited Rome to celebrate the year 2000.

TIMELINE

	1929 Lateran Treaty creates a separate Vatican state	**1946** National referendum establishes Italy as a Republic; King Umberto II exiled
1915 Italy enters World War I	**1926** Opposition parties banned	**1944** Allies liberate Rome from Germans

1900	**1915**	**1930**	**1945**

| **1911** Victor Emmanuel Monument is completed | **1922** Fascists march on Rome. Mussolini becomes Prime Minister | *Poster for EUR* | **1940** Italy enters World War II; work begins on EUR zone |

Three Tenors Concert (1990)
Combining Italy's love for music and football, this opera recital at the Baths of Caracalla was broadcast live during the World Cup.

Poster for La Dolce Vita
In the 1950s and '60s Rome was Europe's Hollywood. Ben-Hur, Quo Vadis? *and* Cleopatra *were made at the Cinecittà studios, as well as Italian films like Fellini's* La Dolce Vita.

Valentino Model
While not as important as Milan for fashion, Rome is still home to some of the industry's leading designers.

City-Centre Traffic
Rome's streets are congested, and many buildings have been damaged by pollution. There are plans to close the historic centre to traffic.

1960 Olympic Games are held in Rome	**1978** Premier Aldo Moro kidnapped, then killed by Red Brigades; Karol Wojtyla is elected Pope John Paul II	**1990** Rome hosts soccer World Cup finals		**2002** The Euro becomes legal tender
1960	1975	1990	2000	2010
1962 Second Vatican Council brings about Church reforms	**1981** Assassination attempt on Pope John Paul II in St Peter's Square	**1993** Francesco Rutelli becomes Rome's first elected mayor	**2000** Rome enters the 21st century with millions of pilgrims celebrating the Holy Year, known as the Jubilee	
1957 Treaty of Rome initiates European Common Market				

ROME AT A GLANCE

ROM ITS EARLY DAYS as a settlement of shepherds on the Palatine hill, Rome grew to rule a vast empire stretching from northern England to North Africa. Later, after the empire had collapsed, Rome became the centre of the Christian world and artists and architects flocked to work for the popes. The legacy of this history can be seen all over the city. The following pages are a time-saving summary of some of the best Rome has to offer. There are sections on churches, museums and galleries, fountains and obelisks, and celebrated visitors and residents in Rome. Below are the top attractions that no visitor should miss.

ROME'S TOP TOURIST ATTRACTIONS

Capitoline Museums
See pp70–73.

Colosseum
See pp92–5.

Sistine Chapel
See pp244–7.

Raphael Rooms
See pp242–3.

Trevi Fountain
See p159.

Spanish Steps
See p134.

Castel Sant'Angelo
See pp248–9.

Pantheon
See pp110–11.

St Peter's
See pp230–33.

Roman Forum
See pp78–87.

Piazza Navona
See p120.

Interior of the Pantheon, by Giovanni Paolo Pannini (1691–1765)

Rome's Best: Churches and Temples

As THE CENTRE of Christianity, Rome has a vast wealth of beautiful and interesting churches. These range from magnificent great basilicas, built to assert the importance of the medieval and Renaissance Catholic church, to smaller, humbler buildings where the first Christians gathered, often in secret. Among the most fascinating early churches are those converted from ancient Roman temples. Additions to these over the years have resulted in some intriguing, many-layered buildings. A more detailed historical overview of Rome's churches is on pages 44–5.

Pantheon
This monumental 2,000-year-old building is one of the largest surviving temples of ancient Rome.

St Peter's
At 136 m (450 ft) high, Michelangelo's dome is the tallest in the world. Sadly, the artist died before seeing his work completed.

Piazza di Spagna

Vatican

Piazza della Rotonda

Piazza Navona

Santa Maria in Trastevere
Built over a very early Christian foundation, this church is famous for its ornate mosaics.

Janiculum

Campo de' Fiori

Cap

Trastevere

Santa Cecilia in Trastevere
This statue of Cecilia, showing her as she lay when her tomb was uncovered, was sculpted in 1599 by Stefano Maderno.

Santa Maria in Cosmedin
The decorations in this 6th-century church are 12th-century and earlier. A restored painting in the apse shows the Virgin, Child and saints.

Santa Maria Maggiore
Rich mosaics and relics contrast with the sober interior form of Santa Maria Maggiore. Among its treasures are vestments bearing the Borghese coat of arms.

Sant'Andrea al Quirinale
Bernini made maximum use of strong, dynamic curves in this oval interior (1658–70), creating a small masterpiece of the Roman Baroque.

Santa Prassede
Magnificent Byzantine mosaics cover the walls and ceilings of this 9th-century church. This Christ with angels is in the Chapel of St Zeno.

Santa Croce in Gerusalemme
Saints adorn the façade of Santa Croce. Inside are relics of the Cross, brought from Jerusalem by St Helena.

Via Veneto

Quirinal

Forum

Esquiline

Palatine

Aventine

Caracalla

Lateran

0 metres 500
0 yards 500

San Clemente
Different archaeological layers lie beneath the 12th-century church. This sarcophagus dates from the 4th century.

San Giovanni in Laterano
The original church was built by Constantine, the first Christian emperor. The Chapel of St Venantius mosaics include the figure of St Venantius himself.

Exploring Churches and Temples

THERE ARE MORE CHURCHES in Rome than there are days of the year, so you'll have to be selective. Catholic pilgrims have always been drawn to the seven major basilicas: **St Peter's**, the heart of the Roman Catholic church, **San Giovanni in Laterano**, **San Paolo fuori le Mura**, **Santa Maria Maggiore**, **Santa Croce in Gerusalemme**, **San Lorenzo fuori le Mura** and **San Sebastiano**. These have a wealth of relics, tombs and magnificent works of art from many different periods. Smaller churches can be equally fascinating, especially those that have preserved their original character.

13th-century fresco by Pietro Cavallini in Santa Cecilia

ANCIENT TEMPLES

ONE PAGAN TEMPLE survives virtually unaltered since it was erected in the 2nd century AD. The **Pantheon**, "Temple of all the Gods", has a domed interior quite different in structure from any other church in Rome. It was reconsecrated as a Christian church in the 7th century.

Other Roman temples have been incorporated into Christian churches at various times. Two of these are in the Forum; **Santi Cosma e Damiano** was established in the Temple of Romulus in 526, while San Lorenzo in Miranda was built on to the ruins of the **Temple of Antoninus and Faustina** in the 11th century. The Baroque façade, built in 1602, looms behind the columns of the temple.

Another church that clearly shows its ancient Roman origins is **Santa Costanza**, built as a mausoleum for Constantine's daughter. It is a round church with some splendid 4th-century mosaics.

EARLY CHRISTIAN AND MEDIEVAL CHURCHES

SOME EARLY BASILICAS – the 5th-century **Santa Maria Maggiore** and **Santa Sabina**, for example – retain much of their original structure. Other, even earlier, churches such as the 4th-century **San Paolo fuori le Mura** and **San Giovanni in Laterano** still preserve their original basilica shape. San Paolo was rebuilt after a fire in 1823 destroyed the original building, and the San Giovanni of today dates from a 1646 reconstruction by Borromini. Both these churches still have their medieval cloisters.

The impressive domed interior of the Pantheon, which became a church in 609

Santa Maria in Trastevere and **Santa Cecilia in Trastevere** were built over houses where the earliest Christian communities met and worshipped in secret to avoid persecution. One church where the different layers of earlier structures can clearly be seen is **San Clemente**. At its lowest level, it has a Mithraic temple of the 3rd century AD. Other early churches include **Santa Maria in Cosmedin,** with its impressive Romanesque bell tower, and the fortified convent of **Santi Quattro Coronati**. Many Roman churches, most notably **Santa Prassede**, contain fine early Christian and medieval mosaics.

Cloister of San Giovanni in Laterano

UNUSUAL FLOORPLANS

The design of Rome's first churches was based on the ancient basilica, a rectangular building divided into three naves. Since then there have been many bold departures from this plan, including round churches, square churches based on the shape of the Greek cross, as in Bramante's plan for St Peter's, and, in the Baroque period, even oval and hexagonal ones.

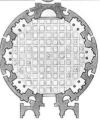

Pantheon (2nd century)

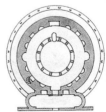

Santa Costanza (4th century)

RENAISSANCE

The greatest undertaking of the Renaissance popes was the rebuilding of **St Peter's**. Disagreements on the form it should take meant that, although work started in 1506, it was not completed until well into the 17th century. Fortunately, this did not prevent the building of Michelangelo's great dome. As well as working on St Peter's, Michelangelo also provided the **Sistine Chapel** with its magnificent frescoes.

On a completely different scale, another key work of Renaissance architecture is Bramante's tiny **Tempietto** (1499) on the Janiculum. **Santa Maria della Pace** has a Bramante cloister, some frescoes by Raphael and a charming portico by Pietro da Cortona. Also of interest is Michelangelo's imaginative use of the great vaults of the Roman Baths of Diocletian in the church of **Santa Maria degli Angeli**.

There are other churches worth visiting for the sake of

Michelangelo's dramatic dome crowning the interior of St Peter's

their outstanding paintings and sculptures. **Santa Maria del Popolo**, for example, has two great paintings by Caravaggio, the Chigi Chapel designed by Raphael, and a series of 15th-century frescoes by Pinturicchio. **San Pietro in Vincoli**, besides having the chains with which St Peter was bound in prison, also has Michelangelo's awe-inspiring statue of Moses, while **San Luigi dei Francesi** has three Caravaggios depicting St Matthew and frescoes by Domenichino.

BAROQUE

Interior of Rosati's dome in San Carlo ai Catinari (1620)

THE COUNTER-REFORMATION inspired the exuberant, lavish style of churches such as the **Gesù** and **Sant' Ignazio di Loyola**. The best-loved examples of Roman Baroque are the later works associated with Bernini, such as the great colonnade and baldacchino he built for **St Peter's**. Of the smaller churches he designed, perhaps the finest is **Sant' Andrea al Quirinale**, while **Santa Maria della Vittoria** houses his truly astonishing Cornaro Chapel with its sculpture of the *Ecstasy of St Teresa*. The late Baroque was not all Bernini, however. You should also look out for churches such as **San Carlo**

ai Catinari with its beautiful dome by Rosato Rosati and the many churches by Bernini's rival, Borromini. **Sant'Agnese in Agone** and **San Carlo alle Quattro Fontane** are famed for the dramatic concave surfaces of their façades, while the complex structure of **Sant'Ivo alla Sapienza** makes it one of the miniature masterpieces of the Baroque.

Bramante's St Peter's (1503)

Sant'Andrea al Quirinale (1658)

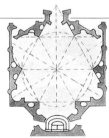

Sant'Ivo alla Sapienza (1642)

Rome's Best: Museums and Galleries

THE MUSEUMS OF ROME are among the richest in the world; the Vatican alone contains incomparable collections of Egyptian, Etruscan, Greek, Roman and Early Christian artifacts, as well as frescoes by Michelangelo and Raphael, priceless manuscripts and jewels. Excavations in the 19th century added treasures from ancient Rome which are now on show in museums throughout the city. The finest Etruscan collections in the world can be enjoyed in the Villa Giulia. More details of Rome's museums and galleries are given on pages 48–9.

Villa Giulia
Etruscan treasures from Rome's early history are displayed in this beautiful Renaissance villa.

Vatican Museums
The galleries and long corridors hold priceless artifacts such as this 9th-century mosaic showing scenes from the life of Christ.

0 metres   500

0 yards   500

Piazza Spagn

Vatican

Piazza Navona

Piazz della Rotonc

Galleria Spada
This collection's strength lies in its 17th- and 18th-century paintings. Earlier works include a Visitation *by Andrea del Sarto (1486–1530).*

Campo de' Fiori

Janiculum

Trastevere

Palazzo Corsini
Included here are works by Caravaggio, Rubens and Van Dyck, as well as a painting of the Baroque sculptor Bernini – a rare portrait by Il Baciccia (1639–1709).

Galleria Doria Pamphilj
Most of the great names of the Renaissance are represented on this gallery's crowded walls. Titian (1485–1576) painted Salomé *early in his career.*

Museo e Galleria Borghese
The ground-floor museum houses ancient Greek and Roman sculpture as well as early Bernini masterpieces such as his David (1619). Upstairs are paintings by Titian, Rubens and other masters.

Museo Nazionale Romano
This fresco, from Livia's Villa (1st century AD) outside Rome, is one of a huge collection of finds from archaeological sites throughout the city.

Palazzo Barberini
The works of art here date mainly from the 13th to the 16th centuries. This figure of Providence comes from Pietro da Cortona's The Triumph of Divine Providence (1633–9).

Palazzo Venezia
The highlights of Rome's most important museum of decorative arts are its Byzantine and medieval collections, including this Byzantine enamel of Christ dating from the 13th century.

Via Veneto

Quirinal

Esquiline

Capitol

Forum

Palatine

Caracalla

Lateran

ntine

Capitoline Museums: Palazzo dei Conservatori
Pietro da Cortona's Rape of the Sabine Women (1629) is one of many Baroque paintings in the picture gallery.

Capitoline Museums: Palazzo Nuovo
Among the sculptures is this head of Giulia Domna (wife of Septimius Severus) from the 2nd century AD.

Exploring Museums and Galleries

ROME'S MUSEUMS and galleries have two major strengths: Greek and Roman archaeological treasures, and paintings and sculptures of the Renaissance and the Baroque. The Vatican Museums have superb collections of both, as do, on a smaller scale, the Capitoline Museums. Fine paintings can also be found scattered throughout Rome in museums, galleries and churches *(see pp44–5)*.

Etruscan clay head, Villa Giulia

ETRUSCAN ARTIFACTS

5th-century BC Etruscan gold plate with inscription, Villa Giulia

T**HE ETRUSCANS** inhabited an area stretching from Florence to Rome from the 8th century BC, and ruled Rome from the late 7th century BC *(see pp16–17)*. It was the Etruscan custom to bury the dead along with their possessions, and as a result Etruscan artifacts have been excavated from tombs all over central Italy. Three main collections can be seen in Rome. The **Villa Giulia** has been the home of the Museo Nazionale Etrusco since 1889. The villa, designed by Vignola for Pope Julius III for summer outings, is one of Rome's prettiest Renaissance buildings. Its gardens contain a reconstructed Etruscan temple. Not

all objects here are Etruscan, however; some of the pottery, statuettes and artifacts are relics of the Faliscans, Latins and other tribes who inhabited central Italy before the Romans. The Gregorian Etruscan Museum in the **Vatican Museums** was opened in 1837 to house Etruscan finds from tombs on church-owned land. The Museo Barracco in the **Piccola Farnesina** has statues from the much older civilizations of ancient Egypt and Assyria.

ANCIENT ROMAN ART

T**he** archaeological zone in Rome forms a huge open-air museum of evidence of ancient Roman life, while the porticoes and cloisters of the city's churches are filled with ancient sarcophagi and fragments of statuary. The largest important collection can be seen in the **Museo Nazionale Romano** at the Baths of Diocletian and its new branch Palazzo Massimo. The museum's many ancient artifacts include, most notably, a sarcophagus from Livia's Villa at Prima Porta just north of Rome. Also on display are some wonderfully well-preserved mosaics. The museum's great collection of Roman statues is now housed in the recently restored **Palazzo Altemps**. The most important statues are in the **Vatican Museums**, which also have the best of the great Greek works, such as the *Laocoön*, brought to Rome around

Victory banner, Museo della Civiltà Romana

the 1st century AD. It had tremendous influence on the subsequent development of Roman art. Splendid copies of Greek originals can be seen in the **Capitoline Museums**.

In the Forum, occupying two floors of the church of Santa Francesca Romana, is the **Antiquarium Forense** with restored finds from the excavations. For those who enjoy history, the large scale model at the **Museo della Civiltà Romana** in EUR gives an excellent idea of what ancient Rome looked like in the 4th century AD.

Centurion's breast-plate, Museo della Civiltà Romana

ART GALLERIES

Muses in Raphael's *Parnassus* (1508–11), Vatican Museums

I**N THE PAST,** many of Rome's great aristocratic families owned magnificent private collections of paintings and sculpture. Some of these are still housed in ancestral palazzi, which are open to the public. One is the **Galleria Doria Pamphilj**, which has the greatest concentration of paintings of any palazzo in Rome. It's well worth searching through the various rooms to find the pearls of the collection, which include works by Raphael,

Filippo Lippi, Caravaggio, Titian and Claude Lorrain, and a portrait of Pope Innocent X Pamphilj by the Spanish artist Velázquez. The **Galleria Spada** collection, begun by Bernardino Spada in 1632, is still housed in the fine original gallery built for it. The paintings demonstrate 17th-century Roman taste and include works by Rubens, Guido Reni, Guercino and Jan Brueghel the Elder. The **Galleria Colonna** contains a collection of art dating from the same period.

Hellenistic faun, Museo Borghese

Other old family residences are now showcases for state art collections. The Galleria Nazionale d'Arte Antica is divided between **Palazzo Barberini** and **Palazzo Corsini**. Palazzo Barberini, built between 1625 and 1633 by Bernini and others for the Barberini family, houses paintings from the 13th to the 16th centuries. It also has *objets d'art* acquired by the state from various private collections. At some future date, the 17th- and 18th-century paintings exhibited in the Palazzo Corsini, on the south side of the Tiber, will

be transferred to join the Palazzo Barberini collection. Another wonderful private collection was that of the Borghese family, also now managed by the state. The **Museo e Galleria Borghese** contains a sculpture collection, including the technically amazing *Apollo and Daphne* by the youthful genius Bernini and the famous statue of Pauline Borghese by Canova. On the first floor is the picture collection with paintings by Titian, Correggio and others.

The **Capitoline Museums** hold collections that were gifts of the popes to the people of Rome. The Pinacoteca (art gallery) in the **Palazzo dei Conservatori** contains works by Titian, Guercino and Van Dyck. There is an art gallery at the **Vatican Museums**, but lovers of Renaissance art will head straight for the Sistine Chapel and the Raphael Rooms. Rome's main modern art collection is in the **Galleria Nazionale d'Arte Moderna**.

SMALLER MUSEUMS

THE MOST IMPORTANT of the smaller collections is the beautifully laid-out medieval museum in **Palazzo Venezia**, with exhibits ranging from ceramics to sculpture. Rome has a wealth of specialist museums like the **Museum of Musical Instruments**, the **Museo di Roma in Trastevere**, with tableaux showing life in Rome during the last century, and the **Burcardo Theatre Museum**.

For those with an interest in the English Romantic poets who lived in Rome in the 19th century, there is the **Keats-Shelley Memorial House**, a museum in the house where John Keats died. Focusing on the French Empire, the **Museo Napoleonico** has relics and paintings

Laocoön (1st century AD) in the Vatican's Pio-Clementine Museum

of Napoleon and members of his family, many of whom came to live in Rome.

Portrait of Pauline Borghese painted by Kinson (c.1805), now in the Museo Napoleonico

The Deposition (1604) by Caravaggio, the Vatican

Rome's Best: Fountains and Obelisks

R OME HAS SOME of the loveliest fountains in the world.
Many of them are the work of the greatest sculptors of
the Renaissance and Baroque. Some fountains are
flamboyant displays, others restful trickles of water. Many
are simply drinking fountains, while a few cascade from
the sides of buildings. Obelisks date from far earlier in
the city's history. Although some of them were
commissioned by Roman emperors, many are even
older and were brought to Rome by triumphant,
conquering armies. A more detailed overview of
Rome's fountains and obelisks is on pages 52–3.

Piazza San Pietro
*Twin fountains give
life to the splendid
monumental piazza
of St Peter's. Maderno
designed the one on
the Vatican side in
1614; the other was
later built to match.*

Piazza del Popolo
*Nineteenth-century
marble lions and
fountains surround an
ancient obelisk in the
centre of the piazza.*

Vatican

*Piaz
del
Rotor*

*Piazza
Navona*

Fontana dei Quattro Fiumi
*The fountain of the four
rivers is the work of Bernini.
The four figures represent
the Ganges, the Plate, the
Danube and the Nile.*

*Campo
de' Fiori*

Janiculum

Trastevere

**Obelisk of Santa Maria
sopra Minerva**
*The Egyptian obelisk,
held up by Bernini's
marble elephant, dates
from the 6th century BC.*

Fontana delle Tartarughe
*One of Rome's more secret fountains,
this jewel of Renaissance sculpture
shows youths helping tortoises into a basin.*

Fontana della Barcaccia
This elegant fountain of 1627 is probably the work of Pietro Bernini, father of the more famous Gian Lorenzo.

Trevi Fountain
The Trevi, inspired by Roman triumphal arches, was designed by Nicola Salvi in 1732. Tradition has it that a coin thrown into the water guarantees a visitor's return to Rome.

0 metres   500

0 yards   500

iazza pagna

Via Veneto

Quirinal

Esquiline

apitol

Forum

Palatine

Lateran

Caracalla

ventine

Fontana delle Naiadi
When this fountain was unveiled in 1901, the realistically sensual bronze nymphs caused a storm of protest.

Obelisk of Piazza San Giovanni in Laterano
The oldest obelisk in Rome dates from the 14th century BC. It came to Rome in AD 357, brought here on the orders of Constantine II.

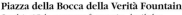

Piazza della Bocca della Verità Fountain
In this 18th-century fountain, built by Carlo Bizzaccheri for Pope Clement XI, water spills over a craggy rock formation where two Tritons hold aloft a large shell.

Exploring Fountains and Obelisks

Fountain of the Amphorae (1920s)

THE POPES who restored the ancient Roman aqueducts used to build fountains to commemorate their deeds of munificence. As a result, fountains of all sizes and shapes punctuate the city, drawing grateful crowds on hot summer days. Ancient obelisks provide powerful reminders of the debt Roman civilization owed to the Egyptians. Architects have learnt to incorporate them into Roman piazzas in fascinating ways.

FOUNTAINS

THE TREVI FOUNTAIN is one of the most famous of all. It is a *mostra*, a monumental fountain built to mark the end of an aqueduct – in this case the Acqua Vergine, built by Marcus Agrippa in 19 BC, although the Trevi itself was only completed in 1762. Other *mostre* are the **Fontana dell'Acqua Paola,** built for Pope Paul V in 1612 on the Janiculum, and the **Moses Fountain**, commemorating the opening of the Acqua Felice by Pope Sixtus V in 1587.

Almost all Rome's famous piazzas have fountains. In **Piazza San Pietro** there is a matching pair of powerful fountains. Piazza Navona has Bernini's wonderful Baroque **Fontana dei Quattro Fiumi** (fountain of the four rivers) as its main attraction. The fountain's four figures each represent one of the principal rivers of the four continents then known. To the south of this is the smaller **Fontana del Moro** (the Moor), also by Bernini, showing an Ethiopian struggling with a dolphin. At the north end, Neptune

wrestles with an octopus on a 19th-century fountain. In Piazza Barberini is the magnificent Bernini creation of 1642–3: the **Fontana del Tritone** with its sea god blowing through a shell.

More recently, large piazzas have been redesigned around fountains. Valadier's great design for **Piazza del Popolo** (1816–20) has marble lions and fountains surrounding the

Fountain of the Four Tiaras located behind St Peter's

The Pantheon Fountain

central obelisk plus two more fountains on the east and west sides of the square. The early 20th century saw the opening of the **Fontana delle Naiadi** (nymphs) in Piazza della Repubblica; its earthy figures caused great scandal at the time. The highly original **Fountain of the Amphorae** (map 8 D2) was erected in Piazza dell'Emporio during the 1920s. The same designer, Pietro Lombardi, also created the **Fountain of the Four Tiaras** (map 3 C3) behind the colonnade of St Peter's.

The city also has a number of smaller, and often very charming, fountains. At the foot of the Spanish Steps is the **Fontana della Barcaccia** (the leaking boat) of 1627; the **Fontana delle Tartarughe**

Fontana dei Cavalli Marini

THE TREVI FOUNTAIN

Appropriately for a fountain resembling a stage set, the theatrical Trevi has been the star of many films set in Rome, including romantic films like *Three Coins in a Fountain* and *Roman Holiday*, but also *La Dolce Vita*, Fellini's satirical portrait of Rome in the 1950s. Whatever liberties Anita Ekberg took then, paddling in the fountains of Rome is now forbidden, however tempting it could be in the summer heat.

Anita Ekberg in *La Dolce Vita* (1960)

(the tortoise fountain) has been in the tiny Piazza Mattei since 1581, and by Santa Maria in Domnica is the **Fontana della Navicella** (little boat), created out of an ancient Roman sculpture in the 16th century. In the forecourt of **Santa Sabina** (map 8 D2) water gushes from a huge mask set in an ancient basin. The **Pantheon Fountain** (map 4 F4), from 1575, is by Jacopo della Porta. **Le Quattro Fontane** (four fountains) have stood at the Quirinal hill crossroads since 1593.

Fountains in parks and gardens include the **Galleon Fountain** (1620–21) at the Vatican, and the **Fontana dei Cavalli Marini** (seahorses), of 1791, at Villa Borghese. The somewhat decayed 16th-century terraced gardens of the **Villa d'Este**, with their display of over 500 fountains, are still worth the journey.

Piazza Navona with Fontana dei Quattro Fiumi, by Pannini (1691–1765)

brought to Rome in the time of Augustus and also erected in the Circus Maximus. The slightly smaller **Obelisk of Piazza Montecitorio** was another of Augustus's trophies. The bronze ball and spike at the top recall its past use as a gnomon for a sundial of vast proportions.

Other obelisks, such as the one at the top of the Spanish Steps, are Roman imitations of Egyptian originals. The **Obelisk of Piazza dell' Esquilino** and the one in **Piazza del Quirinale** (map 5 B4) first stood at the entrance to the Mausoleum of Augustus. When re-erected, most obelisks were mounted on decorative bases, often with statues and fountains at their foot. Others became parts of sculptures.

The Ovato Fountain at Villa d'Este

OBELISKS

THE MOST ANCIENT and tallest of Rome's obelisks is the **Obelisk of Piazza di San Giovanni in Laterano**. Built of red granite, 31 m (100 ft) high, it came from the Temple of Ammon at Thebes, erected in the 14th century BC. It was brought to Rome in AD 357 by the order of Constantine II and put up in the Circus Maximus. In 1587 it was rediscovered, broken into three pieces, and was re-erected in the following year. Next in age is the obelisk in **Piazza del Popolo**, from the 12th or 13th century BC. It was

Obelisk in Piazza del Popolo

Bernini was the creator of the marble elephant balancing the Egyptian **Obelisk of Santa Maria sopra Minerva** on its back, and the **Fontana dei Fiumi**, with an obelisk from the Circus of Maxentius. Another obelisk was added to the remodelled Pantheon Fountain in 1711. The obelisk in **Piazza San Pietro** is Egyptian but does not have the usual hieroglyphics.

Wall fountain at Villa d'Este

Celebrated Visitors and Residents

Rome exerts a powerful fascination and foreigners throughout history have succumbed to its charms, often staying for long periods or even taking up permanent residence. The list of famous visitors is almost endless: painters, sculptors and architects from Rome's very earliest days; writers, poets, musicians, exiles, pilgrims, religious teachers, philosophers, aesthetes, archaeologists – all have passed through. Their orchestral works, operas, paintings, drawings, drama and literary journals testify to Rome's inspirational effect.

Martin Luther *(1483–1546)*
The religious reformer from Germany came to the convent at Santa Maria del Popolo in 1511. His horror at the corruption he saw led to the Reformation.

J W von Goethe *(1749–1832)*
The German poet, philosopher, artist, playwright, botanist and courtier lived at No. 20 Via del Corso, now a museum.

Sant'Ignazio di Loyola
(1491–1556)
He came to Rome from Spain in 1537 and founded the Jesuits near what is now the Gesù, the first Jesuit church.

Queen Christina
(1626–89)
The Swedish queen abdicated in 1654, and came to live in Palazzo Corsini on Via Lungara.

Vatican

Piazza Navona

Janiculum

Piazza Popo

Piazz della Rot

Campo de' Fie

Trastevere

T I B E R

St Dominic *(1170–1221)*
Founder of the Dominican order, St Dominic was born in Spain. The order's headquarters were at Santa Sabina on the Aventine.

Jean-Auguste-Dominique Ingres *(1780–1867)*
The 19th-century French painter, leader of the Neo-Classical tradition, lived in Rome from 1806 until 1820. He returned in 1834 as director of the French Academy at Villa Medici.

Pauline Borghese
(1780–1825)
Napoleon's sister was the subject of scandal in 1805, when she posed semi-nude for a statue by Canova, which is now in Museo Borghese.

Via Veneto

The Exiled Stuarts
James Stuart (1688–1766), unsuccessful claimant to the British throne, came to Rome as an exile. He was presented with Palazzo Balestra by Pope Clement XI and died here.

Quirinal

itol

Forum

Esquiline

Palatine

Lateran

Caracalla

ventine

Lord Byron *(1788–1824)*
Though the English poet's stay in the city was brief, the influence on his work was long-lasting. Stanzas in Childe Harold's Pilgrimage *and* Manfred *were inspired by seeing the Colosseum by moonlight.*

| 0 metres | 500 |
| 0 yards | 500 |

Percy Bysshe Shelley
(1792–1822)
The great English Romantic poet wrote his drama Prometheus Unbound *in the calm of the ruined Baths of Caracalla in 1819.*

Artists and Writers Inspired by Rome

ARTISTS AND WRITERS have been attracted to Rome since Classical times. Many came to work for the emperors; the poets Horace, Virgil and Ovid, for example,

all enjoyed the patronage of Emperor Augustus. Later on, especially in the Renaissance and Baroque periods, the greatest artists and architects came to Rome to compete for commissions from the popes. However, patronage was not the only magnet. Since the Renaissance, Rome's Classical past and its picturesque ruins have drawn artists, architects and writers from all over Italy and abroad.

The prolific love poet Ovid (43 BC–AD 17)

PAINTERS, SCULPTORS AND ARCHITECTS

Diego Velázquez, one of many great 17th-century artists to visit Rome

IN THE EARLY 16th century, artists and architects were summoned from all parts of Italy to realize the grandiose building projects of the popes. From Urbino came Bramante (1444–1514) and Raphael (1483–1520); from Perugia Perugino (1450–1523); from Florence Michelangelo (1475–1564) and many others. They worked in the Vatican, on the new St Peter's and the decoration of the Sistine Chapel. Artists were often well rewarded, but they also lived in dangerous times. Florentine sculptor and goldsmith Benvenuto Cellini (1500–71) helped defend Castel Sant' Angelo *(see pp248–9)* during the Sack of Rome (1527), but was later imprisoned there and made a dramatic escape. His memoirs tell the story.

Towards the end of the 16th century church patronage was generous to the

Milanese-born Caravaggio (1571–1610) despite his violent character and unruly life. The Carracci family from Bologna also flourished – especially brothers Annibale (1560–1609) and Agostino (1557–1602).

The work of Gian Lorenzo Bernini (1598–1680) can be seen all over Rome. He succeeded Carlo Maderno (1556–1629) as architect of St Peter's, and created its great bronze baldacchino, the splendid colonnade *(see pp230–31)* and numerous fountains, churches and sculptures. His rival for the title of leading architect of the Roman Baroque was Francesco Borromini (1599–1667), whose highly original genius can be appreciated in many Roman churches and palazzi.

In the 17th century it became more common for artists from outside Italy to come and work in Rome. Diego Velázquez (1599–1660), King Philip IV of Spain's court painter, came in 1628 to study

Self-portrait by the 18th-century artist Angelica Kauffmann, c.1770

the art treasures of the Vatican. Rubens (1577–1640) came from Antwerp to study, and carried out various commissions. The French artists Nicolas Poussin (1594–1665) and Claude Lorrain (1600–82) lived here for many years.

The Classical revival of the 18th century attracted artists to Rome in unprecedented numbers. From Britain came the Scottish architect Robert Adam (1728–92) and the Swiss artist Angelica Kauffmann (1741–1807), who settled here and was buried with great honour in Sant'Andrea delle Fratte. After the excesses of the Baroque, sculpture also turned to the simplicity of Neo-Classicism. A leading exponent of this movement was Antonio Canova (1757–1821). Sculptors from all over Europe were influenced by him, including the Dane Bertel Thorvaldsen (1770–1844) who lived in Rome for many years.

Claude Lorrain's view of the Forum, painted in Rome in 1632

WRITERS

Dante (1262–1321) visited Rome during his exile from Florence and in the *Inferno* describes the great influx of pilgrims for the first Holy Year (1300). The poet Petrarch (1304–74), born in Arezzo, came to the city in much happier circumstances to be crowned with laurels on the Capitol in 1341. The poet Torquato Tasso (1544–95), from Sorrento, was invited to receive a similar honour, but died soon after his arrival. He is buried in Sant'Onofrio *(see p219)* on the Janiculum.

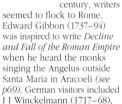

Torquato Tasso

Two of the first writers from abroad to visit Rome were the French essayist Montaigne (1533–92) and English poet John Milton (1608–74). Then, by the early 18th century, writers seemed to flock to Rome. Edward Gibbon (1737–94) was inspired to write *Decline and Fall of the Roman Empire* when he heard the monks singing the Angelus outside Santa Maria in Aracoeli *(see p69)*. German visitors included J J Winckelmann (1717–68),

who wrote influential studies of ancient art, and the poet J W von Goethe (1749–1832).

In the Romantic period Rome teemed with English writers: poets Keats, Shelley and Byron, followed by the Brownings and the novelist Charles Dickens. Travel writers in the 19th century included Augustus Hare (1834–1903) and the German historian Ferdinand Gregorovius (1821–91). Much of *The Portrait of a Lady* by American Henry James (1843–1916) is set in Rome.

Modern life in Rome is brilliantly captured by the Roman novelist and short-story writer Alberto Moravia (1907–90).

MUSICIANS

Giovanni luigi da Palestrina (1525–94), from the town of that name, became choir-master and organist to the Vatican and composed some of the greatest unaccompanied choral music ever written. In 1770 the 14-year-old Mozart heard Gregorio Allegri's unpublished *Miserere* in the Sistine Chapel and wrote it down from memory. Arcangelo

Portrait of the poet John Keats painted by his friend Joseph Severn in 1819

Corelli (1653–1713), the great violinist and composer of the Baroque age, worked in Rome under the patronage of Cardinal Ottoboni. One of his first commissions was to provide a festival of music for Queen Christina of Sweden.

During the 19th century the Prix de Rome brought many French musicians to study here at the Villa Medici *(see p135)*. Hector Berlioz (1803–69) owed the inspiration for his popular *Roman Carnival,* the overture to his opera *Benvenuto Cellini,* to his two-year stay in Rome. Georges Bizet (1838–75) and Claude Debussy (1862–1918) were also Prix de Rome winners. Franz Liszt (1811–86), after his 50th year, settled in Rome, took minor orders and became known as Abbé Liszt. He wrote *Fountains of the Villa d'Este* while staying at the villa in Tivoli.

Giacomo Puccini

Twentieth-century musical associations with Rome include the popular works by Ottorino Respighi (1870–1936): *The Fountains of Rome* and *The Pines of Rome,* while Giacomo Puccini (1858–1924) used Roman settings when creating his dramatic, tragic opera *Tosca.*

ROMAN CINEMA

The Cinecittà studios, built in 1937 just outside Rome, are most famous for the films made here in the 1940s – classics of Italian Neo-Realism such as Roberto Rossellini's *Roma Città Aperta* and Vittorio De Sica's *Sciuscià* and *Ladri di Biciclette.* The director most often linked with Roman cinema is Federico Fellini, through films like *La Dolce Vita* (1960) and *Roma* (1972). However, perhaps the most famous artist associated with Rome is the controversial writer-turned-film-maker Pier Paolo Pasolini (1922–75), widely known for his films *Teorema* (1968) and *Il Decamerone* (1971).

Since the 1950s, Rome and Cinecittà have also been much used for foreign films: from *Ben-Hur* and *Spartacus* in the 1950s through to *Gladiator* and Scorsese's *Gangs of New York.*

Pier Paolo Pasolini

ROME THROUGH THE YEAR

THE BEST TIMES to visit Rome are spring and autumn when the weather is usually warm, and sometimes even hot enough to sunbathe and swim at the beaches and lakes outside the city. In the winter months, the weather tends to be grey and wet, while in high summer, most people (including Romans, who leave the city in their droves) find the heat unbearable. Easter and Christmas are obviously very special in Rome, but there are other religious festivals worth seeing at other times in the year, as well as some enjoyable secular events like the Festa de' Noantri in Trastevere and the Flower Festival in Genzano. In villages outside Rome, local celebrations are held to welcome new crops such as strawberries and beans in the spring, and grapes and truffles in the autumn.

SPRING

EASTER, falling in March or April, marks the official beginning of the tourist season in Rome. Catholics from all over the world flock into the city to make their pilgrimages to the main basilicas and to hear the pope's Easter Sunday address outside St Peter's, while the less devout come simply to take advantage of the mild weather. Meanwhile, Romans pile into their cars and head for the coast and countryside, so you can expect the roads, beaches and restaurants of the Castelli Romani and Lake Bracciano to be busy.

Temperatures tend to be around 18° C (66° F), but can hit 28° C (82° F), so by mid-May it is usually possible to lunch and dine outside. However, there can still be sudden downpours and temperature swings, so do bring warm clothes and an umbrella.

Crowds gathering in St Peter's Square at Easter

In April tubs full of colourful azaleas are ranged on the Spanish Steps and along Via Veneto, and once the roses start to flower in the city's Rose Garden overlooking the Circus Maximus, it is opened to the public.

For a fortnight from mid-May Via dei Coronari is lit by candles, lined with plants and hung with banners for the street's antiques fair, while Via Margutta hosts an outdoor art show. In the first week of May the International Horse Show is held in the Villa Borghese. Also usually in May, many world-class tennis players flock to Rome to compete in the International Tennis Championships held annually at the Foro Italico.

EVENTS

Festa di Santa Francesca Romana (9 March), Santa Francesca Romana. Blessing of the city's vehicles (see p87).
Festa di San Giuseppe (19 March), in the Trionfale area. St Joseph's (and Father's) Day celebrated in the streets.
Rome Marathon (late March), through the city (see p351).
Good Friday (March/April), Colosseum. Procession of the Cross at 9pm led by the Pope.
Easter Sunday (March/April), St Peter's Square. Address made by the Pope (see p231).
Rome's Birthday (Sunday before 21 April), Piazza del Campidoglio.
Festa della Primavera (March/April), Spanish Steps and Trinità dei Monti. Azaleas in the street and concerts.
Art exhibition (April/May), Via Margutta (see p339).
International Horse Show (early May), Villa Borghese (see p350).
Antiques Fair (mid–late May), Via dei Coronari (see p324).
International Tennis Championships (usually May), Foro Italico (see p350).

International Horse Show in Villa Borghese in May

Average Daily Hours of Sunshine

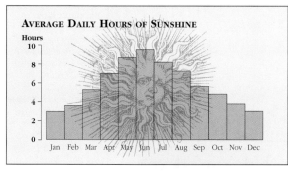

Hours
10
8
6
4
2
0

Jan Feb Mar Apr May Jun Jul Aug Sep Oct Nov Dec

Sunshine Chart
Rome is famous for its light. June is the sunniest month but it is also very dry, and without the odd shower the bright heat can feel intense. In autumn, Rome's southerly position means that the sun can still be enjoyably warm at midday.

Summer

In JUNE a season of concerts begins, with performances in some of the city's most beautiful palaces, churches and courtyards. In July and August opera and drama are staged at Ostia Antica *(see pp270–71)* and in various outdoor locations. During the summer there are also contemporary cultural events – film, music of all kinds, dance and theatre. On midsummer evenings there are stalls and amusements on the Tiber embankments by Castel Sant'Angelo, while in the last two weeks of July Trastevere becomes an open-air party as the Noantri festival is celebrated with trinket stalls, dining in the street and fireworks.

Summer vegetables

The sales *(saldi)* begin in mid-July, and the relatively new Alta Moda Fashion Show is usually held mid- to late July at the Spanish Steps.

Many Romans leave the city at the end of June, when schools close, but as June and July are peak tourist months, hotels, cafés, restaurants and all the main places of interest and other attractions are packed out. In August,

Flower-carpeted streets in Genzano

when the temperature often soars to over 40° C (104° F), virtually all Romans flee the city for the seaside, meaning that many cafés, shops and restaurants close for the entire month.

Events

Flower Festival *(June, the Sunday after Corpus Domini)*, Genzano, Castelli Romani, south of Rome. Streets are carpeted with flowers.
Festa di San Giovanni *(23–24 June)*, Piazza di Porta San Giovanni. Celebrated with meals of snails in tomato sauce, suckling pig, a fair and firework display.
Festa di San Pietro *(29 June)*, many churches. Celebrations mark the feast of St Peter.
Tevere Expo *(end June–mid-July)*, along the Tiber.

Crafts, food and wine, music and fireworks *(see p339)*.
Festa de' Noantri *(last two weeks in July)*, the streets of Trastevere. Food and entertainment *(see p339 and p341)*.
Alta Moda Fashion Show *(usually mid- to late July)*, Spanish Steps *(see p339)*.
Estate Romana *(July/ August)*, Villa Ada, Ostia Antica, in parks, by the Tiber. Opera, concerts, drama, dance and film *(see p341)*.
Festa della Madonna della Neve *(5 August)*, Santa Maria Maggiore. Fourth-century snowfall re-enacted with white flower petals *(see p172)*.
Ferragosto *(15 August)*, Santa Maria in Trastevere. Midsummer holiday. Almost everything closes down. Celebrations are held for the Feast of the Assumption.

The heat of an August afternoon in front of St Peter's

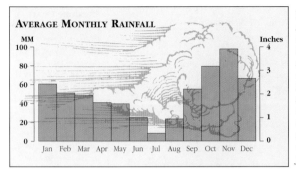

AVERAGE MONTHLY RAINFALL

MM · Inches

Rainfall Chart
Autumn is Rome's rainiest season, with heavy downpours, sometimes lasting for days, especially in November. Rain in summer tends to come in violent – but often extremely refreshing – storms. In winter and early spring expect a few dull, drizzly days.

AUTUMN

SEPTEMBER AND OCTOBER are the best – and among the most popular – months to visit Rome. The fiery heat of July and August will have cooled a little, but midday can be very hot, and you can still eat and drink outside without feeling chilly until late at night. Visiting Rome in November is not recommended: it is the wettest month of the year and Roman rainstorms are often very strong and heavy.

At the beginning of October an artisans' fair is held on Via dell'Orso and adjacent streets, while nearby the antiques galleries of Via dei Coronari hold open house. There are also October antiques fairs in Orvieto and Perugia, two of the loveliest Umbrian hill towns, which are about an hour's drive north of Rome. In November, there's yet another prestigious antiques fair at the papal palace of Viterbo, 65 km (40 m) north of Rome *(see p271)*.

Autumn is the season of harvest festivals, so head out to the small towns around Rome to sample delicacies such as local cheeses, sausages, chestnuts and mushrooms.

A roast chestnut stall in autumn

Another reason for taking a trip out of Rome is the wine festival in Marino, in the Castelli Romani, south of the city. There are many opportunities to sample the wines of this region that was once the home to luxurious 16th- and 17th-century country residences but now is renowned particularly for its white wines.

Throughout the autumn and winter in Rome freshly roasted chestnuts can be bought from vendors on street corners, and occasionally there is a stand on Campo de' Fiori where you can sample *vino novello*, the new season's wine. On All Saints' and All Souls' Days, which fall on 1 and 2 November

respectively, the Romans make pilgrimages to the tombs of relatives who are buried in the cemeteries of Prima Porta and Verano. Chrysanthemums are then traditionally placed on their graves and for this reason they should definitely not be given as thank-you presents. On a much happier note, the classical concert and opera seasons begin again in October and November. Details of performances can be found in listings magazines such as *Time Out Roma, Trovaroma* and *Roma c'è (see p340)*, in daily newspapers, such as *La Repubblica (see p367)*, and on posters around the city.

EVENTS

RomaEuropa *(autumn)*. Films, dance, theatre and concerts in venues around Rome *(see p341)*.
Art fair *(September)*, Via Margutta *(see p339)*.
Crafts fair *(last week September/first week October)*, Via dell'Orso *(see p339)*.
Marino Wine Festival *(first Sunday in October)*, Marino. Celebrations include tastings and street entertainment.
Antiques Fair *(mid-October)*, Via dei Coronari *(see p339)*.
All Saints' and All Souls' Days *(1, 2 November)*, Prima Porta and Verano cemeteries. The Pope usually celebrates Mass in the Verano cemetery.
Festa di Santa Cecilia *(22 November)*, Santa Cecilia in Trastevere and Catacombs of San Callisto.
Vino Novello tasting *(late November)*, Campo de' Fiori.

Autumn in the Villa Doria Pamphilj park

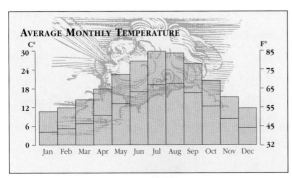

Average Monthly Temperature

Temperature Chart
The chart shows the average minimum and maximum monthly temperatures. July and August can be unbearably hot, making sightseeing a chore. The fresher days of spring and autumn are ideal to visit Rome, but there are some dull and rainy spells.

Winter

DURING THE WINTER Rome is bracingly chilly but the temperature rarely drops below freezing. Not all buildings are centrally heated so if you are staying in a small hotel bring warm clothes and request extra blankets as soon as you arrive, as they can be in short supply. Warm up in cafés with hot chocolate and cappuccino.

The run-up to Christmas is great fun in Rome, especially if you have children. Manger scenes, *presepi*, are set up in many churches, piazzas and public places and from mid-December to Twelfth Night

Rome during one of its rare snowfalls

Market on Piazza Navona

Piazza Navona hosts a market where you can buy manger scenes, decorations and toys. Unless you have friends in Rome, Christmas itself can be rather lonely, as it is very much a family event. On New Year's Eve, however, everyone is out on the street to drink sparkling wine and let off fireworks.

La Befana, on 6 January, is a traditional holiday when a witch, called La Befana, delivers sweets to children.

The Carnival season runs from late January through to February, celebrated largely by children with fancy-dress

parties and parades along Via Nazionale, Via Cola di Rienzo and the Pincio. Keep out of the way of teenagers with shaving-cream spray cans and water-filled balloons.

Events

Festa della Madonna Immacolata *(8 December)*, Piazza di Spagna. Firemen climb up a ladder to place a wreath on the statue of the Virgin Mary.
Christmas Market *(mid-December – 6 January)*, Piazza Navona. Christmas and children's market *(see p120)*.
Nativity scenes *(mid-December – mid-January)*, many churches. Life-size scene in St Peter's Square, collection at Santi Cosma e Damiano.
Midnight Mass *(24 December)*, at most churches.
Christmas Day *(25 December)*, St Peter's Square. Blessing by the Pope.
New Year's Eve *(31 December)*, all over city. Firework displays, furniture thrown out.
La Befana *(6 January)*, all over city. Parties for children.

Public Holidays
New Year's Day (1 Jan)
Epiphany (6 Jan)
Easter Monday
Liberation Day (25 Apr)
Labour Day (1 May)
Day of the Republic (2 Jun)
SS Peter & Paul (29 Jun)
Ferragosto (15 Aug)
All Saints' Day (1 Nov)
Immaculate Conception (8 Dec)
Christmas Day (25 Dec)
Santo Stefano (26 Dec)

Via Condotti at Christmas

ROME AREA BY AREA

CAPITOL

THE TEMPLE OF JUPITER on the Capitol, the southern summit of the Capitoline hill, was the centre of the Roman world. Reached by a zig-zag path up from the Forum, the temple was the scene of all the most sacred religious and political ceremonies. The hill and its temple came to symbolize Rome's authority as *caput mundi*, head of the world, and the concept of a "capital" city is derived from the Capitol. Throughout the city's history, the Capitol (Campidoglio), has remained the seat of municipal government. Today's city council, the Comune di Roma, meets in the Renaissance splendour of Palazzo Senatorio. The Capitol also serves as Rome's Registry Office. Rome's position as a modern capital is forcefully expressed in the enormous Victor Emmanuel Monument, which unfortunately blots out the view of the Capitol from Piazza Venezia. The present arrangement on the hill dates from the 16th century, when Michelangelo created a beautiful piazza reached by a flight of steps, the Cordonata. Two of the buildings around the piazza now house the Capitoline Museums.

Hand of colossal statue in Palazzo dei Conservatori

SIGHTS AT A GLANCE

Churches and Temples
Santa Maria in Aracoeli **7**
Temple of Jupiter **8**
San Marco **12**

Museums and Galleries
Capitoline Museums: Palazzo Nuovo pp70–71 **1**
Capitoline Museums: Palazzo dei Conservatori pp72–3 **2**
Palazzo Venezia and Museum **11**

Historic Buildings
Roman Insula **5**

Historic Streets and Piazzas
Piazza del Campidoglio **3**
Cordonata **4**
Aracoeli Staircase **6**

Ancient Sites
Tarpeian Rock **9**

Monuments
Victor Emmanuel Monument **10**

GETTING THERE
All the sights in this area are within walking distance of Piazza Venezia. Bus routes converge here from all parts of the city, as do many thousands of motorists. From Termini station you can catch the 40, 64, or 170; from Piazza Barberini the 63 or 95. From St Peter's and the Vatican the only buses are the 40, 62 and 64. Piazza Venezia is also a stopping-off point for the 110 tourist bus.

```
0 metres      200
0 yards       200
```

KEY

▨ Street-by-Street map

SEE ALSO

• *Street Finder*, maps 5, 12

Statue of Marcus Aurelius on Michelangelo's Piazza del Campidoglio

Street-by-Street: The Capitol and Piazza Venezia

THE CAPITOL, citadel of ancient Rome, is a must for every visitor. A broad flight of steps (the Cordonata) leads up to Michelangelo's spectacular Piazza del Campidoglio. This is flanked by the Palazzo Nuovo and Palazzo dei Conservatori, housing the Capitoline Museums with their fine collections of sculptures and paintings. The absence of cars makes the hill a welcome retreat from the squeal of brakes below, but you should brave the traffic to visit Palazzo Venezia and its museum.

PIAZZA VENEZIA

PIAZZA VENEZIA

PIAZZA VENEZIA

VIA DEL TEATRO DI MARCELLO

Victor Emmanuel Monument
This huge white marble monument to Italy's first king was completed in 1911 ❿

San Marco
The church of the Venetians in Rome has a fine 9th-century apse mosaic ⓬

Palazzo Venezia
The museum's finest exhibits, such as this 13th-century gilded angel decorated with enamel, date from the late Middle Ages ⓫

Roman *Insula*
This is a ruined apartment block dating from Imperial Rome ❺

Cordonata
Michelangelo's great staircase changed the orientation of the Capitol towards the west ❹

Aracoeli Staircase
When it was built in 1348, the staircase became a centre for political debate ❻

KEY

– – – Suggested route

0 metres	75
0 yards	75

★ **Palazzo dei Conservatori**
In this part of the Capitoline Museums a fine series of reliefs from the Temple of Hadrian (see p106) is displayed in the courtyard ❷

Santa Maria in Aracoeli
The treasures hidden behind the church's brick façade include this 15th-century fresco of the Funeral of St Bernardino *by Pinturicchio* **7**

LOCATOR MAP
See Central Rome Map pp12–13

★ Palazzo Nuovo
This bust of Augustus in the Hall of the Emperors is one of many fine Classical sculptures in the Capitoline Museums **1**

Palazzo Senatorio was used by the Roman Senate from about the 12th century. It now houses the offices of the mayor.

★ Piazza del Campidoglio
Michelangelo designed both the geometric paving and the façades of the buildings **3**

Temple of Jupiter
This artist's impression shows the gold and ivory statue of Jupiter that stood in the temple **8**

Tarpeian Rock
In ancient Rome traitors were thrown to their death from this cliff on the Capitol **9**

STAR SIGHTS

★ Palazzo dei Conservatori

★ Palazzo Nuovo

★ Piazza del Campidoglio

Capitoline Museums: Palazzo Nuovo ❶

See pp70–71.

Capitoline Museums: Palazzo dei Conservatori ❷

See pp72–3.

Piazza del Campidoglio ❸

Map 5 A5 & 12 F5. 🚌 *See **Getting There** p65.*

W HEN EMPEROR Charles V visited Rome in 1536, Pope Paul III Farnese was so embarrassed by the muddy state of the Capitol that he asked Michelangelo to draw up plans for repaving the piazza, and for renovating the façades of the Palazzo dei Conservatori and Palazzo Senatorio.

Michelangelo proposed adding the Palazzo Nuovo to form a piazza in the shape of a trapezium, embellished with Classical sculptures chosen for their relevance to Rome. Building started in 1546 but progressed so slowly that Michelangelo only lived to oversee the double flight of steps at the entrance of Palazzo Senatorio. The piazza was completed in the 17th century, the design remaining largely faithful to the original. Pilasters two storeys high and balustrades interspersed with statues link the buildings thematically. The piazza faces west towards St Peter's, the Christian equivalent of the Capitol. At its centre stands a replica of a statue of Marcus Aurelius. The original is in the Palazzo Nuovo *(see pp70–71).*

Cordonata ❹

Map 5 A5 & 12 F5. 🚌 *See **Getting There** p65.*

F ROM PIAZZA VENEZIA, the Capitol is approached by a gently rising, subtly widening ramp – the Cordonata. At the foot is a pair of granite Egyptian lions, and on the left a 19th-century monument to Cola di Rienzo, close to where the dashing 14th-century tyrant was executed. The top of the ramp is guarded by restored Classical statues of the Dioscuri – Castor and Pollux.

Roman *Insula* ❺

Piazza d'Aracoeli. **Map** 5 A5 & 12 F4. 📞 *06-6710 3819.* 🚌 *See **Getting There** p65. **Open** by appt only: permit needed (see p367).*

T WO THOUSAND YEARS ago the urban poor of Rome used to make their homes in *insulae* – apartment blocks.

A statue of one of the Dioscuri at the top of the Cordonata

These were often badly maintained by landlords, and expensive to rent in a city where land costs were high. This 2nd-century AD tenement block, of barrel-vault construction, is the only survivor in Rome from that era. The fourth, fifth and part of the sixth storey remain above current ground level.

In the Middle Ages, a section of these upper storeys was converted into a church; its bell tower and 14th-century Madonna in a niche are visible from the street.

During the Fascist years, the area was cleared, and three lower floors emerged. Some 380 people may have lived in the tenement, in the squalid conditions described by the 1st-century AD satirical writers Martial and Juvenal. The latter mentions that he had to climb 200 steps to reach his garret.

This *insula* may once have had more storeys. The higher you lived, the more dismal the conditions, as the poky spaces of the building's upper levels testify.

The Cordonata in an 18th-century painting by Antonio Canaletto

Aracoeli Staircase ➏

Piazza d'Aracoeli. **Map** 5 A5 & 12 F4.
🚌 See **Getting There** p65.

THE ARACOELI Staircase numbers 124 marble steps (122 if you start from the right) and was completed in 1348, some say in thanks for the passing of the Black Death, but probably in view of the 1350 Holy Year.

The 14th-century tribune-turned-tyrant Cola di Rienzo used to harangue the masses from the Aracoeli Staircase; in the 17th century foreigners used to sleep on the steps, until Prince Caffarelli, who lived on the hill, scared them off by rolling barrels filled with stones down them.

Popular belief has it that by climbing the steps on your knees you can win the Italian national lottery. From the top there is a good view of Rome, with the domes of Sant' Andrea della Valle and St Peter's slightly to the right.

Aracoeli Staircase

Santa Maria in Aracoeli ➐

Piazza d'Aracoeli (entrances via Aracoeli Staircase and door behind Palazzo Nuovo). **Map** 5 A5 & 12 F4. ☏ 06-679 81 55. 🚌 See **Getting There** p65. **Open** 9am–12.30pm, 3–6pm daily.

DATING FROM AT LEAST the 6th century, the church of Santa Maria in Aracoeli, or St Mary of the Altar in the Sky, stands on the northern summit of the Capitoline, on the site of the ancient temple

Ceiling commemorating Battle of Lepanto in Santa Maria in Aracoeli

to Juno. Its 22 columns were taken from various ancient buildings; the inscription on the third column to the left tells us that it comes *"a cubiculo Augustorum"* – from the bedroom of the emperors.

The church of the Roman senators and people, Santa Maria in Aracoeli has been used to celebrate many triumphs over adversity. Its ceiling, with naval motifs, commemorates the Battle of Lepanto (1571), and was built under Pope Gregory XIII Boncompagni, whose family crest, the dragon, can be seen towards the altar end.

Many other Roman families and individuals are honoured by memorials in the church. To the right of the entrance door, the tombstone of archdeacon Giovanni Crivelli, rather than being set into the floor of the church, stands eternally to attention, partly so that the signature "Donatelli" (by Donatello) can be read at eye-level.

The frescoes in the first chapel on the right, painted by Pinturicchio in the 1480s in the beautifully clear style of the early Renaissance, relate the life and death of St Bernardino of Siena. On the left-hand wall, the perspective of *The Burial of the Saint* actually slants to the right, taking into account the position of the viewer standing just outside the chapel.

The church is most famous, however, for an icon with apparently miraculous powers, the *Santo Bambino*, a 15th-century olive-wood figure of the Christ Child which was carved out of a tree from the garden of Gethsemane. Its powers are said to include resurrecting the dead, and it is sometimes summoned to the bedsides of the gravely ill. The original figure was stolen in 1994 but has been replaced by a replica.

At Christmas the Christ Child takes its place in the centre of a picturesque crib (second chapel to the left) but is usually to be found in the sacristy, as is the panel of the *Holy Family* from the workshop of Giulio Romano.

The miraculous olive-wood Christ Child at Santa Maria in Aracoeli

Capitoline Museums: Palazzo Nuovo ❶

A COLLECTION of Classical statues has been kept on the Capitoline hill since the Renaissance. The first group of bronze sculptures was given to the city by Pope Sixtus IV in 1471 and more additions were made by Pope Pius V in 1566. The Palazzo Nuovo was designed by Michelangelo as part of the renovation of the Piazza del Campidoglio, and after its completion in 1655, a number of the statues were transferred here. In 1734 Pope Clement XII Corsini decreed that the building be turned into the world's first public museum.

Hall of the Philosophers
The hall contains a rich mix of portraits of Greek politicians, scientists and literary figures. They are Roman copies that decorated the libraries, villas and gardens of the wealthy in ancient times.

MUSEUM GUIDE

The Palazzo Nuovo is devoted chiefly to sculpture, and most of its finest works, such as the Capitoline Venus, are Roman copies of Greek masterpieces. For visitors keen to identify the philosophers and poets of ancient Greece and the rulers of ancient Rome, there are collections of busts assembled in the 18th century. Admission price also includes entry to the Palazzo dei Conservatori opposite. A gallery below Piazza del Campidoglio links the two buildings.

Portrait of a Flavian Lady
The woman wears the fanciful and elaborate hairstyle popular among the female aristocracy of the 1st century AD.

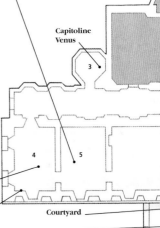

Capitoline Venus

First floor   **Courtyard**

★ **Marcus Aurelius**
This bronze equestrian statue of the emperor dates from the 2nd century AD. It used to stand on a pedestal in the centre of the Campidoglio, but has now been restored and is housed in the Palazzo Nuovo. A copy stands on the square.

Ground floor

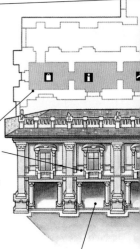

The façade of Palazzo Nuovo was designed by Michelangelo, but the work was actually finished in 1655 by the brothers Carlo and Girolamo Rainaldi.

Main entrance

STAR SCULPTURES

★ **Marcus Aurelius**

★ **Discobolus**

★ **Dying Galatian**

KEY TO FLOORPLAN

▨ Non-exhibition space

☐ Exhibition space

Mosaic of the Doves
This charming, naturalistic mosaic once decorated the floor of Hadrian's Villa at Tivoli (see p269). It shows doves drinking water from a vase.

★ **Discobolus**
The twisted torso was part of a Greek statue of a discus thrower. An 18th-century French sculptor, Monnot, made the additions that turned him into a wounded warrior.

Red Faun
Found at Tivoli, the famous red marble satyr is a 2nd-century AD version of a Greek original – an example of Hadrian's fondness for all things Greek.

Stairs to ground floor

7   8

Stairs to galleries below the Senate and connecting with Palazzo dei Conservatori

Stairs to first floor

★ **Dying Galatian**
Great compassion is conveyed in this Roman copy of an original Greek work of the 3rd century BC.

Alexander Severus as Hunter
In this marble of the 3rd century AD, the emperor's pose is a pastiche of Perseus, holding up the head of Medusa the Gorgon after he had killed her in her sleep.

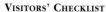

Capitoline Museums: Palazzo dei Conservatori ❷

THE PALAZZO DEI CONSERVATORI was the seat of the city's magistrates during the late Middle Ages. Its frescoed halls are still used occasionally for political meetings and the ground floor houses the municipal register office. The palazzo was built by Giacomo della Porta who carried out Michelangelo's designs for the Piazza del Campidoglio in the mid-16th century. While much of the palazzo is given over to sculpture, the art galleries on the second floor hold works by Veronese, Guercino, Tintoretto, Rubens, Caravaggio, Van Dyck and Titian.

Façade of Palazzo dei Conservatori
Work began on this Michelangelo design in 1563, the year before his death.

MUSEUM GUIDE

The museum is being reorganized, so some items might move. The first-floor rooms have original 16th- and 17th-century decoration and Classical statues. The second-floor gallery holds paintings and a porcelain collection; two newly opened rooms (10 and 11) house the Capitol medal and coin collection.

Burial and Glory of St Petronilla
This huge Baroque altar-piece was painted in 1622–3 by Guercino to hang in St Peter's.

★ St John the Baptist
Painted in 1595–6, Caravaggio's sensual portrait of the young saint presents a highly unorthodox image of the forerunner of Christ.

Second-floor art gallery

7
6
5
4
3
2
1
9
9

Stairs to second floor

Stairs to first floor

15
14
13
1
12

Courty

The Horatii and Curatii
D'Arpino's fresco was painted in 1613 and depicts a duel taken from early Roman legend.

KEY TO FLOORPLAN

☐ Garden
☐ Non-exhibition space
☐ Undergoing restoration
☐ Exhibition space

Main entrance

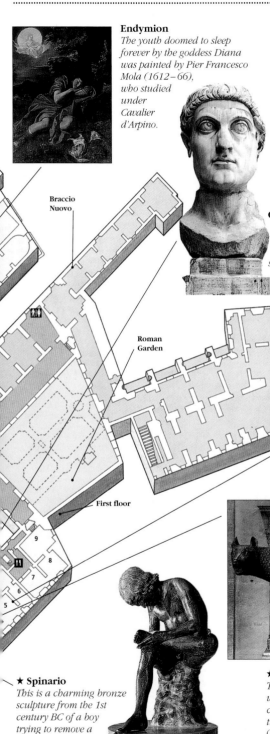

Endymion
The youth doomed to sleep forever by the goddess Diana was painted by Pier Francesco Mola (1612–66), who studied under Cavalier d'Arpino.

STAR EXHIBITS

★ **St John the Baptist by Caravaggio**

★ **Spinario**

★ **She-Wolf**

Braccio Nuovo

Constantine I
The head of a colossal 4th-century AD statue of the emperor has survived, along with a hand and other odd fragments.

Roman Garden

Medusa
This bust by Bernini of the mythological Medusa is in Room 5.

First floor

★ Spinario
This is a charming bronze sculpture from the 1st century BC of a boy trying to remove a thorn from his foot.

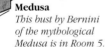

★ She-Wolf
The Etruscan bronze of the wolf dates from the early 5th century BC. The legendary twins Romulus and Remus (see pp16–17) were probably added in the 15th century.

Temple of Jupiter

Via del Tempio di Giove. **Map** 5 A5 & 12 F5. 🚌 See **Getting There** p65.

THE TEMPLE of Jupiter, the most important in ancient Rome, was founded in honour of the arch-god around 509 BC on the southern summit of the Capitoline hill. From the few traces that remain, archaeologists have been able to reconstruct the rectangular, Greek appearance of the temple as it once stood. In places you can see remnants of its particularly Roman feature, the podium. Most of this lies beneath the Museo Nuovo wing of the Palazzo dei Conservatori *(see pp72–3)*.

By walking around the site, from the podium's south-western corner in Via del Tempio di Giove to its south-eastern corner in Piazzale Caffarelli, you can see that the temple was about the same size as the Pantheon.

Sabine soldiers crushing the treacherous Tarpeia with their shields

his men, bribed Tarpeia to let them up on to the Capitol. As the Augustan historian Livy records, the Sabines used to wear heavy gold bracelets and jewelled rings on their left hands, and Tarpeia's reward for her treachery was to be "what they wore on their shield-arms".

The Sabines kept to the letter of the bargain if not to its spirit – they repaid Tarpeia not with their jewellery but by crushing her to death between their shields. Tarpeia was possibly the only casualty of her act of treachery – as the invading warriors met the Roman defenders, the Sabine women leapt between the two opposing armies, forcing a reconciliation. Traitors and other condemned criminals were subsequently executed by being thrown over the sheer face of the rock.

The place has been considered dangerous and used to be fenced off, but restoration work is now under way.

Ancient coin showing the
Temple of Jupiter

Tarpeian Rock

Via di Monte Caprino and Via del Tempio di Giove. **Map** 5 A5 & 12 F5. 🚌 See **Getting There** p65.

THE SOUTHERN TIP of the Capitoline is called the Tarpeian Rock (Rupe Tarpea), after Tarpeia, the young daughter of Spurius Tarpeius, defender of the Capitol in the 8th-century BC Sabine War.

The Sabines, bent on vengeance for the rape of their women by Romulus and

Victor Emmanuel Monument

Piazza Venezia. **Map** 5 A5 & 12 F4. 📞 06-699 17 18. 🚌 See **Getting There** p65. **Open** 9.30am–4pm daily (to 5pm summer).

KNOWN AS Il Vittoriano, this monument was begun in 1885 and inaugurated in 1911 in honour of Victor Emmanuel II of Savoy, the first king of a unified Italy. The king is depicted here in a gilt bronze equestrian statue, oversized like the monument itself – the statue is 12 m (39 ft) long.

The edifice also contains a museum of the Risorgimento, the events that led to unification *(see pp36–7)*. Built in austere white Brescian marble, the "wedding cake" or "typewriter" (two of the many insulting nicknames given to this white elephant) will never mellow into the ochre tones of surrounding buildings. It is widely held to be the epitome of self-important, insensitive architecture, though the views that it offers are spectacular.

Victor Emmanuel Monument in Piazza Venezia

Palazzo Venezia and Museum ⓫

Via del Plebiscito 118. **Map** 5 A4 & 12 E4. **☎** 06-6999 4318 **▦** See **Getting There** p65. **Open** 9am–7pm Tue–Sun (last adm: 30 mins before closing). **Closed** 1 Jan, 1 May, 25 Dec. **Adm charge**. **☒** Temporary exhibitions.

Palazzo Venezia with Mussolini's balcony in the centre

Iℕ ONE OF THE first Renaissance civic buildings in Rome, the arched windows and doors are so harmonious that the façade was once attributed to the great Humanist architect Leon Battista Alberti (1404–72). It was more probably built by Giuliano da Maiano, who is known to have carved the fine doorway on to the piazza.

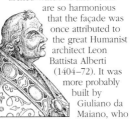

Pope Paul II

Palazzo Venezia was built in 1455–64 for the Venetian cardinal Pietro Barbo, who later became Pope Paul II. It was at times a papal residence, but it also served as the Venetian Embassy to Rome before passing into French hands in 1797. Since 1916 it has belonged to the state; in the Fascist era Mussolini used it as his head-quarters and addressed crowds from the central balcony.

The interior is best seen by visiting the Museo del Palazzo Venezia, Rome's most underrated museum. It holds first-class collections of early Renaissance painting; painted wood sculptures and Renaissance chests from Italy; tapestries from all of Europe; majolica; silver; Neapolitan ceramic figurines; Renaissance bronzes; arms and armour; Baroque terracotta sculptures by Bernini, Algardi and others; and 17th- and 18th-century Italian painting. There is a marble screen from the Aracoeli convent, destroyed to make way for the Victor Emmanuel Monument, and a bust of Paul II, showing him to rank with Martin V and Leo X among the fattest-ever popes. The building also hosts major temporary exhibitions.

San Marco ⓬

Piazza San Marco 48. **Map** 5 A4 & 12 F4. **☎** 06-679 52 05. **▦** See **Getting There** p65. **Open** 7.30am–12.30pm, 4–7pm, Mon–Sat, 8am–1.15pm, 4–7pm Sun. **✛**

Tℍᴇ CHURCH of San Marco was founded in 336 by Mark, the then pope, in honour of St Mark the Evangelist. The relics of Pope Mark lie under the altar. The church was restored by Pope Gregory IV in the 9th century – the magnificent apse mosaics date from this period.

Further major rebuilding took place in 1455–71, when Pope Paul II Barbo made San Marco the church of the Venetian commu-

Coat of arms of Pope Paul II

nity in Rome. The blue and gold coffered ceiling is decorated with Pope Paul's heraldic crest, the lion rampant, recalling the lion of St Mark, the patron saint of Venice. The appearance of the rest of the interior, with its colonnades of Sicilian jasper, was largely the creation of Filippo Barigioni in the 1740s. Complemented by an interesting array of funerary monuments in the aisles, the taste is typical of the late Roman Baroque.

Leon Battista Alberti, whose name is also mentioned tentatively in connection with Palazzo Venezia, may have been the architect of the elegant travertine arcade and loggia of the façade.

San Marco's apse mosaic of Christ, with Gregory IV on the far left

FORUM

THE FORUM was the centre of political, commercial and judicial life in ancient Rome. The largest buildings were the basilicas, where legal cases were heard. According to the playwright Plautus, the area teemed with "lawyers and litigants, bankers and brokers, shopkeepers and strumpets, good-for-nothings waiting for a tip from the rich". As

Figure of barbarian on the Arch of Constantine

Rome's population boomed, the Forum became too small. In 46 BC Julius Caesar built a new one, setting a precedent that was followed by emperors from Augustus to Trajan. As well as the Imperial Fora, emperors also erected triumphal arches to themselves, and just to the east Vespasian built the Colosseum, centre of entertainment after the business of the day.

SIGHTS AT A GLANCE

Churches and Temples
Temple of Saturn **5**
Temple of Castor
  and Pollux **8**
Temple of Vesta **9**
Temple of Antoninus
  and Faustina **11**
Temple of Romulus and Santi
  Cosma e Damiano **12**
Santa Francesca Romana **14**
Temple of Venus and Rome **17**

Historic Buildings
Basilica Aemilia **1**
Curia **2**
Basilica Julia **7**

House of the Vestal Virgins **10**
Basilica of Constantine
  and Maxentius **13**
Trajan's Markets pp88–9 **18**
Torre delle Milizie **20**
Casa dei Cavalieri di Rodi **21**
Mamertine Prison **24**
Colosseum pp92–5 **27**

Museums
Antiquarium Forense **15**

KEY

	Tour of the Forum maps
M	Metro station
i	Tourist information

Arches and Columns
Arch of Septimius Severus **4**
Column of Phocas **6**
Arch of Titus **16**
Trajan's Column **19**
Arch of Constantine **26**

Ancient Sites
Rostra **3**
Forum of Augustus **22**
Forum of Caesar **23**
Forum of Nerva **25**

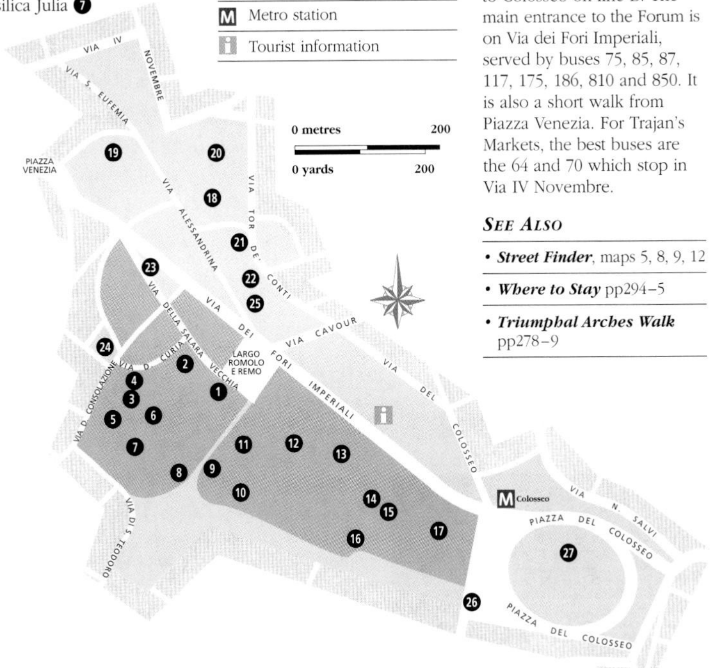

GETTING THERE
The simplest way is by Metro to Colosseo on line B. The main entrance to the Forum is on Via dei Fori Imperiali, served by buses 75, 85, 87, 117, 175, 186, 810 and 850. It is also a short walk from Piazza Venezia. For Trajan's Markets, the best buses are the 64 and 70 which stop in Via IV Novembre.

SEE ALSO
• *Street Finder*, maps 5, 8, 9, 12

• *Where to Stay* pp294–5

• *Triumphal Arches Walk* pp278–9

0 metres   200

0 yards   200

PIAZZA
VENEZIA

LARGO
ROMOLO
E REMO

Colosseo

PIAZZA DEL COLOSSEO

PIAZZA DEL COLOSSEO

View of the Forum with the Colosseum rising behind the bell tower of Santa Francesca Romana

A Tour of the Roman Forum: West

To APPRECIATE THE LAYOUT of the Forum before visiting its confusing patchwork of ruined temples and basilicas, it is best to view the whole area from above, from the back of the Capitol. From there you can make out the Via Sacra (the Sacred Way), the route followed through the Forum by religious and triumphal processions towards the Capitol. Up until the 18th century when archaeological excavations began, the Arch of Septimius Severus and the columns of the Temple of Saturn lay half-buried underground. Excavation of the Forum continues, and the ruins uncovered date from many different periods of Roman history.

The Temple of Vespasian was the point from where Piranesi made this 18th-century engraving of the Forum. Its three columns were then almost completely buried.

Temple of Concord

Portico of the Dii Consentes

Temple of Saturn
The eight surviving columns of this temple stand close by the three columns of the Temple of Vespasian ❺

Rostra
These are the ruins of the platform used for public oratory in the Forum ❸

Basilica Julia
Named after Julius Caesar, who ordered its construction, the basilica housed important law courts ❼

Column of Phocas
One of the very last monuments erected in the Forum, this single column dates from AD 608 ❻

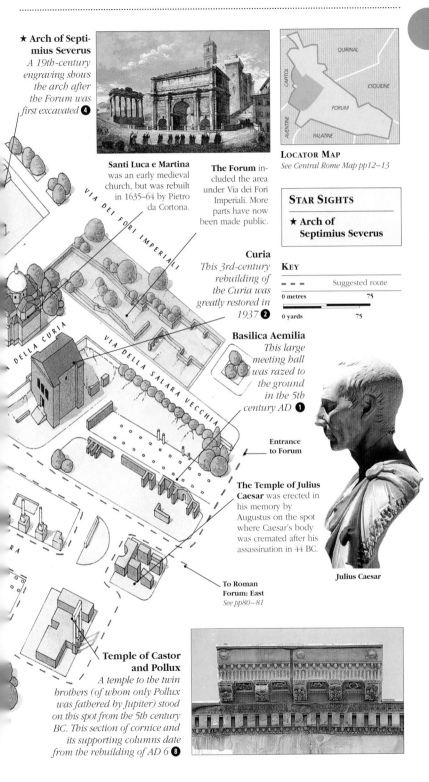

★ **Arch of Septimius Severus**
A 19th-century engraving shows the arch after the Forum was first excavated ❹

LOCATOR MAP
See Central Rome Map pp12–13

Santi Luca e Martina was an early medieval church, but was rebuilt in 1635–64 by Pietro da Cortona.

The Forum included the area under Via dei Fori Imperiali. More parts have now been made public.

STAR SIGHTS

★ **Arch of Septimius Severus**

VIA DEI FORI IMPERIALI

Curia
This 3rd-century rebuilding of the Curia was greatly restored in 1937 ❷

KEY

- - - Suggested route

0 metres   75

0 yards   75

VIA DELLA CURIA

VIA DELLA SALARA VECCHIA

Basilica Aemilia
This large meeting hall was razed to the ground in the 5th century AD ❶

Entrance to Forum

The Temple of Julius Caesar was erected in his memory by Augustus on the spot where Caesar's body was cremated after his assassination in 44 BC.

Julius Caesar

To Roman Forum: East
See pp80–81

Temple of Castor and Pollux
A temple to the twin brothers (of whom only Pollux was fathered by Jupiter) stood on this spot from the 5th century BC. This section of cornice and its supporting columns date from the rebuilding of AD 6 ❽

A Tour of the Roman Forum: East

THE EASTERN END of the Roman Forum is dominated by the massive barrel-vaulted ruins of the Basilica of Constantine. To picture the building as it was in the 4th century AD, you must imagine marble columns, floors and statues, and glittering tiles of gilt bronze. The remains of the other important buildings are scanty, though the garden and ponds in the centre of the House of the Vestal Virgins make it a very attractive spot. The two churches in this part of the Forum cannot be reached from within the archaeological area, but are accessible from the road outside.

The Regia was the office of the Pontifex Maximus, the chief priest of ancient Rome.

To Forum entrance

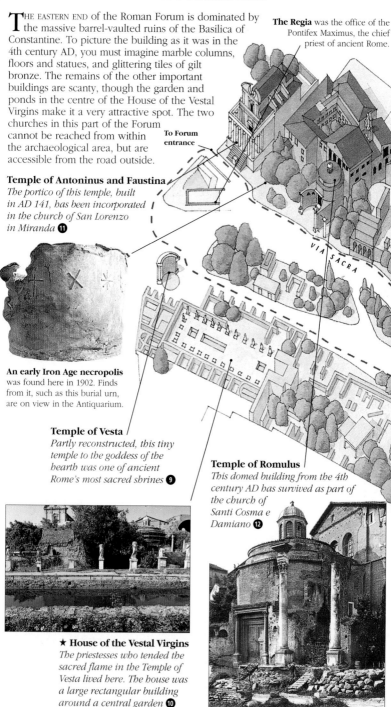

Temple of Antoninus and Faustina
The portico of this temple, built in AD 141, has been incorporated in the church of San Lorenzo in Miranda ⑪

VIA SACRA

An early Iron Age necropolis was found here in 1902. Finds from it, such as this burial urn, are on view in the Antiquarium.

Temple of Vesta
Partly reconstructed, this tiny temple to the goddess of the hearth was one of ancient Rome's most sacred shrines ⑨

Temple of Romulus
This domed building from the 4th century AD has survived as part of the church of Santi Cosma e Damiano ⑫

★ House of the Vestal Virgins
The priestesses who tended the sacred flame in the Temple of Vesta lived here. The house was a large rectangular building around a central garden ⑩

★ **Basilica of Constantine and Maxentius**
The stark remains of the basilica's huge arches and ceilings give some idea of the original scale and grandeur of the Forum's public buildings ⓭

LOCATOR MAP
See Central Rome Map pp12–13

Santa Francesca Romana
The church takes its name from a saint who cared for the Roman poor in the 15th century ⓮

Antiquarium Forense
A small museum houses archaeological finds made in the Forum. They include this frieze of Aeneas and the Founding of Rome *from the Basilica Aemilia* ⓯

Colonnade surrounding Temple of Venus and Rome

Temple of Venus and Rome
These extensive ruins are of a magnificent temple, built here in AD 121 by the Emperor Hadrian, largely to his own design ⓱

Arch of Titus
This 19th-century reconstruction shows how the arch may have looked when it spanned the flagstoned roadway of the Via Sacra ⓰

VIA DEI FORI IMPERIALI

VIA SACRA

To the Palatine

Ruined Baths

STAR SIGHTS

★ **House of the Vestal Virgins**

★ **Basilica of Constantine**

KEY

– – – Suggested route

0 metres   75

0 yards   75

Remains of the Basilica Julia, a Roman court of civil law

Basilica Julia ❼

See Visitors' Checklist, p82.

THIS IMMENSE basilica, which occupied the area between the Temple of Saturn and the Temple of Castor and Pollux, was begun by Julius Caesar in 54 BC and completed after his death by his great nephew Augustus. It was damaged by fire almost immediately afterwards in 9 BC, but was subsequently repaired and dedicated to the emperor's grandsons, Gaius and Lucius.

After numerous sackings and pilferings, only the steps, pavement and column stumps remain. Nevertheless the ground plan is fairly clear. The basilica had a central hall, measuring 80 m by 18 m

(260 ft by 59 ft), surrounded by a double portico. The hall was on three floors, while the outer portico had only two.

The Basilica Julia was the seat of the *centumviri*, a body of 180 magistrates who tried civil law cases. They were split into four chambers of 45 men, and unless a case was particularly complicated they would all sit separately.

The four courts were, however, divided only by screens or curtains, and the voices of lawyers and cheers and boos of spectators in the upper galleries echoed through the building. Lawyers used to hire crowds of spectators, who would applaud every time the lawyer who was paying them made a point and jeer at his opponents. The clappers and booers must have had a good deal of time on their hands: scratched into the steps are chequerboards where they played dice and other gambling games to while away the time between cases.

Temple of Castor and Pollux ❽

See Visitors' Checklist, p82.

THE THREE SLENDER fluted columns of this temple form one of the Forum's most beautiful ruins. The first temple here was probably dedicated in 484 BC in honour of the mythical twins and patrons of horsemanship, Castor and Pollux. During the battle of Lake Regillus (499 BC) against the ousted Tarquin kings, the Roman dictator Postumius promised to build a temple to the twins if the Romans were victorious. Some said the twins appeared on the battlefield, helped the Romans to victory and then materialized in the Forum – the temple marks the spot – to announce the news.

The temple, like most buildings in the Forum, was rebuilt many times. The three surviving columns date from the last occasion on which it was rebuilt – by the future Emperor Tiberius after a fire in AD 6. For a long period the temple housed the city's office of weights and measures, and it was also used at times by a number of bankers.

Corinthian columns of the Temple of Castor and Pollux

Temple of Vesta ❾

See Visitors' Checklist, p82.

THE FORUM'S most elegant temple, a circular building originally surrounded by a ring of 20 fine fluted columns, dates from the 4th century AD, though there had been a temple on the site for far longer. It was partially reconstructed in 1930.

The cult of the Vestals was one of the oldest in Rome, and centred on six Vestal Virgins, who were required to

TEMPLE OF VESTA
The temple preserved the shape of an original primitive structure made of wooden posts with a thatched roof.

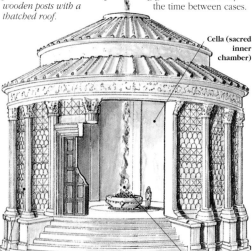

Cella (sacred inner chamber)

Ring of Corinthian columns

Sacred flame

keep alight the sacred flame of Vesta, the goddess of the hearth. This responsibility was originally entrusted to the daughters of the king, but it then passed to the Vestals, the only group of women priests in Rome. It was no easy task, as the flame was easily blown out. Any Vestal who allowed the flame to die was whipped by the high priest (Pontifex Maximus) and dismissed.

The girls, who had to belong to noble families, were selected when they were between 6 and 10 years old. They served for 30 years: the first ten were spent learning their duties, the next ten performing them and the final ten teaching novices. They enjoyed high status and financial security, but had to remain virgins. The penalty for transgressing was to be buried alive, although only ten Vestals are recorded as ever having suffered this fate. The men concerned were whipped to death. When Vestals retired, they were free to live the rest of their lives as ordinary citizens. If they wished they could marry, but few ever did.

Another of the Vestals' duties was to guard the Palladium, a sacred statue of the goddess Pallas Athenae. The irreverent Emperor Heliogabalus burgled the temple in the 3rd century AD. He thought he had succeeded in stealing the Palladium, but the Vestals had been warned of his intention and had replaced it with a replica.

Restored section of Temple of Vesta

Central courtyard of the House of the Vestal Virgins

House of the Vestal Virgins ⑩

See Visitors' Checklist, p82.

AS SOON AS a girl became a Vestal she came to live in the House of the Vestal Virgins. Originally this was an enormous complex with about 50 rooms on three storeys. The only substantial remains today are some of the rooms around the central courtyard. This space is perhaps the most evocative part of the Forum. Overlooking ponds of water lilies and plump goldfish is a row of eroded, and mostly headless, statues of senior Vestals, dating from the 3rd and 4th centuries AD. The better-preserved examples were transferred to the Museo Nazionale Romano *(see p163).* On one of the pedestals the inscription has been removed because the Vestal in question suffered some disgrace. It is thought she may have been a certain Claudia, known to have betrayed the cult by converting to Christianity.

Though many of the rooms surrounding the courtyard are well preserved – some even retain flights of steps leading to an upper floor – you are not allowed inside them. If you peep into the series of rooms along the south side, however, you might be able to see the remains of a mill,

Honorary statue of a Vestal Virgin

used for grinding the grain with which the Vestals made a special sacrificial cake. The bakery was next door.

Temple of Antoninus and Faustina ⑪

See Visitors' Checklist, p82. **Church open** *10am–noon Thu; ring the bell.*

ONE OF THE FORUM'S oddest sights is the Baroque façade of the church of San Lorenzo in Miranda rising above the porch of a Roman temple. First dedicated in AD 141 by the Emperor Antoninus Pius to his late wife Faustina, the temple was rededicated to them both on the death of the emperor. In the 11th century it was converted into a church because it was believed that San Lorenzo (St Lawrence) had been condemned to death there. The current church dates from 1601.

Temple of Antoninus and Faustina

Temple of Romulus and Santi Cosma e Damiano ⑫

See Visitors' Checklist, p82. **Santi Cosma e Damiano**
📞 *06-692 04 41.*
Open *9am–1pm, 3–7pm daily.*
Crib *closed Mon and Wed am.*
Adm charge *for crib.* 🚻 ♿

NO ONE IS SURE to whom the Temple of Romulus was dedicated, but it was probably to the son of Emperor Maxentius, and not to Rome's founder.

The temple is a circular brick building, topped by a cupola, with two rectangular side rooms and a concave porch. The heavy, dull bronze doors are original.

Since the 6th century the temple has acted as a vestibule to the church of Santi Cosma e Damiano, which itself occupies an ancient building – a hall in Vespasian's Forum of Peace. The entrance to the church is on Via dei Fori Imperiali. The beautiful carved figures of its 18th-century Neapolitan *presepio* (crib or Nativity scene) are back on view now, and the church has a vivid Byzantine apse mosaic with Christ pictured against orange clouds.

Roof of the Temple of Romulus

Basilica of Constantine and Maxentius ⑬

See Visitors' Checklist, p82.

THE BASILICA's three vast, coffered barrel vaults are powerful relics of what was the largest building in the Forum. Work began in AD 308 under the Emperor Maxentius. When he was deposed by Constantine after the Battle of the Milvian Bridge in AD 312, work on the massive project continued under the new regime. The building, which, like other Roman basilicas, was used for the administration of justice and for carrying on business, is often referred to simply as the Basilica of Constantine.

The area covered by the basilica was roughly 100 m by 65 m (330 ft by 215 ft). It was originally designed to have a long nave and aisles running from east to west, but Constantine switched the axis around to create three short broad aisles with the main entrance in the centre of the long south wall. The height of the building was 35 m (115 ft). In the apse at the western end, where it could be seen from all over the building, stood a 12-m (39-ft) statue of the emperor, made partly of wood and partly of marble. The giant head, hand and foot are on display in the courtyard of the Palazzo dei Conservatori *(see pp72–3)*. The roof of the basilica glittered with gilded tiles until the 7th century when they were stripped off to cover the roof of the old St Peter's.

The three barrel-vaulted aisles of the basilica were used as law courts.

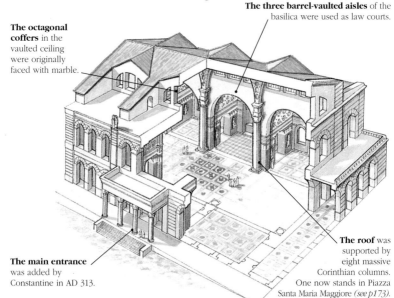

The octagonal coffers in the vaulted ceiling were originally faced with marble.

The main entrance was added by Constantine in AD 313.

The roof was supported by eight massive Corinthian columns. One now stands in Piazza Santa Maria Maggiore *(see p173)*.

Santa Francesca Romana ⑭

Piazza di Santa Francesca Romana.
Map 5 B5. 📞 06-679 55 28.
🚌 85, 87, 117, 175, 810. 🚋 3.
Ⓜ Colosseo. **Open** 9.30am–noon,
3–5pm daily. 🏛 🔔

Bell tower of Santa Francesca

EVERY YEAR on 9 March devout Roman drivers try to park as close as possible to this Baroque church with a Romanesque bell tower. The aim of their pilgrimage is to have their vehicles blessed by Santa Francesca Romana, the patron saint of motorists. During the 15th century, Francesca of Trastevere founded a society of pious women devoted to helping the less fortunate. After her canonization in 1608 the church, originally named Santa Maria Nova, was rededicated to Francesca.

The most curious sight inside the church is a flagstone with what are said to be the imprints of the knees of St Peter and St Paul. A magician, Simon Magus, decided to prove that his powers were superior to those of the Apostles by levitating above the Forum. As Simon was in mid-air, Peter and Paul fell to their knees and prayed fervently for God to humble him, and Simon immediately plummeted to his death.

Antiquarium Forense ⑮

See Visitors' Checklist, p82.

THE FORMER CONVENT of Santa Francesca Romana is now occupied by the offices in charge of the excavations of the Forum and a small museum. The latter is currently being reorganized, and only a couple of rooms are open. They contain Iron Age burial urns, graves and their skeletal occupants along with some ancient bric-a-brac exhumed from the Forum's drains. When the reorganization is complete you should be able to see fragments of statues, capitals, friezes and other architectural decoration taken from the Forum's buildings.

Frieze of Aeneas in the Antiquarium Forense

Arch of Titus ⑯

See Visitors' Checklist, p82.

THIS TRIUMPHAL ARCH was erected in AD 81 by the Emperor Domitian in honour of the victories of his brother, Titus, and his father, Vespasian, in Judaea. In AD 66 the Jews, weary of being exploited by unscrupulous Roman officials, rebelled. A bitter war broke out which ended 2 years later in the fall of Jerusalem and the Jewish Diaspora.

Although the reliefs inside the arch are badly eroded, you can make out a triumphant procession of Roman soldiers carrying off spoils from the Temple of Jerusalem. The booty includes the altar, silver trumpets and a golden seven-branched candelabrum.

Dedication to Titus and Vespasian on the Arch of Titus

Temple of Venus and Rome ⑰

See Visitors' Checklist, p82.

THE EMPEROR Hadrian designed this temple to occupy what had been the vestibule to Nero's Domus Aurea (see p175). Many of the columns have been re-erected, and though there is no access, there is a good view as you leave the Forum and from the upper tiers of the Colosseum. The temple, the largest in Rome, was dedicated to Roma, the personification of the city, and to Venus because she was the mother of Aeneas, father of Romulus and Remus. Each goddess had her own cella (shrine). When the architect Apollodorus pointed out that the seated statues in the niches were too big (had they tried to "stand" their heads would have hit the vaults), Hadrian had him put to death.

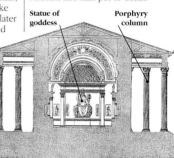

Statue of goddess   **Porphyry column**

Cross-section of Temple of Venus and Rome

Trajan's Markets ⑱

ORIGINALLY CONSIDERED among the wonders of the Classical world, Trajan's Markets now show only a hint of their former splendour. Emperor Trajan and his architect, Apollodorus of Damascus, built this visionary new complex of 150 shops and offices (probably used for administering the corn dole) in the early 2nd century AD. It was the ancient Roman equivalent of the modern shopping centre, selling everything from silks and spices imported from the Middle East to fresh fish, fruit and flowers.

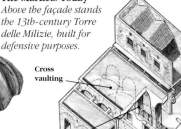

The Markets Today
Above the façade stands the 13th-century Torre delle Milizie, built for defensive purposes.

Cross vaulting

Trajan
The emperor was a benevolent ruler and a successful general.

Main Hall
Twelve shops were built on two floors, and the corn dole was shared out on the upper storey. This was a free corn ration given to Roman men to prevent hunger.

Via Biberatica
The main street which runs through the market is named after the drinking inns which once lined it.

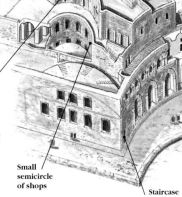

Small semicircle of shops

Staircase

TIMELINE

AD 100–112 Building of Trajan's Markets	**472** Invasion by Ricimer the Suevian. Some of his Germanic troops stationed here		**1200s** Torre delle Milizie built on top of the markets	**1572** Convent of Santa Caterina da Siena built over part of markets	**1924** Many medieval houses demolished
AD 100	**AD 500**	**1000**	**1300**	**1800**	**1950**
AD 117 Death of Trajan **AD 98** Trajan succeeds Nerva as emperor	**552** Byzantine takeover of Rome. Markets occupied and fortified by the army		**1300s** Annibaldi and Caetani families vie for control of the area	**1828** First tentative excavations, but value of site not recognized	**1911–14** Convent demolished **1930–33** Markets finally excavated

VISITORS' CHECKLIST

Mercati Traianei, Via IV Novembre.
Map 5 B4. 📞 06-679 00 48.
🚌 64, 70, 170 and many routes
to Piazza Venezia. **Open** 9am–
4.30pm Tue–Sun (to 6.30pm
summer). Last adm: 30 mins before
closing. **Closed** 1 Jan, 25 Dec.
Adm charge. Newly excavated
parts of Trajan's Markets can be
seen by prior arrangement. 📷 ♿

The Markets in the 16th Century
*This fanciful fresco depicts a gladiatorial combat
taking place in front of the partly buried remains
of Trajan's Markets.*

A Market Shop
*Shops were built with
arched entrances, with
jambs and lintels
creating rectangular
portals and windows.
A wooden mezzanine
was used for storage.*

Upper Corridor
*Shops on this upper level
were thought to have sold
wine and oil, since a
number of storage jars were
discovered here.*

The terrace
over the archway
spanning Via
Biberatica has
a good view of
the Forum
of Trajan
below.

**Wall dividing market area
from Forum of Trajan**

**Large hall with
semidomed ceiling**

Forum of Trajan, built in front of the markets
in AD 107–113, was flanked by the Basilica Ulpia.
The basilica, measuring 170 m (558 ft) by 60 m
(197 ft), was the largest in Rome. A small portion
of the Forum has been excavated; unfortunately,
however, the rest of it remains buried beneath
modern Rome's busy city streets.

MARKET SHOPPING
Shops opened early and closed about
noon. The best ones were decorated
with mosaics of the goods they sold.
Almost all the shopping was done
by men, though women visited the
dressmaker and cobbler. The
tradesmen were almost all male.
In employment records for the
period AD 117–193, the only
female shopkeepers mentioned
are three wool-sellers, two
jewellers, a greengrocer
and a fishwife.

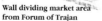

Fish mosaic

Trajan's Markets ⑱

See pp88–9.

Trajan's Column ⑲

Via dei Fori Imperiali. **Map** 5 A4 & 12 F4. *See Visitors' Checklist for Trajan's Markets, p89.*

Detail of Trajan's Column

This elegant marble column was inaugurated by Trajan in AD 113, and celebrates his two campaigns in Dacia (Romania) in AD 101–3 and AD 107–8. The column, base and pedestal are 40 m (131 ft) tall – precisely the same height as the spur of the Quirinal hill which was excavated to make room for Trajan's Forum. Spiralling up the column are minutely detailed scenes from the campaigns, beginning with the Romans preparing for war and ending with the Dacians being ousted from their homeland. The column is pierced with small windows to illuminate its internal spiral staircase (closed to the public). If you wish to see the reliefs in detail there is a complete set of casts in the Museo della Civiltà Romana at EUR *(see p266).*

When Trajan died in AD 117 his ashes, along with those of his wife Plotina, were placed in a golden urn in the column's hollow base. The column's survival was largely thanks to the intervention of Pope Gregory the Great (reigned 590–604). He was so moved by a relief showing Trajan helping a woman whose son had been killed that he begged God to release the emperor's soul from hell. God duly

appeared to the pope to say that Trajan had been rescued, but asked him not to pray for the souls of any more pagans.

According to legend, when Trajan's ashes were exhumed his skull and tongue were not only intact, but his tongue told of his release from hell. The land around the column was then declared sacred and the column itself was spared. The statue of Trajan remained on top of the column until 1587, when it was replaced with one of St Peter.

Torre delle Milizie ⑳

Mercati Traianei, Via IV Novembre. **Map** 5 B4. ☎ 06-679 00 48. **Open** *by appt only.*

For centuries this massive brick tower was thought to have been the one in which Nero stood watching Rome burn, after he had set it alight to clear the city's slums. It is uncertain whether arson was among Nero's crimes, but it is certain that he did not watch the fire from this tower – it was built in the 13th century.

Casa dei Cavalieri di Rodi ㉑

Piazza del Grillo 1. **Map** 5 B5. ☎ 06-6710 3622. ▭ 84, 85, 87, 117, 175, 186, 810, 850. **Open** *by appt only.*

Loggia, Casa dei Cavalieri di Rodi

Since the 12th century the crusading order, the Knights of St John, also known as the Knights of Rhodes (Rodi) or Malta, have had their priorate in this medieval house above the Forum of Augustus. If you are lucky enough to get inside, ask to see the beautiful Cappella di San Giovanni (Chapel of St John).

Forum of Augustus ㉒

Piazza del Grillo 1. **Map** 5 B5 & 12 F5. *See Visitors' Checklist for Trajan's Markets, p89.* **Open** *by appt only.*

Podium of the Temple of Mars in the Forum of Augustus

The forum of Augustus was built to celebrate Augustus's victory over Julius Caesar's assassins, Brutus and Cassius, at the Battle of Philippi in 41 BC. The temple in its centre was dedicated to Mars the Avenger. The forum stretched from a high wall at the foot of the sleazy Suburra quarter to the edge of the Forum of Caesar. At least half of it is now concealed below Mussolini's Via dei Fori Imperiali. The temple is easily identified, with its cracked steps and four Corinthian columns. Originally it had a statue of Mars which looked very like Augustus. In case anyone failed to notice the resemblance, a giant statue of Augustus himself was placed against the Suburra wall.

Forum of Caesar ㉓

Via del Carcere Tulliano. **Map** 5 A5. ☎ 06-3996 7700. ▭ 84, 85, 87, 175, 186, 810, 850. **Open** *by appt only.*

The first of Rome's Imperial fora was built by Julius Caesar. He spent a fortune – most of it booty from his conquest of Gaul – buying up and demolishing houses on the site. Pride of place went to a temple dedicated in 46 BC to the goddess Venus Genetrix, from whom Caesar claimed descent. The temple contained statues of Caesar and Cleopatra as well as of Venus. All that remains of this temple to vanity is a platform and three Corinthian columns. The forum was enclosed by a double colonnade which sheltered a row of shops, but this burnt down in AD 80 and was rebuilt by Domitian and Trajan. Trajan also added the Basilica Argentaria and a heated public lavatory.

The forum is only open to the public by appointment, but parts are visible from above in Via dei Fori Imperiali.

Mamertine Prison ㉔

Clivo Argentario 1. **Map** 5 A5.
06-679 29 02. 84, 85, 87, 175, 186, 810, 850. **Open** 9am–12.30pm, 2–5pm daily (2.30–6.30pm summer). **Donation** expected.

19th-century engraving of guards visiting prisoners in the Mamertine

BELOW THE 16th-century church of San Giuseppe dei Falegnami (St Joseph of the Carpenters) is a dank dungeon in which, according to Christian legend, St Peter was imprisoned. He is said to have caused a spring to bubble up into the cell, and used the water to baptize his guards.

The prison, also known as Tullianum, was in an old cistern with access to the city's main sewer (the Cloaca Maxima). The lower cell was used for executions and bodies were thrown into the sewer. Among the enemies of Rome to be executed here was the Gaulish leader Vercingetorix, defeated by Julius Caesar in 52 BC.

17th-century view of the ruined Forum of Nerva

Forum of Nerva ㉕

Piazza del Grillo 1 (reached through Forum of Augustus). **Map** 5 B5.
06-3996 7700. 84, 85, 87, 175, 186, 810, 850. **Open** by appt only.

THE FORUM of Nerva was begun by his predecessor, Domitian, and completed in AD 97. Little more than a long corridor with a colonnade along the sides and a Temple of Minerva at one end, it was also known as the Forum Transitorium because it lay between the Forum of Peace built by the Emperor Vespasian in AD 70 and the Forum of Augustus. Vespasian's forum is almost completely covered by Via dei Fori Imperiali, as is much of the Forum of Nerva itself. Excavations have unearthed Renaissance shops and

Medallion on the Arch of Constantine

taverns, but only part of the forum can be seen, including the base of the temple and two columns that were part of the original colonnade. These support a relief of Minerva above a frieze of young girls learning to sew and weave.

Arch of Constantine ㉖

Between Via di San Gregorio and Piazza del Colosseo. **Map** 8 F1.
75, 85, 87, 175, 673, 810.
3. Colosseo.

THIS TRIUMPHAL ARCH was dedicated in AD 315 to celebrate Constantine's victory three years before over his co-emperor, Maxentius. Constantine claimed he owed his victory to a vision of Christ, but there is nothing Christian about the arch – in fact, most of the medallions, reliefs and statues were scavenged from earlier monuments.

There are statues of Dacian prisoners taken from Trajan's Forum and reliefs of Marcus Aurelius, including one where he distributes bread to the poor. Inside the arch are reliefs of Trajan's victory over the Dacians. These were probably by the artist who worked on Trajan's Column.

Colosseum ㉗

See pp92–5.

North side of the Arch of Constantine, facing the Colosseum

Colosseum  ㉗

Rome's greatest amphitheatre was commissioned by the Emperor Vespasian in AD 72 on the marshy site of a lake in the grounds of Nero's palace, the Domus Aurea *(see p175)*. Deadly gladiatorial combats and wild animal fights were staged free of charge by the emperor and wealthy citizens for public viewing.

Outer Wall of the Colosseum
Stone plundered from the façade in the Renaissance was used to build several palaces, bridges and parts of St Peter's.

The Colosseum was built to a practical design, with its 80 arched entrances allowing easy access to 55,000 spectators, but it is also a building of great beauty. The drawing here shows how it looked at the time of its opening in AD 80. It was one of several similar amphitheatres built in the Roman Empire, and some survive at El Djem in North Africa, Nîmes and Arles in France and Verona in northern Italy. Despite being damaged over the years by neglect and theft, it remains a majestic sight.

The Founder of the Colosseum
Vespasian was a professional soldier who became emperor in AD 69, founding the Flavian dynasty.

The outer walls are made of travertine.

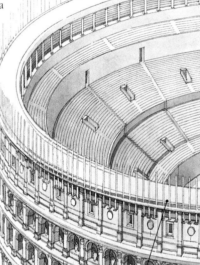

Flora of the Colosseum

By the 19th century the Colosseum was heavily overgrown. Different micro-climates in various parts of the ruin had created an impressive variety of herbs, grasses and wild flowers. Several botanists were inspired to study and catalogue them and two books were published, one listing 420 different species. **Borage, a herb**

The bollards anchored the velarium.

The velarium was a huge awning which shaded spectators from the sun. Supported on poles fixed to the upper storey of the building, it was then hoisted into position with ropes anchored to bollards outside the stadium.

Timeline

80 Vespasian's son, Titus, stages inaugural festival in the amphitheatre. It lasts 100 days

AD 70		100

72 Emperor Vespasian begins work on the Colosseum

81–96 Amphitheatre completed in reign of Domitian

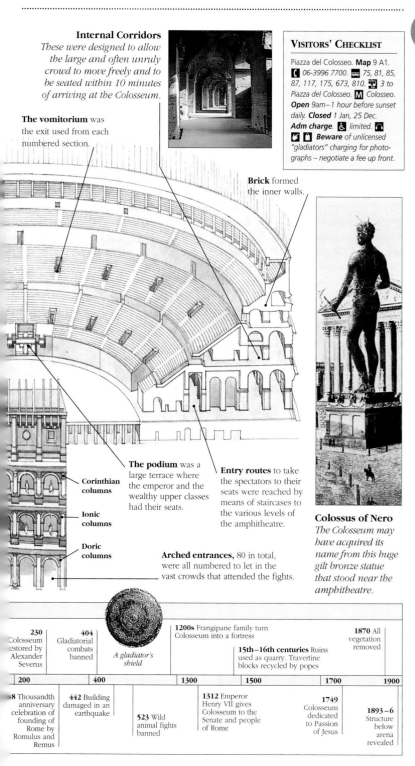

Internal Corridors
These were designed to allow the large and often unruly crowd to move freely and to be seated within 10 minutes of arriving at the Colosseum.

The vomitorium was the exit used from each numbered section.

VISITORS' CHECKLIST

Piazza del Colosseo. **Map** 9 A1.
06-3996 7700. 75, 81, 85, 87, 117, 175, 673, 810. 3 to Piazza del Colosseo. Colosseo. **Open** 9am–1 hour before sunset daily. **Closed** 1 Jan, 25 Dec. **Adm charge.** limited. **Beware** of unlicensed "gladiators" charging for photographs – negotiate a fee up front.

Brick formed the inner walls.

Corinthian columns

Ionic columns

Doric columns

The podium was a large terrace where the emperor and the wealthy upper classes had their seats.

Entry routes to take the spectators to their seats were reached by means of staircases to the various levels of the amphitheatre.

Arched entrances, 80 in total, were all numbered to let in the vast crowds that attended the fights.

Colossus of Nero
The Colosseum may have acquired its name from this huge gilt bronze statue that stood near the amphitheatre.

| **230** Colosseum restored by Alexander Severus | **404** Gladiatorial combats banned | *A gladiator's shield* | **1200s** Frangipane family turn Colosseum into a fortress | | **1870** All vegetation removed |
| | | | **15th–16th centuries** Ruins used as quarry. Travertine blocks recycled by popes | | |

200	**400**		**1300**	**1500**	**1700**	**1900**
48 Thousandth anniversary celebration of founding of Rome by Romulus and Remus	**442** Building damaged in an earthquake	**523** Wild animal fights banned	**1312** Emperor Henry VII gives Colosseum to the Senate and people of Rome		**1749** Colosseum dedicated to Passion of Jesus	**1893–6** Structure below arena revealed

How Fights were Staged in the Arena

THE EMPERORS HELD shows here which often began with animals performing circus tricks. Then on came the gladiators, who fought each other to the death. When one was killed, attendants dressed as Charon, the mythical ferryman of the dead, carried his body off on a stretcher, and sand was raked over the blood ready for the next bout. A badly wounded gladiator would surrender his fate to the crowd. The "thumbs up" sign from the emperor meant he could live, "thumbs down" that he die, and the victor became an instant hero. Animals were brought here from as far away as North Africa and the Middle East. The games held in AD 248 to mark the thousandth anniversary of Rome's founding saw the death of a host of lions, elephants, hippos, zebras and elks.

Beneath the Arena
Late 19th-century excavations exposed the network of underground rooms where the animals were kept.

Interior of the Colosseum
The stadium was built in the form of an ellipse, with tiers of seats around a vast central arena.

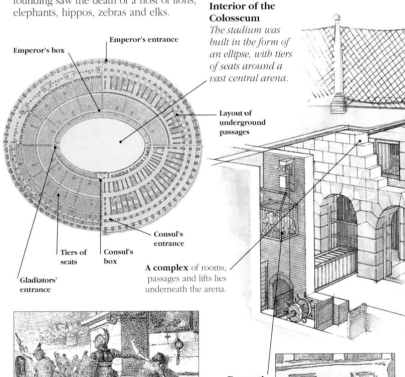

Emperor's box

Emperor's entrance

Layout of underground passages

Tiers of seats

Consul's box

Consul's entrance

Gladiators' entrance

A complex of rooms, passages and lifts lies underneath the arena.

Dramatic Entrances
Below the sand was a wooden floor through which animals, men and scenery appeared in the arena.

Roman Gladiators
These were usually slaves, prisoners of war or condemned criminals. Most were men, but there were a few female gladiators.

The Colosseum by Antonio Canaletto

This 18th-century view of the Colosseum shows the Meta Sudans fountain (now demolished). Water "sweated" from a metal ball on top of its brick cone.

Metal fencing kept animals penned in, while archers stood by just in case any escaped.

Seating was tiered, and different social classes were segregated.

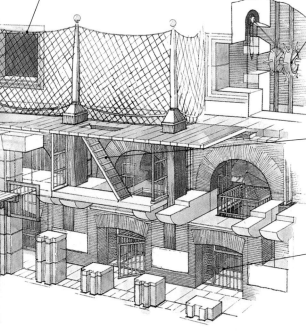

A winch brought the animal cages up to arena level when they were due to fight.

A ramp and trap door enabled the animal to reach the arena after walking along a corridor.

Cages were like three-sided lifts which went up to the next level where the animals were released.

SEA BATTLES IN THE ARENA

The historian Dion Cassius, writing in the 4th century AD, relates how, 150 years earlier, the Colosseum's arena was flooded to stage a mock sea battle. Scholars now believe that he was mistaken. The spectacle probably took place in the Naumachia of Augustus, a water-filled arena situated across the Tiber in Trastevere.

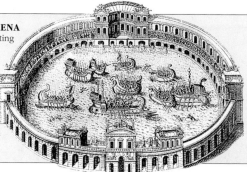

PALATINE

According to legend, Romulus and Remus were brought up here by a wolf in a cave. Traces of Iron Age huts, dating from the 9th century BC, have been found on the Palatine hill, providing archaeological support for the area's legendary links with the founding of Rome. The Palatine was a very desirable place to live, becoming home to some of the city's most famous inhabitants. The great orator Cicero had a house here, as did the lyric poet Catullus. Augustus was born on the hill and continued to live here in very modest

Fresco of mask in the House of Augustus

circumstances even when he became emperor. The two buildings identified as the House of Augustus and the House of Livia, his wife, are among the best preserved here. The first emperor's example of frugality was ignored by his successors, Tiberius, Caligula and Domitian, who all built extravagant palaces here. The ruins of Tiberius's palace lie beneath the 16th-century Farnese Gardens. The most extensive ruins are those of the Domus Augustana and Domus Flavia, the two wings of Domitian's palace, and the later extension built by Septimius Severus.

SIGHTS AT A GLANCE

Temples
Temple of Cybele ❻

Historic Buildings
Domus Flavia ❶
Domus Augustana ❸
House of Livia ❺

Ancient Sites
Cryptoporticus ❷
Stadium ❹
Huts of Romulus ❼

Parks and Gardens
Farnese Gardens ❽

SEE ALSO

• *Street Finder*, map 8

GETTING THERE

There are two ways of getting on to the Palatine hill; either through the Roman Forum (from Via dei Fori Imperiali) or through the entrance in Via di San Gregorio. A separate ticket for the Palatine is needed, even if you come through the Forum. The best buses are the 75, 85, 87, 117, 175, 186, 810, 850; all stop in Via dei Fori Imperiali near the main entrance. Tram 3 and Colosseo Metro station (*see p77*) are also handy.

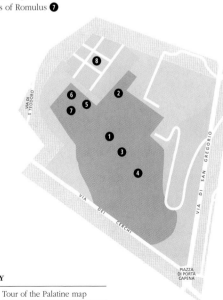

KEY

Tour of the Palatine map

0 metres 200
0 yards 200

Towering ruins of the Palace of Septimius Severus on the Palatine hill

A Tour of the Palatine

SHADED ON ITS LOWER SLOPES with pines, and scattered in spring with wild flowers, the Palatine is the most pleasant and relaxing of the city's ancient sites. You can reach the hill by walking up from the Roman Forum *(see pp76–7)*. The area is dominated by the ruins of the Domus Flavia and the Domus Augustana, two parts of Domitian's huge palace built at the end of the 1st century AD. What you are able to see depends on where excavations are taking place at the time.

Huts of Romulus
These are traces of a 9th-century BC village on the Palatine ❼

To Farnese Gardens
See p101

House of Augustus

Temple of Cybele
Also known as the Temple of the Magna Mater, this was the centre of an important fertility cult ❻

★ House of Livia
Many of the wall paintings have survived in the house where Augustus lived with his wife Livia ❺

STAR SIGHTS

★ House of Livia

★ Domus Flavia

KEY

– – –   Suggested route

0 metres   75

0 yards   75

★ Domus Flavia
This oval fountain was designed to be seen from the dining hall of the palace ❶

Domus Augustana
The Roman emperors lived in this part of the palace, while the Domus Flavia was used for public functions ❸

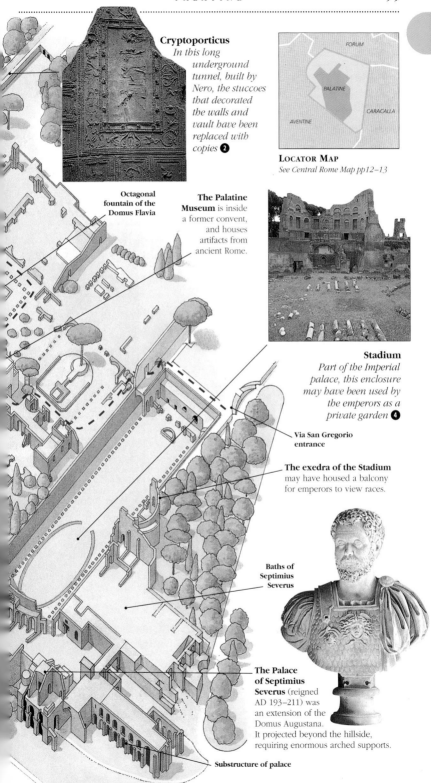

Cryptoporticus
In this long underground tunnel, built by Nero, the stuccoes that decorated the walls and vault have been replaced with copies ②

LOCATOR MAP
See Central Rome Map pp12–13

FORUM

PALATINE

CARACALLA

AVENTINE

Octagonal fountain of the Domus Flavia

The Palatine Museum is inside a former convent, and houses artifacts from ancient Rome.

Stadium
Part of the Imperial palace, this enclosure may have been used by the emperors as a private garden ④

Via San Gregorio entrance

The exedra of the Stadium may have housed a balcony for emperors to view races.

Baths of Septimius Severus

The Palace of Septimius Severus (reigned AD 193–211) was an extension of the Domus Augustana. It projected beyond the hillside, requiring enormous arched supports.

Substructure of palace

Domus Flavia ❶

See Visitors' Checklist.

**Marble pavement in the courtyard
of the Domus Flavia**

In AD 81 Domitian, the third
of the Flavian dynasty of
emperors, decided to build a
splendid new palace on the
Palatine hill. But the western
peak, the Germalus, was
covered with houses and
temples, while the eastern
peak, the Palatium, was very
steep. So the emperor's
architect, Rabirius, flattened
the Palatium and used the
soil to fill in the cleft between
the two peaks, burying (and
preserving) a number of
Republican-era houses.

The palace had two wings –
one official (the Domus
Flavia), the other private (the
Domus Augustana). It was
the main Imperial palace for
300 years. At the front of the
Domus Flavia, the surviving
stubs of columns and fragments of walls trace the
shapes of three adjoining
rooms. In the first of these, the
Basilica, Domitian dispensed
his personal brand of justice.

The central Aula Regia was a
throne room decorated with
12 black basalt statues. The
third room (now covered
with corrugated plastic) was
the Lararium, a shrine for the
household gods known as
Lares (usually the owner's
ancestors). It may have been
used for official ceremonies
or by the palace guards.

Fearing assassination,
Domitian had the walls of the
courtyard covered with shiny
marble slabs designed to act
as mirrors so that he could
see anyone lurking behind
him. In the event, he was
assassinated in his bedroom,
possibly on the orders of his
wife, Domitia. The courtyard
is now a pleasant place to
pause; the flower beds in the
centre follow the maze pattern
of a sunken fountain pool.

Cryptoporticus ❷

See Visitors' Checklist.

The CRYPTOPORTICUS, a series
of underground corridors,
was built by Nero to connect
his Domus Aurea *(see p175)*
with the palaces of earlier
emperors on the Palatine. A
further branch leading to the
Palace of Domitian was added
later. Its vaults are decorated
with delicate stucco reliefs –
copies of originals now kept
in the Palatine's museum.

Domus
Augustana ❸

See Visitors' Checklist.

This PART of Domitian's
palace was called the
Domus Augustana because it
was the private residence of
the "august" emperors. On
the upper level a high brick

wall remains, and you can
make out the shape of its two
courtyards. The far better-
preserved lower level is closed
to the public, though you can
look down on its sunken
courtyard with the geometric
foundations of a fountain in
its centre. Sadly, you can't see
the stairs linking the two levels
(once lit by sunlight falling
on a mirror-paved pool),
nor the surrounding rooms,
paved with coloured marble.

Stadium ❹

See Visitors' Checklist.

Stadium viewed from the south

The STADIUM on the Palatine
was laid out at the same
time as the Palace of Domitian.
It is not clear whether it was a
public stadium, a private track
for exercising horses, or
simply a large garden. The
alcove in the eastern wall
looks as though it may have
held a box from which the
emperor could have watched
races. It is, however, known
that the Stadium was used for
foot races by the Ostrogothic
king, Theodoric, in the 6th
century – he added the small
oval-shaped enclosure at the
southern end of the site.

Remains of the Domus Augustana and the Palace of Septimius Severus

House of Livia ❺

See Visitors' Checklist. If closed, apply to custodian.

Fresco in the House of Livia

THIS HOUSE dating from the 1st century BC is one of the best preserved on the Palatine. It was probably part of the house in which the Emperor Augustus and his wife Livia lived. Compared with later Imperial palaces, it is a relatively modest home. According to Suetonius, the biographer of Rome's early emperors, Augustus slept in the same small bedroom for 40 years on a low bed which had "a very ordinary coverlet". He wore home-made clothes (woven by Livia, his sister Octavia and daughter Julia), but he was vain enough to wear shoes with extremely thick soles to conceal the fact that he was rather short.

Detail of floor mosaic

The ground level of the Palatine is now above the house, so you walk down a flight of steps and along a mosaic-paved corridor into a courtyard. Its imitation-marble wall frescoes have been detached in order to preserve them, but they still hang in situ. Though they are very faded, you can still make out the veining patterns. Leading off the courtyard are three small reception rooms. The frescoes in the central one include a faded scene of Hermes coming to the rescue of Zeus's beloved Io, who is guarded by the 100-eyed Argos. In the left-hand room you can make out frescoed figures of griffins and other beasts, while the decor in the right-hand room includes land-scapes and cityscapes.

Temple of Cybele ❻

See Visitors' Checklist.

OTHER THAN a platform with a few column stumps and capitals, there is little to see of the Temple of Cybele, a popular fertility goddess imported to Rome from Asia. The priests of the cult castrated themselves in the belief that if they sacrificed their own fertility it would guarantee that of the natural world. The annual festival of Cybele, in early spring, culminated with frenzied eunuch-priests slashing their bodies to offer up their blood to the god-dess, and the ceremonial castration of novice priests.

Statue of the goddess Cybele

Huts of Romulus ❼

See Visitors' Checklist.

ACCORDING TO LEGEND, after killing his brother Remus, Romulus founded a village on the Palatine. In the 1940s a series of holes was found filled with earth lighter in colour than the surrounding soil. Archaeologists deduced that these holes must originally have held the supporting poles of three Iron Age huts – the first foundations of Rome *(see pp16–17)*.

Farnese Gardens ❽

See Visitors' Checklist.

IN THE MID-16TH century Cardinal Alessandro Farnese, grandson of Pope Paul III, bought the ruins of Tiberius's palace on the Palatine. He filled in the ruined building and had Vignola, architect of the interior of the Gesù church, design a garden for him. The result was one of the first botanical gardens in Europe, its terraces linked by steps stretching from the House of Vestal Virgins in the Forum to the Palatine's Germalus peak. The gardeners introduced a number of plants to Italy and Europe, among them *Acacia farnesiana*. Farnese was at the centre of a glittering set which included a number of courtesans, so the parties here are likely to have been somewhat unholy.

The area was dug up during the excavation of the Palatine and re-landscaped afterwards. Nevertheless the tree-lined avenues, rose gardens and glorious views still make it an ideal place to unwind.

Farnese pavilions, relics of the age when the Palatine was a private garden

PIAZZA DELLA ROTONDA

THE PANTHEON, one of the great buildings in the history of European architecture, has stood at the heart of Rome for nearly 2,000 years. The historic area around it has seen uninterrupted economic and political activity throughout that time. Palazzo di Montecitorio, built for Pope Innocent XII as a papal tribunal in 1694,

Bitter-style apéritif, popular in Roman cafés

is now the Italian parliament and many nearby buildings are government offices. This is also the main financial district of Rome with banking headquarters and the stock exchange. Not many people live here, but in the evenings, Romans stroll in the narrow streets and fill the lively restaurants and cafés that make this a focus for the city's social life.

SIGHTS AT A GLANCE

Churches and Temples
Temple of Hadrian ❶
Sant'Ignazio di Loyola ❸
Gesù pp114–15 ❾
Santa Maria sopra Minerva ⓫
Pantheon pp110–11 ⓭
Sant'Eustachio ⓮
La Maddalena ⓯
Santa Maria in
  Campo Marzio ⓲
San Lorenzo in Lucina ⓴

Historic Streets and Piazzas
Piazza di Sant'Ignazio ❷
Via della Gatta ❼

Historic Buildings
Palazzo del Collegio
  Romano ❹
Palazzo Doria Pamphilj ❻
Palazzo Altieri ❽
Palazzo Baldassini ⓱
Palazzo Borghese ⓳
Palazzo di Montecitorio ㉑
Palazzo Capranica ㉔

Columns, Obelisks and Statues
Pie' di Marmo ❿
Obelisk of Santa Maria
  sopra Minerva ⓬
Obelisk of Montecitorio ㉒
Column of Marcus Aurelius ㉓

Fountains
Fontanella del Facchino ❺

Cafés and Restaurants
Caffè Giolitti ⓰

KEY

	Street-by-Street map
P	Parking

GETTING THERE
The area has no Metro station, but is about 20 minutes' walk from Spagna or Barberini Metro stops. Buses that stop in Via del Plebiscito include the 46, 64, 70, 186, 492 and 810. Piazza Colonna is served by the 117, 119, 492 and all buses that go up Via del Corso or stop at Piazza S. Silvestro. The only bus that passes through the narrow streets of the area is the 116 electric minibus, which stops right outside the Pantheon.

0 metres   200
0 yards   200

SEE ALSO

Piazza della Rotonda seen through the granite columns of the Pantheon

Street-by-Street: Piazza della Rotonda

IF YOU WANDER THROUGH this area, sooner or later you will emerge into Piazza della Rotonda with its jumble of open-air café tables in front of the Pantheon. The refreshing splash of the fountain makes it a welcome resting place. In this warren of narrow streets, it can be hard to realize just how close you are to some of Rome's finest sights. The magnificent art collection of Palazzo Doria Pamphilj and the Baroque splendour of the Gesù are just a few minutes' walk from the Pantheon. At night there is always a lively buzz of activity, as people dine in style or enjoy the coffee and ice creams for which the area is famous.

Temple of Hadrian
The columns of this Roman temple now form the façade of the stock exchange ❶

Piazza di Sant'Ignazio
The square is a rare example of stylish domestic architecture from the early 18th century ❷

La Tazza d'Oro enjoys a reputation for the wonderful coffee consumed on its premises as well as for its freshly ground coffee to take away. *(See p319.)*

Santa Maria sopra Minerva
The rich decoration of Rome's only Gothic church was added in the 19th century ⓫

★ **Pantheon**
The awe-inspiring interior of Rome's best-preserved ancient temple is only hinted at from the outside ⓭

PIAZZA DI SANT'IGNAZIO

VIA DI SANT' IGNAZIO

VIA DEL SEMINARIO

PIAZZA DELLA ROTONDA

PIAZZA DELLA MINERVA

Obelisk of Santa Maria sopra Minerva
In 1667 Bernini dreamed up the idea of mounting a recently discovered obelisk on the back of a marble elephant ⓬

★ **Sant'Ignazio di Loyola**
Andrea Pozzo painted this glorious Baroque ceiling (1685) to celebrate St Ignatius and the Jesuit order ❸

LOCATOR MAP
See Central Rome Map pp12–13

Palazzo del Collegio Romano
Up until 1870, the college educated many leading figures in the Catholic Church ❹

Fontanella del Facchino
The water in this small 16th-century fountain spurts from a barrel held by a porter ❺

★ **Palazzo Doria Pamphilj**
Among the masterpieces in the art gallery of this magnificent family palazzo is this portrait of Pope Innocent X by Velázquez (1650) ❻

Via della Gatta
The street is named after the statue of a cat ❼

Palazzo Altieri
This enormous 17th-century palazzo is decorated with the arms of Pope Clement X ❽

★ **Gesù**
The design of the first-ever Jesuit church had a great impact on religious architecture ❾

Pie' di Marmo
This marble foot is a stray fragment from a gigantic Roman statue ❿

STAR SIGHTS

★ **Pantheon**

★ **Sant'Ignazio di Loyola**

★ **Palazzo Doria Pamphilj**

★ **Gesù**

KEY

--- --- Suggested route

0 metres   75
0 yards   75

Temple of Hadrian ❶

La Borsa, Piazza di Pietra. **Map** 4 F3 & 12 E2. 🚌 *117, 119, 492 and routes along Via del Corso or stopping at Piazza S. Silvestro.* **Closed** to public.

THIS TEMPLE honours the emperor Hadrian as a god and was dedicated by his son and successor Antoninus Pius in AD 145. The remains of the temple are visible on the southern side of Piazza di Pietra, incorporated in a 17th-century building. This was originally a papal customs house, completed by Carlo Fontana and his son in the 1690s. Today the building houses the Roman stock exchange (La Borsa).

Eleven marble Corinthian columns 15 m (49 ft) high stand on a base of *peperino*, a volcanic rock quarried from the Alban hills to the south of Rome. The columns decorated the northern flank of the temple enclosing its inner shrine, the *cella*. The *peperino* wall of the *cella* is still visible behind the columns, as is part of the coffered portico ceiling.

A number of reliefs from the temple, representing conquered Roman provinces, are now in the courtyard of the Palazzo dei Conservatori *(see pp72–3)*. They reflect the mostly peaceful foreign policy of Hadrian's reign.

Remains of Hadrian's Temple

Piazza di Sant'Ignazio ❷

Map 4 F4 & 12 E3. 🚌 *117, 119, 492 and routes along Via del Corso or stopping at Piazza S. Silvestro.*

ONE OF THE MAJOR works of the Roman Rococo, the piazza (1727–8) is Filippo Raguzzini's masterpiece. It offsets the imposing façade of the church of Sant'Ignazio

Illusionistic ceiling in the crossing of Sant'Ignazio

with the intimacy of the houses belonging to the bourgeoisie. The theatrical setting, the curvilinear design and the playful forms of its windows, balconies and balusters mark the piazza as one of a highly distinct group of structures. Along with Palazzo Doria Pamphilj (1731), the façade of La Maddalena (1735) and the aristocratic Spanish Steps (1723), it belongs to the moment when Rome's bubbly Rococo triumphed over conservative Classicism.

Sant'Ignazio di Loyola ❸

Piazza di Sant'Ignazio. **Map** 4 F4 & 12 E3. 📞 *06-679 44 06.* 🚌 *117, 119, 492 and along Via del Corso.* **Open** 7.30am–12.30pm, 3–7.30pm daily. 🛗

THE CHURCH was built by Pope Gregory XV in 1626 in honour of St Ignatius of Loyola, founder of the Society of Jesus and the man who most embodied the zeal of the Counter Reformation.

Together with the Gesù *(see pp114–15)*, Sant'Ignazio forms the centre of the Jesuit area in Rome. Its vast interior, lined with precious stones, marble, stucco and gilt, creates a sense of theatre. The church has a Latin-cross plan, with an apse and many side chapels.

A cupola was planned but never built, so the space it would have filled was covered by a fake perspective painting. The piers built to uphold the cupola support the observatory of the Collegio Romano.

Palazzo del Collegio Romano ❹

Piazza del Collegio Romano. **Map** 5 A4 & 12 E3. 🚌 *117, 119, 492 and along Via del Corso or stopping at Piazza Venezia.* **Not open** to the public.

ON THE SAME BLOCK as the church of Sant'Ignazio is the palazzo used by Jesuits as a college where many future bishops, cardinals and popes studied. The college was confiscated in 1870 and turned into an ordinary school. The portals bear the coat of arms of its founder, Pope Gregory XIII of Boncompagni (reigned 1572–85). The façade is also adorned with a bell, a clock, and two sundials. On the right is a tower built in 1787 as a meteorological observatory. Until 1925 its time signal regulated all the clocks within the city.

Portal of the Collegio Romano

Fontanella del Facchino ❺

Via Lata. **Map** 5 A4 & 12 E3.
🚌 *64, 81, 85, 117, 119, 492 and many other routes.*

IL FACCHINO (the Porter), once in the Corso, now set in the wall of the Banco di Roma, was one of Rome's "talking statues" like Pasquino *(see p124)*. Created around 1590, the fountain may have been based on a drawing by painter Jacopino del Conte. The statue of a man holding a barrel most likely represents a member of the Università degli Acquaroli (Fraternity of Water-carriers), though it is also said to be of Martin Luther, or of the porter Abbondio Rizzio, who died carrying a barrel.

The Facchino drinking fountain

Palazzo Doria Pamphilj ❻

Piazza del Collegio Romano 2. **Map** 5 A4 & 12 E3. 📞 *06-679 73 23.* 🚌 *64, 81, 85, 117, 119, 492 and many other routes.* **Open** *10am–5pm Fri–Wed.* **Closed** *25 Dec, 1 Jan, Easter Sun, 1 May, 15 Aug.* **Adm charge.** ♿ 📷 *compulsory for private apartments.* 🎧 🎵 **Concerts** 🌐 *www.doriapamphilj.it*

PALAZZO DORIA PAMPHILJ is a great island of stone in the heart of Rome, the oldest parts dating from 1435. Through the Corso entrance you can see the 16th-century porticoed courtyard with the coat of arms of the della Rovere family. The Aldobrandini were the next owners. Between 1601 and 1647 the mansion acquired a second courtyard and flanking wings at the expense of a public bath that stood nearby.

When the Pamphilj family took over, they completed the Piazza del Collegio Romano

façade and the Via della Gatta wing, a splendid chapel and a theatre inaugurated by Queen Christina of Sweden in 1684.

In the first half of the 18th century, Gabriele Valvassori created the gallery above the courtyard and a new façade along the Corso, using the highly decorative style of the period known as *barocchetto*, which now dominates the building. The stairways and salons, the Mirror Gallery and the picture gallery all radiate a joyous sense of light and space.

The family collection in the Doria Pamphilj gallery has over 400 paintings dating from the 15th to the 18th century, including the famous portrait of Pope Innocent X Pamphilj by Velázquez. There are also works by Titian, Caravaggio, Lorenzo Lotto, Guercino and Claude Lorrain. The rooms in the private apartment have many of their original furnishings, including splendid Brussels and Gobelin tapestries.

Via della Gatta ❼

Map 5 A4 & 12 E3. 🚌 *62, 63, 64, 70, 81, 87, 186, 492 & routes along Via del Plebiscito & Corso Vittorio Emanuele II.*

THIS NARROW STREET runs between the Palazzo Doria Pamphilj and the smaller Palazzo Grazioli. The ancient

marble sculpture of a cat *(gatta)* that gives the street its name is on the first cornice on the corner of Palazzo Grazioli.

Via della Gatta's marble cat

Palazzo Altieri ❽

Via del Gesù 93. **Map** 4 F4 & 12 E3.
🚌 *46, 62, 63, 64, 70, 81, 87, 186, 492 and routes along Via del Plebiscito and Corso Vittorio Emanuele II.* 🚋 *8.*

THE ALTIERI FAMILY is first mentioned in Rome's history in the 9th century. This palazzo was built by the last male heirs, the brothers Cardinal Giambattista di Lorenzo Altieri and Cardinal Emilio Altieri, later Pope Clement X (reigned 1670–76). Many surrounding houses had to be demolished, but an old woman called Berta refused to leave, so her hovel was incorporated in the palazzo. Its windows are still visible on the west end of the building. Part of the palazzo is occupied by Mirabilia, a ticket agency *(see p340)*.

Gesù ❾

See pp114–15.

Caravaggio's *Rest during the Flight into Egypt* **in Palazzo Doria Pamphilj**

Marble foot from a Roman statue

Pie' di Marmo ⑩

Via di Santo Stefano del Cacco. **Map**
4 F4 & 12 E3. 🚌 62, 63, 64, 70, 81,
87, 116, 186, 492 and other routes
along Via del Corso, Via del Plebiscito
and Corso Vittorio Emanuele II.

I⊤ WAS POPULARLY believed in
the Middle Ages that half
the population of ancient Rome
was made up of bronze and
marble statues. Fragments of
these giants, usually gods or
emperors, are scattered over
the city. This piece, a marble
foot (pie' di marmo), comes
from an area dedicated to the
Egyptian gods Isis and Serapis
and was probably part of a
temple statue. Statues were
painted and covered with
jewels and clothes given by the
faithful – a great fire risk with
unattended burning tapers.

Santa Maria sopra Minerva ⑪

Piazza della Minerva 42. **Map** 4 F4 &
12 E3. 📞 06-679 39 26. 🚌 116 and
along Via del Corso, Via del Plebiscito
and Corso Vittorio Emanuele II. **Open**
7am–7pm daily (occasionally closed Sun
pm). **Cloister open** 9am–12.30pm,
4–6.30pm Mon–Sat. ✝ 🎵 **Concerts**.

FEW OTHER CHURCHES display
such a complete and im-
pressive record of Italian art.
Dating from the 13th century,
the Minerva is one of the few
examples of Gothic architecture in Rome. It was the
traditional stronghold of the
Dominicans, whose anti-
heretical zeal earned them the
nickname of Domini Canes
(the hounds of the Lord).
   Built on ancient ruins,
supposed to have been the
Temple of Minerva, the
simple T-shaped vaulted
building acquired rich chapels
and works of art by which its

many patrons wished to be
remembered. Note the
Cosmatesque 13th-century
tombs and the exquisite
works of 15th-century Tuscan
and Venetian artists. Native
Roman talent of the period
can be admired in Antoniazzo
Romano's Annunciation,
featuring Cardinal Juan de
Torquemada, uncle of the
infamous Spanish Inquisitor.
   The more monumental style
of the Roman Renaissance is
well represented in the tombs
of the 16th-century Medici
popes, Leo X and his cousin
Clement VII, and in the richly
decorated Aldobrandini
Chapel. Near the steps of
the choir is the celebrated
sculpture of the Risen Christ,
started by Michelangelo but
completed by Raffaele da
Montelupo in 1521.
   There are also splendid
works of art from the
Baroque period, including a
tomb and a bust by Bernini.
The church is visited not
only for its art, but also
because it contains
the tombs of many
famous Italians: St
Catherine of Siena,
who died here in 1380;
the Venetian sculptor
Andrea Bregno (died
1506); the Humanist
Cardinal Pietro Bembo
(died 1547); and Fra
Angelico, the Dominican
friar and painter, who
died in Rome in 1455.

Obelisk of Santa Maria sopra Minerva ⑫

Piazza della Minerva. **Map** 4 F4 & 12
D3. 🚌 116 and routes along Via del
Corso and Corso Vittorio Emanuele II.

ORIGINALLY MEANT to decorate
Palazzo Barberini as a
joke, this exotic elephant and
obelisk sculpture is typical of
Bernini's inexhaustible
imagination. (The elephant was
actually sculpted by Ercole
Ferrata to Bernini's design.)
When the ancient obelisk
was found in the garden of
the monastery of Santa
Maria sopra Minerva, the
friars wanted the monument
erected in their piazza. The
elephant was provided with
its enormous saddle-cloth
because of a friar's insis-
tence that the gap under
the animal's abdomen
would undermine its
stability. Bernini knew
better: you need
only look at the
Fontana dei
Quattro Fiumi (see
p120) to appreciate
his use of empty
space. The elephant,
an ancient symbol
of intelligence and
piety, was chosen as
the embodiment of
the virtues on which
Christians should
build true wisdom.

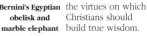

Bernini's Egyptian obelisk and marble elephant

Nave of Santa Maria sopra Minerva

Pantheon ⑬

See pp110–11.

Sant'Eustachio ⑭

Piazza Sant'Eustachio. **Map** 4 F4 & 12 D3. [06-686 5334. ▭ *116 and routes along Corso Vittorio Emanuele II.* **Open** *9am–noon, 3.30–7.30pm daily.*

THE ORIGINS of this church date to early Christian times, when it offered relief to the poor. In medieval times, many charitable brotherhoods elected Sant'Eustachio as their patron and had chapels here.

The Romanesque bell tower is one of the few surviving remains of the medieval church, which was completely redecorated in the 17th and 18th centuries.

Nearby is the excellent Caffè Sant'Eustachio *(see p319)*.

Bell tower of Sant'Eustachio

La Maddalena ⑮

Piazza della Maddalena. **Map** 4 F3 & 12 D2. [06-679 77 96. ▭ *116 and many routes along Via del Corso and Corso Vittorio Emanuele II.* **Open** *8am–noon, 5–7.30pm daily.*

SITUATED IN a small piazza near the Pantheon, the Maddalena's Rococo façade, built in 1735, epitomizes the love of light and movement of the late Baroque. Its curves are reminiscent of Borromini's San Carlo alle Quattro Fontane *(see p161)*. The façade has been lovingly restored, despite the protests of die-hard Neo-Classicists who dismiss its painted stucco as icing sugar.

The small size of the Maddalena did not deter the

The old-fashioned *salone* **of the Caffè Giolitti**

17th- and 18th-century decorators who filled the interior with ornaments from the floor to the top of the elegant cupola. The organ loft and choir are particularly powerful examples of the Baroque's desire to fire the imagination of the faithful.

Many of the paintings and sculptures adopt the Christian imagery of the Counter-Reformation. In the niches of the nave, the statues are personifications of virtues such as Humility and Simplicity. There are also scenes from the life of San Camillo, who died in the adjacent convent in 1614. The church belonged to his followers, the Camillians, a preaching order active in Rome's hospitals. Like the Jesuits, they commissioned powerful works of art to convey the force of their religious message.

La Maddalena's stuccoed façade

Caffè Giolitti ⑯

Via degli Uffici del Vicario 40. **Map** 4 F3 & 12 D2. [06-699 12 43. ▭ *116 and many routes along Via del Corso and Corso Rinascimento.* **Open** *7am–1am daily.*

FOUNDED IN 1900, the Caffè Giolitti is the heir to the *Belle Époque* cafés that lined the nearby Via del Corso in Rome's first days as capital of the new Italian state. Its *salone* holds tourists in summer and Roman families at weekends, and on weekdays is frequented by local workers from a wide range of industries. Its ice creams are especially good.

Palazzo Baldassini ⑰

Via delle Coppelle 35. **Map** 4 F3 & 12 D2. ▭ *116 and many routes along Via del Corso and Corso Rinascimento.* **Not open** *to the public.*

MELCHIORRE BALDASSINI commissioned Antonio da Sangallo the Younger to build his home in Florentine Renaissance style in 1514–20. With its cornices marking the different floors and wrought-iron window grilles, this is one of the best examples of an early 16th-century Roman palazzo. It stands in the part of Rome still known as the Renaissance Quarter, which flourished around the long straight streets such as Via di Ripetta and Via della Scrofa built at the time of Pope Leo X (reigned 1513–21).

Pantheon ⑬

IN THE MIDDLE AGES the Pantheon, the Roman temple of "all the gods", became a church; in time this magnificent building with its awe-inspiring domed interior became a symbol of Rome itself. The rectangular portico screens the vast hemispherical dome: only from inside can its true scale and beauty be appreciated. The rotunda's height and diameter are equal: 43.3 m (142 ft). The hole at the top of the dome, the *oculus*, provides the only light. We owe this marvel of Roman engineering to the emperor Hadrian, who designed it (AD 118–125) to replace an earlier temple built by Marcus Agrippa, son-in-law of Augustus. The shrines that now line the wall of the Pantheon range from the Tomb of Raphael to those of the kings of modern Italy.

★ Interior of Dome
The dome was cast by pouring concrete mixed with tufa and pumice over a temporary wooden framework.

The portico, enclosed by granite columns

The walls of the drum supporting the dome are 6 m (19 ft) thick.

The immense portico is built on the foundations of Agrippa's temple.

STAR FEATURES

★ **Interior of the Dome**

★ **Tomb of Raphael**

Bell Towers
This 18th-century view by Bernardo Bellotto shows Bernini's much-ridiculed turrets, which were removed in 1883.

Floor Patterning
The marble floor, restored in 1873, preserves the original Roman design.

RAPHAEL AND LA FORNARINA

Raphael, at his own request, was buried here when he died in 1520. He had lived for years with his model, La Fornarina (*see p210*), seen here in a painting by Giulio Romano, but she was excluded from the ceremony of his burial. On the right of his tomb is a memorial to his fiancée, Maria Bibbiena, niece of the artist's patron, Cardinal Dovizi di Bibbiena.

VISITORS' CHECKLIST

Piazza della Rotonda. **Map** 4 F4 & 12 D3. 06-68 30 02 30. 116 and many routes along Via del Corso, Corso Vittorio Emanuele II & Corso del Rinascimento. **Open** 8.30am–7.30pm Mon–Sat, 9am–6pm Sun. **Closed** 1 Jan, 1 May, 25 Dec.

Oculus

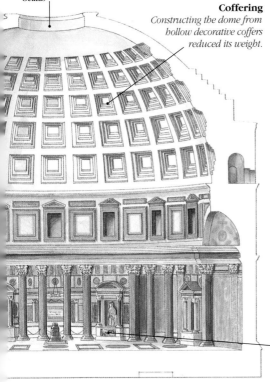

Coffering
Constructing the dome from hollow decorative coffers reduced its weight.

Relieving Arches
Brick arches embedded in the structure of the wall act as internal buttresses, distributing the weight of the dome.

★ Tomb of Raphael
The artist's body rests below a Madonna by Lorenzetto (1520).

TIMELINE

Inscription on pediment

27–25 BC Marcus Agrippa builds first Pantheon	**735** Gregory III roofs the Pantheon in lead	**1309–77** While papal seat is in Avignon, Pantheon is used as a fortress and poultry market	**1888** Tomb of King Vittorio Emanuele II completed
30 BC	**AD 100**	**600**	**1100**	**1600**
118–25 Hadrian builds new Pantheon	**609** Pope Boniface IV consecrates Pantheon as church of Santa Maria ad Martyres	**663** Byzantine Emperor Constans II strips gilded tiles from the roof	**1632** Urban VIII melts down bronze from portico for Bernini's baldacchino in St Peter's

Bernini's curving southern façade of Palazzo di Montecitorio

Santa Maria in Campo Marzio ⑱

Piazza in Campo Marzio 45. **Map** 4 F3
& 12 D2. 🚌 116 and many routes on
Via del Corso and Corso Rinascimento.
Closed for renovation.

Around the courtyard through which you enter the church, there are fascinating remnants of medieval houses, once the property of the original monastery. The church itself was rebuilt in 1685 by Antonio de Rossi, using a square Greek-cross plan with a cupola. Above the altar is a 12th-century painting of the Madonna, which gives the church its name.

Palazzo Borghese ⑲

Largo della Fontanella di Borghese.
Map 4 F3 & 12 D1. 🚌 81, 117, 492,
628. **Closed** to the public.

The palazzo was acquired in about 1605 by Cardinal Camillo Borghese, just before he became Pope Paul V. Flaminio Ponzio was hired to enlarge the building and give it the grandeur appropriate to the residence of the pope's family. He added a wing overlooking Piazza Borghese and the delightful porticoed courtyard inside. Subsequent enlargements included the building and decoration of a great *nymphaeum* known as the Bath of Venus. For more than two centuries this palazzo housed the Borghese family's renowned collection of paintings, which was bought

by the Italian state in 1902 and transferred to the Galleria Borghese *(see pp260–61).*

Pope Paul V, who commissioned Palazzo Borghese for his family

San Lorenzo in Lucina ⑳

Via in Lucina 16A. **Map** 4 F3 & 12 E1.
📞 06-687 14 94. 🚌 81, 117,
492, 628. **Open** 7.30am–noon,
4.30–8pm daily. ⛪

The church is one of Rome's oldest Christian places of worship, and was probably built on a well sacred to Juno, protectress of women. It was rebuilt in the 12th century, and today's external appearance is quite typical of the period featuring a portico with re-used Roman columns crowned by medieval capitals, a plain triangular pediment and a Romanesque bell tower with coloured marble inlay.

The interior was totally rebuilt in 1856–8. The old basilical plan was destroyed and the two side naves were replaced

by Baroque chapels. Do not miss the fine busts in the Fonseca Chapel, designed by Bernini, or the *Crucifixion* by Guido Reni above the main altar. There is also a 19th-century monument honouring French painter Nicolas Poussin, who died in Rome in 1655 and was buried in the church.

Palazzo di Montecitorio ㉑

Piazza di Montecitorio. **Map** 4 F3 &
12 E2. 🚌 116 and all routes along
Via del Corso or stopping at Piazza
S. Silvestro. **Open** 10am–6pm
1st Sun each month; no bookings.
📞 06-676 01.
🌐 www.camera.it

The palazzo's first architect, Bernini, got the job after he presented a silver model of his design to the wife of his patron, Prince Ludovisi. The building was completed in 1694 by Carlo Fontana and became the Papal Tribunal of Justice. In 1871 it was chosen to be Italy's new Chamber of Deputies and by 1927 it had doubled in size with a second grand façade. The 630 members of parliament are elected by a majority system with proportional representation.

The church of San Lorenzo in Lucina

Emperor Augustus's obelisk

Obelisk of Montecitorio ㉒

Piazza di Montecitorio. **Map** 4 F3 & 12 E2. 🚌 116 and routes along Via del Corso or to Piazza S. Silvestro.

THE MEASUREMENT of time in ancient Rome was always a rather hit-and-miss affair: for many years the Romans relied on an imported (and therefore inaccurate) sundial, a trophy from the conquest of Sicily. In 10 BC the Emperor Augustus laid out an enormous sundial in the Campus Martius. Its centre was roughly in today's Piazza di San Lorenzo in Lucina. The shadow was cast by a huge granite obelisk that he had brought back from Heliopolis in Egypt. Unfortunately this sundial too became inaccurate after only 50 years, possibly due to subsidence.

The obelisk was still in the piazza in the 9th century, but then disappeared until it was rediscovered lying under medieval houses in the reign of Pope Julius II (1503–13). The pope was intrigued, because Egyptian hieroglyphs were thought to hold the key to the wisdom of Adam before the Fall, but it was only under Pope Benedict XIV (reigned 1740–58) that the obelisk was finally unearthed. It was erected in its present location in 1792 by Pope Pius VI.

Column of Marcus Aurelius ㉓

Piazza Colonna. **Map** 5 A3 & 12 E2. 🚌 116 and routes along Via del Corso or to Piazza S. Silvestro.

CLEARLY AN IMITATION of the Column of Trajan (see p90), this monument was erected after the death of Marcus Aurelius in AD 180 to commemorate his victories over the barbarian tribes of the Danube. The 80-year lapse between the two works produced a great artistic change: the wars of Marcus Aurelius are rendered with simplified pictures in stronger relief, sacrificing Classical proportions for the sake of clarity and immediacy. The spirit of the work is more akin to the 4th-century Arch of Constantine (see p91) than to Trajan's monument. Gone are the heroic qualities of the Roman soldiers, by now mostly barbarian mercenaries, and a sense of respect for the vanquished. A new emphasis on the supernatural points to the end of the Hellenistic tradition and the beginning of Christianity.

Composed of 28 drums of marble, the column was restored in 1588 by Domenico Fontana on the orders of Pope Sixtus V. The emperor's statue on the summit was replaced by a bronze of St Paul. The 20 spirals of the low relief chronicle the German war of AD 172–3, and (above) the Sarmatic war of AD 174–5. The column is almost 30 m (100 ft) high and 3.7 m (12 ft) in diameter. An internal staircase leads to the top. The easiest way to appreciate the sculptural work, however, is to visit the Museo della Civiltà Romana at EUR (see p266) and study the casts of the reliefs.

Palazzo Capranica ㉔

Piazza Capranica. **Map** 4 F3 & 12 D2. 🚌 116 and routes along Via del Corso or to Piazza S. Silvestro.

Windows of Palazzo Capranica

ONE OF ROME'S small number of surviving 15th-century buildings, the palazzo was commissioned by Cardinal Domenico Capranica both as his family residence and as a college for higher education. Its fortress-like appearance is a patchwork of subsequent additions, not unusual in the late 15th century, when Rome was still hovering between medieval and Renaissance taste. The Gothic-looking windows on the right of the building show the cardinal's coat of arms and the date 1451 is inscribed on the doorway underneath. The palazzo is now a shell housing a good restaurant.

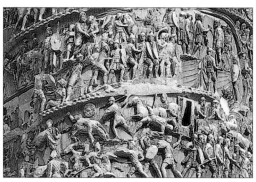

Relief of the emperor's campaigns on the Column of Marcus Aurelius

Gesù ⓿

DATING FROM BETWEEN 1568 and 1584, the Gesù was the first Jesuit church to be built in Rome. Its design epitomizes Counter-Reformation Baroque architecture and has been much imitated throughout the Catholic world. The layout proclaims the church's two major functions: a large nave with side pulpits for preaching to great crowds, and a main altar as the centrepiece for the celebration of the mass. The illusionistic decoration in the nave and dome was added a century later. Its message is clear and confident: faithful, Catholic worshippers will be joyfully uplifted into the heavens while Protestants and other heretics are flung into hell's fires.

★ Chapel of Sant'Ignazio
Above its altar is a statue of the saint, framed by gilded lapis lazuli columns. The chapel was built in 1696–1700 by Andrea Pozzo, a Jesuit artist.

Triumph of Faith Over Idolatry
This vivid Baroque allegory sculpted by Théudon illustrates the great ambition of Jesuit theology.

ST IGNATIUS AND THE JESUIT ORDER

Spanish soldier Ignatius Loyola (1491–1556) joined the Church after being wounded in battle in 1521. He came to Rome in 1537 and founded the Jesuits, sending missionaries and teachers all over the world to win souls for Catholicism.

Main entrance

STAR FEATURES

★ Chapel of Sant'Ignazio

★ Monument to San Roberto Bellarmino

★ Nave Ceiling Decorations

Allegorical Figures
Antonio Raggi made these stuccoes, which were designed by Il Baciccia to complement the figures on his own nave frescoes.

Madonna della Strada
This 15th-century image, the Madonna of the Road, was originally displayed on the façade of Santa Maria della Strada which once stood on this site.

VISITORS' CHECKLIST
Piazza del Gesù. **Map** 4 F4 & 12 E4. 06-69 70 01.
H, 46, 62, 64, 70, 81, 87, 186, 492, 628, 810 and other routes. 8.
Open 6am–12.30pm, 4–7.15pm daily.

★ Monument to San Roberto Bellarmino
Bernini captured the forceful personality of this anti-Protestant theologian, who died in 1621.

The Chapel of St Francis Xavier is a memorial to the great missionary who died alone on an island off China in 1552.

★ Nave Ceiling Decorations
The figures in Il Baciccia's astonishing fresco of the Triumph of the Name of Jesus *spill out on to the coffered vaulting of the nave.*

Cupola Frescoes
The cupola was completed by della Porta to Vignola's design. The frescoes, by Il Baciccia, feature Old Testament figures.

TIMELINE

	1540 Founding of the Society of Jesus (the Jesuits)	**1571** Giacomo della Porta's design chosen for the façade **1584** Church's consecration	**1696–1700** The Chapel of Sant' Ignazio is designed by Andrea Pozzo, a Jesuit artist	**1773** Pope Clement XIV orders the suppression of the Jesuit order
1500		**1600**		**1700**
1545–63 Council of Trent defines the new Catholic orthodoxy **1556** Ignatius Loyola dies		**1568–71** Vignola builds the church up to the crossing under the patronage of Cardinal Alessandro Farnese	**1622** Ignatius Loyola is canonized	**1670–83** Giovanni Battista Gaulli (Il Baciccia) paints the nave vault, dome and apse

Piazza Navona

THE FOUNDATIONS of the buildings surrounding the elongated oval of Piazza Navona were the ruined grandstands of the vast Stadium of Domitian. The piazza still provides a dramatic spectacle today with the obelisk of the Fontana dei Quattro Fiumi in front of the church of Sant' Agnese in Agone as its focal

Lion on Fontana dei Quattro Fiumi

point. The predominant style of the area is Baroque, many of its finest buildings dating from the reign of Innocent X Pamphilj (1644–55), patron of Bernini and Borromini. Of special interest is the complex of the Chiesa Nuova, headquarters of the Filippini, the order founded by San Filippo Neri, the 16th-century "Apostle of Rome".

Sights at a Glance

Churches and Temples
Sant'Agnese in Agone ❹
Santa Maria dell'Anima ❺
Santa Maria della Pace ❻
San Luigi dei Francesi ❼
Sant'Ivo alla Sapienza ❾
Sant'Andrea della Valle ❿
Chiesa Nuova ⓰
Oratorio dei Filippini ⓰
San Salvatore in Lauro ⓴

Museums
Palazzo Braschi ⓬
Museo Napoleonico ㉑

Historic Buildings
Palazzo Pamphilj ❸
Palazzo Madama ❽
Palazzo Massimo
  alle Colonne ⓫
Torre dell'Orologio ⓱
Palazzo del Banco
  di Santo Spirito ⓲
Palazzo Altemps ㉓

Fountains and Statues
Fontana dei Quattro Fiumi ❶
Pasquino ⓭

Historic Streets and Piazzas
Piazza Navona ❷
Via del Governo Vecchio ⓮
Via dei Coronari ⓳

Restaurants
Hostaria dell'Orso ㉒

See Also
- **Street Finder**, maps 4, 11, 12
- **Where to Stay** pp294–5
- **Restaurants** pp310–11

Getting There
This central area is within walking distance of many parts of the city and it is easily reached by bus. The principal routes along Corso Vittorio Emanuele II are the 64 from Termini station to St Peter's and the 46. Corso del Rinascimento, which runs parallel to Piazza Navona, is served by several useful routes, including the 70, 81, 116, 186 and 492.

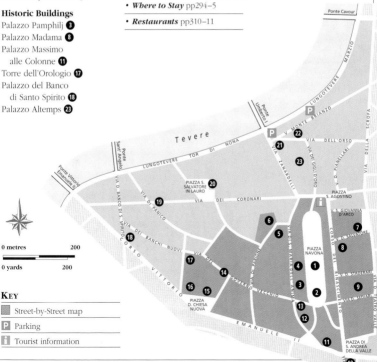

Key

▦	Street-by-Street map
🅿	Parking
ℹ	Tourist information

Piazza Navona, with the Fontana del Moro and church of Sant'Agnese in Agone

Street-by-Street: Piazza Navona

No other piazza in Rome can rival the theatricality of Piazza Navona. Day and night there is always something going on in the pedestrian area around its three flamboyant fountains. The Baroque is also represented in many of the area's churches. To discover an older Rome, walk along Via del Governo Vecchio to admire the façades of its Renaissance buildings and browse in the fascinating antiques shops.

Oratorio dei Filippini
The musical term oratorio comes from this place of informal worship **⑯**

Torre dell' Orologio
This clock tower by Borromini (1648) is part of the Convent of the Filippini **⑰**

VIA DEL CORALLO

Chiesa Nuova
This church was rebuilt in the late 16th century for the order founded by San Filippo Neri **⑮**

To Corso Vittorio Emanuele II

Via del Governo Vecchio
This street preserves a large number of fine Renaissance houses **⑭**

Santa Maria della Pace
This medallion shows Pope Sixtus IV who reigned 1471–84 and under whose orders the church was built **⑥**

Pasquino
Romans hung satirical verses and dialogues on this weather-beaten statue **⑬**

Palazzo Pamphilj
This grand town house was built for Pope Innocent X and his family in the mid-17th century **❸**

Palazzo Braschi
A late 18th-century building with a splendid balcony, the palazzo houses the Museo di Roma **⑫**

Palazzo Massimo alle Colonne
The magnificent curving colonnade (1536) is by Baldassarre Peruzzi **⑪**

STAR SIGHTS

★ **San Luigi dei Francesi**

★ **Piazza Navona**

★ **Sant'Andrea della Valle**

KEY

— — — Suggested route

| 0 metres | 75 |
| 0 yards | 75 |

Sant'Agnese in Agone
Borromini's startling concave façade (1657) dominates one side of Piazza Navona ❹

Santa Maria dell'Anima
For four centuries this has been the German church in Rome ❺

Palazzo Madama
A spread-eagled stone lion skin decorates the central doorway of the palazzo, now the Italian Senate ❽

Fontana dei Quattro Fiumi
This fountain supporting an Egyptian obelisk was designed by Bernini ❶

★ **San Luigi dei Francesi**
An 18th-century statue of St Louis stands in a niche in the façade ❼

★ **Piazza Navona**
This unique piazza owes its shape to a Roman racetrack and its stunning decor to the genius of the Roman Baroque ❷

The Fontana del Moro was remodelled in 1653 by Bernini, who designed the central sea god.

Sant'Ivo alla Sapienza
This tiny domed church is one of Borromini's most original creations. He worked on it between 1642 and 1650 ❾

★ **Sant'Andrea della Valle**
The church, with its grandiose façade by Carlo Rainaldi (1665), has gained fame outside Rome as the setting of the first act of Puccini's Tosca ❿

To Campo de' Fiori

Fontana dei Quattro Fiumi ❶

Piazza Navona. **Map** 4 E4 & 11 C3.
🚌 *46, 62, 64, 70, 81, 87, 116, 492, 628.*

B UILT FOR POPE Innocent X
Pamphilj, this magnificent
fountain in the centre of
Piazza Navona was unveiled
in 1651. The pope's coat of
arms, the dove and the olive
branch, decorate the pyramid
rock formation supporting the
Roman obelisk, which once
stood in the Circus of
Maxentius on the Appian
Way. Bernini designed the
fountain, which was paid for
by means of taxes on bread
and other staples. The great
rivers – the Ganges, the
Danube, the Nile and the
River Plate – are represented
by four giants. The Nile's
veiled head symbolizes the
river's unknown source, but
there is also a legend that the
veil conveys Bernini's dislike
for the nearby Sant'Agnese in
Agone, designed by his rival
Borromini. Similarly, the

**Palazzo Pamphilj, the largest
building in Piazza Navona**

athletic figure of the River
Plate, cringing with arm
upraised, is supposed to
express Bernini's fear that the
church will collapse. Sadly,
these widely believed stories
can have no basis in fact:
Bernini had completed the
fountain before Borromini
started work on the church.

Piazza Navona ❷

Map 4 E3 & 11 C2. 🚌 *46, 62, 64,
70, 81, 87, 116, 492, 628.*

R OME'S MOST beautiful
Baroque piazza follows
the shape of Domitian's
Stadium which once stood on
this site – some of its arches
are still visible below the
church of Sant'Agnese in
Agone. The *agones*
were athletic contests
held in the 1st-century
stadium, which could
seat 33,000 people.
The word "Navona"
is thought to be a
corruption of *in
agone*. The piazza's
unique appearance

and atmosphere were created
in the 17th century with the
addition of the Fontana dei
Quattro Fiumi. The other
fountains date from the previous century but have been
altered several times since.
The basin of the Fontana di
Nettuno, at the northern end,
was built by Giacomo della
Porta in 1576, while the
statues of Neptune and the
Nereids date from the 19th
century. The Fontana del
Moro, at the southern end,
was also designed by della
Porta, though Bernini altered
it later, adding a statue of a
Moor fighting a dolphin.
   Up until the 19th century,
Piazza Navona was flooded
during August by stopping
the fountain outlets. The
rich would splash around
in carriages, while street
urchins paddled after them.
Today, with its numerous
shops and cafés, the piazza is
a favourite in all seasons. In
summer it is busy with street
entertainers, while in winter
it fills with colourful stalls
selling toys and sweets for
the feast of the Befana.

Palazzo Pamphilj ❸

Piazza Navona. **Map** 4 E4 & 11 C3.
🚌 *46, 62, 64, 70, 81, 87, 116, 492,
628.* **Not open** to the public.

**Family dove and olive branch on
façade of Palazzo Pamphilj**

I N 1644 Giovanni Battista
Pamphilj became Pope
Innocent X. During his 10-
year reign, he heaped riches
on his own family, especially
his domineering sister-in-law,
Olimpia Maidalchini. The
"talking statue" Pasquino *(see
p124)* gave her the nickname
"Olim-Pia", Latin for "formerly
virtuous". She lived in the
grand Palazzo Pamphilj,
which has frescoes by Pietro
da Cortona and a gallery by
Borromini. The building is
now the Brazilian embassy
and cultural centre.

Symbolic figure of the River Ganges in the Fontana dei Quattro Fiumi

Sant'Agnese in Agone ❹

Piazza Navona. **Map** 4 E4 & 11 C3.
(06-6819 2134. **⁌** 46, 62, 64,
70, 81, 87, 116, 492, 628. **Open**
9am–noon, 4–7pm Tue–Sat,
10am–1pm Sun. **↑** **&**

THIS CHURCH is believed to
have been founded on the
site of the brothel where, in
AD 304, the young St Agnes
was exposed naked to force
her to renounce her faith.
A marble relief in the crypt
shows the miraculous growth
of her hair, which fell around
her body to protect her
modesty. She was martyred
on this site and is buried
in the catacombs that bear
her name along the Via
Nomentana *(see p264)*.

Today's church was
commissioned by Pope
Innocent X in 1652. The first
architects were father and
son, Girolamo and Carlo
Rainaldi, but they were
replaced by Borromini
in 1653. He stuck
more or less to the
Rainaldi scheme
except for the
concave façade
designed to
emphasize the
dome. A statue
of St Agnes on the
façade is said to
be reassuring
the Fontana dei
Quattro Fiumi's
statue of the River
Plate that the
church is stable.

**Statue of St Agnes
on façade of Sant'
Agnese in Agone**

Carlo Saraceni's *Miracle of St Benno and the Keys of Meissen Cathedral*

Santa Maria dell'Anima ❺

Via della Pace 24. **Map** 4 E4 & 11 C2.
(06-682 8181. **⁌** 46, 62, 64,
70, 81, 87, 116, 492, 628.
Open 8am–1pm, 2pm–7.30pm daily.
↑ **&**

POPE ADRIAN VI (reigned
1522–3), son of a ship-
builder from Utrecht, was the
last non-Italian pope before
John Paul II. He would have
disapproved of his superb

tomb by Baldassarre Peruzzi
in Santa Maria dell'Anima. It
stands to the right of
Giulio Romano's
damaged altarpiece and
is redolent of the
pagan Renaissance
spirit the pope had so
condemned during
his brief, rather
gloomy reign, when
patronage of the arts
ground to a halt. Santa
Maria dell'Anima is
the German church in
Rome and some of its
paintings, such as the
Miracle of St Benno by
Carlo Saraceni (1618),
illustrate events connected
with the history of Germany.

Santa Maria della Pace ❻

Vicolo dell'Arco della Pace 5.
Map 4 E3 & 11 C2. **(** 06-686
1156. **⁌** 46, 62, 64, 70, 81, 87,
116, 492, 628. **Open** 10am–12.45pm
Tue–Fri. **↑** **&** 2 steps.
Exhibitions, concerts.

A DRUNKEN SOLDIER allegedly
pierced the breast of a
painted Madonna on this site,

causing it to bleed. Pope
Sixtus IV della Rovere
(reigned 1471–84) placated
the Virgin by ordering Baccio
Pontelli to build her a church
if she would bring the war
with Turkey to an end. Peace
was restored and the church
was named Santa Maria della
Pace (St Mary of Peace).

The cloister was added by
Bramante in 1504. As in his
famous Tempietto *(see p219)*,
he scrupulously followed
Classical rules of proportion
and achieved a monumental
effect in a relatively small
space. Pietro da Cortona
may have had Bramante's
Tempietto in mind when he
added the church's charming
semi-circular portico in 1656.
The interior, a short nave
ending under an octagonal
cupola, houses Raphael's
famous frescoes of four *Sybils*,
and four *Prophets* by his pupil
Timoteo Viti, painted for the
banker Agostino Chigi in
1514. Baldassarre Peruzzi also
did some work in the church
(fresco in the first chapel on
the left), as did the architect
Antonio da Sangallo the
Younger, who designed the
second chapel on the right.

San Luigi dei Francesi ❼

Piazza di San Luigi dei Francesi 5.
Map 4 F4 & 12 D2. 06-68 82 71.
70, 81, 87, 116, 186, 492, 628.
Open 8.30am–12.30pm, 3.30–7pm
daily. **Closed** Thu pm.

THE FRENCH national church was founded in 1518, but it took until 1589 to complete, with contributions by Giacomo della Porta and Domenico Fontana. The church serves as a last resting place for many illustrious French people, including Chateaubriand's lover Pauline de Beaumont.

Three Caravaggios hang in the fifth chapel on the left, all dedicated to St Matthew. Painted between 1597 and 1602, these were Caravaggio's first great religious works: the *Calling of St Matthew*, the *Martyrdom of St Matthew* and *St Matthew and the Angel*. The first version of this last painting was rejected because of its vivid realism; never before had a saint been shown as a tired old man with dirty feet. All three works display very disquieting realism and a highly dramatic use of light.

Caravaggio, whose paintings of St Matthew hang in San Luigi dei Francesi

Shield linking symbols of France and Rome on facade of San Luigi

Palazzo Madama ❽

Corso del Rinascimento. **Map** 4 F4 & 12 D3. 06-670 61. 70, 81, 87, 116, 186, 492, 628. **Open** 10am–6pm first Sat of month.
www.senato.it

THIS 16TH-CENTURY palazzo was built for the Medici family, who had owned a bank here in the previous century. It was the residence of Medici cousins Giovanni and Giuliano, both of whom became popes: Giovanni as Leo X and Giuliano as Clement VII. Caterina de' Medici, Clement VII's niece, also lived here before she was married to Henry, son of King Francis I of France in 1533.

The palazzo takes its name from Madama Margherita of Austria, illegitimate daughter of Emperor Charles V, who married Alessandro de' Medici and, after his death, Ottavio Farnese. Thus part of the art collection of the Florentine Medici family was inherited by the Roman Farnese family.

The spectacular façade was built in the 17th century by Paolo Maruccelli. He gave it an ornate cornice and whimsical decorative details on the roof. Since 1871 the palazzo has been the seat of the upper house of the Italian parliament.

Cornice of Palazzo Madama

Sant'Ivo alla Sapienza ❾

Corso del Rinascimento 40.
Map 4 F4 & 12 D3. 06-686 4987.
40, 46, 64, 70, 81, 87, 116, 186, 492, 628. **Open** 10am–4.30pm Mon–Fri, 10am–1pm Sat, 9am–noon Sun.

THE CHURCH'S lantern is crowned with a cross on top of a dramatic twisted spiral – a highly distinctive landmark from Rome's roof terraces. No other Baroque church is quite like this one, made **Lantern and spire of Sant'Ivo** by Borromini. Based on a ground design of astonishing geometrical complexity, the walls are a breathtaking combination of concave and convex surfaces. The church stands in the small courtyard of the Palazzo della Sapienza, seat of the old University of Rome from the 15th century until 1935.

Sant'Andrea della Valle ⑩

Piazza Sant'Andrea della Valle. **Map** 4 E4 & 12 D4. 📞 *06-686 1339.* 🚌 *H, 40, 46, 62, 64, 70, 81, 87, 116, 186, 492, 628.* 🚋 *8.* **Open** *7.30am– 12.30pm, 4.30pm–7.30pm daily.* 🔓

Dome of Sant'Andrea della Valle

The church is the scene of the first act of Puccini's opera *Tosca*, though opera fans will not find the Attavanti chapel, a poetic invention. The real church has much to recommend it – the recently restored façade shows the flamboyant Baroque style at its best. Inside, a golden light filters through high windows, showing off the gilded interior. Here lie the two popes of the Sienese Piccolomini family: on the left of the central nave is the tomb of Pius II, the first Humanist pope (reigned 1458–64); Pope Pius III lies opposite – he reigned for less than a month in 1503.

The church is famous for its beautiful dome, the largest in Rome after St Peter's. It was built by Carlo Maderno in 1622–5 and was painted with splendid frescoes by Domenichino and Giovanni Lanfranco. The latter's extravagant style, to be seen in the dome fresco *Glory of Paradise*, won him most of the commission, and the jealous Domenichino is said to have tried to kill his colleague. He failed, but Domenichino's jealousy was unnecessary, as shown by his two beautiful paintings of

scenes from the life of St Andrew around the apse and altar. In the Strozzi Chapel, built in the style of Michelangelo, the altar has copies of the *Leah* and *Rachel* by Michelangelo in San Pietro in Vincoli *(see p170).*

Palazzo Massimo alle Colonne ⑪

Corso Vittorio Emanuele II 141. **Map** 4 F4 & 11 C3. 🚌 *40, 46, 62, 64, 70, 81, 87, 116, 186, 492, 628.* **Chapel open** *7am–noon 16 Mar.*

Roman column, Palazzo Massimo

During the last two years of his life, Baldassarre Peruzzi built this palazzo for the Massimo family, whose home had been destroyed in the 1527 Sack of Rome. Peruzzi displayed great ingenuity in dealing with an awkwardly shaped site. The previous building had stood on the ruined Theatre of Domitian, which created a curve in the great processional Via Papalis. Peruzzi's convex colonnaded façade follows the line of the street. His originality is also evident in the small square upper windows, the court-yard and the stuccoed vestibule. The Piazza de' Massimi entrance has a Renaissance-style, frescoed façade. A single column from the theatre has been set up in the piazza.

The Massimo family traced its origins to Quintus Fabius Maximus, conqueror of Hannibal in the 3rd century BC, and their

coat of arms is borne by an infant Hercules. Over the years the family produced many great Humanists, and in the 19th century, it was a Massimo who negotiated peace with Napoleon. On 16 March each year the family chapel opens to the public to commemorate young Paolo Massimo's resurrection from the dead by San Filippo Neri in 1538.

Palazzo Braschi ⑫

Piazza San Pantaleo 10. **Map** 4 E4 & 11 C3. 📞 *06-6710 8346.* 🚌 *40, 46, 62, 64, 70, 81, 87, 116, 186, 492, 628.* **Open** *9am–7pm Tue–Sun.* ♿ 🎫 🏛 📷

On one side of Piazza San Pantaleo is the last Roman palazzo to be built for the family of a pope. Palazzo Braschi was built in the late 18th century for Pope Pius VI Braschi's nephews by the architect Cosimo Morelli. He gave the building its imposing façade which looks out on to the piazza.

The palazzo now houses the municipal Museo di Roma. It holds collections of pictures, drawings and everyday objects illustrating life in the city from medieval times until the 19th century.

Angel with raised wing by Ercole Ferrata, flanking the façade of Sant'Andrea della Valle

Pasquino ⑬

Piazza di Pasquino. **Map** 4 E4 &
11 C3. 🚌 *40, 46, 62, 64, 70, 81, 87,
116, 492, 628.*

**Pasquino, the most famous of
Rome's satirical "talking statues"**

THIS ROUGH CHUNK of marble
is all that remains of a
Hellenistic group, probably
representing the incident in
Homer's *Iliad* in which Mene-
laus shields the body of the
slain Patroclus. For years it
lay as a stepping stone in a
muddy medieval street until it
was erected on this corner in
1501, near the shop of an
outspoken cobbler named
Pasquino. Freedom of speech
was not encouraged in papal
Rome, so the cobbler wrote
out his satirical comments on
current events and attached
them to the statue.

Other Romans followed suit,
hanging their maxims and
verses on the statue by night to
escape punishment. Despite
the wrath of the authorities,
the sayings of the "talking

statue" (renamed Pasquino)
were part of popular culture up
until the 19th century. Other
statues started to "talk" in the
same vein; Pasquino used to
conduct dialogues with the
statue Marforio in Via del
Campidoglio (now in the courtyard of Palazzo Nuovo, *see
pp70–71*) and with the Babuino
in Via del Babuino *(see p135)*.
Pasquino still speaks on
occasion and Rome's English-
language cinema is named
after him *(see p347)*.

Via del Governo
Vecchio ⑭

Map 4 E4 & 11 B3.
🚌 *40, 46, 62, 64.*

THE STREET TAKES its name
from Palazzo del Governo
Vecchio, the seat of papal
government in the 17th and
18th centuries. Once part of
the Via Papalis, which led
from the Lateran to St Peter's,
the street is lined with 15th-
and 16th-century houses and
small workshops. Particularly
interesting are those at No.
104 and No. 106. The small
palazzo at No. 123 was once
thought to have been the
home of Bramante.
Opposite is Palazzo del
Governo Vecchio. It is
also known as Palazzo
Nardini, from the name of
its founder, which is inscribed
on the first-floor windows
along with the date 1477.

Via del Governo Vecchio

Chiesa Nuova ⑮

Piazza della Chiesa Nuova.
Map 4 E4 & 11 B3. 📞 *06-687 52 89.*
🚌 *40, 46, 62, 64.* **Open** *8am–noon,
4.30–7pm daily.* ⛪

Façade of the Chiesa Nuova

SAN FILIPPO NERI (St Philip
Neri) is the most appealing
of the Counter-Reformation
saints. A highly unconventional
reformer, he required his
noble Roman followers to
humble themselves in public.
He made aristocratic young
men parade through the
streets of Rome in rags or even
with a fox's tail tied behind
them, and set noblemen to
work as labourers building
his church. With the help of
Pope Gregory XIII, his church
was built in place of an old
medieval church, Santa Maria
in Vallicella, and it has been
known ever since as the
Chiesa Nuova (new church).
Begun in 1575 by Matteo da
Città di Castello and continued
by Martino Longhi the Elder,
it was consecrated in 1599
(although the façade, by Fausto
Rughesi, was only finished
in 1606). Against San Filippo's
wishes, the interior was
decorated after his death;
Pietro da Cortona frescoed the
nave, dome and apse, taking
nearly 20 years. There are
also three paintings by Rubens:
Madonna and Angels above
the altar, *Saints Domitilla,
Nereus and Achilleus* on the
right of the altar, and *Saints
Gregory, Maurus and Papias*
on the left. San Filippo is
buried in his own chapel, to
the left of the altar.

Borromini's façade of the Oratorio

Oratorio dei Filippini 🔟

Piazza della Chiesa Nuova. **Map** 4 E4 & 11 B3. 🚌 *46, 62, 64*. **Not open to the public.**

WITH THE ADJOINING church and convent, the oratory formed the centre of Filippo Neri's religious order, founded in 1575. Its members are commonly known as Filippini. The musical term "oratorio" (a religious text sung by solo voices and chorus) derives from the services that were held here.

Filippo Neri came to Rome aged 18 to work as a tutor. The city was undergoing a period of religious strife and an economic slump after the Sack of Rome in 1527. There was also an outbreak of the plague. It was left to newcomers like Neri and Ignazio di Loyola to revive the spiritual life of the city.

Neri formed a brotherhood of laymen who worshipped together and helped pilgrims and the sick (*see Santissima Trinità dei Pellegrini p147*). He founded the Oratory as a centre for religious discourse. Its conspicuous curving brick façade was built by Borromini in 1637–43.

Torre dell' Orologio 🔟

Piazza dell'Orologio. **Map** 4 E4 & 11 B3. 🚌 *40, 46, 62, 64*.

BORROMINI BUILT this clock tower to decorate one corner of the Convent of the Oratorians of San Filippo Neri in 1647–9. It is typical of Borromini in that the front and rear are concave and the sides convex. The mosaic of the Madonna beneath the clock is by Pietro da Cortona, while on the corner of the building is a small tabernacle to the Madonna flanked by angels in the style of Bernini.

Pietro da Cortona (1596–1669)

Palazzo del Banco di Santo Spirito 🔟

Via del Banco di Santo Spirito. **Map** 4 D4 & 11 A2. 🚌 *40, 46, 62, 64*. **Open normal banking hours.**

FORMERLY THE MINT of papal Rome, this palazzo is often referred to as the Antica Zecca (old mint). The upper storeys of the façade, built by Antonio da Sangallo the Younger in the 1520s, are in the shape of a Roman triumphal arch. Above it stand two Baroque statues symbolizing Charity and Thrift, and in the centre of the arch above the main entrance an inscription records the founding of the Banco di Santo Spirito by Pope Paul V Borghese in 1605.

Pope Paul was a very shrewd financier and he encouraged Romans to deposit their money at the bank by offering the vast estates of the Hospital of Santo Spirito (*see p226*) as security. The system catered only for the rudimentary banking requirements of the population, but business was brisk as people deposited money here safe in the knowledge that they could get it out simply by presenting a chit. The hospital coffers also gained from the system. The Banco di Santo Spirito still exists, but is now part of the Banca di Roma.

Façade of the Banco di Santo Spirito, built to resemble a Roman arch

Via dei Coronari ⓳

Map 4 D3 & 11 B2. 🚌 40, 46, 62, 64, 70, 81, 87, 116, 186, 280, 492.

LARGE NUMBERS of medieval pilgrims making their way to St Peter's walked along this street to cross over the Tiber at Ponte Sant'Angelo. Of the businesses that sprang up to try to part the pilgrims from their money, the most enduring was the selling of rosaries, and the street is still named after the rosary sellers *(coronari)*. The street followed the course of the ancient Roman Via Recta (straight street), which originally ran from today's Piazza Colonna to the Tiber.

Making one's way through the vast throng of people in Via dei Coronari could be extremely hazardous. In the Holy Year of 1450, some 200 pilgrims died, crushed by the crowds or drowned in the Tiber. Following the tragedy, Pope Nicholas V demolished the Roman triumphal arch that stood at the entrance to Ponte Sant'Angelo. In the late 15th century, Pope Sixtus IV encouraged the building of private houses and palaces along the street.

Although the rosary sellers have been replaced by antiques dealers, the street still has many original buildings from the 15th and 16th centuries. One of the earliest, at Nos. 156–7, is known as the House of Fiammetta, the mistress of Cesare Borgia.

Antiques shop, Via dei Coronari

Cloister, San Salvatore in Lauro

San Salvatore in Lauro ⓴

Piazza San Salvatore in Lauro 15. **Map** 4 E3 & 11 B2. 📞 06-687 51 87. 🚌 70, 81, 87, 116, 186, 280, 492. **Open** 5–7pm daily; also 8am–1pm Sun. 🚻

THE CHURCH is named "in Lauro" after the laurel grove that grew here in ancient times. The church standing here today was constructed at the end of the 16th century by Ottaviano Mascherino. The bell tower and sacristy were 18th-century additions by Nicola Salvi, famous for the Trevi Fountain *(see p159)*.

The church contains the first great altarpiece by the 17th-century artist Pietro da Cortona, *The Birth of Jesus*, in the first chapel to the right.

The adjacent convent of San Giorgio, to the left, has a pretty Renaissance cloister, a frescoed refectory and the monument to Pope Eugenius IV (reigned 1431–47), moved here when the old St Peter's was pulled down. An extravagant Venetian, Eugenius would willingly spend thousands of ducats on his gold tiara, but requested a "simple, lowly burial place" near his predecessor Pope Eugenius III. His portrait, painted by Salviati, hangs in the refectory.

In 1669 the church became the seat of a pious association, the Confraternity of the Piceni, inhabitants of the Marche region. Fanatically loyal to the pope, the Piceni were traditionally employed as papal soldiers and tax collectors.

Museo Napoleonico ㉑

Piazza di Ponte Umberto 1. **Map** 4 E3 & 11 C1. 📞 06-6880 6286. 🚌 70, 81, 87, 116, 186, 280, 492. **Open** 9am–7pm Tue–Sun. **Closed** 1 Jan, 1 May, 25 Dec. **Adm charge**. ⊘ ♿ 📷 🚻

THIS MUSEUM contains memorabilia and portraits of Napoleon Bonaparte and his family. Personal relics of Napoleon himself include an Indian shawl he wore during his exile on St Helena.

After his death in 1821, the pope allowed many of the Bonaparte family to settle in Rome, including his mother Letizia, who lived in Palazzo Misciattelli on Via del Corso, and his sister Pauline who married the Roman Prince Camillo Borghese. The museum has a cast of her right breast, made by Canova in 1805 as a study for his statue of her as a reclining Venus, now in the Museo Borghese *(see p261)*. Portraits and personal effects of other members of the family are on display, including uniforms, court dresses, and a penny-farthing bicycle that belonged to Prince Eugène, the son of Emperor Napoleon III.

The last male of the Roman branch of the family was Napoleon Charles, portrayed in a late 19th-century painting by Guglielmo de Sanctis. The collection was assembled in 1927 by the Counts Primoli, the sons of Charles's sister, Carlotta Bonaparte.

Façade of San Salvatore in Lauro

The palace next door, in Via Zanardelli houses the Racolta Praz, an impressive selection of over a thousand *objets d'art*, paintings and pieces of furniture. Dating from the 17th and 18th centuries, they were collected by the art historian and literary critic Mario Praz.

Side relief of the Ludovisi Throne, Palazzo Altemps

Entrance to Museo Napoleonico

Hostaria dell'Orso ㉒

Via dei Soldati 25. **Map** 4 E3 & 11 C2. 70, 81, 87, 116, 186, 204, 280, 492, 628. **Not open** to the public.

THIS ANCIENT INN has a 15th-century portico and loggia built with columns taken from Roman ruins. Luminaries who have used the inn include the 16th-century French writers Rabelais and Montaigne. Dante is also said to have stayed here.

Palazzo Altemps ㉓

Piazza Sant'Apollinare 46. **Map** 4 E3 & 11 C2. 06-3996 7700. 70, 81, 87, 116, 280, 492, 628. **Open** 9am–7.45pm Tue–Sun (last adm: 1 hour before closing.) **Adm charge**.

AN EXTRAORDINARY collection of Classical sculpture is housed in this branch of the Museo Nazionale Romano.

Restored as a museum during the 1990s, the palazzo was originally built for Girolamo Riario, nephew of Pope Sixtus IV in 1480. The Riario coat of arms can still be seen in the janitor's room. In the popular uprising that followed the pope's death in 1484, the building was sacked and Girolamo fled the city.

In 1568 the palazzo was bought by Cardinal Marco Sittico Altemps. His family was of German origin – the name is an Italianization of Hohenems – and influential in the church. The palazzo was renovated by Martino Longhi the Elder in the 1570s. He added the great belvedere, crowned with obelisks and a marble unicorn.

The Altemps family were ostentatious collectors; the courtyard and its staircase are lined with ancient sculptures. These form part of the museum's collection, together with the Ludovisi collection of ancient sculptures, which was previously housed in the Museo Nazionale Romano in the Baths of Diocletian *(see p163)*. Located on the ground floor is the Greek statue of Athena Parthenos and the Dionysius group, a Roman copy of the Greek original. On the first floor, at the far end of the courtyard, visitors can admire the Painted Loggia, dating from 1595. The Ludovisi throne, a Greek original carved in the 5th century BC, is on the same floor. It is decorated with reliefs, one of which shows a young woman rising from the sea, who is thought to represent Aphrodite. In the room which is known as the Salone del Camino is the powerful statue *Galata's Suicide*, a marble copy of a group originally made in bronze. Nearby is the Ludovisi Sarcophagus, dating from the 3rd century AD.

Galata's Suicide in the Palazzo Altemps

PIAZZA DI SPAGNA

BY THE 16th century, the increase in numbers of visiting pilgrims and ecclesiastics was making life in Rome's already congested medieval centre unbearable. A new triangle of roads was built, still in place today, to help channel pilgrims as quickly as possible from the city's north gate, the Porta del Popolo, to the Vatican. By the 18th century hotels had sprung up all over

Lion fountain in Piazza del Popolo

the district. Today this attractive area offers much more: the superb works of Renaissance and Baroque art in Santa Maria del Popolo and Sant' Andrea delle Fratte, the magnificent reliefs of the restored Ara Pacis, art exhibitions in the Villa Medici, fine views of the city from the Spanish Steps and the Pincio Gardens and Rome's most famous shopping streets, centred around Via Condotti.

SIGHTS AT A GLANCE

Churches
Sant'Andrea delle Fratte **1**
Trinità dei Monti **10**
All Saints **12**
Santa Maria dei Miracoli and
  Santa Maria in Montesanto **14**
*Santa Maria del
  Popolo pp138–9* **17**
San Rocco **21**
Santi Ambrogio e Carlo
  al Corso **22**

Museums and Galleries
Keats-Shelley
  Memorial House **7**
Casa di Goethe **13**

Historic Buildings
Palazzo di Propaganda
  Fide **2**
Villa Medici **11**

Arches, Gates and Columns
Colonna dell'Immacolata **3**
Porta del Popolo **18**

Historic Streets and Piazzas
Via Condotti **4**
Piazza di Spagna **6**

Spanish Steps **9**
Piazza del Popolo **16**

Monuments and Tombs
Ara Pacis **19**
Mausoleum of Augustus **20**

Parks and Gardens
Pincio Gardens **15**

Cafés and Restaurants
Caffè Greco **5**
Babington's Tea Rooms **8**

GETTING THERE
For Piazza di Spagna and the shops around Via Condotti, Spagna Metro station on line A is more convenient than the main bus routes along Via del Corso and Via del Tritone. Stay on until Flaminio Metro if you wish to visit Piazza del Popolo. For getting around locally, the 116 and 117 minibuses are very handy.

KEY
▧	Street-by-Street map
M	Metro station
P	Parking
—	City Wall
ℹ	Tourist information

SEE ALSO
- **Street Finder**, maps 4, 5
- **Where to Stay** pp294–5
- **Restaurants** pp310–11
- **Shops** pp322–37

The Spanish Steps leading up to the church of Trinità dei Monti

Street-by-Street: Piazza di Spagna

THE NETWORK of narrow streets between Piazza di Spagna and Via del Corso is one of the liveliest areas in Rome, drawing throngs of tourists and Romans to its discreet and elegant shops. In the 18th century the area was full of hotels for frivolous English aristocrats doing the Grand Tour, but there were also artists, writers and composers, who took the city's history and culture more seriously.

Caffè Greco
Busts and portraits recall the café's former artistic patrons ⑤

★ **Piazza di Spagna**
For almost three centuries the square with its curious Barcaccia fountain in the centre has been the chief meeting place for visitors to Rome ⑥

Via delle Carrozze took its name from the carriages of wealthy tourists that used to queue up here for repairs.

Via Condotti
This shadowy, narrow street has the smartest shops in one of the smartest shopping areas in the world ④

Bulgari sells very expensive jewellery behind an austere shopfront in Via Condotti.

0 metres	75
0 yards	75

KEY

- - - Suggested route

Ⓜ Metro station

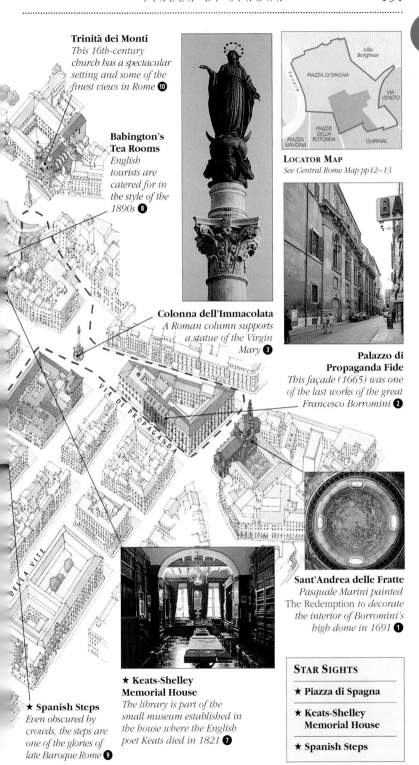

Trinità dei Monti
This 16th-century church has a spectacular setting and some of the finest views in Rome ⑩

Babington's Tea Rooms
English tourists are catered for in the style of the 1890s ⑧

Colonna dell'Immacolata
A Roman column supports a statue of the Virgin Mary ③

LOCATOR MAP
See Central Rome Map pp12–13

Palazzo di Propaganda Fide
This façade (1665) was one of the last works of the great Francesco Borromini ②

Sant'Andrea delle Fratte
Pasquale Marini painted The Redemption *to decorate the interior of Borromini's high dome in 1691* ①

★ Keats-Shelley Memorial House
The library is part of the small museum established in the house where the English poet Keats died in 1821 ⑦

★ Spanish Steps
Even obscured by crowds, the steps are one of the glories of late Baroque Rome ⑨

STAR SIGHTS

★ Piazza di Spagna

★ Keats-Shelley Memorial House

★ Spanish Steps

Sant'Andrea delle Fratte ❶

Via Sant'Andrea delle Fratte 1.
Map 5 A3. ☎ 06-679 31 91. 🚍 116,
117. Ⓜ Spagna. **Open** 6.30am–
12.30pm, 4–7pm daily. ✝

W HEN SANT'ANDREA delle
Fratte was built in the
12th century, this was the
northernmost edge of Rome.
Though the church is now
firmly embedded in the city,
its name (*fratte* means thickets)
recalls its original setting.

The church was completely
rebuilt in the 17th century,
partly by Borromini. His bell
tower and dome, best viewed
from the higher ground further
up Via Capo le Case, are
remarkable for the complex
arrangement of concave and
convex surfaces. The bell
tower is particularly fanciful,
with angel caryatids, flaming
torches, and exaggerated

scrolls like semi-folded hearts
supporting a spiky crown.

In 1842, the Virgin Mary
appeared in the church to a
Jewish banker, who promptly
converted to Christianity and
became a missionary. Inside,
the chapel of the Miraculous
Madonna is the first thing you
notice. The church is better
known, however, for the
angels that Borromini's rival,
Bernini, carved for the Ponte
Sant'Angelo. Pope Clement IX
declared they were too lovely
to be exposed to the weather,
so they remained with Bernini's
family until 1729, when they
were moved to the church.

Palazzo di Propaganda Fide ❷

Via di Propaganda 1. **Map** 5 A2.
☎ 06-6987 9299. **FAX** 06-6988 0118.
🚍 116, 117. Ⓜ Spagna. **Open** by
appt (via fax).

T HE POWERFUL JESUIT Congregation for the Propagation
of the Faith was
founded in 1622.
Their head-
quarters had to
be a remarkable
building, and
Bernini was
commissioned.
But Innocent X,
who became
pope in 1644,
preferred the
style of Borromini
who was asked
to continue. His
extraordinary
west façade,
completed in
1662, must
have out-
stripped
everyone's expectations.
It is striped with broad
pilasters, between which
the first-floor windows
bend in, and the
central bay bulges.
A rigid band divides
its floors, and the
cornice above the con-
vex central bay swerves
inwards. The more you look
at it, the more restless it
seems; a sign perhaps of
the increasing unhappiness
of the architect who
committed suicide in 1667.

**Angel by Bernini,
Sant'Andrea delle Fratte**

Entrance to the Jesuit College

Colonna dell'Immacolata ❸

Piazza Mignanelli. **Map** 5 A2.
🚍 116, 117. Ⓜ Spagna.

I NAUGURATED IN 1857, the
column commemorates
Pope Pius IX's proclamation of
the doctrine of the Immaculate
Conception, holding that the
Virgin Mary was the only
human being ever to have
been born "without the stain
of original sin". The column
itself dates from ancient, pagan
Rome but is crowned with a
statue of the Virgin Mary.

On 8 December the Pope,
assisted by the fire brigade,
places a wreath around the
head of the statue (*see p61*).

**Portrait of Pope Pius IX
(reigned 1846–78)**

Via Condotti ❹

Map 5 A2. 🚌 *81, 116, 117, 119, 492 and many routes along via del Corso or stopping at Piazza S. Silvestro.* Ⓜ *Spagna. See* **Shops and Markets** *pp322–33.*

NAMED AFTER the conduits that carried water to the Baths of Agrippa near the Pantheon, Via Condotti is now home to the most traditional of Rome's designer clothes shops. Stores selling shoes and other leather goods are also well represented. The street is extremely popular for early evening strolls, when elegant Italians mingle with tourists in shorts and trainers.

Slightly younger designers such as Laura Biagiotti and the Fendi sisters have shops on the parallel Via Borgognona, while Valentino and Giorgio Armani both have shops on Via Condotti itself. Valentino has a second branch on Via Bocca di Leone, which crosses Via Condotti just below Piazza di Spagna, and Versace also has a shop here. Giorgio Armani has a second store on nearby Via del Babuino, among the discreet art galleries, exclusive antique shops and furnishing stores.

View along Via Condotti towards the Spanish Steps

Caffè Greco ❺

Via Condotti 86. **Map** 5 A2. 📞 *06-678 5474.* 🚌 *81, 116, 117, 119, 492.* Ⓜ *Spagna.* **Open** *8am–8.30pm daily.* **Closed** *1 Jan, 1 May, 2 weeks in Aug, 25–26 Dec.* ♿

THIS CAFÉ was opened by a Greek (hence *greco*) in 1760, and throughout the 18th

Caffè Greco, around 240 years old

century it was a favourite meeting place for foreign artists. Writers such as Keats, Byron and Goethe and composers like Liszt, Wagner and Bizet all breakfasted and drank here. So too did Casanova, and mad King Ludwig of Bavaria. Today, Italians stand in the crowded foyer to sip a quick espresso coffee, and foreigners sit in a cosy back room, whose walls are studded with portraits of the café's illustrious customers.

Piazza di Spagna ❻

Map 5 A2. 🚌 *116, 117, 119.* Ⓜ *Spagna.*

SHAPED LIKE a crooked bow tie and surrounded by tall, shuttered houses painted in muted shades of ochre, cream and russet, Piazza di Spagna (Spanish square) is crowded all day and (in summer) most of the night. It is the most famous square in Rome, and has long been the haunt of foreign visitors and expatriates.

In the 17th century Spain's ambassador to the Holy See had his headquarters on the square, and the area around it was deemed to be Spanish territory. Foreigners who unwittingly trespassed were liable to be dragooned into the Spanish army. In the 18th and 19th centuries Rome was almost as popular with

Pope Urban VIII's arms, with the Barberini bees

visitors as it is today, and the square stood at the heart of the city's main hotel district. Some of the travellers came in search of knowledge and artistic inspiration, but most were more interested in gambling, collecting ancient statues and conducting love affairs with Italian women.

Not surprisingly, the wealthy travellers attracted hordes of beggars, who were usually supplied with tear-jerking letters by scribes who worked in the square.

The Fontana della Barcaccia in the square is the least showy of Rome's Baroque fountains, and it is often completely screened from view by people resting on its rim. It was designed either by the famous Gian Lorenzo Bernini or by his father Pietro. Because the pressure from the aqueduct that feeds the fountain is extremely low there are no spectacular cascades or spurts of water. Instead, Bernini constructed a leaking boat – *barcaccia* means useless, old boat – which lies half submerged in a shallow pool.

The bees and suns that decorate the Fontana della Barcaccia are taken from the family coat of arms of Pope Urban VIII Barberini, who commissioned the fountain.

The Fontana della Barcaccia at the foot of the Spanish Steps

Bust of Shelley by Moses Ezekiel

Keats-Shelley Memorial House ●

Piazza di Spagna 26. **Map** 5 A2.
C 06-678 4235. 🚌 116, 117, 119.
M Spagna. **Open** 9am–1pm, 3–6pm
Mon–Fri, 11am–2pm, 3–6pm Sat.
Closed at Christmas and
New Year. **Adm charge.** 📷
🎫 book in advance. 📱
🌐 www.keats-shelley-house.org

IN NOVEMBER 1820 the English
poet John Keats came to
stay with his friend, the
painter Joseph Severn, in a
dusty pink house, the Casina
Rossa, on the corner of the
Spanish Steps. Suffering from
consumption, Keats had been
sent to Rome by his doctor, in
the hope that the mild, dry
climate would help the young
man's recovery. Depressed
because of scathing criticism of
his work and tormented by his
love for a young girl named
Fanny Brawne, Keats died the
following February aged 25.
  His death inspired fellow
poet Percy Bysshe Shelley
to write the poem *Mourn
not for Adonais*. In July 1822
Shelley himself was drowned
in a boating accident in the
Gulf of La Spezia off the
coast of Liguria. Keats,
Shelley and Severn are all
buried in Rome's Protestant
Cemetery *(see p205)*.
  In 1906 the house was
bought by an Anglo-American
association and preserved as
a memorial and library in
honour of English Romantic

poets. The relics include a
lock of Keats's hair, some
fragments of Shelley's bones
in a tiny urn and a garish
carnival mask picked up by
Lord Byron as a souvenir of
a trip to Venice. You can visit
the room where Keats died,
though all the original
furniture was burnt after
his death, on papal orders.

Babington's Tea Rooms ●

Piazza di Spagna 23. **Map** 5 A2.
C 06-678 6027. 🚌 116, 117, 119.
M Spagna. **Open** 9am–8.15pm
Wed–Mon. **Closed** 25 Dec. 🚻

THESE AUGUST, old-fashioned
tea rooms were opened in
1896 by two Englishwomen,
Anna Maria and Isabel Cargill
Babington, to serve homesick
British tourists with scones,
jam and pots of Earl Grey tea.
The food remains homely –
shepherd's pie and chicken
supreme for lunch, muffins
and cinnamon toast for tea –
although these days the menu
offers pancakes with maple
syrup for breakfast as well as
the traditional bacon and egg.

**Purveyors of English breakfasts to
homesick exiles since 1896**

Spanish Steps ●

Scalinata della Trinità dei Monti,
Piazza di Spagna. **Map** 5 A2. 🚌 116,
117, 119. **M** Spagna.

IN THE 17TH century the
French owners of Trinità dei
Monti decided to link the
church with Piazza di Spagna
by building a magnificent
new flight of steps. They also
planned to place an equestrian
statue of King Louis XIV at the
top. Pope Alexander VII Chigi
was not too happy at the

The Spanish Steps in spring with azaleas in full bloom

prospect of erecting a statue of a French monarch in the papal city, and the arguments continued until the 1720s when an Italian architect, Francesco de Sanctis, produced a design that satisfied both parties. The steps, completed in 1726, combine straight sections, curves and terraces to create one of the city's most dramatic and distinctive landmarks.

When the Victorian novelist Charles Dickens visited Rome, he reported that the Spanish Steps were the meeting place for artists' models, who would dress in colourful traditional costumes, hoping to catch the attention of a wealthy artist. The steps are now a popular place to sit, write postcards, take photos, flirt, busk or watch the passers-by, but eating there is not allowed.

Trinità dei Monti ⑩

Piazza della Trinità dei Monti.
Map 5 A2. ☎ *06-679 4179.*
▦ *116, 117, 119.* Ⓜ *Spagna.*
Open *9am–1pm, 3–7pm daily.*

Trinità dei Monti's bell towers

THE VIEWS of Rome from the platform in front of the twin bell-towered façade of Trinità dei Monti are so beautiful that the church itself is often ignored. It is, however, unusual for Rome, for it was founded by the French in 1495, and although it was later badly damaged, there are still traces of attractive late Gothic latticework in the vaults of the transept. The interconnecting side chapels are decorated with Mannerist paintings, including two fine works by Daniele da Volterra.

19th-century engraving of the inner façade of the Villa Medici

A pupil of Michelangelo, Volterra had to paint clothes on the nudes in the *Last Judgment* in the Sistine Chapel, in response to the objections of Pope Pius IV.

Michelangelo's influence is obvious in the powerfully muscled bodies shown in the *Deposition* (second chapel on the left). The circles of gesturing figures and dancing angels surrounding the Virgin Mary in the *Assumption* (third chapel on the right) have more in common with the graceful style of Raphael.

Villa Medici ⑪

Accademia di Francia a Roma,
Viale della Trinità dei Monti 1.
Map 5 A2. ☎ *06-676 11.*
▦ *117, 119.* Ⓜ *Spagna.*
Open *for exhibitions and concerts.*
Adm charge.

SUPERBLY POSITIONED on the Pincio hill above Piazza di Spagna, this 16th-century villa has kept the name it assumed when Cardinal Ferdinando de' Medici bought it in 1576. From the terrace you can look across the city to Castel Sant'Angelo, from where Queen Christina of Sweden is said to have fired the large cannon ball which now sits in the basin of the fountain.

The villa is now home to the French Academy. This was founded by Louis XIV in 1666 to give a few select painters the chance to study in Rome. Nicolas

Poussin was one of the first advisers to the Academy, Ingres was a director and ex-students include Fragonard and Boucher.

After 1803 when the French Academy moved to the Villa Medici, musicians were also admitted; both Berlioz and Debussy came to Rome as students of the Academy.

All Saints ⑫

Via del Babuino 153B. **Map** 4 F2.
☎ *06-3600 1881.* ▦ *117, 119.*
Open *8am–noon Mon–Fri and for services on Sun.*

IN 1816 THE POPE gave English residents and visitors the right to hold Anglican services in Rome, but it wasn't until the early 1880s that they acquired a site to build their own church. The architect was G E Street, best known in Britain for his Neo-Gothic churches and the London Law Courts. All Saints is also built in Victorian Neo-Gothic, and the interior, though splendidly decorated with different coloured Italian marbles, has a very English air. Street also designed St-Paul's-within-the-Walls in Via Nazionale, whose interior is a jewel of British Pre-Raphaelite art.

The street on which All Saints stands got its name from the Fontana del Sileno, known as Babuino (baboon) due to the sad condition in which it was found.

Fontana del Sileno, on Via del Babuino since 1957

Casa di Goethe ⑬

Via del Corso 18. **Map** 4 F1. *06-3265 0412.* 95, 117, 119, 490, 495, 628, 926. 2. **M** *Flaminio.* **Open** 10am–6pm Tue–Sun. **Adm charge.** W www.casadigoethe.it

THE GERMAN POET, dramatist and novelist Johann Wolfgang von Goethe (1749–1832) lived in this house from 1786 until 1788 and worked on a journal that eventually formed part of his travel book *The Italian Journey*. Rome's noisy street life irritated him, especially during Carnival time. He was a little perturbed by the number of murders in his neighbourhood, but Rome energised him and his book became one of the most influential ever written about Italy.

Santa Maria dei Miracoli and Santa Maria in Montesanto ⑭

Piazza del Popolo. **Map** 4 F1. 95, 117, 119, 490, 495, 628, 926. 2. **M** *Flaminio.* **Santa Maria dei Miracoli** *06-361 0250.* **Open** 6.30am–1pm, 4–7.30pm Mon–Sat, 8am–1.30pm, 4.30–7.30pm Sun & public hols. **Santa Maria in Montesanto** *06-361 0594.* **Open** 4–7pm Mon–Sat, 11am–1pm Sun.

THE TWO CHURCHES at the south end of Piazza del Popolo were designed by the architect Carlo Rainaldi (1611–91), proof that he could be as ingenious as his peers, Bernini and Borromini. To provide a focal point for the piazza, the churches had to appear

Portrait of Goethe in the Roman countryside by Tischbein (1751–1821)

symmetrical, but the site on the left was narrower. So, Rainaldi gave Santa Maria dei Miracoli (on the right) a circular dome and Santa Maria in Montesanto an oval one to squeeze it into the narrower site, while keeping the sides of the supporting drums that face the piazza identical.

Pincio Gardens ⑮

Il Pincio. **Map** 4 F1. 95, 117, 119, 490, 495, 628, 926. 2. **M** *Flaminio.*

THE PINCIO GARDENS lie above Piazza del Popolo on a hillside that has been so skilfully terraced and richly planted with trees that, from below, the zig-zagging road climbing to the gardens is virtually invisible. In ancient Roman times, there were magnificent gardens on the Pincio hill, but the present gardens were designed in the early 19th century by Giuseppe Valadier (who also redesigned the Piazza

The Pincio Gardens water clock

del Popolo). The broad avenues, lined with umbrella pines, palm trees and evergreen oaks soon became a fashionable place to stroll, and even this century such diverse characters as Gandhi and Mussolini, Richard Strauss and King Farouk of Egypt patronized the Casina Valadier, an exclusive café and restaurant in the grounds.

From the Pincio's main square, Piazzale Napoleone I, the panoramic views of Rome stretch from the Monte Mario to the Janiculum. For full effect, approach the gardens from the grounds of Villa Borghese (*see pp258–9*) above the Pincio, or along Viale della Trinità dei Monti.

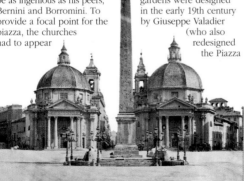

The twin churches of Santa Maria di Montesanto (left) and Santa Maria dei Miracoli in a 19th-century view of Piazza del Popolo

The panorama is particularly beautiful at sunset, the traditional time for tourists to take a stroll in the gardens.

One of the most striking features of the park itself is an Egyptian-style obelisk which Emperor Hadrian erected on the tomb of his favourite, the beautiful male slave Antinous. After the slave's premature death (according to some accounts he died saving the emperor's life), Hadrian deified him.

The 19th-century water clock on Via dell'Orologio was designed by a Dominican monk. It was displayed at the Paris Exhibition of 1889.

Traditional carnival band in Piazza del Popolo

The Casina Valadier restaurant in the Pincio Gardens

Piazza del Popolo 🔟

Map 4 F1. 🚌 95, 117, 119, 490, 495, 926. 🚋 2. Ⓜ Flaminio.

A VAST COBBLED OVAL standing at the apex of the triangle of roads known as the Trident, Piazza del Popolo forms a grand symmetrical antechamber to the heart of Rome. Twin Neo-Classical façades stand on either side of the Porta del Popolo; an Egyptian obelisk rises in the centre; and the matching domes and porticoes of Santa Maria dei Miracoli and Santa Maria di Montesanto flank the beginning of Via del Corso.

Although it is now one of the most unified squares in Rome, Piazza del Popolo evolved gradually over the centuries. In 1589 the great town-planning pope, Sixtus V, had the obelisk erected in the centre by Domenico Fontana.

Over 3,000 years old, the obelisk was originally brought to Rome by Augustus to adorn the Circus Maximus after the conquest of Egypt. Almost a century later Pope Alexander VII commissioned Carlo Rainaldi to build the twin Santa Marias.

In the 19th century the piazza was turned into a grandiose oval by Giuseppe Valadier, the designer of the Pincio Gardens. He also encased Santa Maria del Popolo in a Neo-Classical shell to make its south façade fit in better with the overall appearance of the piazza.

In contrast to the piazza's air of ordered rationalism, many of the events staged here were barbaric. In the 18th and 19th centuries, public executions were held in Piazza del Popolo, often as part of the celebration of Carnival. Condemned men were sometimes hammered to death by repeated blows to the temples. The last time a criminal was executed in this way was in 1826, even though the guillotine had by then been adopted as a more scientific means of execution.

The riderless horse races from the piazza down Via del Corso were scarcely more humane: the performance of the runners was enhanced by feeding the horses stimulants, wrapping them in nail-studded ropes, and letting off fireworks at their heels.

Santa Maria del Popolo 🔽

See pp138–9.

Porta del Popolo 🔴

Between Piazzale Flaminio and Piazza del Popolo. **Map** 4 F1. 🚌 95, 117, 119, 490, 495, 926. 🚋 2. Ⓜ Flaminio.

T HE VIA FLAMINIA, built in 220 BC to connect Rome with Italy's Adriatic coast, enters the city at Porta del Popolo, a grand 16th-century gate built on the orders of Pope Pius IV Medici. The architect, Nanni di Baccio Bigio, modelled it on a Roman triumphal arch. The outer face has statues of St Peter and St Paul on either side and a huge Medici coat of arms above.

A century later, Pope Alexander VII commissioned Bernini to decorate the inner face to celebrate the arrival in Rome of Queen Christina of Sweden. Lesser visitors were often held up while customs officers rifled their luggage. The only way to speed things up was with a bribe.

Porta del Popolo's central arch

Santa Maria del Popolo ⓱

Oᴺᴇ ᴏꜰ ʀᴏᴍᴇ'ꜱ greatest stores of artistic treasures, this early Renaissance church was commissioned by Pope Sixtus IV della Rovere in 1472. Among the artists who worked on the building were Andrea Bregno and Pinturicchio. Later additions were made by Bramante and Bernini. Many illustrious families have chapels here, all decorated with appropriate splendour. The Della Rovere Chapel has delightful Pinturicchio frescoes, the Cerasi Chapel has two Caravaggio masterpieces, *The Conversion of St Paul* and *The Crucifixion of St Peter*, but the finest of all is the Chigi Chapel designed by Raphael for his patron, the banker Agostino Chigi. The most striking of the church's many Renaissance tombs are the two by Andrea Sansovino behind the main altar.

★ Chigi Chapel
Raphael designed this chapel, which has an altarpiece by Sebastiano del Piombo. Niches on either side of the altar house sculptures by Bernini and Lorenzetto. Mosaics in the dome show God as creator of the seven heavenly bodies.

Kneeling Skeleton
This floor mosaic of the figure of death was added to the Chigi Chapel in the 17th century.

Nero's Ghost

Nero lived on in the imagination of the people long after the fall of the Roman Empire. In the Middle Ages a legend arose that a walnut tree growing here on the spot where his ashes were buried was haunted by the emperor. Ravens roosting in the tree were thought to be demons tormenting him for his hideous crimes. When the first church was built here in 1099 by Pope Paschal II, the tree was cut down, supposedly putting an end to the supernatural events that had terrified local people.

Entrance

Cybo Chapel

Della Rovere Chapel
Pinturicchio painted the frescoes in the lunettes and the Nativity above the altar in 1490.

Star Features

★ **Chigi Chapel**

★ **Caravaggio Paintings in Cerasi Chapel**

★ **Delphic Sibyl**

VISITORS' CHECKLIST

Piazza del Popolo 12. **Map** 4 F1.
06-361 0836. 95, 117,
119, 490, 495, 926. 2.
Flaminio. **Open** 7am–noon,
4–7pm Mon–Sat, 7.30am–
1.30pm, 4.30–7.30pm Sun.

★ **Caravaggio Paintings in Cerasi Chapel**
One of two Caravaggios in the Cerasi Chapel, The Crucifixion of St Peter uses dramatic fore-shortening to highlight the sheer effort involved in turning the saint's crucifix upside down.

The altarpiece of *The Assumption* is by Annibale Carracci (1540–1609).

Stained Glass
In 1509 French artist Guillaume de Marcillat was invited to provide Rome's first two stained-glass windows.

The Tomb of Ascanio Sforza, who died in 1505, is by Andrea Sansovino.

★ **Delphic Sibyl**
This is one of a series of frescoes by Pinturicchio, some Classical and others Biblical, painted in 1508–10 to decorate the ceiling of the apse.

The altar houses the 13th-century painting known as the *Madonna del Popolo*.

The Tomb of Giovanni della Rovere (1483) is by pupils of Andrea Bregno.

TIMELINE

1090	1200	1300	1400	1500
	1213–27 Church enlarged under Gregory IX	*Pinturicchio (c.1454–1513)*	**1485–9** Della Rovere Chapel painted by Pinturicchio	**1513–16** Raphael designs and executes Chigi Chapel
1099 Paschal II builds chapel over tombs of the Domitia family (which included Nero) in honour of the Madonna		*Pope Paschal II (reigned 1099–1118)*	**1472–8** Sixtus IV builds church (one of the first Renaissance churches in Rome) **1473** Main altar built	**1530–34** Chigi Chapel altarpiece built by Sebastiano del Piombo

Ara Pacis

Via di Ripetta. **Map** 4 F2. 06-
6880 6848. 70, 81, 117, 119,
186, 628. **Closed** for restoration.
Call ahead for new opening hours.

RECONSTRUCTED at great
expense over a period
of many years, the Ara Pacis
(Altar of Peace) is one of the
most significant monuments
of ancient Rome. It celebrates
the peace created throughout
the Mediterranean area by
Emperor Augustus after his
victorious campaigns in Gaul

Frieze on south wall showing procession with the family of Augustus

Marcus Agrippa (right)

and Spain. The monument was
commissioned by the Senate
in 13 BC and completed four
years later. It was positioned so
that the shadow of the huge
obelisk sundial on Campus
Martius *(see p113)* would fall
upon it on Augustus' birthday.
It is a square enclosure on a
low platform with the altar in
the centre. All surfaces are
decorated with magnificent
friezes and reliefs carved
in Carrara marble, most
likely by Greek craftsmen.
The reliefs on the north
and south walls depict a
procession that took
place on 4 July 13 BC,

in which the members of the
emperor's family can be identified, ranked by their position
in the succession. At the time
the heir apparent was Marcus
Agrippa, husband of Augustus's
daughter Julia. All the portraits
in the relief are carved with
extraordinary realism, even
the innocent toddler clinging
to his mother's skirts.

The tale of the rediscovery
of the Ara Pacis dates back to
the 16th century, when the first
panels were unearthed. One
section ended up in Paris,
another in Florence. Further
discoveries were made in
the late 19th century, when
archaeologists finally realized

just what they had found.
What we see today has all
been pieced together since
1938, in part original, in part
facsimile. In 1999 the architect
Richard Meier was called upon
to design a new building to
house the monument.

**Livia (right), Augustus's wife and
the mother of Tiberius, with an
unidentified member of the family**

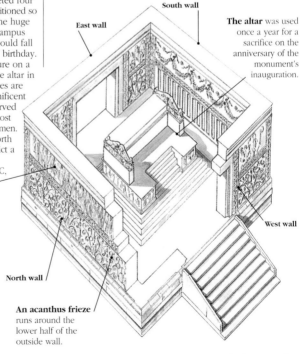

South wall

East wall

The altar was used
once a year for a
sacrifice on the
anniversary of the
monument's
inauguration.

West wall

North wall

An acanthus frieze
runs around the
lower half of the
outside wall.

**Augustus's young
grandson, Lucius**

Mausoleum of Augustus ⑳

Piazza Augusto Imperatore.
Map 4 F2. 📞 06-6710 3819. 🚌 81, 117, 492, 628, 926. **Open** by appt only: permit needed (see p367).

NOW JUST a weedy mound ringed with cypresses and sadly strewn with litter, this was once the most prestigious burial place in Rome. Augustus had the mausoleum built in 28 BC, the year he became sole ruler, as a tomb for himself and his descendants. The circular building was 87 m (285 ft) in diameter with two obelisks (now in Piazza del Quirinale and Piazza dell'Esquilino) at the entrance.

Inside were four concentric passageways linked by corridors where the urns containing the ashes of the Imperial family were placed. The first to be buried here was Augustus's favourite nephew, Marcellus, who had married Julia, the emperor's daughter. He died in 23 BC, possibly poisoned by Augustus's second wife Livia, who felt that her son, Tiberius, would make a more reliable emperor. When Augustus died in AD 14, his ashes were placed in the mausoleum, Tiberius duly became emperor, and dynastic poisonings continued to fill the family vault with urns.

This sinister monument was later used as a medieval fortress, a vineyard, a private garden, and even, in the 18th century, as an auditorium and a theatre.

Augustus, the first Roman emperor

Madonna, San Rocco and Sant'Antonio with Victims of the Plague by Il Baciccia (1639–1709)

San Rocco ㉑

Largo San Rocco 1. **Map** 4 F2.
📞 06-689 6416. 🚌 81, 117, 492, 628, 926. **Open** 7.30–9am, 4.30–7.30pm daily. **Closed** 17–31 Aug. ✝

THIS CHURCH, with a restrained Neo-Classical façade by Giuseppe Valadier, the designer of Piazza del Popolo, began life as the chapel of a 16th-century hospital with beds for 50 men – San Rocco was a healer of the plague-stricken. A maternity wing was added for the wives of Tiber bargees to save them from having to give birth in the insanitary conditions of a boat. The hospital came to be used by unmarried mothers, and one section was set aside for women who wished to be unknown. They were even permitted to wear a veil for the duration of their stay. Unwanted children were sent to an orphanage, and if any mothers or children died they were buried in anonymous graves. The hospital was abandoned in the early 20th century, and demolished in the 1930s during the excavation of the Mausoleum of Augustus.

The church sacristy is an interesting Baroque altarpiece (c.1660) by Il Baciccia, the artist who decorated the ceiling of the Gesù *(see pp114–15).*

Santi Ambrogio e Carlo al Corso ㉒

Via del Corso 437. **Map** 4 F2.
📞 06-687 8335.
🚌 81, 117, 492, 628, 926.
Open 7am–7pm daily.
Ring porter's door to left of church if closed. 🚫

THIS CHURCH belonged to the Lombard community in Rome, and is dedicated to two canonized bishops of Milan, Lombardy's capital. In 1471, Pope Sixtus IV gave the Lombards a church which they dedicated to Sant'Ambrogio, who died in 397. Then in 1610, when Carlo Borromeo was canonized, the church was rebuilt in his honour. Most of the new church was the work of father and son, Onorio and Martino Longhi, but the fine dome is by Pietro da Cortona. The altarpiece by Carlo Maratta (1625–1713) is the *Gloria dei Santi Ambrogio e Carlo*. An ambulatory leads behind the altar to a chapel housing the heart of San Carlo in a richly decorated reliquary.

Statue of San Carlo by Attilio Selva (1888–1970) behind the apse of Santi Ambrogio e Carlo

CAMPO DE' FIORI

ETWEEN Corso Vittorio Emanuele II and the Tiber, the city displays many distinct personalities. The open-air market of Campo de' Fiori preserves the lively, bohemian atmosphere of the medieval inns that once flourished here, while the area also contains Renaissance palazzi, such as Palazzo Farnese and Palazzo Spada, where powerful Roman families built their fortress-like houses near the route of papal processions. Close by, overlooking the picturesque Tiber Island, lies the former Jewish Ghetto, where many traces of daily life from past centuries can still be seen. The Portico of Octavia and the Theatre of Marcellus are spectacular examples of the city's many-layered history, built up over the half-ruined remains of ancient Rome.

18th-century Madonna in Campo de' Fiori

SIGHTS AT A GLANCE

Churches and Temples
Santissima Trinità dei Pellegrini ❺
Santa Maria dell'Orazione e Morte ❼
San Girolamo della Carità ❾
Sant'Eligio degli Orefici ❿
Santa Maria in Monserrato ⓫
San Carlo ai Catinari ⓭
Santa Maria in Campitelli ⓴
San Nicola in Carcere ㉑
San Giovanni dei Fiorentini ㉙

Museums and Galleries
Palazzo Spada ❻
Piccola Farnesina ⓮
Burcardo Theatre Museum ⓯

Historic Buildings
Palazzo Pio Righetti ❷
Palazzo del Monte di Pietà ❸
Palazzo Farnese ❽
Palazzo Ricci ⓬
Palazzo della Cancelleria ⓭
Casa di Lorenzo Manilio ㉕
Palazzo Cenci ㉖

Fountains
Fontana delle Tartarughe ⓳

Historic Streets and Piazzas
Campo de' Fiori ❶
Ghetto and Synagogue ㉔
Tiber Island ㉗
Via Giulia ㉘

Famous Theatres
Teatro Argentina ⓰

Ancient Sites
Sotterranei di San Paolo alla Regola ❹
Area Sacra dell'Argentina ⓱
Theatre of Marcellus ㉒
Portico of Octavia ㉓

GETTING THERE
Only bus 116 can manage the narrow streets around Campo de' Fiori, but many routes, including the 40, 46, 62 and 64, and tram 8, converge on Largo Argentina. This is a useful starting point for exploring the area. Only the 40, 46, 62 and 64 run the full length of Corso Vittorio Emanuele II while 23 and 280 run along Lungotevere.

SEE ALSO

• **Street Finder**, maps 4, 8, 11, 12

• **Where to Stay** pp294–5

• **Restaurants** pp310–11

• **Via Giulia Walk** pp276–7

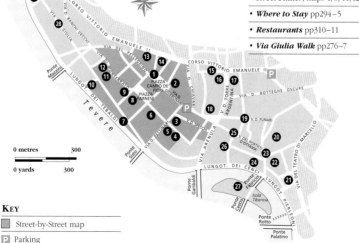

KEY

▨ Street-by-Street map

P Parking

Fruit stalls surrounding the statue of Giordano Bruno in the Campo de' Fiori market

Street-by-Street: Campo de' Fiori

THIS FASCINATING PART of Renaissance Rome is
also an exciting area for shopping and night life,
centred on the market square of Campo de' Fiori. Its
stalls supply many nearby restaurants, and young
people shop for clothes in Via dei Giubbonari.
Popular restaurants keep the area alive late
into the night, when overcrowding and
drunks can become problems. By day
there are great buildings to admire, though
few are open to the public. Two exceptions
are the Piccola Farnesina, with its collection of
Classical statues, and Palazzo Spada,
home to many important paintings.

**Sant'Eligio
degli Orefici**
*A small Renaissance
church designed by
Raphael is concealed
behind a later façade* ❿

Palazzo Ricci
*Painted Classical scenes
were a favourite form of
decoration for the façades
of Renaissance houses* ⓬

**San Girolamo
della Carità**
*The chief attraction
of this church is
Borromini's fabulous
Spada Chapel* ❾

**Santa Maria in
Monserrato**
*This church, which has
strong connections with
Spain, houses a Bernini
bust of Cardinal Pedro
Foix de Montoya* ⓫

**Santa Maria
dell'Orazione
e Morte**
*A pair of
dramatic winged
skulls flank the
doorway to this
church dedicated to
the burial of the dead* ❼

KEY

– – – Suggested route

0 metres   75

0 yards   75

Palazzo Farnese
*Michelangelo and other
great artists helped create
this monumental
Renaissance palazzo* ❽

Palazzo della Cancelleria
The papal administration ran the affairs of the church from this vast building  **⓭**

Piccola Farnesina
This plaque honours Giovanni Barracco. His sculpture collection is housed in the palazzo ⓮

LOCATOR MAP
See Central Rome Map pp12–13

★ Campo de' Fiori
This colourful market makes Piazza Campo de' Fiori one of Rome's most entertaining squares ❶

Palazzo Pio Righetti
Heraldic eagles stare down from the pediments of the palazzo's windows ❷

Palazzo del Monte di Pietà
This was a papal institution, where the poor pawned their possessions in order to borrow small sums of money ❸

Sotterranei di San Paolo alla Regola
Remains of a Roman house have survived in the basement of an old palace ❹

★ Palazzo Spada
The picture gallery houses a collection started by two wonderfully eccentric 17th-century cardinals ❻

Santissima Trinità dei Pellegrini
The principal role of this church was one of charity, looking after poor pilgrims arriving in Rome ❺

STAR SIGHTS
★ Campo de' Fiori
★ Palazzo Spada

Campo de' Fiori ❶

Piazza Campo de' Fiori. **Map** 4 E4 & 11 C4. 116 and routes to Largo di Torre Argentina or Corso Vittorio Emanuele II. See **Markets** p338.

T HE CAMPO DE' FIORI (field of flowers), once a meadow, occupies the site of the open space facing the Theatre of Pompey. Cardinals and noblemen used to rub shoulders with fishmongers and foreigners in the piazza's market, making it one of the liveliest areas of medieval and Renaissance Rome. Today's market retains much of the traditional lively atmosphere.

In the centre of the square is a statue of the philosopher Giordano Bruno, burnt at the stake for heresy here in 1600. The hooded figure is a grim reminder of the executions that were held here.

The piazza was surrounded by inns for pilgrims and other travellers. Many of these were once owned by the successful 15th-century courtesan, Vannozza Catanei, mistress of Pope Alexander VI Borgia. On the corner between the piazza and Via del Pellegrino you can see Catanei's shield, which she had decorated with her own coat of arms and those of her husband and her lover, the Borgia pope.

Market stalls in Campo de' Fiori

Palazzo Pio Righetti ❷

Piazza del Biscione 89. **Map** 4 E5 & 11 C4. 116 and routes to Largo Torre Argentina or Corso Vittorio Emanuele II. **Not open to the public.**

T HE VAST 17th-century Palazzo Pio Righetti was built over the ruined Theatre

Window pediment with heraldic lion and pine cones, Palazzo Pio Righetti

of Pompey. The windows of the palazzo are decorated with lions and pine cones from the coat of arms of the Pio da Carpi family who lived here.

The curve of the Theatre of Pompey, completed in 55 BC, is followed by Via di Grotta Pinta. Rome's first permanent theatre was built of stone and concrete and in the basement of the Pancrazio restaurant you can see early examples of *opus reticulatum* – small square blocks of tufa (porous rock) set diagonally as a facing for a concrete wall.

Palazzo del Monte di Pietà ❸

Piazza del Monte di Pietà 33. **Map** 4 E5 & 11 C4. 06-68 441. 116 and routes to Largo di Torre Argentina or Corso Vittorio Emanuele II. 8. **Chapel open** only by appt. Ring above number between 8.30am and 1.30pm.

T HE MONTE, as it is known, is a public institution, founded in 1539 by Pope Paul III Farnese as a pawn-shop to staunch the usury then rampant in the city. The building still has offices and auction rooms for the sale of unredeemed goods.

The stars with diagonal bands on the huge central plaque decorating the façade are the coat of arms of Pope Clement VIII Aldobrandini, added when Carlo Maderno enlarged the palace in the 17th century. The clock on the left was added later.

Within, the chapel is a jewel of Baroque architecture, adorned with gilded stucco, marble panelling and reliefs. The decoration makes a perfect setting for the sculptures by Domenico Guidi – a bust of San Carlo Borromeo and a

relief of the *Pietà*. There are also splendid reliefs by Giovanni Battista Théudon and Pierre Legros of biblical scenes illustrating the charitable nature of the institution.

Relief by Théudon of *Joseph Lending Grain to the Egyptians* in Palazzo del Monte di Pietà

Sotterranei di San Paolo alla Regola ❹

Via di San Paolo alla Regola. **Map** 11 C5. 06-6710 3819. FAX 06-679 07 95. 23, 116, 280 and routes to Largo di Torre Argentina. 8. **Adm** by request in advance via fax.

A N OLD PALACE hides the perfectly conserved re-mains of an ancient Roman house, dating from the 2nd–3rd centuries. Restoration works are being carried out in order to open this site to the public, but at present it is only possible to visit by special arrangement.

A ramp leads down well below today's street level, to reveal the locations of shops of the time. One level above is the Stanza della Colonna, at one time an open courtyard, with traces of frescoes and mosaics on its walls.

Guido Reni's *Holy Trinity*, in Santissima Trinità dei Pellegrini

Santissima Trinità dei Pellegrini ❺

Piazza della Trinità dei Pellegrini.
Map 4 E5 & 11 C5. 📞 06-686 8451.
🚌 23, 116, 280 and routes to
Largo di Torre Argentina. 🚋 8.
Open 11am–1pm Sun.

THE CHURCH was donated in the 16th century to a charitable organization founded by San Filippo Neri to care for the poor and sick, in particular the thousands of paupers who flocked in pilgrimage to Rome during the special holy years known as Jubilees. The 18th-century façade has niches with statues of the Evangelists by Bernardino Ludovisi. The interior, with Corinthian columns, ends in a horseshoe vault and apse, dominated by Guido Reni's striking altarpiece of the Holy Trinity (1625). The frescoes in the lantern are also by Reni. Other interesting paintings include *St Gregory the Great Freeing Souls from Purgatory*, by Baldassarre Croce (third chapel to the left); Cavalier d'Arpino's *Virgin and Saints* (second chapel to the left); and a painting by Borgognone (1677) of the Virgin and recently canonized saints, including San Filippo Neri. In the sacristy are depictions of the nobility washing the feet of pilgrims, a custom which was started by San Filippo.

Palazzo Spada ❻

Piazza Capo di Ferro 13.
Map 2 F5. 📞 06-686 1158 (Palazzo)
or 06-32 810 (Galleria).
🚌 23, 116, 280 and routes to Largo
di Torre Argentina. 🚋 8. **Galleria
Spada Open** 9am–7pm Tue–Sat,
9am–1pm Sun. **Closed** 1 Jan, 1 May,
25 Dec. **Adm charge.** 🚫 ♿ 📷 📱
🌐 www.galleriaborghese.it

THIS MAJESTIC PALAZZO, built around 1550 for Cardinal Capo di Ferro, has an elegant stuccoed courtyard and façade decorated with reliefs evoking Rome's glorious past.
Cardinal Bernardino Spada, who lived here in the 17th century with his brother Virginio (also a cardinal), hired architects Bernini and Borromini to work on the building. The brothers' whimsical delight in false perspectives resulted in a colonnaded gallery by Borromini that appears four times longer than it really is.
The cardinals also amassed a superb private collection of paintings, which is now on display in the Galleria Spada. The collection features a wide range of artists, including Rubens, Dürer and Guido Reni. The most important works on display include *The Visitation* by Andrea del Sarto (1486–1530), *Cain and Abel* by Giovanni Lanfranco (1582–1647) and *The Death of Dido* by Guercino (1591–1666).

Santa Maria dell'Orazione e Morte ❼

Via Giulia. **Map** 4 E5 & 11 B4.
📞 06-6880 2715. 🚌 23, 116, 280.
Open 4–6.30pm Sun. 🚹

A PIOUS CONFRATERNITY was formed here in the 16th century to collect the bodies of the unknown dead and give them a Christian burial. The theme of death is stressed in this church, dedicated to St Mary of Prayer and Death. The doors and windows of Ferdinando Fuga's dramatic Baroque façade are decorated with winged skulls. Above the central entrance there is a *clepsydra* (an ancient hourglass) – symbolic of death.

Offertory box in Santa Maria dell'Orazione e Morte

Palazzo Farnese ❽

Piazza Farnese. **Map** 4 E5 & 11 B4.
🚌 23, 116, 280 and routes to
Corso Vittorio Emanuele II.
Not open to the public.

THE PROTOTYPE for many princely palaces, the imposing Palazzo Farnese was originally built for Cardinal Alessandro Farnese (who became Pope Paul III in 1534). He commissioned the greatest artists to work on it, starting with Antonio da Sangallo the Younger as architect in 1517. Michelangelo, who took over after him, contributed the great cornice and central window of the main façade, and the third level of the courtyard.
Michelangelo had a plan for the Farnese gardens to be connected by a bridge to the Farnese home in Trastevere, Villa Farnesina *(see pp220–21)*. The elegant arch spanning Via Giulia belongs to this sadly unrealized scheme. The palazzo was completed in 1589, on a less ambitious scale, by Giacomo della Porta. It is now the home of the French Embassy, which moved in as early as 1635.

Majestic façade of Palazzo Farnese

Spada Chapel in San Girolamo

San Girolamo della Carità **⑨**

Via di Monserrato 62A.
Map 4 E5 & 11 B4.
(06-687 9786.
▨ 23, 40, 46, 62, 64, 116, 280.
Open 10.30–11.30am Sun. **⬆**

T HE CHURCH was built on the site of the home of San Filippo Neri, the 16th-century saint from Tuscany who renewed Rome's spiritual and cultural life by his friendly, open approach to religion. He would have loved the frolicking putti shown surrounding his statue, in his chapel, reminding him of the Roman urchins he had cared for during his lifetime.

The breathtaking Spada Chapel was designed by Borromini, and is unique both

Statue of San Filippo Neri by Pierre Legros

as a work of art and as an illustration of the spirit of the Baroque age. All architectural elements are concealed so that the space of the chapel's interior is defined solely by decorative marblework and statues. Veined jasper and precious multicoloured marbles are sculpted to imitate flowery damask and velvet hangings. Even the altar rail is a long swag of jasper drapery held up by a pair of kneeling angels with wooden wings.

Although there are memorials to former members of the Spada family, oddly there is no indication as to which of the Spadas was responsible for endowing the chapel. It was probably art-lover Cardinal Virginio Spada, a follower of San Filippo Neri.

Sant'Eligio degli Orefici **⑩**

Via di Sant'Eligio 8A. **Map** 4 D4 & 11 B4. **(** 06-686 8260. **▨** 23, 40, 46, 62, 64, 116, 280. **Open** 10am–1pm Mon, Tue, Thu & Fri. Ring bell at No. 7 or No. 9. Telephone booking preferred. **Closed** Aug. **⬆**

T HE NAME of the church still records the fact that it was commissioned by a rich corporation of goldsmiths (orefici) in the early 16th century. The original design was by Raphael, who, like his master Bramante, had acquired a sense of the grandiose from the remains of Roman antiquity. The influence of some of Bramante's works, such as the choir of Santa Maria del Popolo (see pp138–9), is evident in the simple way the arches and pilasters define the structure of the walls.

The cupola of Sant' Eligio is attributed to Baldassarre Peruzzi, while the façade was added in the early 17th century by Flaminio Ponzio. Among the various 16th-century painters who decorated the interior was Taddeo Zuccari, who worked on Palazzo Farnese (see p147).

Santa Maria in Monserrato **⑪**

Via di Monserrato. **Map** 4 E4 & 11 B3. **(** 06-686 5865. **▨** 23, 40, 46, 62, 64, 116, 280. **Open** for mass only, 10am–1pm Sun. **Closed** to the public except by special permission: ring the above number. **⬆**

An early bust by Bernini of Cardinal Pedro Foix de Montoya

T HE ORIGINS of the Spanish national church in Rome go back to 1506, when a hospice for Spanish pilgrims was begun by a brotherhood of the Virgin of Montserrat in Catalonia. Inside is Annibale Carracci's painting San Diego de Alcalà and, in the third chapel on the left, a copy of a Sansovino statue of St James. Some beautiful 15th-century tombs by Andrea Bregno and Luigi Capponi are in the courtyard and side chapels. Don't miss Bernini's bust of Pedro Foix de Montoya, the church's benefactor, in the annexe.

San Diego by Annibale Carracci

Palazzo Ricci 🕛

Piazza de' Ricci. **Map** 4 D4 & 11 B4.
🚌 *23, 40, 46, 62, 64, 116, 280, 870.*
Not open to the public.

PALAZZO RICCI was famous
for its frescoed façade –
now rather faded – originally
painted in the 16th century
by Polidoro da Caravaggio,
a follower of Raphael.
   In Renaissance Rome it
was common to commission
artists to decorate the outsides
of houses with heroes of
Classical antiquity. A fresco
by a leading artist such as
Polidoro, reputedly the inventor of this style of painting,
was a conspicuous status
symbol, in the nobility's
attempts to outshine each
other with their palazzi.

Part of the frescoed façade of Palazzo Ricci

Palazzo della Cancelleria 🕔

Piazza della Cancelleria.
Map 4 E4 & 11 C3.
📞 *06-6989 3491.* 🚌 *40, 46, 62,
64, 70, 81, 87, 116, 492.*
Open by appointment.

THE PALAZZO, a supreme
example of the confident
architecture of the Early
Renaissance, was begun in
1485. It was financed partly
with the gambling winnings
of Cardinal Raffaele Riario.
Roses, the emblem of the
Riario family, adorn the vaults
and capitals of the beautiful
Doric courtyard. The palazzo's
interior was decorated after
the Sack of Rome in 1527.
Giorgio Vasari boasted that he
had completed work on one
enormous room in just 100
days; Michelangelo allegedly
retorted: "It looks like it."
Other Mannerist artists, Perin
del Vaga and
Francesco Salviati,
frescoed the rooms of
the cardinal in charge
of the Papal
Chancellery, the office
that gave the palazzo
its name when it was
installed here by Pope
Leo X. On the right of
the main entrance is the
unobtrusive and rather quaint
church of San Lorenzo in
Damaso, founded by Pope

Damasus (reigned 366–84). It
was reconstructed in 1495 and
although Bernini made alter-
ations to the transept and apse
in 1638, it was later restored
to its 15th-century lines. Its
porticoes housed libraries for
the first Papal Archives.

Piccola Farnesina 🕕

Corso Vittorio Emanuele II 168.
Map 4 E4 & 11 C3. 📞 *06-6880
6848.* 🚌 *40, 46, 62, 64, 70, 81, 87,
116, 492.* **Open** *9am–7pm Tue–Sat,
9am–1pm Sun.*
Adm charge. 🚫

THIS DELIGHTFUL miniature
palazzo acquired its name
from the lilies decorating
its cornices. These were
mistakenly identified as part
of the Farnese family crest. In
fact they were part of the coat
of arms of a French clergyman,
Thomas Le Roy, for whom
the palazzo was built in 1523.
   The entrance is in a new
façade built to overlook
Corso Vittorio Emanuele II
when the road was constructed
at the turn of the century.
The original façade on the
left of today's entrance is
attributed to Antonio da
Sangallo the Younger.
Note the asymmetrical
arrangement of its
windows and ledges.
The elegant central
courtyard also retains
its original appearance.
The Piccola Farnesina
now houses the Museo
Barracco, a collection
of ancient sculpture assembled
during the last century by the
politician Baron Giovanni
Barracco. A bust of the baron

**Lily on façade
of the Piccola
Farnesina**

can be seen in the courtyard.
The collection includes an
ancient Egyptian relief of the
scribe Nofer, some Assyrian
artifacts and, among the
Etruscan exhibits, a delicate
ceramic female head. On the
first floor is the Greek collection with a head of Apollo.

Inner courtyard, Piccola Farnesina

Burcardo Theatre Museum 🕔

Via del Sudario 44. **Map** 4 F4 & 12
D4. 📞 *06-681 9471.* 🚌 *40, 46,
62, 64, 70, 81, 186, 492.* 🚋 *8.*
Museum and library Open
9am–1.30pm Mon–Fri. **Closed** *Aug.*
🚫 W www.burcardo.siae.it

THIS LATE 15th-century house
belonged to Johannes
Burckhardt, chamberlain to
Pope Alexander VI Borgia and
author of a diary of Rome under
the Borgias. His house now
holds Rome's most complete
collection of theatre literature,
plus Chinese puppets and
comic masks from the various
regions of Italy.

Teatro Argentina ⑯

Largo di Torre Argentina 56. **Map** 4
F4 & 12 D4. 📞 *06-6880 4601.* 🚌
*40, 46, 62, 64, 70, 81, 87, 186, 492,
810.* 🚋 *8.* **Plays** *performed Oct–Jun.
See* **Entertainment** *pp346–7.*
🔲 *www.teatrodiroma.it*

O NE OF ROME'S most
important theatres was
founded by the powerful
Sforza Cesarini family in 1732,
though the façade dates from
a century later. Many famous
operas, including those of
Verdi, were first performed
here. In 1816, the theatre
saw the ill-fated début of
Rossini's *Barber of Seville*,
during which the composer
insulted the unappreciative
audience, who then pursued
him, enraged, through the
streets of Rome.

Detail of façade, Teatro Argentina

Area Sacra dell'Argentina ⑰

Largo di Torre Argentina. **Map** 4 F4 &
12 D4. 🚌 *40, 46, 62, 64, 70, 81,
87, 186, 492, 810.* 🚋 *8.* **Open** *by
appt only: permit needed (see p367).*

T HE REMAINS of four temples
were discovered here in
the 1920s. Dating from the
Republican era, they are
among the oldest in Rome.
They are known as A, B, C and
D. The oldest (temple C) dates
from the early 3rd century BC.
It was placed on a high platform preceded by an altar and
is typical of Italic plans. Temple
A is from later in the 3rd
century BC. In medieval times
the church of San Nicola de'
Cesarini was built over its
podium: remains of its two
apses are still visible. The north
column stumps belonged to a
great portico, the Hecatostylum
(portico of 100 columns). In

San Carlo at Prayer by Guido Reni

Imperial times two marble
lavatories were built here –
the remains of one are visible
behind temple A. Behind
temples B and C are remains of
a great platform of tufa blocks
identified as part of the Curia
of Pompey – a rectangular
building with a statue of
Pompey. It was here that the
Senate met and Julius Caesar
was murdered on 15 March 44
BC. At the south-west corner
of the site is a cat sanctuary,
home to Rome's abandoned
felines (visits on request).

**Area Sacra, with circular ruins of
temple B in the foreground**

San Carlo ai Catinari ⑱

Piazza B Cairoli. **Map** 4 F5 & 12 D4.
📞 *06-6880 3554.* 🚌 *see Area
Sacra.* 🚋 *8.* **Open** *7.30am–noon,
4–7pm daily.* 🛈

I N 1620, ROME'S Milanese
congregation decided
to honour Cardinal Carlo
Borromeo with this great

church. It was called "ai
Catinari" on account of the
bowl-makers' *(catinari)*
shops in the area. The
solemn travertine façade
was completed in 1638 by
the Roman architect Soria.
The 16th-century basilican
plan is flanked by chapels.
The St Cecilia chapel was
designed and decorated by
Antonio Gherardi, who
added a family portrait.
The church's paintings and
frescoes by Pietro da Cortona
and Guido Reni are mature
works of the Counter-
Reformation, depicting the
life and acts of the recently
canonized San Carlo.
The ornate crucifix on the
sacristy altar, inlaid with
marble and mother-of-pearl,
is by the 16th-century
sculptor, Algardi.

Sacristy altar, San Carlo ai Catinari

Fontana delle Tartarughe ⑲

Piazza Mattei. **Map** 4 F5 & 12 D4.
🚌 *46, 62, 63, 64, 70, 87, 186,
492, 810.* 🚋 *8.*

T HE DELIGHTFUL Fontana
delle Tartarughe
(*tartarughe* are tortoises) was
commissioned by the Mattei
family to decorate "their"
piazza between 1581 and
1588. The design was by
Giacomo della Porta, but the
fountain owes much of its
charm to the four bronze
youths each resting one foot
on the head of a dolphin,
sculpted by Taddeo Landini.
Nearly a century later an

Della Porta's graceful Fontana delle Tartarughe

unknown sculptor added the struggling tortoises to complete the composition.

Santa Maria in Campitelli ⑳

Piazza di Campitelli 9.
Map 4 F5 & 12 E5. 06-6880 3978.
40, 46, 62, 63, 64, 70, 87, 186, 780, 810. **Open** 7.30am–noon, 4–7pm daily.

IN 17TH-CENTURY ROME the plague could still strike fiercely and there were no reliable, effective remedies. Many Romans simply prayed for a cure to a sacred medieval icon of the Virgin, the Madonna del Portico. When a particularly lethal outbreak of plague abated in 1656, popular gratitude was so strong that a new church was built to house the icon.

Lavish altar tabernacle in Santa Maria in Campitelli

The church, designed by a pupil of Bernini, Carlo Rainaldi, was completed in 1667. The main elements of the lively Baroque façade are the graceful columns, symbolizing the supporters of the true faith.

Inside the church stands a fabulously ornate, gilded altar tabernacle with spiral columns which was designed by Giovanni Antonio de Rossi to contain the image of the Virgin. The side chapels are decorated by some of Rome's finest Baroque painters: Sebastiano Conca, Giovanni Battista Gaulli (known as Il Baciccia) and Luca Giordano.

Façade and medieval bell tower of San Nicola in Carcere

San Nicola in Carcere ㉑

Via del Teatro di Marcello 46.
Map 5 A5 & 12 E5. 06-686 99 72. 44, 63, 81, 95, 160, 170, 628, 780, 781. **Open** 9am–7pm daily.

THE MEDIEVAL CHURCH of San Nicola in Carcere stands on the site of three Roman temples of the Republican era which were converted into a prison (carcere) in the Middle Ages. The temples of Juno, Spes and Janus faced a city gate leading from the Forum Holitorium, the city's vegetable and oil market, to the road down to the port on the Tiber. The columns embedded in the walls of the church belonged to two flanking temples whose platforms are now marked by grass lawns. The church

was rebuilt in 1599 and restored in the 19th century, but the bell tower and Roman columns are part of the original design.

The Theatre of Marcellus by Thomas Hartley Cromek (1809–73)

Theatre of Marcellus ㉒

Via del Teatro di Marcello.
Map 4 A5 & 12 E5. 06-6710 3819. 44, 63, 81, 95, 160, 170, 628, 780, 781. **Open** 9am–1 hour before sunset daily.

THE CURVED OUTER WALL of this vast amphitheatre has supported generations of Roman buildings. It was built by the Emperor Augustus (27 BC–AD 14), who dedicated it to Marcellus, his nephew and son-in-law, who had died aged 19 in 23 BC.

The Middle Ages were a turbulent time of invasions and local conflicts (see p28) and by the 13th century the theatre had been converted into the fortress of the Savelli family. In the 16th century Baldassarre Peruzzi built a great palace on the theatre ruins for the Orsini family. This included a garden that faced the Tiber. The lower arches were later occupied by humble dwellings and workshops.

Close to the theatre stand three beautiful Corinthian columns and a section of frieze. These are from the Temple of Apollo, which housed many great works of art that the Romans had plundered from Greece in the 2nd century BC.

Portico of Octavia ㉓

Via del Portico d'Ottavia.
Map 4 F5 & 12 E5. 46, 62, 63, 64, 70, 87, 186, 780, 810.

BUILT IN HONOUR of Octavia (the sister of Augustus and the abandoned wife of Mark Antony), this is the only surviving portico of what used to be the monumental piazza of Circus Flaminius. The rectangular portico enclosed temples dedicated to Jupiter and Juno, decorated with bronze statues. The part we see today is the great central atrium originally covered by marble facings.

In the Middle Ages a great fish market and a church, Sant'Angelo in Pescheria, were built in the ruins of the portico. As the church was associated with the fishing activities of the nearby river port, aquatic flora and fauna feature in many of its inlays. Links with the Tiber are also apparent in the stucco façade on the adjacent Fishmonger's Oratory, built in 1689. The church has a fresco of the Madonna and angels by the school of Benozzo Gozzoli.

Narrow lane in the Jewish Ghetto

Ghetto and Synagogue ㉔

Synagogue, Lungotevere dei Cenci. **Map** 4 F5 & 12 E5. 06-6840 0661. 23, 63, 280, 780 and routes to Largo di Torre Argentina. 8. **Open** 9am–4.30pm (Oct–Apr), 9am–7.30pm (May–Sep) Mon–Thu, 9am–1.30pm Fri, 9am–noon Sun. **Closed** on Jewish public hols. **Adm charge**. Ghetto, main street is Via del Portico d'Ottavia.

THE FIRST Jews came to Rome as traders in the 2nd century BC and there has been a Jewish community in Rome

Synagogue overlooking the Tiber

ever since. Jews were much appreciated for their financial and medical skills during the time of the Roman Empire.

Systematic persecution began in the 16th century. From 25 July 1556 all Rome's Jews were forced to live inside a high-walled enclosure erected on the orders of Pope Paul IV. The Ghetto was in an unhealthy part of Rome. Inhabitants were only allowed out during the day, and on Sundays they were driven into the Church of Sant'Angelo in Pescheria to listen to Christian sermons – a practice abolished only in 1848.

Persecution started again in 1943 with the German occupation. Although many Jews were helped to escape or hidden by Roman citizens, thousands were deported to German concentration camps.

Today many Jews still live in the former Ghetto and the medieval streets retain much of their old character. The imposing Synagogue on Lungotevere was completed in 1904. It houses a Jewish museum which describes the history of the community through plans, torahs and other artifacts.

Casa di Lorenzo Manilio ㉕

Via del Portico d'Ottavia 1D. **Map** 4 F5 & 12 D5. 46, 62, 63, 64, 70, 87, 186, 780, 810. **Not open** to the public.

BEFORE THE RENAISSANCE, most Romans had only vague ideas of their city's past, but the 15th-century revival of interest in the philo-sophy and arts of antiquity inspired some to build houses recalling the splendour of ancient Rome. In 1468 a certain Lorenzo Manilio built a great house for his family, decorating it with an

elegant Classical plaque. The Latin inscription dates the building according to the ancient Roman method – 2,221 years after the foundation of the city – and gives the owner's name. Original reliefs are embedded in the façades as well as a fragment of an ancient sarcophagus. The Piazza Costaguti façade's windows are inscribed *Ave Roma* (Hail Rome).

Balcony of Palazzo Cenci

Palazzo Cenci ㉖

Vicolo dei Cenci. **Map** 4 F5 & 12 D5. *See Ghetto and Synagogue.* **Not open** to the public.

PALAZZO CENCI belonged to the family of Beatrice Cenci, who was accused, together with her brothers and stepmother, of witchcraft and the murder of her tyrannical father. She was condemned to death and beheaded at Ponte Sant'Angelo in 1599.

Row of Roman busts decorating the Casa di Lorenzo Manilio

Tiber Island, with Ponte Cestio linking it to Trastevere

Most of the original medieval palazzo has been demolished, and the building you see today dates back to the 1570s, though its rather forbidding appearance seems medieval. Heraldic half-moons decorate the main façade on Via del Progresso while pretty balconies open on the opposite side where a medieval arch joins the palace to Palazzetto Cenci, designed by Martino Longhi the Elder. Inside is a traditional courtyard with an Ionic-style loggia; many of the rooms retain the original 16th-century decoration that the unfortunate Beatrice would have known as a child.

Tiber Island ⑳

Isola Tiberina. **Map** 8 D1 & 12 D5.
🚌 23, 63, 280, 780. 🚋 8.

IN ANCIENT TIMES the island, which lay opposite the city's port, had large structures of white travertine at either end built to resemble the stern and prow of a ship.

Since 293 BC, when a temple was dedicated here to Aesculapius, the god of healing and protector against the plague, the island has been associated with the sick and there is still a hospital here.

San Bartolomeo all'Isola, the church in the island's central piazza, was built on the ruins of the Temple of Aesculapius in the 10th century. Its Romanesque bell tower is clearly visible from across the river.

From the Ghetto area you can reach the island by a footbridge, the Ponte Fabricio. The oldest original bridge over the Tiber still in use, it was built in 62 BC. In medieval times the Pierleoni,

and then the Caetani, two powerful families, controlled this strategic point by means of a tower, still in situ. The other bridge to the island, the Ponte Cestio, is inscribed with the names of the Byzantine emperors associated with its restoration in AD 370.

Via Giulia ⑳

Map 4 D4 & 11 A3.
🚌 23, 116, 280, 870.

THIS PICTURESQUE street was laid out by Bramante for Pope Julius II della Rovere. Lined with 16th–18th century aristocratic palazzi, as well as fine churches and antique shops, Via Giulia makes a fascinating walk (see pp276–7).

Mask fountain in Via Giulia

San Giovanni dei Fiorentini ⑳

Via Acciaioli 2. **Map** 4 D4 & 11 A2.
📞 06-6889 2059. 🚌 23, 40, 46, 62, 64, 116, 280, 870. **Open** 9am–1pm, 4–7pm daily. 🔲

THE CHURCH of St John of the Florentines was built for the large Florentine community living in this area. Pope Leo X wanted it to be an expression of the cultural superiority of Florence over Rome. Started in the early 16th century, the church took over a century to build. The principal architect was Antonio da Sangallo the Younger, but many others contributed before Carlo Maderno's elongated cupola was finally completed in 1620. The present façade was added in the 18th century.

The church was decorated mainly by Tuscan artists. One interesting exception is the 15th-century statue of San Giovannino by the Sicilian Mino del Reame in a niche above the sacristy. The spectacular high altar houses a marble group by Antonio Raggi, the *Baptism of Christ*. The altar itself is by Borromini, who is buried in the church along with Carlo Maderno.

This and San Lorenzo in Lucina (see p112) are the only churches in Rome which admit animals: the faithful can bring their pets, and an Easter lamb-blessing takes place.

Antonio Raggi's *Baptism of Christ* in San Giovanni dei Fiorentini

Quirinal

ONE OF THE original seven hills of Rome, the Quirinal was a largely residential area in Imperial times. To the east of the hill were the vast Baths of Diocletian, still standing in front of what is now the main rail station. Abandoned in the Middle Ages, the district returned to favour in the late 16th century. The prime site

1st-century BC stucco in the Museo Nazionale Romano

was taken by the popes for Palazzo del Quirinale. Great families such as the Colonna and the Aldobrandini had their *palazzi* lower down the hill. With the end of papal rule in 1870, the surrounding area, especially Via Nazionale, was redeveloped as the Quirinal became the residence of the kings of Italy, then of the Italian president.

SIGHTS AT A GLANCE

Churches
Santi Apostoli **4**
San Marcello al Corso **5**
Santa Maria in Trivio **7**
Santi Vincenzo e Anastasio **9**
Sant'Andrea al Quirinale **11**
San Carlo alle Quattro Fontane **12**
Santa Maria degli Angeli **15**
Santa Maria dei Monti **20**
Sant'Agata dei Goti **21**
Santi Domenico e Sisto **23**

Museums and Galleries
Accademia Nazionale di San Luca **8**
Museo Nazionale Romano (Palazzo Massimo) **16**

Museo delle Paste Alimentari **10**
Palazzo delle Esposizioni **19**

Historic Piazzas
Piazza della Repubblica **18**

Historic Buildings
Palazzo del Quirinale **2**
Palazzo Colonna **3**
Baths of Diocletian **17**

Fountains and Statues
Castor and Pollux **1**
Trevi Fountain **6**
Le Quattro Fontane **13**
Moses Fountain **14**

Parks and Gardens
Villa Aldobrandini **22**

GETTING THERE
The area has Metro stops at Repubblica and Cavour. Buses include the 40 (only one stop), 64 and 70 along Via Nazionale and the 71, 116T and 117, which go through the Traforo Umberto I tunnel. Many buses run along Via del Tritone but there is no bus to the top of the Quirinal. You have to walk up Via XXIV Maggio.

KEY

Street-by-Street map

M Metro station

P Parking

i Tourist information

0 metres 300
0 yards 300

SEE ALSO

Fontana delle Naiadi in Piazza della Repubblica

Street-by-Street: The Quirinal Hill

Even though Palazzo del Quirinale is closed to the public, it is well worth walking up the hill to the palace to see the giant Roman statues of Castor and Pollux in the piazza and enjoy fine views of the city below. Come down the hill by way of the narrow streets and stairways that lead to one of Rome's unforgettable sights, the Trevi Fountain. Many small churches lie hidden away in the back streets. Towards Piazza Venezia there are grand palazzi, including that of the Colonna, one of Rome's most ancient and powerful families.

Santa Maria in Via is famous for its medieval well and miraculous 13th-century icon of the Madonna.

Santa Maria in Trivio
The attractive façade of this tiny church conceals a rich Baroque interior ❼

Accademia Nazionale di San Luca
The art academy has works by famous former members, such as Canova and Angelica Kauffmann ❽

★ **Trevi Fountain**
Rome's grandest and best-known fountain almost fills the tiny Piazza di Trevi ❻

Santi Vincenzo e Anastasio
The grand façade of this small Baroque church is on a corner facing the Trevi Fountain ❾

San Marcello al Corso
This stark Crucifixion *by Van Dyck hangs in the sacristy of the church* ❺

Palazzo Odescalchi has a Bernini façade from 1664, with a balustrade and richly decorated cornice. The building faces Santi Apostoli.

Museo delle Cere, a wax museum opened in 1953, places its emphasis on horror.

To Piazza Venezia

Museo delle Paste Alimentari
All worth knowing about pasta is explained in this museum ⓾

LOCATOR MAP
See Central Rome Map pp12–13

Palazzo del Quirinale
The old papal palace is now the home of the president of Italy. Palace guards in colourful dress uniform can often be seen outside ❷

VIA DELLA DATARIA

PIAZZA DEL QUIRINALE

PIAZZA DELLA PILOTTA

Castor and Pollux
The statues are grouped with an obelisk and a fountain ❶

Piazza della Pilotta is dominated by the imposing façade of the Gregorian University.

Santi Apostoli
The figures of Christ and the Apostles on the balustrade were added by Carlo Rainaldi in 1681 ❹

Palazzo Colonna
One of the art gallery's finest old masters is Annibale Carracci's The Bean Eater ❸

STAR SIGHT

★ **Trevi Fountain**

KEY

- - - Suggested route

0 metres   75

0 yards   75

Castor and Pollux ❶

Piazza del Quirinale. **Map** 5 B4.
🚌 H, 40, 64, 70, 170 and many routes along Via del Tritone.

Quirinal fountain and obelisk with Roman statues of Castor and Pollux

Castor and pollux – the patrons of horsemanship – and their prancing horses stand in splendour in the Piazza del Quirinale. Over 5.5 m (18 ft) high, these statues are huge Roman copies of 5th-century BC Greek originals. They once stood at the entrance to the nearby Baths of Constantine. Pope Sixtus V had them restored and placed here in 1588. Formerly known as the "horse tamers", they gave the square its familiar name of Monte Cavallo (horse hill).

The obelisk which stands between them was brought here in 1786 from the Mausoleum of Augustus. In 1818 the composition was completed by the addition of a massive granite basin, once a cattle trough in the Forum.

Palazzo del Quirinale ❷

Piazza del Quirinale. **Map** 5 B3.
📞 06-469 91. 🚌 H, 40, 64, 70, 170 and many routes along Via del Tritone.
Open 8.30am–12.30pm Sun. **Closed** Aug & public hols. **Adm charge.**
🌐 www.quirinale.it

By the 1500s, the Vatican had a reputation as an unhealthy location because of the high incidence of malaria, so

Pope Gregory XIII chose this site on the highest of Rome's seven hills as a papal summer residence. Work began in 1573. Piazza del Quirinale has buildings on three sides while the fourth is open, with a splendid view of the city. Many great architects worked on the palace before it assumed its present form in the 1730s. Domenico Fontana designed the main façade, Carlo Maderno the huge chapel and Bernini the narrow wing on Via del Quirinale.

Following the unification of Italy in 1870, it became the official residence of the king, then, in 1947, of the president of the republic.

Just across the piazza are the Scuderie Papali, a new exhibition space housed in the ex-stables of the Palazzo del Quirinale.

Canova's monument to Pope Clement XIV in Santi Apostoli, with figures of Humility and Modesty

Palazzo del Quirinale, official residence of the president of Italy

Palazzo Colonna ❸

Via della Pilotta 17. **Map** 5 A4 & 12 F3. 📞 06-679 4362. 🚌 H, 40, 64, 70, 170 and many routes to Piazza Venezia. **Open** 9am–1pm Sat only (last adm: noon). **Closed** Aug & public hols. **Adm charge.** 🚫

Pope martin v Colonna (reigned 1417–31) began building the palazzo, but most of the structure dates from the 18th century. The art gallery, built by Antonio del Grande between 1654 and 1665, is the only part open to the public. The pictures are numbered but unlabelled, so pick up a guide on the way in. Go up the stairs

and through the antechamber leading to a series of three gleaming marble rooms with prominent yellow columns, the Colonna family emblem (*colonna* means column).

The ceiling frescoes celebrate Marcantonio Colonna's victory over the Turks at the Battle of Lepanto (1571). On the walls are 16th- to 18th-century paintings, including Annibale Carracci's *The Bean Eater (see p157)*. The room of landscape paintings, many by Poussin's brother-in-law Gaspare Dughet, reflects the 18th-century taste of Cardinal Girolamo Colonna. Beyond is a room with a ceiling fresco of *The Apotheosis of Martin V*. The throne room has a chair reserved for visiting popes and a copy of Pisanello's portrait of Martin V. The gallery also offers a fine view of the private palace garden, site of the ruined Temple of Serapis.

Santi Apostoli ❹

Piazza dei Santi Apostoli. **Map** 5 A4 & 12 F3. 📞 06-679 4085. 🚌 H, 40, 64, 70, 170 and many other routes to Piazza Venezia. **Open** 7am–noon, 4pm–7pm daily. 🚹

The original 6th-century church on this site was rebuilt in the 15th century by Popes Martin V Colonna and

Sixtus IV della Rovere, whose oak-tree crest decorates the capitals of the late 15th-century portico. Inside the portico on the left is Canova's 1807 memorial to the engraver Giovanni Volpato. The church itself contains a much larger monument by Canova, his Tomb of Clement XIV (1789).

The Baroque interior by Francesco and Carlo Fontana was completed in 1714. Note the 3-D effect of Giovanni Odazzi's painted *Rebel Angels*, who really look as though they are falling from the sky. A huge 18th-century altarpiece by Domenico Muratori shows the martyrdom of the Apostles James and Philip, whose tombs are in the crypt.

Detail of Triton and "sea-horse" at Rome's grandest fountain, the Trevi

San Marcello al Corso ❺

Piazza San Marcello 5. **Map** 5 A4 & 12 F3. **C** 06-69 93 01. 🚌 62, 63, 81, 85, 95, 117, 119, 160, 175, 492, 628. **Open** 7am–noon, 4–7pm Mon–Sat, 8.30am–noon, 4–7pm Sun. 🚹

THIS CHURCH was originally one of the first places of Christian worship in Rome, which were known as *tituli*. A later Romanesque building

burned down in 1519, and was rebuilt by Jacopo Sansovino with a single nave and many richly decorated private chapels on either side. The imposing travertine façade was designed by Fontana in late Baroque style.

The third chapel on the right has fine frescoes of the Virgin Mary by Francesco Salviati. The decoration of the next chapel was interrupted by the Sack of Rome in 1527. Raphael's follower Perin del Vaga fled, leaving the ceiling frescoes to be completed by

Daniele da Volterra and Pellegrino Tibaldi when peace returned to the city. In the nave stands a splendid Venetian-style double tomb by Sansovino, a memorial to Cardinal Giovanni Michiel (victim of a Borgia poisoning in 1503) and his nephew, Bishop Antonio Orso.

Trevi Fountain ❻

Fontana di Trevi. **Map** 5 A3 & 12 F2. 🚌 52, 53, 61, 62, 63, 71, 80, 95, 116, 119 and many other routes along Via del Corso and Via del Tritone.

MOST VISITORS gathering around the coin-filled fountain assume that it has always been here, but by the standards of the Eternal City, the Trevi is a fairly recent creation. Nicola Salvi's theatrical design for Rome's largest and most famous fountain *(see p52)* was completed only in 1762. The central figures are Neptune, flanked by two Tritons. One struggles to master a very unruly "sea-horse", the other leads a far more docile animal. These symbolize the two contrasting moods of the sea.

The site originally marked the terminal of the Aqua Virgo aqueduct built in 19 BC. One of the first-storey reliefs shows a young girl (the legendary virgin after whom the aqueduct was named) pointing to the spring from which the water flows.

Chapel in San Marcello al Corso, decorated by Francesco Salviati

Façade of Santa Maria in Trivio

Santa Maria in Trivio ❼

Piazza dei Crociferi 49. **Map** 5 A3 &
12 F2. 📞 06-678 9645. 🚌 52,
53, 61, 62, 63, 71, 80, 95, 116,
119. **Open** 8am–noon, 4–7.30pm
daily. 🏛

IT HAS BEEN SAID that Italian
architecture is one of
façades, and nowhere is this
clearer than in the 1570s
façade of Santa Maria in Trivio,
delightfully stuck on to the
building behind it. Note the
false windows. There is
illusion inside too, particularly
in the ceiling frescoes, which
show scenes from the New
Testament by Antonio
Gherardi (1644–1702).

The name of the tiny church
probably means "St Mary-at-
the-meeting-of-three-roads".

Accademia Nazionale di San Luca ❽

Piazza dell'Accademia di San Luca 77.
Map 5 A3 & 12 F2. 📞 06-679 8850.
🚌 52, 53, 61, 62, 63, 71, 80, 95,
116, 119 and many other routes
along Via del Corso and Via del
Tritone. **Open** 10am–12.30pm
Mon–Sat.

ST LUKE IS supposed to have
been a painter, hence the
name of Rome's academy of
fine arts. Appropriately, the
gallery contains a painting of
*St Luke Painting a Portrait of
the Virgin* by Raphael and his
followers. The academy's
heyday was in the 17th and
18th centuries, when many

members gave their work to
the collection. Canova donated
a model for his famous marble
group, *The Three Graces.*

Of particular interest are
three fascinating self-portraits
painted by women: the
17th-century Italian Lavinia
Fontana; the 18th-century
Swiss Angelica Kauffmann,
whose painting is copied
from a portrait of her by
Joshua Reynolds; and
Elisabeth Vigée-Lebrun, the
French painter of the years
before the 1789 Revolution.

Santi Vincenzo e Anastasio ❾

Vicolo dei Modelli 73. **Map** 5 A3 &
12 F2. 📞 06-678 3098. 🚌 52, 53,
61, 62, 63, 71, 80, 95, 116, 119.
Open 7.30am–noon, 4–7pm daily. 🏛

OVERLOOKING the Trevi
Fountain is one of the
most over-the-top Baroque
façades in Rome. Its thickets
of columns are crowned by
the huge coat of arms of
Cardinal Raimondo Mazzarino,
who commissioned Martino
Longhi the Younger to build
the church in 1650. The female
bust above the door is of one

of the cardinal's famous nieces,
either Louis XIV's first love,
Maria Mancini (1639–1715),
or her younger sister, Ortensia.
In the apse, memorial plaques
record the popes whose *prae-
cordia* (a part of the heart) are
enshrined behind the wall.
This gruesome tradition was
started at the end of the 16th
century by Pope Sixtus V and
continued until Pius X stopped
it in the early 20th century.

Museo delle Paste Alimentari ❿

Piazza Scanderbeg 117. **Map** 5 A3 &
12 F2. 📞 06-699 1119. 🚌 52, 53,
61, 62, 63, 71, 80, 95, 116, 119.
Open 9.30am–5.30pm daily. **Closed**
public hols. 🚫 🏛 ♿ W www.
pastainmuseum.com

THE ROLE OF PASTA in Italian
cuisine cannot be exag-
gerated, and this entertaining
museum presents everything
there is to know about the beloved staple. Its rooms focus
on various aspects, such as
the history of pasta, how it is
made and the background of
the different shapes, while
others exhibit photography
and art with a pasta theme.

Self-portrait by Lavinia Fontana in the Accademia Nazionale di San Luca

Interior of Bernini's oval Sant'Andrea al Quirinale

Sant'Andrea al Quirinale

Via del Quirinale 29. **Map** 5 B3.
06-4890 3187. 116, 117 and
routes to Via del Tritone. **Open**
8am–noon, 4–6pm Wed–Mon
(closed afternoons in August).
Gratuity expected by sacristan for
showing St Stanislas's rooms.

KNOWN AS the "Pearl of the Baroque" because of its beautiful roseate marble interior, Sant'Andrea was designed by Bernini and executed by his assistants between 1658 and 1670. It was built for the Jesuits, hence the many IHS emblems (*Jesus Hominum Salvator* – Jesus Saviour of Mankind).

The site for the church was wide but shallow, so Bernini pointed the long axis of his oval plan not towards the altar, but towards the sides; he then leads the eye round to the altar end. Here he ordered works of art in various media which function not in isolation, but together. The crucified St Andrew (Sant' Andrea) of the altarpiece looks up at a stucco version of himself, who in turn ascends towards the lantern and the Holy Spirit.

Do not miss the rooms of St Stanislas Kostka in the adjacent convent. The quarters of the Jesuit novice, who died in 1568 aged 19, reflect not his own spartan taste, but the richer style of the 17th-century Jesuits. The Polish saint has been brilliantly immortalized in marble by Pierre Legros (1666–1719).

San Carlo alle Quattro Fontane

Via del Quirinale 23. **Map** 5 B3.
06-488 3261. 116, 117 and many
routes to Piazza Barberini. M
Barberini. **Open** 10am–1pm daily;
3–6pm Mon–Sat.

IN 1634, the Spanish Trinitarians, an order whose role was to pay the ransom of Christian hostages to the Arabs, commissioned Borromini to design a church and convent at the Quattro Fontane crossroads. The church, so small it would fit inside one of the piers of St Peter's, is also known as "San Carlino".

Although dedicated to Carlo Borromeo, the 16th-century Milanese cardinal canonized in 1620, San Carlo is as much a monument to Borromini. Both the façade and interior employ bold curves that give light and life to a small, cramped site. The oval dome and tiny lantern are particularly ingenious. The undulating lines of the façade are decorated with angels and a statue of San Carlo. Finished in 1667, the façade is one of Borromini's very last works.

There are further delights in the playful inverted shapes in the cloister and the stucco work in the refectory (now the sacristy), which houses a painting of San Carlo by Orazio Borgianni (1611).

In a small room off the sacristy hangs a portrait of Borromini himself wearing the Trinitarian cross. Borromini committed suicide in 1667, and in the crypt (which is now open to the public) a small curved chapel reserved for him remains empty.

Dome of San Carlo alle Quattro Fontane, lit by concealed windows

Fountain of Strength (or Juno)

Le Quattro Fontane ⑬

Intersection of Via delle Quattro Fontane and Via del Quirinale. **Map** 5 B3. 🚌 *Routes to Piazza Barberini or Via Nazionale.* Ⓜ *Barberini.*

THESE FOUR small fountains are attached to the corners of the buildings at the intersection of two narrow, busy streets. They date from the great redevelopment of Rome in the reign of Sixtus V (1585–90). Each fountain has a statue of a reclining deity. The river god accompanied by the she-wolf is clearly the Tiber; the other male figure may be the Arno. The female figures represent Strength and Fidelity or the goddesses Juno and Diana.

The crossroads is at the highest point of the Quirinal hill and commands splendid views of three distant landmark obelisks: those placed by Sixtus V in front of Santa Maria Maggiore and Trinità dei Monti, and the one that stands in Piazza del Quirinale.

Moses Fountain ⑭

Fontana dell'Acqua Felice, Piazza San Bernardo. **Map** 5 C2. 🚌 *36, 60, 61, 62, 84, 175, 492.* Ⓜ *Repubblica.*

OFFICIALLY KNOWN as the Fontana dell'Acqua Felice, this fountain owes its popular name to the grotesque statue of Moses in the central niche. The massive structure with its three elegant arches was designed by Domenico Fontana to mark the terminal of the Acqua Felice aqueduct, so called because it was one of the many great improvements commissioned by Felice Peretti, Pope Sixtus V. Completed in 1587, it brought clean piped water to this quarter of Rome for the first time.

The notorious statue of Moses striking water from the rock is larger than life and the proportions of the body are obviously wrong. Sculpted either by Prospero Bresciano or Leonardo Sormani, it is a clumsy attempt at recreating the awesome appearance of Michelangelo's Moses in the church of San Pietro in Vincoli *(see p170).* As soon as it was unveiled, it was said to be frowning at having been brought into the world by such an inept sculptor.

Fontana's Moses Fountain

The side reliefs also illustrate water stories from the Old Testament: Aaron leading the Israelites to water and Joshua pointing the army towards the Red Sea. The fountain's four lions are copies of Egyptian originals (now in the Vatican Museums), which Sixtus V had put there for public "convenience" and "delight".

Gold coin with head of the Emperor Diocletian (AD 285–305)

Santa Maria degli Angeli ⑮

Piazza della Repubblica. **Map** 5 C3. 🄲 *06-488 0812.* 🚌 *36, 60, 61, 62, 64, 84, 90, 116, 170, 492, 910.* Ⓜ *Repubblica, Termini.* **Open** *7am–6.30pm daily.* 🚻 ♿ 🄲

PARTS OF THE RUINED Baths of Diocletian *(right)* provided building material and setting for this church, constructed by Michelangelo in 1563. The church was so altered in the 18th century that it has lost most of its original character.

An exhibition in the sacristy gives a detailed account of Michelangelo's original design.

Fidelity (or Diana) with her attendant dog, one of the Quattro Fontane

Museo Nazionale Romano (Palazzo Massimo) ⑯

Part of the Museo Nazionale Romano in the Baths of Diocletian

Palazzo Massimo, Largo di Villa Peretti 1. **Map** 6 D3. 🦻 06-3996 7700. 🚌 36, 38, 40, 64, 86, 170, 175, H and other routes to Piazza dei Cinquecento. Ⓜ Repubblica, Termini. **Open** 9am–7.45pm Tue–Sun. **Closed** 1 Jan, 1 May, 25 Dec. **Adm charge** (the biglietto cumulativo gives entry to the museum's five branches). 🦻 🗸 🗋 🗋

Founded in 1889, the Museo Nazionale Romano holds most of the antiquities found in Rome since 1870 as well as pre-existing collections, and is one of the world's leading museums of Classical art. It now has five branches: its original site, occupying part of the Baths of Diocletian; the Palazzo Massimo; the Palazzo Altemps (see p127); the Aula Ottagona (near the Baths of Diocletian); and Crypta Balbi at Via delle Botteghe Oscure 31, excavated in the foyer of the Augustean Balbus' Theatre and housing findings from medieval Rome.

The Palazzo Massimo, built in 1883–7 on the site of a villa which belonged to Sixtus V, used to be a Jesuit college. In 1981–97 it was restored to house a significant proportion of the museum's collections. The exhibits, contained on four floors, are originals dating from the 2nd century BC to the end of the 4th century AD.

The basement contains an excellent display of ancient coins, precious artifacts and the only mummified child to be found in the ancient city. The ground floor is devoted to Roman statuary, with funeral monuments in Room 2 and Emperor Augustus in Pontifex Maximus guise in Room 5. Upstairs there are statues from Nero's summer villa in Anzio and Roman copies of famous Greek originals, such as the *Discobolos Ex-Lancellotti*. The real joy of the museum, however, is on the second floor, where entire rooms of wall paintings have been brought from various villas excavated in and around Rome. A guided tour of the wall paintings is necessary, which you can book at the museum entrance. The most incredible frescoes are from Livia's Villa at Prima Porta. Her triclinium (dining room) was decorated with an abundance of trees, plants and fruit, painted in a totally naturalistic style to fool guests that they were eating alfresco, rather than indoors. Other marvels include rooms brought from the first Villa Farnesina: the children's room has a predominantly white design, while the adults' bedroom is red, complete with erotic paintings. Equally impressive is the museum's display of mosaics on the same floor.

Baths of Diocletian ⑰

Terme di Diocleziano, Viale E de Nicola 79. **Map** 6 D3. 🦻 06-3996 7700. 🚌 36, 60, 61, 62, 84, 90. Ⓜ Repubblica, Termini. **Open** 9am–7pm Tue–Sun.

Built in AD 298–306 under the infamous Emperor Diocletian, who murdered thousands of Christians, the baths (see pp22–3) were the most extensive in Rome and could accommodate up to 3,000 bathers at a time.

Part of the Museo Nazionale Romano, the complex houses a vast collection of Roman statues and inscriptions and incorporates a former Carthusian monastery which has a beautiful cloister designed by Michelangelo.

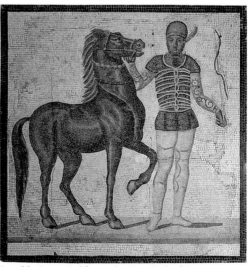

One of the Quattro Aurighe mosaics, Museo Nazionale Romano

Piazza della Repubblica ⑱

Map 5 C3. 🚌 *36, 60, 61, 62, 64, 84, 90, 170, 175, 492, 646, 910.* Ⓜ *Repubblica.*

ROMANS OFTEN refer to the piazza by its old name, Piazza Esedra, so called because it follows the shape of an *exedra* (a semicircular recess) that was part of the Baths of Diocletian. The piazza was part of the great redevelopment undertaken when Rome became capital of a unified Italy. Under its sweeping 19th-century colonnades there were once elegant shops, but they have been ousted by banks, travel agencies and cafés.

In the middle of the piazza stands the Fontana delle Naiadi. Mario Rutelli's four naked bronze nymphs caused something of a scandal when they were unveiled in 1901. Each reclines on an aquatic creature symbolizing water in its various forms: a sea-horse for the oceans, a water snake for rivers, a swan for lakes, and a curious frilled lizard for subterranean streams. The figure in the middle, added in 1911, is of the sea god Glaucus, who represents man victorious over the hostile forces of nature.

Piazza della Repubblica and the Fontana delle Naiadi

Palazzo delle Esposizioni ⑲

Via Nazionale 194 (second entrance in Via Milano). **Map** 5 B4. 📞 *06-474 5903.* 🚌 *40, 60, 64, 70, 116T, 170.* **Open** *10am–9pm Wed–Mon (last adm: 8.30pm).* **Closed** *1 Jan, 1 May, 25 Dec.* **Adm charge**. 🚫 ♿ *from Via Piacenza entrance.* **Concerts**, **lectures**, **films**. See **Entertainment** *pp346–7.* 🍴 🖥 📷 🌐 *www.palazzoesposizioni.it*

Façade of the Palazzo delle Esposizioni

THIS grandiose building, with wide steps, Corinthian columns and statues, was designed as an exhibition centre by the architect Pio Piacentini and built by the city of Rome in 1882 during the reign of Umberto I. The main entrance looks like a triumphal arch.

The palazzo is still used to house exhibitions today and the exhibition space has recently been modernized. The exhibitions are changed every three months and include a variety of sculpture and paintings. Live performances, films and lectures also take place here *(see p346)*. Foreign films are usually shown in the original language.

Santa Maria dei Monti ⑳

Via Madonna dei Monti 41. **Map** 5 B4. 📞 *06-48 55 31.* 🚌 *75, 84, 117.* Ⓜ *Cavour.* **Open** *7am–noon, 5–7.30pm Mon–Sat, 8.30am–1pm, 5–7.30pm Sun.* 🍴 ♿

DESIGNED BY Giacomo della Porta, this church, dating from 1580, has a particularly splendid dome. Over the high altar is a stunning medieval painting of the Madonna, patroness of this quarter of Rome. The altar in the left transept houses the tomb and effigy of the unworldly French saint Benoît-Joseph Labre, who died here in 1783, having spent his life as a solitary pilgrim. He slept rough in the ruins of the Colosseum, gave away any charitable gifts he received, and came regularly to Santa Maria dei Monti to worship. His faith could not sustain his body: still in his mid-thirties, he collapsed and died outside the church. The foul rags he wore are preserved.

One of the bronze nymphs of the fountain in Piazza della Repubblica

Sant'Agata dei Goti ㉑

Via Mazzarino 16 and Via Panisperna.
Map 5 B4. 06-488 8061.
40, 60, 64, 70, 71, 117, 170.
Open 7–9am, 4–7pm Mon–Sat,
9am–noon, 4–6pm Sun.

THE GOTHS who gave their
name to this church (*Goti*
are Goths) occupied Rome in
the 6th century AD. They were
Aryan heretics who denied the
divinity of Christ. The church
was founded between AD 462
and 470, shortly before the
main Gothic invasions, and the
beautiful granite columns date
from this period. The main altar
has a well-preserved 12th-cen-
tury Cosmatesque tabernacle,
but the most delightful part of
the church is the charming
18th-century courtyard built
around an ivy-draped well.

Villa Aldobrandini ㉒

Via Panisperna. Entrance to gardens:
Via Mazzarino 1. **Map** 5 B4.
40, 60, 64, 70, 71 117, 170.
Gardens open dawn–dusk daily.
Villa not open to the public.

BUILT IN the 16th century for
the Dukes of Urbino and
acquired for his family by Pope
Clement VIII Aldobrandini
(reigned 1592–1605), the
villa is now government
property and houses an
international law library.

The villa itself, decorated
with the family's six-starred
coat of arms, is closed to the
public, but the gardens and
terraces, hidden behind a
high wall that runs along Via
Nazionale, can be reached
through an iron gate in Via
Mazzarino. Steps lead up past
2nd-century AD ruins into the
recently renovated gardens,
highly recommended as an
oasis of tranquillity in the
centre of the city. Gravel
paths lead between formal
lawns and clearly marked
specimen trees, and benches
are provided for the weary.
Since the garden is raised
some 10 m (30 ft) above street
level, the views are excellent.

18th-century courtyard of Sant'Agata dei Goti

Santi Domenico e Sisto ㉓

Largo Angelicum 1.
Map 5 B4. 06-670 21.
40, 60, 64, 70, 71 117, 170.
Open by appointment.

Chapel in Santi Domenico e Sisto

THE CHURCH has a tall,
slender Baroque façade
rising above a steep flight of
steps. This divides into two
curving flights that sweep up
to the terrace in front of the
entrance. The pediment of the
façade is crowned by eight
flaming candlesticks.

The interior has a vaulted
ceiling with a large fresco
of *The Apotheosis of
St Dominic* by
Domenico Canuti
(1620–84). The
first chapel on
the right was
decorated by
Bernini, who
may also have
designed the
sculpture of Mary
Magdalene
meeting the
risen Christ in
the Garden of
Gethsemane.
This fine marble
group was
executed by

**Façade of Santi
Domenico
e Sisto**

Antonio Raggi (1649). Above
the altar is a 15th-century
terracotta plaque of the Virgin
and Child. On the left over a
side altar is a large painting of
the Madonna from the same
period, attributed to Benozzo
Gozzoli (1420–97), a pupil of
Fra Angelico.

ESQUILINE

THE ESQUILINE is the largest and highest of Rome's seven hills. In Imperial Rome the western slopes overlooking the Forum housed the crowded slums of the Suburra. On the eastern side there were a few villas belonging to wealthy citizens like Maecenas, patron of the arts and adviser to Augustus. The essential character of the place has persisted through two millennia; it is still one of the poorer quarters

Michelangelo's
Rachel **in San**
Pietro in Vincoli

of the city. The area is now heavily built up, except for a rather seedy park on the Colle Oppio, a smaller hill to the south of the Esquiline, where you can see the remains of the Baths of Titus, the Baths of Trajan and Nero's Domus Aurea. The area's main interest, however, lies in its churches. Many of these were founded on the sites of private houses where Christians met to worship secretly in the days when the religion was banned.

SIGHTS AT A GLANCE

Churches

San Martino ai Monti ❶
San Pietro in Vincoli ❷
Santa Pudenziana ❸
Santa Maria Maggiore
  pp172–3 ❹
Santa Prassede ❺
Santa Bibiana ❼

Museums

Museo Nazionale d'Arte
  Orientale ❾

Historic Piazzas

Piazza Vittorio Emanuele II ❽

Ancient Sites

Auditorium of Maecenas ❿
Domus Aurea ⓬
Sette Sale ⓫

Arches

Arch of Gallienus ❻

GETTING THERE

This area is close to Termini station and has several other Metro stops: Vittorio Emanuele and Manzoni on line A, Cavour and Colosseo on line B. Bus routes here are a little confusing. Among the most useful are the 16, 75 and 714 from Stazione Termini and the 84. Tram 3 runs along Via Labicana.

SEE ALSO

KEY

	Street-by-Street map
FS	Railway station
M	Metro station
P	Parking
i	Tourist information

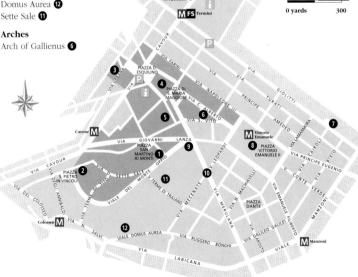

0 metres   300
0 yards   300

Street-by-Street: The Esquiline Hill

THE SIGHT that draws most people to this rather scruffy part of Rome is the great basilica of Santa Maria Maggiore. But it is also well worth searching out some of the smaller churches on the Esquiline: Santa Pudenziana and Santa Prassede with their celebrated mosaics, and San Pietro in Vincoli, home to one of Michelangelo's most famous sculptures. To the south, in the Colle Oppio park, are the scattered remains of the Baths of Trajan.

Santa Pudenziana
The apse of this ancient church has a magnificent 4th-century mosaic of Christ surrounded by the Apostles ❸

Piazza dell'Esquilino
was furnished with an obelisk in 1587 by Pope Sixtus V. This helped to guide pilgrims coming from the north to the important church of Santa Maria Maggiore.

To the Colosseum

VIA SFORZA

VIA DEI QUATTRO CANTI

VIA GIOVANNI LANZA

PIAZZA S
MARTINO A

VIA IN SELCI

PIAZZA DI SAN PIETRO IN VINCOLI

★ **San Pietro in Vincoli**
The church's treasures include Michelangelo's Moses and the chains that bound St Peter ❷

VIALE DEL MONTE OPP

The **Baths** of **Trajan** (AD 109) were the first to be built on the massive scale later used in the Baths of Diocletian and of Caracal

★ Santa Maria Maggiore
This imposing rear façade was added by Baroque architect Carlo Rainaldi in 1673. Santa Maria's interior is one of the most richly decorated in Rome ❹

LOCATOR MAP
See Central Rome Map pp12–13

The Tomb of Pius V (died 1572) by Domenico Fontana stands in this less well-known Sistine Chapel, under the northeast dome of Santa Maria Maggiore.

Arch of Gallienus
This was built in the 3rd century AD to replace an entrance in the old Servian Wall ❻

To Vittorio Emanuele Metro

★ Santa Prassede
The 9th-century mosaics in the Chapel of San Zeno are among the finest in Rome ❺

The Torre dei Capocci, a restored medieval tower, is one of the area's most distinctive landmarks.

San Martino ai Monti
The frescoes include 17th-century Roman landscapes and scenes from the life of Elijah by Gaspare Dughet ❶

VIA DELL'ESQUILINO

PIAZZA DI SANTA MARIA MAGGIORE

VIA CARLO ALBERTO

VIA MERULANA

LMATA

KEY

- - - - Suggested route

0 metres   75

0 yards   75

STAR SIGHTS

★ San Pietro in Vincoli

★ Santa Maria Maggiore

★ Santa Prassede

San Martino ai Monti ❶

Viale del Monte Oppio 28. **Map** 6 D5.
C 06-487 3126. 🚌 16, 714.
M Cavour, Vittorio Emanuele.
Open 7.30am–noon, 4.30–6.30pm
Mon–Sat, 8am–12.30pm, 4.30–
7.30pm Sun. 🚻 ♿

**Fresco of old San Giovanni in
Laterano in San Martino ai Monti**

CHRISTIANS have been
worshipping on the site
of this church since the 3rd
century, when they used to
meet in the house of a man
named Equitius. In the 4th
century, after Constantine had
legalized Christianity, Pope
Sylvester I built a church, one
of very few things he did
during his pontificate. In fact
he was so insignificant that
in the 5th century a more
exciting life was fabricated
for him – which included
tales of him converting
Constantine, curing him of
leprosy and forcing him to
close all pagan temples.
Pope Sylvester's fictional life
was further enhanced in the
8th century, with the
forgery of a document in
which Constantine offered
him the Imperial crown.

Pope Sylvester's church
was replaced in about
AD 500 by St Symmachus,
rebuilt in the 9th century
and then transformed
completely in the 1630s.
The only immediate signs of
its age are the ancient
Corinthian columns dividing
the nave and aisles. The most
interesting interior features
are a series of frescoed
landscapes of the countryside
around Rome (campagna
romana) by the 17th-century

French artist Gaspare Dughet,
Poussin's brother-in-law, in
the right aisle. The frescoes
by Filippo Gagliardi, at either
end of the left aisle, show old
St Peter's and the interior of
San Giovanni in Laterano
before Borromini's redesign.
If you can find the sacristan,
you can go beneath the church
to see the remains of
Equitius's house.

San Pietro in Vincoli ❷

Piazza di San Pietro in Vincoli 4A.
Map 5 C5. **C** 06-488 28 65. 🚌
75, 84, 117. **M** Cavour, Colosseo.
Open 7am–12.30pm, 3.30–7pm
(Oct–Mar: 6pm) daily. 🚻 ♿ 🅿

ACCORDING TO TRADITION, the
two chains (vincoli) used
to shackle St Peter while he
was being held in the depths

Michelangelo's Moses in San Pietro

Reliquary with St Peter's chains

of the Mamertine Prison (see
p91) were subsequently taken
to Constantinople. In the 5th
century, Empress Eudoxia
deposited one in a church in
Constantinople and sent the
other to her daughter Eudoxia
in Rome. She in turn gave hers
to Pope Leo I, who had this
church built to house it. Some
years later the second chain
was brought to Rome,
where it linked miraculously
with its partner.

The chains are still here,
displayed below the high
altar, but the church is now
best known for Michelangelo's
Tomb of Pope Julius II. When
it was commissioned in 1505,
Michelangelo spent 8 months
searching for perfect blocks
of marble at Carrara in
Tuscany, but Pope Julius
became more interested in
the building of a new St
Peter's and the project
was laid aside. After the
pope's death in 1513,
Michelangelo resumed
work on the tomb, but
had only finished the
statues of Moses and
The Dying Slaves when Pope
Paul III persuaded him to
start work on the Sistine
Chapel's Last Judgment.
Michelangelo had planned
a vast monument with
over 40 statues, but the
tomb that was built –
mainly by his pupils –
is simply a façade with
six niches for statues.
The Dying Slaves are in
Paris and Florence, but
the tremendous bearded
Moses is here. The horns
on Moses' head should
really be beams of light
– they are the result of
the Hebrew original from
the Old Testament being
wrongly translated.

Santa Pudenziana ❸

Via Urbana 160. **Map** 5 C4.
☎ 06-481 4622.
🚌 16, 75, 84, 105, 714.
Ⓜ Cavour.
Open 8am–1pm, 3–6pm daily. ⬆

Cᴴᴜʀᴄʜᴇs tend to be dedicated to existing saints, but in this case, the church, through a linguistic accident, created a brand new saint. In the 1st century AD a Roman senator called Pudens lived here, and, according to legend, allowed St Peter to lodge with him. In the 2nd century a bath house was built on this site and in the 4th century a church was established inside the baths, known as the *Ecclesia Pudentiana* (the church of Pudens). In time it was assumed that "Pudentiana" was a woman's name and a life was created for her – she became the sister of Prassede and was credited with caring for Christian victims of persecution. In 1969 both saints were declared invalid, though their churches both kept their names.

The 19th-century façade of the church retains an 11th-century frieze depicting both Prassede and Pudenziana dressed as crowned Byzantine empresses. The apse has a remarkable 4th-century mosaic, clearly influenced by Classical pagan art in its use of subtle colours. The Apostles are represented as Roman senators in togas but a clumsy attempt at restoration in the 16th century destroyed two of the Apostles and left other figures without legs.

Apse mosaics in Santa Prassede, showing the saint with St Paul

Santa Maria Maggiore ❹

See pp172–3.

Santa Prassede ❺

Via Santa Prassede 9A. **Map** 6 D4.
☎ 06-488 24 56. 🚌 16, 70, 71, 75, 714. Ⓜ Vittorio Emanuele. **Open** 7.30am–noon, 4pm–6.30pm daily (afternoons only, Aug). ⬆ ♿

Tʜᴇ ᴄʜᴜʀᴄʜ was founded by Pope Paschal II in the 9th century, on the site of a 2nd-century oratory. Although the interior has been altered and rebuilt, the structure of the original design of the 9th-century church is clearly visible. Its three naves are separated by rows of granite columns. In the central nave, there is a round stone slab covering the well where, according to the legend, St Prassede would have buried the remains of 2,000 martyrs.

Artists from Byzantium decorated the church with glittering, jewel-coloured mosaics. Those in the apse and choir depict stylized white-robed elders, the haloed elect looking down from the gold and blue walls of heaven, spindly legged lambs, feather-mop palm trees and bright red poppies.

In the apse, Santa Prassede and Santa Pudenziana stand on either side of Christ, with the fatherly arms of St Paul and St Peter on their shoulders. Beautiful mosaics of saints, the Virgin and Christ and the Apostles also cover the walls and vault of the Chapel of St Zeno, built as a mausoleum for Pope Paschal's mother, Theodora. Part of a column brought back from Jerusalem, allegedly the one to which Christ was bound and flogged, also stands here.

11th-century frieze and medallions on the façade of Santa Pudenziana

Santa Maria Maggiore ❹

Of all the great Roman basilicas, Santa Maria has the most successful blend of different architectural styles. Its colonnaded triple nave is part of the original 5th-century building. The Cosmatesque marble floor and delightful Romanesque bell tower, with its blue ceramic roundels, are medieval. The Renaissance saw a new coffered ceiling, and the Baroque gave the church twin domes and its imposing front and rear façades. The mosaics are Santa Maria's most famous feature. From the 5th century come the biblical scenes in the nave and the spectacular mosaics on the triumphal arch. Medieval highlights include a 13th-century enthroned Christ in the loggia.

★ Cappella Paolina
Flaminio Ponzio designed this richly decorated chapel (1611) for Pope Paul V Borghese.

Obelisk in Piazza dell'Esquilino
The Egyptian obelisk was erected by Pope Sixtus V in 1587 as a landmark for pilgrims.

LEGEND OF THE SNOW
In 356, Pope Liberius had a dream in which the Virgin told him to build a church on the spot where he found snow. When it fell on the Esquiline, on the morning of 5 August in the middle of a baking Roman summer, he naturally obeyed. The miracle of the snow is commemorated each year by a service during which thousands of white petals float down from the ceiling of Santa Maria. Originally roses were used, but nowadays the petals are more usually taken from dahlias.

Coffered Ceiling
The gilded ceiling, possibly by Giuliano da Sangallo, was a gift of Alexander VI Borgia at the end of the 15th century. The gold is said to be the first brought from America by Columbus.

TIMELINE

356 Virgin appears to Pope Liberius

432–40 Sixtus III completes church

420 Probable founding date

Pope Gregory VII

1075 Pope Gregory VII kidnapped by opponents while reading Christmas mass in Santa Maria

Coat of arms of Gregory VII

1347 Cola di Rienzo crowned Tribune of Rome in Santa Maria

1288–92 Nicholas IV adds apse and transepts

1673 Carlo Rainaldi rebuilds apse

1743 Ferdinando Fuga adds main façade on orders of Benedict XIV

300 AD	600	900	1200	1500	1800

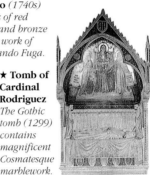

VISITORS' CHECKLIST

Piazza di Santa Maria Maggiore.
Map 6 D4.
06-48 31 95.
16, 70, 71, 714. 14.
Termini, Cavour.
Open 7am–7pm daily.

★ **Coronation of the Virgin Mosaic**
This is the central image of a series of wonderful apse mosaics of the Virgin by Jacopo Torriti (1295).

Baldacchino *(1740s)*
Its columns of red porphyry and bronze were the work of Ferdinando Fuga.

★ **Tomb of Cardinal Rodriguez**
The Gothic tomb (1299) contains magnificent Cosmatesque marblework.

★ **Cappella Sistina**
This Sistine Chapel was built for Pope Sixtus V (1584–87) by Domenico Fontana and houses the pope's tomb.

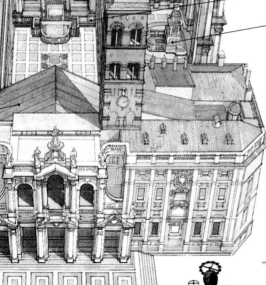

Column in Piazza Santa Maria Maggiore
A bronze of the Virgin and Child was added to this ancient marble column in 1615. The column came from the Basilica of Constantine in the Forum.

STAR FEATURES

★ **Cappella Paolina**

★ **Coronation of the Virgin Mosaic**

★ **Tomb of Cardinal Rodriguez**

★ **Cappella Sistina**

Arch erected in memory of Emperor Gallienus

Arch of Gallienus 6

Via Carlo Alberto. **Map** 6 D4. 🚌 *16, 71, 714.* **M** *Vittorio Emanuele.*

S QUASHED between two buildings just off Via Carlo Alberto is the central arch of an originally three-arched gate erected in memory of Emperor Gallienus, who was assassinated by his Illyrian officers in AD 262. It was built on the site of the old Esquiline Gate in the Servian Wall, parts of which are visible nearby.

Santa Bibiana 7

Via Giovanni Giolitti 154. **Map** 6 F4. 🄲 *06-446 1021.* 🚌 *71.* 🚊 *5, 14.* **M** *Vittorio Emanuele.* **Open** *7.30–11am, 4.30–7.30pm daily.* ✝ ♿

T HE DECEPTIVELY simple façade of Santa Bibiana was Bernini's first foray into architecture. It is a clean, economic design with superimposed pilasters and deeply shadowed archways. The church itself was built on the site of the palace belonging to Bibiana's family. This is where

the saint was buried after being flogged to death with leaded cords during the brief persecution of the Christians in the reign of Julian the Apostate (361–3). Just inside the church is a small column against which Bibiana is said to have been whipped. Her remains, along with those of her mother Dafrosa and her sister Demetria, who also suffered martyrdom, are preserved in an alabaster urn below the altar. In a niche above the altar stands a statue of Santa Bibiana by Bernini – the first fully clothed figure he ever sculpted. He depicts her standing beside a column, holding the cords with which she was whipped, apparently on the verge of a deadly swoon.

Early sculpture by Bernini of the martyr Santa Bibiana (1626)

Piazza Vittorio Emanuele II 8

Map 6 E5. 🚌 *4, 9, 71.* 🚊 *5, 14.* **M** *Vittorio Emanuele.* See **Markets** *p338.*

P IAZZA VITTORIO, as it is called for short, was once one of the city's main open-air food markets, though now it has moved around the corner to new, covered premises. The arcaded square was built in the urban development undertaken after the unification of Italy in 1870. It was named after Italy's first king, but there is nothing regal about its appearance today.

However, the garden area in the centre of the square has recently been restored. It contains a number of mysterious ruins, including a large mound, part of a Roman fountain from the 3rd century AD and the Porta Magica, a curious 17th-century doorway inscribed with alchemical signs and formulae.

Museo Nazionale d'Arte Orientale 9

Via Merulana 248. **Map** 6 D5. 🄲 *06-487 4415.* 🚌 *16, 70, 71, 714.* **M** *Vittorio Emanuele.* **Open** *8.30am–2pm Mon, Wed, Fri, Sat; 8.30am–7.30pm Tue, Thu, Sun.* **Closed** *1st & 3rd Mon of month.* **Adm charge.** ♿

T HE MUSEUM occupies part of the late 19th-century Palazzo Brancaccio, home of the Italian Institute of the Middle and Far East since 1957. The collection ranges from prehistoric Iranian ceramics, sculpture from Afghanistan, Nepal, Kashmir and India to 18th-century Tibetan paintings on vellum. From the Far East there are collections of Japanese screen paintings and Chinese jade. The most unusual exhibits are the finds from the Italian excavation of the ancient civilization of

4th-century relief from Kashmir

Nepalese Bodhisattva in the Museo Nazionale d'Arte Orientale

Swat in northeast Pakistan. This fascinating Gandhara culture lasted from the 3rd century BC to about the 10th century AD. Its wonderfully exotic, sensual reliefs show an unusual combination of Hellenistic, Buddhist and Hindu influences.

Auditorium of Maecenas ⑩

Largo Leopardi 2. **Map** 6 D5.
📞 06-487 3262. 🚌 *16, 714.*
Ⓜ *Vittorio Emanuele.* **Open**
9am–1.30pm Tue–Sun. 🚫 ♿

MAECENAS, fop, gourmet and patron of the arts, was also an astute adviser and colleague of the Emperor Augustus. Fabulously rich, he created a fantastic villa and gardens on the Esquiline hill, most of which has long disappeared beneath the modern city. The partially reconstructed auditorium, isolated on a traffic island, is all that remains.

Inside, a semicircle of tiered seats suggests that it may have been a place for readings and performances. If it was, then Maecenas would have been entertained here by his protégés, the lyric poet Horace and Virgil, author of the *Aeneid*, reading their latest works. However, water ducts have also been discovered and it may well have been a *nympheum* – a kind of summerhouse – with fountains. Traces of frescoes

remain on the walls: you can make out garden scenes and a procession of miniature figures – including one of a characteristically drunken Dionysus (the Greek god of wine) being propped upright by a satyr.

Sette Sale ⑪

Via delle Terme di Traiano. **Map** 5 C5.
📞 *06-6710 3819.* 🚌 *85, 87, 117, 186, 810, 850.* 🚋 *3.* Ⓜ *Colosseo.*
Open *by request; phone in advance.*

NOT FAR FROM Nero's Domus Aurea is the cistern of the Sette Sale. It was built here to supply the enormous quantities of water needed for the Baths of Trajan. These were built for Emperor Trajan in AD 104 on parts of the Domus Aurea damaged by a fire.

A set of stairs leads down into the cistern, well below street level. There is not much to see here now, but a walk through the huge, echoing cistern where light rays illuminate the watery surfaces is still an evocative experience. The nine sections, 30 m (98 ft) long and 5 m (16 ft) wide, had a capacity of 8 million litres.

Domus Aurea ⑫

Viale della Domus Aurea. **Map** 5 C5.
📞 *06-3996 7700.* 🚌 *85, 87, 117, 186, 810, 850.* 🚋 *3.* Ⓜ *Colosseo.*
Open *9am–7.45pm Wed–Mon. Advance booking normally required: phone the above number (listen for Domus Aurea).* 🎧 🎫 🚻 🔊

AFTER ALLEGEDLY setting fire to Rome in AD 64, Nero decided to build himself an outrageous new palace. The Domus Aurea (sometimes called Nero's Golden House) occupied part of the Palatine and most of the Celian and Esquiline hills – an area approximately 25 times the size of the Colosseum. The vestibule on the Palatine side of the complex contained a colossal gilded statue of Nero. There was an artificial lake, with gardens and woods where imported wild beasts

were allowed to roam free. According to Suetonius in his life of Nero, the palace walls were adorned with gold and mother-of-pearl, rooms were designed with ceilings that showered guests with flowers or perfumes, the dining hall rotated and the baths were fed with both sulphurous water and sea water.

Tacitus described Nero's debauched garden parties, with banquets served on barges and lakeside brothels serviced by aristocratic women, though as Nero killed himself in AD 68, he did not have long to enjoy his new home.

Nero's successors, anxious to distance themselves from the monster-emperor, did their utmost to erase all traces of the palace. Vespasian drained the lake and built the Colosseum *(see pp92–5)* in its place, Titus and Trajan each erected a complex of baths over the palace, and Hadrian placed the Temple of Venus and Rome *(see p87)* over the vestibule.

Rooms from one wing of the palace have survived, buried beneath the ruins of the Baths of Trajan on the Oppian hill. Recent excavations have revealed large frescoes and mosaics which are thought to be a panorama of Rome from a bird's-eye perspective. Hopefully more areas will open to the public when considered safe from landslides.

Frescoed room in the ruins of the Domus Aurea

LATERAN

I N THE MIDDLE AGES the Lateran Palace was the residence of the popes, and the basilica of San Giovanni beside it rivalled St Peter's in splendour. After the return of the popes from Avignon at the end of the 14th century, the area declined in importance. Pilgrims still continued to visit San Giovanni and Santa

Cherub from San Giovanni in Laterano

Croce in Gerusalemme, but the area remained sparsely inhabited. Ancient convents slumbered amid gardens and vineyards until Rome became capital of Italy in 1870 and a network of residential streets was laid out here to house the influx of newcomers. Archaeological interest lies chiefly in the Aurelian Wall and the ruins of the Aqueduct of Nero.

SIGHTS AT A GLANCE

Churches

San Giovanni in Laterano pp182–3 ❶
Santa Croce in Gerusalemme ❺
Santi Quattro Coronati ⓫
San Clemente pp186–7 ⓬
Santo Stefano Rotondo ⓭

Shrines

Scala Santa and Sancta Sanctorum ❷

Arches and Gates

Porta Asinaria ❸
Porta Maggiore ❼

Ancient Sites

Amphiteatrum Castrense ❹
Baker's Tomb ❽
Aqueduct of Nero and the Freedmen's Tombs ❾

Museums

Museum of Musical Instruments ❻
Museo Storico della Liberazione di Roma ❿

SEE ALSO

• *Street Finder*, maps 6, 9, 10
• *Restaurants* pp310–11
• *Mosaics Walk* pp280–81

GETTING THERE

San Giovanni Metro station on line A is just outside the city wall, but handy for many of the sights in the area. The 16, 81, 85, 87 and 186 are among the many buses to Piazza di San Giovanni in Laterano. This can also be reached by the 3 tram. This is slow, but its route makes it useful for exploring this part of Rome.

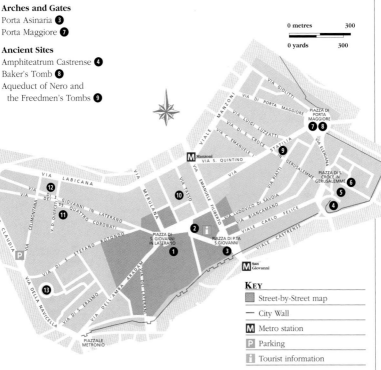

| 0 metres | 300 |
| 0 yards | 300 |

KEY

	Street-by-Street map
—	City Wall
M	Metro station
P	Parking
i	Tourist information

15th-century apse fresco in Santa Croce in Gerusalemme

Street-by-Street: Piazza di San Giovanni

BOTH THE BASILICA of San Giovanni and the Lateran Palace look out over a huge open area, the Piazza di San Giovanni, laid out at the end of the 16th century with an Egyptian obelisk, the oldest in Rome, in the centre. Sadly the traffic streaming in and out of the city through Porta San Giovanni tends to detract from its grandeur. Across the square is the building housing the Scala Santa (the Holy Staircase), one of the most revered relics in Rome and the goal for many pilgrims. The area is also a venue for political rallies, and the feast of St John on 23 June is celebrated with a fair at which Romans consume roast *porchetta* (*see p59*).

The Chapel of Santa Rufina, originally the portico of the baptistry, has a 5th-century mosaic of spiralling foliage in the apse.

VIA DI SANTO STEFANO ROTO

VIA DELL'AMBA ARADAM

VIA DEI LATERANI

The Cloister of San Giovanni fortunately survived the two fires that destroyed the early basilica. A 13th-century masterpiece of mosaic work, the cloister now houses fragments from the medieval basilica.

Piazza di San Giovanni in Laterano boasts an ancient obelisk and parts of Nero's Aqueduct. This 18th-century painting by Canaletto shows how the piazza once looked.

STAR SIGHTS

★ **San Giovanni in Laterano**

KEY

- - -   Suggested route

| 0 metres | 75 |
| 0 yards | 75 |

The Chapel of San Venanzio is decorated with a series of 7th-century mosaics on a gold background. This detail from the apse shows one of the angels flanking the central figure of Christ. San Venanzio was an accomplished 6th-century Latin poet.

LOCATOR MAP
See Central Rome Map pp12–13

The Lateran Palace, residence of the popes until 1309, was rebuilt by Domenico Fontana in 1586.

PIAZZA DI SAN GIOVANNI IN LATERANO

VIA D. FONTANA

PIAZZA DI PORTA SAN GIOVANNI

★ **San Giovanni in Laterano**
Borromini's interior dates from the 17th century, but the grand façade by Alessandro Galilei, with its giant statues of Christ and the Apostles, was added in 1735 ❶

Scala Santa
This door at the top of the holy staircase leads to the Sancta Sanctorum ❷

The Triclinio Leoniano is a piece of wall and a mosaic from the dining hall of 8th-century Pope Leo III.

Porta Asinaria
This minor gateway, no longer in use, is as old as the Aurelian Wall, dating back to the 3rd century AD ❸

San Giovanni in Laterano ❶

See pp182–3.

Scala Santa and Sancta Sanctorum ❷

Piazza di San Giovanni in Laterano 14.
Map 9 C1. 🄲 *06-772 6641.* 🚌 *16, 81, 85, 87, 186 and other routes to Piazza di San Giovanni in Laterano.*
🚋 *3.* Ⓜ *San Giovanni.*
Open *6.30am–noon, 3–6pm (3.30–6.30pm in summer).* 🚹

Devout Christians climbing the Scala Santa on their knees

O N THE EAST SIDE of Piazza di San Giovanni in Laterano, a building designed by Domenico Fontana (1589) houses two surviving parts of the old Lateran Palace. One is the Sancta Sanctorum, the other the holy staircase, the Scala Santa. The 28 steps, said to be those that Christ ascended in Pontius Pilate's house during his trial, are supposed to have been brought from Jerusalem by St Helena, mother of the Emperor Constantine. This belief, however, cannot be traced back any earlier than the 7th century.

The steps were moved to their present site by Pope Sixtus V (reigned 1585–90) when the old Lateran Palace was destroyed. No foot may touch the holy steps, so they are covered by wooden boards. They may only be climbed by the faithful on their knees, a penance that is performed especially on Good Friday. In the vestibule

there are various 19th-century sculptures including an *Ecce Homo* by Giosuè Meli (1874).

The Scala Santa and two side stairways lead to the Chapel of St Lawrence or Sancta Sanctorum (Holy of Holies), built by Pope Nicholas III in 1278. Decorated with fine Cosmatesque marble-work, the chapel contains many important relics, the most precious being an image of Jesus – the *Acheiropoeton* or "picture painted without hands", said to be the work of St Luke, with the help of an angel. It was taken in procession in medieval times to ward off plagues.

On the walls and in the vault, restoration work has revealed 13th-century frescoes which for 500 years had been covered by later paintings. The frescoes, representing the legends of St Nicholas, St Lawrence, St Agnes and St Paul, show signs of the style that would characterize the frescoes of Giotto in Assisi, made a few years later.

Porta Asinaria ❸

Between Piazza di Porta San Giovanni and Piazzale Appio. **Map** 10 D2.
🚌 *16, 81, 85, 87.* 🚋 *3.* Ⓜ *San Giovanni. See **Markets** p339.*

T HE PORTA ASINARIA (Gate of the Donkeys) is one of the minor gateways in the Aurelian Wall *(see p196)*. Twin circular

Porta Asinaria from inside the wall

towers were added and a small enclosure built around the entrance; the remains are still visible. From outside the walls you can see the gate's white travertine façade and two rows of small windows, giving light to two corridors built into the wall above the gateway. In AD 546 treacherous barbarian soldiers serving in the Roman army opened this gate to the hordes of the Goth Totila, who mercilessly looted the city. In 1084 the Holy Roman Emperor Henry IV entered Rome via Porta Asinaria with the antipope Guibert to oust Pope Gregory VII. The gate was badly damaged in the conflicts that followed.

The area close to the gate, especially in the Via Sannio, is the home of a popular flea-market *(see p339)*.

Amphiteatrum Castrense ❹

Between Piazza di Santa Croce in Gerusalemme and Viale Castrense.
Map 10 E1. 🚌 *649.* 🚋 *3.*
Not open *to the public.*

Columns and bricked-up arches of the Amphiteatrum Castrense

T HIS SMALL 3rd-century amphitheatre was used for games and baiting animals. It owes its preservation to the fact that it was incorporated in the Aurelian Wall *(see p196)*, which included several existing high buildings in its fortifications. The graceful arches framed by brick semicolumns were blocked up. The amphitheatre is best seen from outside the walls, from where there is also a good view of the bell tower of Santa Croce in Gerusalemme.

Discovery and Triumph of the Cross, attributed to Antoniazzo Romano, in Santa Croce in Gerusalemme

Santa Croce in Gerusalemme **❺**

Piazza di Santa Croce in Gerusalemme 12. **Map** 10 E1. **[** 06-701 4769. **▦** 16, 81, 649, 810. **▦** 3. **Open** 7am–1pm, 2–7pm daily. **✞ ▣**

E MPEROR CONSTANTINE'S mother St Helena founded this church in AD 320 in the grounds of her private palace. Although the church stood at the edge of the city, the relics of the Crucifixion that St Helena had brought back from Jerusalem made it a centre of pilgrimage. Most

18th-century statue of St Helena on the façade of Santa Croce

important were the pieces of Christ's Cross (*croce* means cross) and part of Pontius Pilate's inscription in Latin, Hebrew and Greek: "Jesus of Nazareth King of the Jews".

In the crypt is a Roman statue of Juno, found at Ostia (*see pp270–71*), transformed into a statue of St Helena by replacing the head and arms and adding a cross. The 15th-century apse fresco shows the medieval legends that arose around the Cross. Helena is shown holding it over a dead youth and restoring him to life. Another episode shows its recovery from the Persians by the Byzantine Emperor Heraclitus after a bloody battle. In the centre of the apse is a magnificent tomb by Jacopo Sansovino made for Cardinal Quiñones, Emperor Charles V's confessor (died 1540).

Museum of Musical Instruments **❻**

Museo degli Strumenti Musicali, Piazza di Santa Croce in Gerusalemme 9a. **Map** 10 E1. **[** 06-701 4796. **▦** 16, 81, 649, 810. **▦** 3. **Open** 8.30am–7.30pm Tue–Sun. **Closed** 1 Jan, 25 Dec. **Adm charge.** **&**

O NE OF ROME'S lesser-known museums, the building stands on the site of the Sessorianum, the great

Imperial villa belonging to Empress St Helena, later included in the Aurelian Wall. Opened in 1974, the museum has a collection of more than 3,000 instruments from all over the world, including instruments typical of the various regions of Italy, and wind, string and percussion instruments of all ages (including Egyptian, Greek and Roman). There are also sections dedicated to church and military music. The greater part of the collection is composed of Baroque instruments: don't miss the gorgeous Barberini harp, remarkably well-preserved, on the first floor in Room 13. There are spinets, harpsichords and clavichords, and one of the first pianos ever made, dating from 1722.

Art Nouveau entrance to the Museum of Musical Instruments

San Giovanni in Laterano ❶

EARLY IN THE 4th century, the Laterani family were disgraced and their land taken by Emperor Constantine to build Rome's first Christian basilica. Today's church retains the original shape, but has been destroyed by fire twice and rebuilt several times. Borromini undertook the last major rebuild of the interior in 1646, and the main façade is an 18th-century addition. Before the pope's move to Avignon in 1309, the adjoining Lateran Palace was the official papal residence, and until 1870 all popes were crowned in the church. The pope is the Bishop of Rome and here in the city's main cathedral he celebrates Maundy Thursday mass and attends the annual blessing of the people.

Cappella di San Venanzio
This chapel is attached to the baptistry and is decorated with 7th-century mosaics.

Entrance to museum

Apse

Papal Altar
Only the Pope can celebrate mass at this altar. The Gothic baldacchino, decorated with frescoes, dates from the 14th century.

★ Cloisters
Built by the Vassalletto family in about 1220, the cloisters are remarkable for their twisted twin columns and inlaid marble mosaics.

TIMELINE

AD 313 Constantine gives Laterani site to Pope Melchiades for a church		**1144** Church dedicated to San Giovanni in Laterano		**1646** Borromini rebuilds interior
314–18 Five-aisled basilical church is built	**896** Church damaged in earthquake	**1309** Papacy moves to Avignon	**1377** Return of popes from Avignon	

AD 300	800	1000	1400

324 Basilica consecrated by Pope Sylvester I and dedicated to the Redeemer	**904–911** Church rebuilt under Pope Sergius III	**1300** First Holy Year proclaimed	**1360** Church burnt down for second time	**1586** Domenico Fontana builds north façade
		1308 Church destroyed by fire	**1730–40** Alessandro Galilei constructs main façade	

★ Baptistry
Though much restored, the domed baptistry dates back to Constantine's time. It assumed its present octagonal shape in AD 432 and the design has served as the model for baptistries throughout the Christian world.

VISITORS' CHECKLIST

Piazza di San Giovanni in Laterano 4. **Map** 9 C2. **[ ]** 06-6988 6452. **[ ]** 16, 81, 85, 87, 186, 650, 850 and other routes to Piazza San Giovanni. **M** San Giovanni. **[ ]** 3. **Church, Cloister open** 7am–6.45pm daily. **Museum open** 9am–1pm Mon–Sat. **Baptistry open** 7.30am–12.30pm, 4–7.30pm daily. **Adm charge** for museum and cloister. **[ ] [ ]**

STAR FEATURES

★ **Baptistry**

★ **Cloisters**

North Façade
This was added by Domenico Fontana in 1586. The pope gives his blessing from the upper loggia.

The original Lateran Palace was almost destroyed by the fire of 1308 which devastated San Giovanni. Pope Sixtus V commissioned Fontana to replace it in 1586.

Statues of Christ and the Apostles

Boniface VIII Fresco
This fragment showing the pope proclaiming the Holy Year of 1300 is attributed to Giotto.

A side door is opened every Holy Year.

The main entrance's bronze doors originally came from the Curia *(see p82).*

TRIAL OF A CORPSE
Fear of rival factions led the early popes to extraordinary lengths. An absurd case took place at the Lateran Palace in 897 when Pope Stephen VI tried the corpse of his predecessor, Formosus, for disloyalty to the Church. The corpse was found guilty, its right hand was mutilated and it was thrown into the Tiber.

Pope Formosus

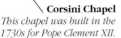

Corsini Chapel
This chapel was built in the 1730s for Pope Clement XII. The altarpiece is a mosaic copy of Guido Reni's painting of Sant'Andrea Corsini.

San Clemente ⓬

SAN CLEMENTE PROVIDES an opportunity to travel back through three layers of history. At street level, there is a 12th-century church; underneath this lies a 4th-century church; and below that are ancient Roman buildings, including a Temple of Mithras. Mithraism, an all-male fertility cult imported from Persia in the 1st century BC, was a rival to Christianity during the age of Imperial Rome.

The upper levels are dedicated to St Clement, the fourth pope, who was exiled to the Crimea and martyred by being tied to an anchor and drowned. His life is illustrated in some of the frescoes in the 4th-century church. The site was taken over in the 17th century by Irish Dominicans, who still continue the excavating work begun by Father Mullooly in 1857.

Entrance to the church is through a door in Via di San Giovanni in Laterano.

Paschal Candlestick
This 12th-century spiralling candlestick, striped with glittering mosaic, is a magnificent example of Cosmati work.

18th-century Façade
Twelfth-century columns were used in the arcade.

★ Cappella di Santa Caterina
The restored frescoes by the 15th-century Florentine artist, Masolino da Panicale, show scenes from the life of the martyred St Catherine of Alexandria.

12th-century church

4th-century church

Piscina
This deep pit was discovered in 1967. It could have been used as a font or fountain.

1st–3rd-century temple and buildings

TIMELINE

2nd century Site possibly used for secret Christian worship

Late 2nd century Temple of Mithras built

867 Reputed transfer of remains of San Clemente to Rome

1108 New church built over 4th-century church

1857 Original 4th-century church rediscovered by Father Mullooly

AD 10	500	1000	1500	1900

c.88–97 Papacy of St Clement

4th century First church built over courtyard of earlier Roman building

1667 Church and convent given to Irish Dominicans

1084 Church destroyed during Norman invasion led by Robert Guiscard

AD 64 Nero's fire destroys area

1861 Church is excavated. Roman ruins discovered

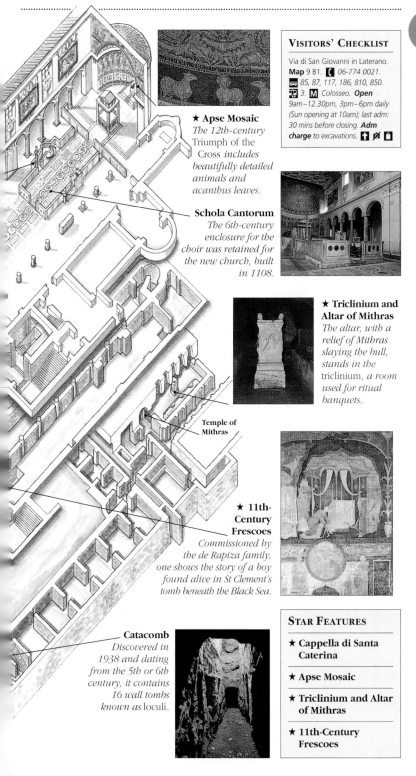

★ Apse Mosaic
The 12th-century
Triumph of the
Cross includes
beautifully detailed
animals and
acanthus leaves.

Schola Cantorum
The 6th-century
enclosure for the
choir was retained for
the new church, built
in 1108.

VISITORS' CHECKLIST

Via di San Giovanni in Laterano.
Map 9 B1. 06-774 0021.
85, 87, 117, 186, 810, 850.
3. Colosseo. **Open**
9am–12.30pm, 3pm–6pm daily
(Sun opening at 10am); last adm:
30 mins before closing. **Adm
charge** to excavations.

**★ Triclinium and
Altar of Mithras**
The altar, with a
relief of Mithras
slaying the bull,
stands in the
triclinium, a room
used for ritual
banquets.

**Temple of
Mithras**

**★ 11th-
Century
Frescoes**
Commissioned by
the de Rapiza family,
one shows the story of a boy
found alive in St Clement's
tomb beneath the Black Sea.

Catacomb
Discovered in
1938 and dating
from the 5th or 6th
century, it contains
16 wall tombs
known as loculi.

STAR FEATURES

★ Cappella di Santa
Caterina

★ Apse Mosaic

★ Triclinium and Altar
of Mithras

★ 11th-Century
Frescoes

IOVINVSALVMNVS

CARACALLA

**Capital from ruins of
Baths of Caracalla**

THE CELIAN HILL overlooks the Colosseum, and takes its name from Caelius Vibenna, the legendary hero of Rome's struggle against the Tarquins *(see pp16–17)*. In Imperial Rome this was a fashionable place to live, and some of its vanished splendour is still apparent in the vast ruins of the Baths of Caracalla. Today, thanks to the Archaeological Zone established at the turn of the 20th century, it is a peaceful area, a green wedge from the Aurelian Wall to the heart of the city. Through it runs the cobbled Via di Porta San Sebastiano, part of the old Via Appia. This road leads to Porta San Sebastiano, one of the best-preserved gates in the ancient city wall.

SIGHTS AT A GLANCE

Churches
Santi Giovanni e Paolo ❶
San Gregorio Magno ❷
Santa Maria in Domnica ❹
San Sisto Vecchio ❻
Santi Nereo e Achilleo ❼
San Cesareo ❽
San Giovanni a Porta Latina ❾
San Giovanni in Oleo ❿
Santa Balbina ⓰

Arches and Gates
Arch of Dolabella ❸
Arch of Drusus ⓭
Aurelian Wall and
  Porta San Sebastiano ⓮
Sangallo Bastion ⓯

Historic Buildings
Baths of Caracalla ⓱

Tombs
Columbarium of
  Pomponius Hylas ⓫
Tomb of the Scipios ⓬

Parks and Gardens
Villa Celimontana ❺

GETTING THERE
Circo Massimo Metro station is handy if you are visiting the churches and parks on the Celian hill. For the Baths of Caracalla and other sights closer to Porta San Sebastiano, take the 628 along Viale delle Terme di Caracalla.

SEE ALSO
• *Street Finder*, maps 8, 9

• *Where to Stay* pp294–5

• *Restaurants* pp310–11

(map)

PIAZZA DEL
COLOSSEO

0 metres   300
0 yards   300

KEY

▨ Street-by-Street map

— City Wall

Ⓜ Metro station

Ⓟ Parking

Mosaic of an athlete from the Baths of Caracalla

Street-by-Street: The Celian Hill

IN THE COURSE OF A MORNING exploring the green
slopes of the Celian hill, you will see a fascinating
assortment of archaeological remains and beautiful
churches. A good starting point is the church of San
Gregorio Magno, from where the Clivo di Scauro leads
up to the top of the hill. The steep narrow street passes
the ancient porticoed church of Santi Giovanni e Paolo
with its beautiful Romanesque bell tower soaring above
the surrounding medieval monastery buildings. Of the
parks on the hill, the best kept and most peaceful is the
Villa Celimontana with its formal walks and avenues.
It is a good place for a
picnic, as there
are few bars or
restaurants
in the area.

Clivo di Scauro, the
Roman *Clivus Scauri*, leads
up to Santi Giovanni e
Paolo, passing under
the flying buttresses
that support
the church.

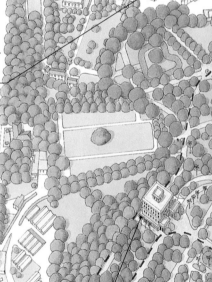

VIA DI SAN GREGORIO

CLIVO DI SCAURO

**To Circo
Massimo
Metro**

La Vignola is a
delightful Renaissance
pavilion, reconstructed
here in 1911 after it
had been demolished
during the creation of
the Archaeological
Zone around the
Baths of Caracalla.

**San Gregorio
Magno**
*A monastery and
chapel were
founded here by
Pope Gregory the
Great at the end of
the 6th century* ❷

★ **Santi Giovanni e Paolo**
*The nave of the church, lit by a blaze
of chandeliers, has been restored
many times, assuming its present
appearance in the 18th century* ❶

★ **Villa Celimontana**
*The delightful 16th-
century villa built for the
Mattei family is now the
centre of a public park* ❺

Trams passing over the Celian hill from the Colosseum rumble up a picturesque narrow track through the Parco del Celio.

LOCATOR MAP
See Central Rome Map pp12–13

Ruins of the Temple of Claudius are visible over a large area of the Celian hill. These travertine blocks have been incorporated in the base of the bell tower of Santi Giovanni e Paolo.

The gateway of San Tommaso in Formis is decorated with a wonderful 13th-century mosaic showing Christ with two freed slaves, one white, one black.

Arch of Dolabella
Built in the 1st century AD, probably as an entrance to the city, this archway was later incorporated in Nero's aqueduct to the Palatine ❸

★ Santa Maria in Domnica
This church is famed for its 9th-century mosaics. These Apostles appear on the triumphal arch above the apse, flanking a medallion containing the figure of Christ ❹

STAR SIGHTS

★ **Santi Giovanni e Paolo**

★ **Villa Celimontana**

★ **Santa Maria in Domnica**

KEY

- - - Suggested route

0 metres   75

0 yards   75

Santi Giovanni e Paolo ❶

Piazza Santi Giovanni e Paolo 13.
Map 9 A1. ☎ *06-772 711.*
🚌 *75, 81, 117, 175, 673.* 🚋 *3.*
Ⓜ *Colosseo or Circo Massimo.*
Open *8.30am–noon, 3.30pm–*
6pm Mon–Sat; 8.30am–12.45pm,
3.30pm–7pm Sun. For timetable
for Roman House, ring 06-7045
4544. 🚻 🚻 *church only.*

Sᴀɴᴛɪ ɢɪᴏᴠᴀɴɴɪ ᴇ ᴘᴀᴏʟᴏ is dedicated to two martyred Roman officers whose house stood on this site. Giovanni (John) and Paolo (Paul) had served the first Christian emperor, Constantine. When they were later called to arms by the pagan emperor Julian the Apostate, they refused and were beheaded in their own house in AD 362.

Built towards the end of the 4th century, the church retains many elements of its original structure. The Ionic portico dates from the 12th century, and the apse and bell tower were added by Nicholas Breakspeare, the only English pope, who reigned as Adrian IV (1154–9). The base of the superb 13th-century Romanesque bell tower was part of the Temple of Claudius that stood on this site. The interior, remodelled in 1718, has granite piers and columns. A tomb slab in the nave marks the burial place of the martyrs, whose relics are preserved in an urn under the high altar. In a tiny room near the altar, a magnificent 13th-century fresco depicts the figure of Christ flanked by his Apostles (ask the sacristan to unlock the door for you).

Excavations beneath the church have revealed two 2nd- and 3rd-century Roman houses used as a Christian burial place. These are well worth a visit. The two-storey construction, with 20 rooms and a labyrinth of corridors, has well-preserved pagan and Christian paintings. The arches to the left of the church were part of a 3rd-century street of shops.

Fresco of Christ and the Apostles in Santi Giovanni e Paolo

San Gregorio Magno ❷

Piazza di San Gregorio. **Map** 8 F2.
☎ *06-700 8227.* 🚌 *75, 81, 117,*
175, 673. 🚋 *3.* Ⓜ *Circo Massimo.*
Open *9am–1pm, 3–6pm daily.* 🚻

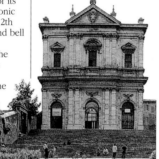

Façade of San Gregorio Magno

Tᴏ ᴛʜᴇ ᴇɴɢʟɪsʜ, this is one of the most important churches in Rome, for it was from here that St Augustine was sent on his mission to convert England to Christianity. The church was founded in AD 575 by San Gregorio Magno (St Gregory the Great), who turned his family home on this site into a monastery. It was rebuilt in medieval times and restored in 1629–33 by Giovanni Battista Soria. The church is reached via a flight of steps from the street.

The forecourt contains some interesting tombs. To the left is that of Sir Edward Carne, who came to Rome several times between 1529 and 1533 as King Henry VIII's envoy to gain the pope's consent to the annulment of Henry's marriage to Catherine of Aragon.

The interior, remodelled by Francesco Ferrari in the mid-18th century, is Baroque, apart from the fine mosaic floor and some ancient columns. At the end of the right aisle is the chapel of St Gregory. Leading off it, another small chapel, believed to have been the saint's own cell, houses his episcopal throne – a Roman chair of sculpted marble. The Salviati Chapel on the left contains a picture of the Virgin said to have spoken to St Gregory.

Outside, amid the cypresses to the left of the church, stand three small chapels, dedicated to St Andrew, St Barbara and St Sylvia (Gregory the Great's mother). Recently restored, they contain frescoes by Domenichino and Guido Reni.

Marble throne of Gregory the Great from the 1st century BC

Arch of Dolabella ❸

Via di San Paolo della Croce.
Map 9 A2. 🚌 81, 117, 673.
🚋 3. Ⓜ Colosseo.

THE ARCH was built in AD 10 by consuls Caius Junius Silanus and Cornelius Dolabella, possibly on the site of one of the old Servian Wall's gateways. It was made of travertine blocks and later used to support Nero's extension of the Claudian aqueduct, built to supply the Imperial palace on the Palatine hill.

The restored Arch of Dolabella

Santa Maria in Domnica ❹

Piazza della Navicella 12.
Map 9 A2. 🄲 06-700 1519.
🚌 81,117, 673. 🚋 3. Ⓜ Colosseo.
Open 9am–noon, 3.30–6pm (winter)
4–7pm (summer) daily. 🚻 ♿

THE CHURCH overlooks the Piazza della Navicella (little boat) and takes its name from the 16th-century fountain.

Dating from the 7th century, the church was made from an ancient stone galley which was probably a temple offering of a Roman traveller for his safe return to the city. In the 16th century Pope Leo X added the portico and the coffered ceiling.

In the apse behind the modern altar is a superb 9th-century mosaic commissioned by Pope Paschal I. Wearing the square halo of the living, the pope appears at the feet of the Virgin and Child. The Virgin, surrounded by a throng of angels, holds a handkerchief like a fashionable lady at a Byzantine court.

Villa Celimontana ❺

Piazza della Navicella.
Map 9 A2. 🚌 81, 117, 673.
Park open 7am–dusk daily.

THE DUKES OF MATTEI bought this land in 1553 and transformed the vineyards that covered the hillside into a formal garden. As well as palms and other exotic trees, the garden has its own Egyptian obelisk. Villa Mattei, built in the 1580s and now known as Villa Celimontana, houses the Italian Geographical Society.

The Mattei family used to open the park to the public on the day of the Visit of the Seven Churches, an annual event instituted by San Filippo Neri in 1552. Starting from the Chiesa Nuova (see p124), Romans went on foot to the city's seven major churches and, on reaching Villa Mattei,

were given bread, wine, salami, cheese, an egg and two apples. The garden, now owned by the city of Rome, still makes an ideal place for a picnic. In summer it hosts an excellent jazz festival (see p344).

Park of Villa Celimontana

San Sisto Vecchio ❻

Piazzale Numa Pompilio 8.
Map 9 A3. 🄲 06-7720 5174.
🚌 160, 628, 671, 714.
Open 9–11am daily. 🚫

THIS SMALL CHURCH is of great historical interest as it was granted to St Dominic in 1219 by Pope Honorius III. The founder of the Dominican order soon moved his own headquarters to Santa Sabina (see p204), San Sisto becoming the first home of the order of Dominican nuns. The church, with its 13th-century bell tower and frescoes, is also a popular place for weddings.

Apse mosaic of the Virgin and Child in Santa Maria in Domnica

Santi Nereo e Achilleo ❼

Via delle Terme di Caracalla 28. **Map** 9 A3. 📞 *06-575 7996.* 🚌 *160, 628, 671, 714.* **Open** *Apr–Oct: 10am–noon, 4–6pm Wed–Mon.* ♿

ACCORDING to legend, St Peter, after escaping from prison, was fleeing the city when he lost a bandage from his wounds. The original church was founded here in the 4th century on the spot where the bandage fell, but later on it was rededicated to the 1st-century AD martyrs St Nereus and St Achilleus.

Detail of mosaic, Santi Nereo e Achilleo

Restored at the end of the 16th century, the church has retained many medieval features, including some fine 9th-century mosaics on the triumphal arch. A magnificent pulpit rests on an enormous porphyry pedestal which was found nearby in the Baths of Caracalla. The walls of the side naves are decorated with a series of rather grisly 16th-century frescoes by Niccolò Pomarancio, showing in clinical detail how each of the Apostles was martyred.

Fresco by Niccolò Pomarancio of the *Martyrdom of St Simon* in Santi Nereo e Achilleo

San Cesareo ❽

Via di Porta San Sebastiano. **Map** 9 A3. 📞 *06-5823 0140.* 🚌 *218, 628.* **Open** *9am–noon Sun & by appt.*

THIS SPLENDID old church was built over Roman ruins of the 2nd century AD. You can still admire Giacomo della Porta's fine Renaissance façade, but by phoning ahead to book a visit, you can also see Cosmatesque mosaic work and carving to rival that of any church in Rome. The episcopal throne, altar and pulpit are decorated with delightful birds and beasts. The church was restored in the 16th century by Pope Clement VIII, whose coat of arms decorates the ceiling.

San Giovanni a Porta Latina ❾

Via di San Giovanni a Porta Latina. **Map** 9 B3. 📞 *06-7049 1777.* 🚌 *218, 360, 628.* **Open** *8am–12.30pm, 3–6.30pm daily.* 🚻 ♿

THE CHURCH of "St John at the Latin Gate" was founded in the 5th century, rebuilt in 720 and restored in 1191. This is one of the most picturesque of the old Roman churches. Classical columns support the medieval portico, and the 12th-century bell tower is superb. A tall cedar tree shades an ancient well standing in the forecourt. The interior has recently been restored, but it preserves the rare simplicity of its early origins with ancient columns of varying styles lining the aisles. Traces of early medieval frescoes can still be seen. There are 12th-century frescoes showing 46 different biblical scenes, from both the Old and New Testaments, which are among the finest of their kind in Rome.

Fresco, San Giovanni a Porta Latina

San Giovanni in Oleo ❿

Via di Porta Latina. **Map** 9 C4. 🚌 *628.* **Adm** *ask at S. Giovanni a Porta Latina.*

Frieze of San Giovanni in Oleo

THE NAME of this charming octagonal Renaissance chapel means "St John in Oil". The tiny building marks the spot where, according to legend, St John was boiled in oil – and came out unscathed, or even refreshed. An earlier chapel is said to have existed on the site; the present one was built in the early 16th century. The design has been attributed to Baldassare Peruzzi or Antonio da Sangallo the Younger. It was restored by Borromini, who altered the roof, crowning it with a cross supported by a sphere decorated with roses. He also added a terracotta frieze of roses and palm leaves. The wall paintings inside the chapel include one of St John in a cauldron of boiling oil.

Niches for funerary urns in the Columbarium of Pomponius Hylas

Columbarium of Pomponius Hylas ⓫

Via di Porta Latina 10. **Map** 9 B4.
🚌 *218, 360, 628.* **Open** *by appt only:
permit needed (see p367).*

KNOWN AS a columbarium because it resembles a dovecote (*columba* is the Latin word for dove), this kind of vaulted tomb was usually built by rich Romans to house the cremated remains of their freedmen. Many similar tombs have been uncovered in this part of Rome, which up until the 3rd century AD lay outside the city wall. This one, ex-cavated in 1831, dates from the 1st century AD. An in-scription informs us that it

is the Tomb of Pomponius Hylas and his wife, Pomponia Vitalinis. Above her name is a "V" which indicates that she was still living when the inscription was made. The tomb was probably a commercial venture. Niches in the interior walls of the columbarium were sold to people who could not afford to build vaults of their own.

Tomb of the Scipios ⓬

Via di Porta San Sebastiano 9.
Map 9 B4. 📞 *06-6710 3819.*
🚌 *218, 360, 628.* **Open** *by appt.
Ring above number.*

THE SCIPIOS were a family of conquering generals. Southern Italy, Corsica, Algeria, Spain and Asia Minor all fell to their victorious Roman armies. The most famous of these generals was Publius Cornelius Scipio Africanus, who defeated the great Carthaginian general Hannibal at the Battle of Zama in 202 BC (*see p21*). Scipio Africanus himself was not buried here in the family tomb, but at Liternum near Naples, where he owned a favourite villa.
   The Tomb of the Scipios was discovered in 1780. It

contained various sarcophagi, statues and niches with terracotta burial urns. Many of the originals have now been moved to the Vatican Museums and copies stand in their place.
   The earliest sarcophagus was that of Cornelius Scipio Barbatus, consul in 298 BC, for whom the tomb was built. Members of his illustrious family continued to be buried here up to the middle of the 2nd century BC. Excavations in the area have revealed a columbarium similar to that of Pomponius Hylas, a Christian catacomb and a three-storey house dating from the 3rd century AD, which was built over the Tomb of the Scipios.

Arch of Drusus ⓭

Via di Porta San Sebastiano.
Map 9 B4. 🚌 *218, 360.*

Arch of Drusus, part of the Aqua Antoniniana aqueduct

ONCE MISTAKENLY identified as a triumphal arch, the so-called Arch of Drusus merely supported the branch aqueduct that supplied the Baths of Caracalla. It was built in the 3rd century AD, so had no connection with Drusus, a stepson of the Emperor Augustus. Its monumental appearance was due to the fact that it carried the aqueduct across the important route, Via Appia. The arch still spans the old cobbled road, just 50 m (160 ft) short of the gateway Porta San Sebastiano.

**Mosaic inscription in the
Columbarium of Pomponius Hylas**

Aurelian Wall and Porta San Sebastiano ⑭

Museo delle Mura, Via di Porta San Sebastiano 18. **Map** 9 B4. 218, 360. 06-7047 5284. **Open** winter: 9am–7pm Tue–Sun (closes 5pm Sun); summer: 9am–2pm Tue–Sun. Last adm: 30 mins before closing. **Closed** 1 Jan, 1 May, 25 Dec. **Adm charge**.

Most of the Aurelian Wall, begun by the emperor Aurelian (AD 270–75) and completed by his successor Probus (AD 276–82), has survived. Aurelian ordered its construction as a defence against Germanic tribes, whose raids were penetrating deeper and deeper into Italy. Some 18 km (11 miles) round, with 18 gates and 381 towers, the wall took in all the seven hills of Rome. It was raised to almost twice its original height by Maxentius (AD 306–12).

The wall was Rome's main defence until 1870, when it was breached by Italian artillery just by Porta Pia, close to today's British Embassy. Many of the gates are still in use, although the city has spread, most of its noteworthy historical and cultural sights still lie within the walls.

Porta San Sebastiano, the gate leading to the Via Appia Antica (see p284), is the largest and best-preserved gateway in the Aurelian Wall. It was rebuilt by Emperor Honorius in the 5th century AD. Originally the Porta Appia, in Christian times it gradually became known as the Porta San Sebastiano, because the Via Appia led to the Basilica and Catacombs of San Sebastiano, which were popular places of pilgrimage.

It was at this gate that the last triumphal procession to enter the city by the Appian Way was received in state – that of Marcantonio Colonna after the victory of Lepanto over the Turkish fleet in 1571. Today the gate's towers house a museum with prints and models showing the walls' history. From here you can take a walk along the restored walls. The views are spectacular.

Pope Paul III Farnese

Sangallo Bastion ⑮

Viale di Porta Ardeatina. **Map** 9 A4. 160. **Closed** for restoration.

Haunted by the memory of the Sack of Rome in 1527 and fearing attack by the Turks, Pope Paul III asked Antonio da Sangallo the Younger to reinforce the Aurelian Wall. Work on the huge projecting bastion began in 1537. For the moment its massive bulk can only be admired from outside.

The high altar of Santa Balbina

Santa Balbina ⑯

Piazza di Santa Balbina 8. **Map** 8 F3. 06-578 0207. 160. 3. **M** Circo Massimo. **Open** 8.30–11.30am Sat & Sun.

Overlooking the Baths of Caracalla, this isolated church is dedicated to Santa Balbina, a 2nd-century virgin martyr. It is one of the oldest in Rome, dating back to the fifth century, and was built on the remains of a Roman villa. Consecrated by Pope Gregory the Great, in the Middle Ages Santa Balbina was a fortified monastery and over time has changed in appearance several times, regaining its Roman-esque aspect in the 1920s.

From the piazza in front of the church, a staircase leads up to a three-arched portico. Inside, light streams in from a series of high windows along the length of the nave. The remains of St Balbina and her father, St Quirinus, are in an urn at the high altar, though the church's real treasure is situated in the far right hand corner: the magnificent sculpted and inlaid tomb of Cardinal Stefanis de Surdis by Giovanni di Cosma (1303).

Other features worth noting are a 13th-century episcopal throne and various fragments of frescoes. These include a lovely Madonna and Child, an example of the school of Pietro Cavallini, in the second chapel on the left. Fragments of first-century Roman mosaics were also discovered in the 1930s. Depicting birds and signs of the zodiac, these are now set in the church floor.

Fortified gateway of Porta San Sebastiano

Baths of Caracalla ⑰

Viale delle Terme di Caracalla 52. **Map**
9 A3. 🚗 06-3996 7700. 🚌 160,
628. 🚋 3. Ⓜ *Circo Massimo.* **Open**
*9am–1hr before sunset Tue–Sun; 9am–
2pm Mon.* **Closed** *1 Jan, 25 Dec.*
Adm charge. 🅿 🚻 ♿

Part of one of the gymnasia in the Baths of Caracalla

COMPLETED by Emperor
Caracalla in AD 217, the
baths functioned for about
300 years, until the plumbing
was destroyed by invading
Goths. Over 1,600 bathers at a
time could enjoy the facilities.
A Roman bath was a serious
business, beginning with a
sort of Turkish bath, followed
by a spell in the *caldarium*,
a large hot
room with
pools of water
to provide
humidity.
Then came
the lukewarm
tepidarium,
a visit to the
large central
meeting place,
known as the
frigidarium, and finally a
plunge into the *natatio*,
an open-air swimming
pool. For the rich,

**Fragment of
mosaic pavement**

this was followed by a rub-
down with scented woollen
cloth. As well as the baths,
there were spaces for
exercise, libraries, art galleries
and gardens – a true
leisure centre. Most
of the rich marble
decorations of the baths
were removed by the
Farnese family in the
16th century to adorn
the interior of Palazzo
Farnese *(see p147)*. Until

recently, open-air operas
were staged here – the vocal
exertions of the performers
are now thought to pose
a threat to the structure of
this ancient monument.

KEY

▢	Caldarium (very hot)
▢	Tepidarium (lukewarm)
▢	Frigidarium (cold)
▢	Natatio (pool)
▢	Garden

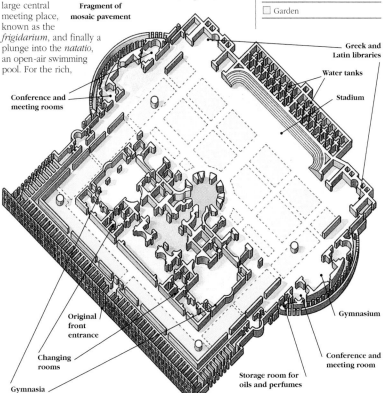

Greek and
Latin libraries

Water tanks

Stadium

Conference and
meeting rooms

Gymnasium

Original
front
entrance

Changing
rooms

Conference and
meeting room

Gymnasia

Storage room for
oils and perfumes

AVENTINE

THIS IS ONE of the most peaceful areas within the walls of the city. Although it is largely residential, there are some unique historic sights. From the top of the Aventine hill, crowned by the magnificent basilica of Santa Sabina, there are fine views across the river to Trastevere and St Peter's. At the

Mask fountain in courtyard of Santa Sabina

foot of the hill, ancient Rome is preserved in the two tiny Temples of the Forum Boarium and the Circus Maximus. The liveliest streets are in Testaccio, which has shops, restaurants and clubs, while to the south, beside Rome's solitary pyramid, the Protestant Cemetery is another oasis of calm.

SIGHTS AT A GLANCE

Churches and Temples
Santa Maria in Cosmedin ❶
San Giorgio in Velabro ❸
San Teodoro ❹
Santa Maria della
    Consolazione ❺
San Giovanni Decollato ❻
Temples of the
    Forum Boarium ❽
Santa Sabina ❾
Santi Bonifacio e Alessio ❿
San Saba ⓯

Historic Buildings
Casa dei Crescenzi ❼

Arches
Arch of Janus ❷

Historic Streets and Piazzas
Piazza dei Cavalieri di Malta ⓫

Ancient Sites
Monte Testaccio ⓬
Circus Maximus ⓰

Monuments and Tombs
Protestant Cemetery ⓭
Pyramid of Caius Cestius ⓮

GETTING THERE
The quickest way is by Metro line B to Piramide or Circo Massimo. For a more interesting trip, take tram 3. Several buses go down from Piazza Venezia, including 81, 160 and 628, while 23 and 280 run along Via Marmorata to Piramide.

KEY
▨ Street-by-Street map
— City Wall
Ⓜ Metro station
Ⓟ Parking

SEE ALSO
• *Street Finder*, maps 7, 8, 12
• *Where to Stay* pp294–5
• *Restaurants* pp310–11

0 metres   300
0 yards   300

Pines and orange trees on the Aventine hill with the dome of St Peter's in the distance

Street-by-Street: Piazza della Bocca della Verità

THE AREA ATTRACTS VISITORS eager to place their hands inside the Bocca della Verità (the Mouth of Truth) in the portico of Santa Maria in Cosmedin. There are many other sights to see in this quiet corner of the city beside the Tiber, which was the site of ancient Rome's first port and its busy cattle market. Substantial Classical remains include two small temples from the Republican age and the Arch of Janus from the later Empire. In the 6th century the area became home to a Greek community from Byzantium, who founded the churches of San Giorgio in Velabro and Santa Maria in Cosmedin.

Sant'Omobono, a late 16th-century church, now stands in isolation in the middle of an important archaeological site. The remains of sacrificial altars and two temples from the 6th century BC have been discovered.

Ponte Rotto, as this forlorn ruined arch in the Tiber is called, means simply "broken bridge". Built in the 2nd century BC, its original name was Pons Aemilius.

Casa dei Crescenzi
This 11th-century building used columns and capitals from ancient Roman temples ❼

★ **Temples of the Forum Boarium**
The tiny round Temple of Hercules and its neighbour, the Temple of Portunus, are the best preserved of Rome's Republican temples ❽

LUNGOTEVERE DEI PIERLEONI

TEVERE

PONTE PALATINO

KEY

- - - Suggested route

0 metres   75
0 yards   75

STAR SIGHTS

★ Santa Maria in Cosmedin

★ Temples of the Forum Boarium

★ **Santa Maria in Cosmedin**
This medieval church has a fine marble mosaic floor and a Gothic baldacchino ❶

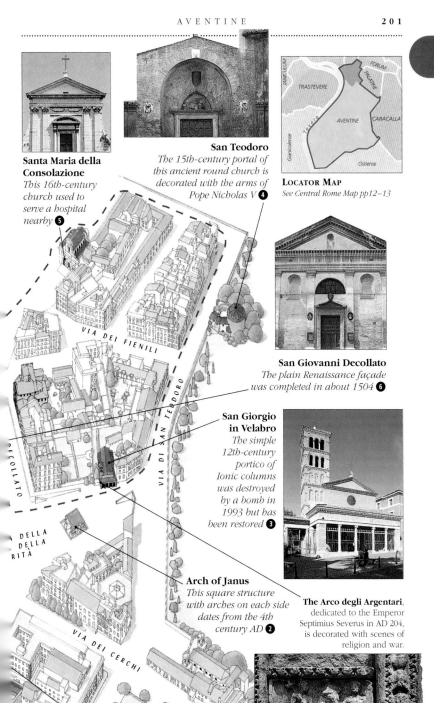

Santa Maria della Consolazione
This 16th-century church used to serve a hospital nearby ❺

San Teodoro
The 15th-century portal of this ancient round church is decorated with the arms of Pope Nicholas V ❹

LOCATOR MAP
See Central Rome Map pp12–13

San Giovanni Decollato
The plain Renaissance façade was completed in about 1504 ❻

San Giorgio in Velabro
The simple 12th-century portico of Ionic columns was destroyed by a bomb in 1993 but has been restored ❸

Arch of Janus
This square structure with arches on each side dates from the 4th century AD ❷

The Arco degli Argentari, dedicated to the Emperor Septimius Severus in AD 204, is decorated with scenes of religion and war.

The Fontana dei Tritoni by Carlo Bizzaccheri was built here in 1715. The style shows the powerful influence of Bernini.

Luminous interior of Santa Sabina

Santa Sabina ❾

Piazza Pietro d'Illiria 1.
Map 8 E2. **C** 06-5794 0600.
🚌 23, 280, 716. **M** Circo Massimo.
Open 6.30am–12.45pm, 3.30–7pm daily. ♿

HIGH ON the Aventine stands an early Christian basilica, founded by Peter of Illyria in AD 425 and restored to its original simplicity in the early 20th century. Light filters through 9th-century windows upon a wide nave framed by white Corinthian columns supporting an arcade decorated with a marble frieze. Over the main door is a 5th-century blue and gold mosaic dedicatory inscription. The pulpit, carved choir and bishop's throne date from the 9th century.

The church was given to the Dominicans in the 13th century and in the nave is the magnificent mosaic tombstone of one of the first leaders of the order, Muñoz de Zamora (died 1300).

The side portico has 5th-century panelled doors carved from cypress wood, representing scenes from the Bible, including one of the earliest Crucifixions in existence.

Santi Bonifacio e Alessio ❿

Piazza di Sant'Alessio 23.
Map 8 D2. **C** 06-574 3446.
🚌 23, 280, 716. **M** Circo Massimo.
Open 8am–8.30pm daily. ♿

THE CHURCH is dedicated to two early Christian martyrs, whose remains lie under the main altar. Legend has it that Alessio, son of a rich senator living on the site, fled East to avoid an impending marriage and become a pilgrim. Returning home after many years, he died as a servant, unrecognized, under the stairs of the family entrance hall, clutching the manuscript of his story for posterity.

The original 5th-century church has undergone many changes over time. Noteworthy are the 18th-century façade with its five arches, the restored Cosmati doorway and pavement, and the magnificent Romanesque five-storey bell tower (1217).

An 18th-century Baroque chapel by Andrea Bergondi houses part of the famous staircase. Other relics include the well from Alessio's family home and the glowing Byzantine Madonna of the Intercession brought from Damascus to Rome at the end of the 10th century.

Piazza dei Cavalieri di Malta ⓫

Map 8 D2. 🚌 23, 280, 716.
M Circo Massimo.

SURROUNDED BY cypress trees, this ornate walled piazza decorated with obelisks and military trophies was designed by Piranesi in 1765. It is named after the Order of the Knights of Malta (Cavalieri di Malta), whose priory (at No. 3) is famous for the bronze keyhole through which there is a miniature view of St Peter's, framed by a tree-lined avenue. The priory church, Santa Maria del Priorato, was restored in Neo-Classical style by Piranesi in the 18th century. To visit the church, ask permission in person at the Order's building at 48 Via Condotti. At the southwest corner of the square is Sant'Anselmo, the international Benedictine church, where Gregorian chant may be heard on Sundays (see p342).

Doorway of the Priory of the Knights of Malta

Monte Testaccio ⓬

Via Galvani. **Map** 8 D4. **M** Piramide.
🚌 23, 95, 673. 🚋 3. **Open** by appt only (see p367).

FROM ABOUT 140 BC to AD 250 this hill was created by dumping millions of testae (hence Testaccio) – pieces of the amphorae used to carry goods to nearby warehouses. The full archaeological significance of this 36-m (118-ft) high artificial hill was not realized until the late 18th century.

Façade of Santi Bonifacio e Alessio

Protestant Cemetery ⑬

Cimitero Acattolico, Via Caio Cestio 6.
Map 8 D4. ☎ 06-574 1900. ⬛ 23,
95, 280. ⬛ 3. Ⓜ Piramide. **Open**
9am–4.30pm (Oct–Mar: 3.30pm)
Tue–Sat, 9am–2pm Sun. **Donation**
expected. ◻

THE PEACE of this well-tended
cemetery beneath the
Aurelian Wall is profoundly
moving. Non-Catholics, mainly
English and German, have
been buried here since 1738.
In the oldest part are
the graves of John
Keats (died 1821),
whose epitaph reads:
"Here lies One
Whose Name was
writ in Water", and
his friend Joseph
Severn (died 1879);
not far away are the
ashes of Percy
Bysshe Shelley
(died 1822).

Goethe's son
Julius is also
buried here.

Tombstone of John Keats

Pyramid of Caius Cestius ⑭

Piazzale Ostiense. **Map** 8 E4. ⬛ 23,
95, 280. ⬛ 3. Ⓜ Piramide.

Memorial pyramid of Caius Cestius

CAIUS CESTIUS, a wealthy
praetor (senior Roman
magistrate), died in 12 BC.
His one claim to fame is his
tomb, an imposing pyramid
faced with white marble set in
the Aurelian Wall near Porta
San Paolo. It stands 36 m
(118 ft) high and, according to
an inscription, took 330 days
to build. Unmistakable as a
landmark, it must have looked
almost as incongruous when
it was built as it does today.

**Detail of carving on sarcophagus
in the portico of San Saba**

San Saba ⑮

Via di San Saba.
Map 8 F3. ☎ 06-574 3352.
⬛ 75, 175, 673. ⬛ 3.
Open 9.30am–noon, 4–7pm daily. ◻

TUCKED AWAY in a residential
street on the Little Aventine
hill, San Saba began life as an
oratory for Palestinian monks
fleeing from Arab invasions in
the 7th century. The existing
church dates from the 10th
century and has undergone
much restoration. The portico
houses a fascinating collection
of archaeological remains.
The church has three naves
in the Greek style and a short
fourth 11th-century nave to
the left with vestiges of 13th-
century frescoes of the life of
St Nicholas of Bari. Particularly
intriguing is a scene of three
naked young ladies lying in
bed, who are saved from
penury by the gift of a bag of
gold from St Nicholas, the
future Santa Claus. The
beautiful marble inlay in the
main door, the floor and the
remains of the choir are all
13th-century Cosmati work.

Circus Maximus ⑯

Via del Circo Massimo.
Map 8 F2. ⬛ 81, 160, 628, 715.
⬛ 3. Ⓜ Circo Massimo.

WHAT WAS ONCE ancient
Rome's largest stadium is
today little more than a long
grassy esplanade. Set in the
valley between the Palatine
and Aventine hills, the Circus
Maximus was continually
embellished and expanded
from the 4th century BC until
AD 549 when the last races
were held. The grandstands
held some 300,000 spectators,
cheering wildly at the horse
and chariot races, athletic
contests and wild animal fights,
betting furiously throughout.
The Circus had a central
dividing barrier *(spina)* with
seven large egg-shaped objects
on it used for counting the
laps of a race. These were
joined in 33 BC by seven
bronze dolphins that served a
similar purpose. In 10 BC
Augustus built the Imperial
box under the Palatine and
decorated the *spina* with the
obelisk that now stands in the
centre of Piazza del Popolo
(see p137). A second obelisk,
which was added in the 4th
century by Constantine II, is
now in Piazza di San Giovanni
in Laterano *(see pp178–9)*.

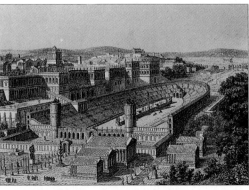

Reconstruction of the Circus Maximus in its heyday

TRASTEVERE

HE PROUD and aggressively independent inhabitants of Trastevere, the area "across the Tiber", consider themselves the most authentic Romans. In one of the most picturesque old quarters of the city, it is still possible to glimpse scenes of everyday life that seem to belong to bygone centuries. There are, however, signs that much of the earthy, proletarian character of the place may soon be destroyed by the proliferation of fashionable restau-

Romanesque bell tower

rants, clubs and boutiques. Some of Rome's most fascinating medieval churches lie hidden away in the patchwork of narrow, cobbled backstreets, the only clue to their location an occasional glimpse of a Romanesque bell tower. Santa Cecilia was built on the site of the martyrdom of the patron saint of music, San Francesco a Ripa commemorates St Francis of Assisi's visit to Rome, and Santa Maria in Trastevere is the traditional centre of the spiritual and social life of the area.

SIGHTS AT A GLANCE

Churches
Santa Maria della Scala ❸
Santa Maria in Trastevere pp212–13 ❺
San Crisogono ❻
Santa Cecilia in Trastevere ❽
San Francesco a Ripa ❿

Museums and Galleries
Sant'Egidio and Museo di Roma in Trastevere ❹

Historic Buildings
Casa della Fornarina ❶
Caserma dei Vigili della VII Coorte ❼
San Michele a Ripa Grande ❾

Bridges
Ponte Sisto ❷

Parks and Gardens
Villa Sciarra ⓫

KEY

	Street-by-Street map
—	City Wall
P	Parking
i	Tourist information

GETTING THERE
The most convenient way is to take tram 8 which starts from Largo di Torre Argentina, crosses the river and runs along the broad, busy Viale di Trastevere. The H bus follows the same route but starts at Stazione Termini. From the Vatican it is best to take a 23 or 280 along Lungotevere.

0 metres   300

0 yards   300

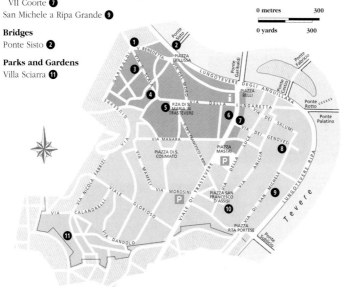

A typical *vicolo* (narrow alleyway) between the densely packed buildings of Trastevere

Street-by-Street: Trastevere

Aᴌᴌ ʏᴇᴀʀ ʀᴏᴜɴᴅ ᴛʀᴀsᴛᴇᴠᴇʀᴇ is a major attraction both for its restaurants, clubs and cinemas, and for its picturesque maze of narrow cobbled alleyways. On summer evenings the streets are packed with jostling groups of pleasure-seekers, especially during the noisy local festival, the Festa de Noantri (see p59). Everywhere café and restaurant tables spill out over pavements, especially around Piazza di Santa Maria in Trastevere and outside the pizzerias along Viale di Trastevere. There are also kiosks selling slices of watermelon and *grattachecca*, a mixture of syrup and grated ice. It is usually easier to appreciate the antique charm of Trastevere's narrow streets in the more tranquil atmosphere of the early morning.

Casa della Fornarina
Raphael's beautiful mistress is said to have lived here. There is now a flourishing restaurant in the back garden ❶

Santa Maria dei Sette Dolori
This church (1643) is a minor work by Borromini.

Santa Maria della Scala
The church's unassuming façade conceals a rich Baroque interior ❸

Sant'Egidio and Museo del Folklore
This 17th-century fresco of Sant' Egidio by Pomarancio decorates the left-hand chapel in the church. The convent next door is a museum of Roman life and customs ❹

★ **Santa Maria in Trastevere**
The church is famous for its mosaics by Pietro Cavallini but it also has earlier works such as this mosaic of the prophet Isaiah to the left of the apse ❺

Star Sight

★ **Santa Maria in Trastevere**

Key

- - -   Suggested route

| 0 metres | 75 |
| 0 yards | 75 |

The fountain of Piazza di Santa Maria in Trastevere by Carlo Fontana (1692) is a popular meeting place. At night it is floodlit and dozens of young people sit on the steps around its octagonal base.

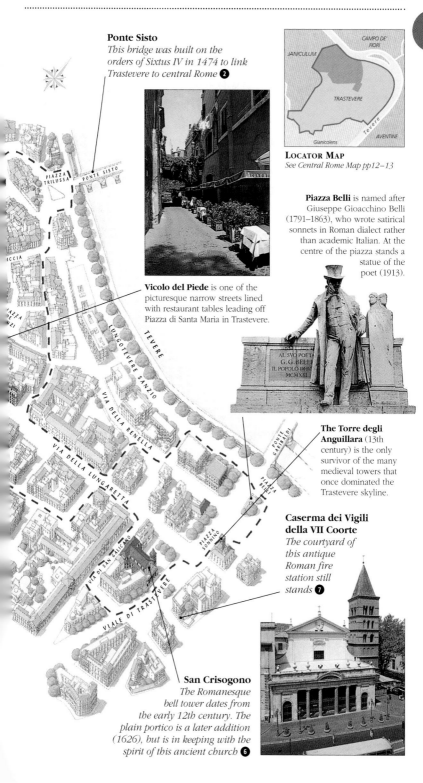

Ponte Sisto
This bridge was built on the orders of Sixtus IV in 1474 to link Trastevere to central Rome ❷

LOCATOR MAP
See Central Rome Map pp12–13

Piazza Belli is named after Giuseppe Gioacchino Belli (1791–1863), who wrote satirical sonnets in Roman dialect rather than academic Italian. At the centre of the piazza stands a statue of the poet (1913).

Vicolo del Piede is one of the picturesque narrow streets lined with restaurant tables leading off Piazza di Santa Maria in Trastevere.

The Torre degli Anguillara (13th century) is the only survivor of the many medieval towers that once dominated the Trastevere skyline.

Caserma dei Vigili della VII Coorte
The courtyard of this antique Roman fire station still stands ❼

San Crisogono
The Romanesque bell tower dates from the early 12th century. The plain portico is a later addition (1626), but is in keeping with the spirit of this ancient church ❻

Casa della Fornarina ❶

Via di Santa Dorotea 20. **Map** 4 D5 & 11 B5. 🚌 *23, 280. See Restaurants p316.*

NOT MUCH is known about Raphael's model and lover, La Fornarina, yet over the centuries she has acquired a name, Margherita, and even a biography. Her father was a Sienese baker (*la fornarina* means the baker's girl) and his shop was here in Trastevere near Raphael's frescoes in the Villa Farnesina (*see pp220–21*).

Margherita earned a reputation as a "fallen woman" and Raphael, wishing to be absolved before dying, turned her away from his deathbed. After his death she took refuge in the convent of Santa Apollonia in Trastevere.

She is assumed to have been the model for Raphael's famous portrait *La Donna Velata* in the Palazzo Pitti in Florence.

Ponte Sisto ❷

Map 4 E5 & 11 B5. 🚌 *23, 280.*

NAMED AFTER Pope Sixtus IV della Rovere (reigned 1471–84), who commissioned it, this bridge was built by Baccio Pontelli to replace an ancient Roman bridge. The enterprising pope also built the Sistine Chapel (*see pp244–7*), the Hospital of Santo Spirito (*see p226*) and restored many churches and monuments. This put him in great financial difficulties and he had to sell personal collections in order to finance his projects.

Another method of financing projects was to levy a tax on the city's prostitutes. Several popes are known to have resorted to this unpopular form of taxation.

Pope Sixtus IV

Gilded Baroque altar of Santa Maria della Scala

Santa Maria della Scala ❸

Piazza della Scala 23. **Map** 4 D5 & 11 B5. 📞 *06-580 6233.* 🚌 *23, 280.* **Church open** *9am–noon, 3.30–6pm daily.* 🛉

THIS CHURCH belongs to a time of great building activity that lasted about 30 years from the end of the 16th to the early 17th century. Its rather simple façade contrasts with a rich interior decorated with multicoloured marbles and a number of spirited Baroque altars and reliefs.

Sant'Egidio and Museo di Roma in Trastevere ❹

Piazza Sant'Egidio 1. **Map** 7 C1. 🚌 *H, 23, 280.* 🚊 *8.* **Church** 📞 *06-58 56 61. Not open to the public.* **Museo di Roma in Trastevere** 📞 *06-581 6563.* **Open** *10am–7pm Tue–Sun.* 🛉

BUILT IN 1630, Sant'Egidio was the church of the adjoining Carmelite convent, one of many founded in the area to shelter the poor and destitute. The convent is now a museum, containing a wealth of material relating to the festivals, pastimes, superstitions and customs of the Romans when they lived under papal rule.

There are old paintings and prints of the city and tableaux showing scenes of everyday life in 18th- and 19th-century Rome, including reconstructions of shops and a tavern.

The museum also has manuscripts by the much-loved poets Belli and Trilussa who wrote in local dialect.

Watercolour of public scribe (1880) in the Museo di Roma in Trastevere

Santa Maria in Trastevere ❺

See pp212–13.

San Crisogono ❻

Piazza Sonnino 44. **Map** 7 C1. 📞 *06-581 82 25.* 🚌 *H, 23, 280, 780.* 🚊 *8.* **Open** *7–11.30am, 4.15–7.30pm, Mon–Sat; 8.30am–1pm, 4.15–7.30pm Sun.* **Adm charge** *for excavations.* 🛉 🛈

THIS CHURCH was built on the site of one of the city's oldest *tituli* (private houses used for Christian worship). An 8th-century church with 11th-century frescoes can still be seen beneath the present church. This dates from the early 12th century, a period of intense building activity in Rome. San Crisogono was decorated by

Apse mosaic in San Crisogono

Pietro Cavallini – the apse mosaic remains. Most of the columns were taken from previous buildings, including the great porphyry ones of the triumphal arch. The mosaic floor is the result of recycling precious marble from various Roman ruins.

Caserma dei Vigili della VII Coorte ❼

Via della VII Coorte.
Map 7 C1. ☎ *06-6710 3819.*
🚌 *H, 23, 280, 780.* 🚊 *8.*
Open by appt.

NOT ALL ROMAN RUINS are Imperial villas or grand temples; one that illustrates the daily life of a busy city is the barracks of the guards of the VII Coorte, the Roman fire brigade. It was built under Augustus's reign, in the 1st century AD, and the excavated courtyard is where the men would rest while waiting for an alarm.

Santa Cecilia in Trastevere ❽

Piazza di Santa Cecilia.
Map 8 D1. ☎ *06-589 9289.*
🚌 *H, 23, 44, 280.* 🚊 *8.* **Open**
9.30am–12.30pm daily.
Adm charge for excavations.
Cavallini fresco can be seen
10.15am–12.15pm daily.

ST CECILIA, ARISTOCRAT and patron saint of music, was martyred here in AD 230. After an attempt at scalding her to death, she was beheaded. A church was founded – perhaps in the 4th century – on the site of her house. (The house, beneath the church with the remains of a Roman tannery, is well worth a visit.) Her body turned up in the Catacombs of San Callisto *(see p265)* and was buried here in the 9th century by Pope Paschal I, who rebuilt the church. A fine apse mosaic survives from this period.

The altar canopy by Arnolfo di Cambio and the fresco of *The Last Judgment* by Pietro Cavallini, reached through the adjoining convent, date from the 13th century, one of the few periods when Rome had

Detail of 13th-century fresco by Pietro Cavallini in Santa Cecilia

a distinctive artistic style of its own. In front of the altar is a statue of St Cecilia by Stefano Maderno, who used her miraculously preserved remains as a model when she was briefly disinterred in 1599.

San Michele a Ripa Grande ❾

Via di San Michele. **Map** 8 D2.
☎ *06-584 31.* 🚌 *23, 44, 75, 280.*
Open for special exhibitions only.

THIS HUGE, IMPOSING complex, now housing the Ministry of Culture, stretches 300 m (985 ft) along the river Tiber. It was built on the initiative of Pope Innocent XII and contained a home for the elderly, a boys' reform school, a woollen mill

and various chapels. Today contemporary exhibitions are often held here.

San Francesco a Ripa ❿

Piazza San Francesco d'Assisi 88.
Map 7 C2. ☎ *06-581 9020.* 🚌 *H, 23, 44, 75, 280.* 🚊 *8.* **Open**
*7am–noon, 4–7pm Mon–Sat,
7am–1pm, 4–7.30pm Sun.* 🚻 ♿

ST FRANCIS OF ASSISI lived here in a hospice when he visited Rome in 1219 and his stone pillow and crucifix are preserved in his cell. The church was rebuilt by his follower, the nobleman Rodolfo Anguillara, who is portrayed on his tombstone wearing the Franciscan habit.

Entirely rebuilt in the 1680s by Cardinal Pallavicini, the church is rich in sculptures. Particularly flamboyant are the 18th-century Rospigliosi and Pallavicini monuments in the transept chapel.

The Paluzzi-Albertoni chapel (fourth on the left, along the nave) contains Bernini's breathtaking *Ecstasy of Beata Ludovica Albertoni.*

Villa Sciarra ⓫

Via Calandrelli 35. **Map** 7 B2. 🚌 *44, 75.* **Park open** 9am–sunset daily.
House closed for restoration. ♿

IN ROMAN TIMES the site of this small, attractive public park was a nymph's sanctuary. It is especially picturesque in spring when its wisterias are in full bloom. The paths through the park are decorated with Romantic follies, fountains and statues, and there are splendid views over the bastions of the Janiculum.

Bernini's *Ecstasy of Beata Ludovica Albertoni* (1674) in San Francesco a Ripa

Santa Maria in Trastevere ❺

Probably the first official Christian place of worship to be built in Rome, this basilica became the focus of devotion to the Virgin Mary. According to legend, the church was founded by Pope Callixtus I in the 3rd century, when Christianity was still a minority cult. Today's church is largely a 12th-century building, remarkable for its mosaics, in particular those by Pietro Cavallini. The 22 granite columns in the nave were taken from the ruins of ancient Roman buildings. Despite some 18th-century Baroque additions, Santa Maria has retained its medieval character. This friendly church has strong links with the local community.

Piazza Santa Maria in Trastevere
The piazza in front of the church is the traditional heart of Trastevere. Today it is surrounded by lively bars and restaurants. Carlo Fontana built the octagonal fountain in the late 17th century.

The floor, relaid in the 1870s, is a recreation of the Cosmatesque mosaic floor of the 13th century.

The bell tower was built in the 12th century. At the top is a small mosaic of the Virgin.

★ **Façade Mosaics**
The 12th-century mosaic shows Mary feeding the baby Jesus and ten women holding lamps. Eight of the lamps are lit, symbolizing virginity; the veiled women whose lamps have gone out are probably widows.

STAR FEATURES

★ **Façade Mosaics**

★ **Cavallini Mosaics**

MODEST DONORS
Many of Rome's mosaics include a portrait of the pope or cardinal responsible for the building of the church. Often the portrait is dwarfed by the rest of the picture, which glorifies the saint to whom the church is dedicated. On the façade of Santa Maria, two tiny unidentified figures kneel at the Virgin's feet. Were they to stand up, the men would barely reach her knees.

Façade mosaic, detail

The portico was remodelled in 1702 by Carlo Fontana. Statues of four popes decorate the balustrade above.

Front entrance

15th-century wall tabernacle by Mino del Reame

Apse Mosaic
The 12th-century mosaic in the basin of the apse shows the Coronation of the Virgin. She sits on Christ's right hand, surrounded by saints.

VISITORS' CHECKLIST

Piazza Santa Maria in Trastevere.
Map 7 C1. ☎ 06-581 4802.
🚌 H & 780 to Piazza S. Sonnino, 23 & 280 along Lungotevere Sanzio. 🚊 8.
Open 7am–9pm daily.
✝ 5.30pm daily. ♿ ⬛

★ **Cavallini Mosaics**
The details in the six mosaics of the Life of the Virgin (1291) display a touching realism.

Madonna della Clemenza
The life-size icon probably dates from the 7th century. A replica is displayed above the altar of the Cappella Altemps.

Tomb of Cardinal Pietro Stefaneschi
The last of his line, Pietro Stefaneschi died in 1417. His tomb is by an otherwise unknown sculptor called Paolo.

TIMELINE

AD 217–22 Church founded by Pope Callixtus I	*Pope Innocent II*	**1291** Pietro Cavallini adds mosaics of scenes from the life of the Virgin for his patron, Bertoldo Stefaneschi	**1617** Domenichino designs coffered ceiling with octagonal panel of the Assumption of the Virgin

30 BC	**AD 200**		**1400**	**1650**	**1900**

38 BC Jet of mineral oil spouts from the ground on this site. Later interpreted as a portent of the coming of Christ	**c1138** Pope Innocent II starts rebuilding the church	**1580** Martino Longhi the Elder restores church and builds family chapel for Cardinal Marco Sittico Altemps	**1702** Pope Clement XI has portico rebuilt
			1866–77 Church restored by Virginio Vespignani

JANICULUM

OVERLOOKING THE TIBER on the Trastevere side of the river, the Janiculum hill has often played its part in the defence of the city. The last occasion was in 1849 when Garibaldi held off the attacking French troops. The park at the top of the hill is filled with monuments to Garibaldi and his men. A popular place for walks, the park provides a welcome escape from the densely packed streets of Trastevere.

Puppets in the park at the top of the Janiculum hill

You will often find puppet shows and other kinds of amusements for children. In medieval times most of the hill was occupied by monasteries and convents. Bramante built his miniature masterpiece, the Tempietto, in the convent of San Pietro in Montorio. The Renaissance also saw the development of the riverside area along Via della Lungara, where the rich and powerful built beautiful houses such as the Villa Farnesina.

SIGHTS AT A GLANCE

Churches and Temples
Sant'Onofrio **6**
San Pietro in Montorio **7**
Tempietto **8**

Museums and Galleries
Palazzo Corsini and Galleria Nazionale d'Arte Antica **2**

Historic Buildings
Villa Farnesina
pp220–21 **1**

Fountains
Fontana dell'Acqua Paola **9**

Monuments
Garibaldi Monument **5**

Arches and Gates
Porta Settimiana **3**

Parks and Gardens
Botanical Gardens **4**

SEE ALSO

- *Street Finder*, maps 3, 4, 7, 11
- *Where to Stay* pp294–5
- *Restaurants* pp310–11

GETTING THERE

The Janiculum (Il Gianicolo) is not the easiest part of Rome to reach by public transport. It can be approached either from the Vatican area *(see p223)* or from Trastevere *(see p207)*. There is only one bus, the 870, that goes up to the top of the hill, but the 44 will take you from Piazza Venezia to Via Giacinto Carini from where you can start your walk up. For sights along Via della Lungara, take the 23 or 280, which go along Lungotevere.

| 0 metres | 300 |
| 0 yards | 300 |

KEY

Tour of the Janiculum map

City Wall

The staircase fountain in the Botanical Gardens

A Tour of the Janiculum

THE LONG HIKE to the top of the Janiculum is rewarded by wonderful views over the city. The park's monuments include a lighthouse and statues of Garibaldi and his wife Anita. There is also a cannon which is fired at noon each day. In Via della Lungara, between the Janiculum and the Tiber, stand Palazzo Corsini with its national art collection and the Villa Farnesina, decorated by Raphael for his friend and patron, the fabulously wealthy banker Agostino Chigi.

Tasso's Oak is a memorial to the poet Torquato Tasso, who liked to sit here in the days before he died in 1595. The tree was struck by lightning in 1843.

The Manfredi Lighthouse, built in 1911, was a gift to the city of Rome from Italians in Argentina.

The Monument to Anita Garibaldi by Mario Rutelli was erected in 1932. The great patriot's Brazilian wife lies buried beneath the statue.

The view from Villa Lante, a beautiful Renaissance summer residence, gives a magnificent panorama of the whole city.

ROMA O MORTE

Garibaldi Monument
The inscription on the base of the equestrian statue says "Rome or Death" ❺

Botanical Gardens
These were established in 1883 when part of the grounds of Palazzo Corsini was given to the University of Rome **4**

★ **Palazzo Corsini**
This 15th-century triptych by Fra Angelico hangs in the Galleria Nazionale d'Arte Antica **2**

LOCATOR MAP
See Central Rome Map pp12–13

★ **Villa Farnesina**
The suburban villa of the banker Agostino Chigi is celebrated for its frescoes by Raphael, Baldassarre Peruzzi and other Renaissance masters **1**

Porta Settimiana
Looking through this Renaissance gateway from Via della Lungara, you catch a glimpse of Trastevere's warren of narrow streets **3**

KEY

– – – Suggested route

0 metres   75

0 yards   75

STAR SIGHTS

★ **Palazzo Corsini and Galleria Nazionale d'Arte Antica**

★ **Villa Farnesina**

Villa Farnesina ❶

See pp220–21.

Palazzo Corsini and Galleria Nazionale d'Arte Antica ❷

Via della Lungara 10. **Map** 4 D5
& 11 A5. 06-6880 2323.
23, 280. **Open** 8.30am–1.45pm
Mon–Sat, 8.30am–7pm Sun.
Closed 1 May, 15 Aug, 25 Dec &
1 Jan. **Adm charge**.
W www.galleriaborghese.it

Queen Christina's bedroom in the Palazzo Corsini

THE HISTORY of Palazzo Corsini is intimately en-twined with that of Rome. Built for Cardinal Domenico Riario in 1510–12, it has boasted among its many distinguished guests Bramante, the young Michelangelo, Erasmus and Queen Christina of Sweden, who died here in 1689. The old palazzo was completely re-built for Cardinal Neri Corsini by Ferdinando Fuga in 1736. As Via della Lungara is too narrow for a good frontal view, Fuga designed the façade so it could be seen from an angle.

Palazzo Corsini houses the Galleria Nazionale d'Arte Antica, also known as Galleria Corsini. This outstanding collection includes paintings by Rubens, Van Dyck, Murillo, Caravaggio and Guido Reni, together with 17th- and 18th-century Italian regional art. The palazzo is also home to the Accademia dei Lincei, a learned society founded in 1603, which once included Galileo among its members.

In 1797 Palazzo Corsini was the backdrop to momentous events: French General Duphot (the fiancé of Napoleon's sister Pauline) was killed here in a skirmish between papal troops and Republicans. The consequent French occupation of the city and the deportation of Pope Pius VI led to the proclamation of a short-lived Roman Republic (1798–9).

Porta Settimiana ❸

Between Via della Scala and Via della Lungara. **Map** 4 D5 & 11 B5.
23, 280.

THIS GATE was built in 1498 by Pope Alexander VI Borgia to replace a minor passageway in the Aurelian Wall. The Porta Settimiana marks the start of Via della Lungara, a long straight road built in the early 16th century.

Botanical Gardens ❹

Largo Cristina di Svezia 24, off Via Corsini. **Map** 4 D5. 06-4991 7107. 23, 280. **Open** Apr–Sep: 9.30am–6.30pm Tue–Sat (Oct–Mar to 5.30pm). **Closed** public hols & Aug. **Adm charge**. (phone to book).

SEQUOIAS, PALM TREES and splendid collections of orchids and bromeliads are housed in Rome's Botanical Gardens *(Orto Botanico)*. These tranquil gardens contain more than 7,000 plant species from all over the world.

Indigenous and exotic species are grouped to illustrate their botanical families and their adaptation to different climates and eco-systems. There are also plants such as the ginkgo that have survived virtually unchanged from earlier eras. The gardens were originally part of the Palazzo Corsini, but since 1983 have belonged to the University of Rome.

Garibaldi Monument ❺

Piazzale Giuseppe Garibaldi. **Map** 3 C5. 870.

Base of the Garibaldi Monument

THIS HUGE equestrian statue is part of a commemorative park, recalling the heroic events witnessed on the Janiculum when the French army attacked the city in 1849. Garibaldi's Republicans fended off the greatly superior French forces for weeks, until the Italians were overwhelmed. Garibaldi and his men escaped. The monument, erected in 1895, was the work of Emilio Gallori. Around the pedestal are four smaller sculptures in bronze showing battle scenes and allegorical figures.

Steps and tiered fountains at the Botanical Gardens

Courtyard of Sant'Onofrio

Sant'Onofrio 6

Piazza di Sant'Onofrio 2. **Map** 3 C4.
📞 06-686 4498. 🚌 870. **Open** at
10am and noon, otherwise phone for
details (Sun for mass). **Closed** Aug,
except Saint's feast day on 12 Aug.
🏛 **Museum open** by appt only.
📞 06-682 8121.

Beato Nicola da Forca
Palena, whose tombstone
guards the entrance, founded
this church in 1419 in honour
of the hermit Sant'Onofrio. It
retains the flavour of the 15th
century in the simple shapes
of the portico and the cloister.
In the early 17th century the
portico was decorated with
frescoes by Domenichino.
    The monastery next to the
church houses a small museum
dedicated to the 16th-century
poet Torquato Tasso.

San Pietro in Montorio 7

Piazza San Pietro in Montorio 2.
Map 7 B1. 📞 06-581 39 40. 🚌 44,
75. **Open** 8.30am–noon, 4–6pm
daily. If closed, ring bell at door to
right of church. 🏛

San Pietro in Montorio – the
church of St Peter on the
Golden Hill – was founded in
the Middle Ages near the spot
where St Peter was presumed
to have been crucified. It was
rebuilt by order of Ferdinand
and Isabella of Spain at the
end of the 15th century, and
decorated by outstanding
artists of the Renaissance.
    The façade is typical of a
time when clean, geometric
shapes derived from Classical
architecture were in vogue.
The single nave ends in a
deep apse that once contained

Raphael's *Transfiguration,*
now in the Vatican. Two wide
chapels, one on either side of
the nave, were decorated by
some of Michelangelo's most
famous pupils. The left-hand
chapel was designed by one
of the few artists Michelangelo
openly admired, Daniele da
Volterra, also responsible for
the altar painting, *The Baptism
of Christ.* The chapel on the
right was the work of Giorgio
Vasari, who included a self-
portrait (in black, on the left)
in his altar painting, *The
Conversion of St Paul.*
    The first chapel to the right
of the entrance contains a
powerful *Flagellation,* by the
Venetian artist Sebastiano del
Piombo (1518); Michelangelo
is said to have provided the
original drawings. Work by
Bernini and his followers can
be seen in the second chapel
on the left and in the flanking
De Raymondi tombs.

Tempietto 8

Piazza San Pietro in Montorio (in courtyard). **Map** 7 B1. 📞 06-581 3940.
🚌 44, 75. **Open** 9.30am–12.30pm,
2–4pm (summer 4–6pm) Tue–Sun.
See **The History of Rome** pp30–31.

Around 1502 Bramante com-
pleted what many consider
to be the first true Renaissance building in Rome – the
Tempietto. The name means
simply "little temple". Its
circular shape echoes early
Christian *martyria,*
chapels built on
the site of a saint's
martyrdom. This
was believed to be
the place where St
Peter was crucified.
    Bramante chose
the Doric order for
the 16 columns
surrounding the
domed chapel.
Above the columns
is a Classical frieze
and a delicate
balustrade. Though
the scale of the
Tempietto is tiny,
Bramante's masterly
use of Classical
proportions creates
a satisfyingly
harmonious whole.

The Tempietto illustrates the
great Renaissance dream that
the city of Rome would once
again relive its ancient glory.

Fontana dell'Acqua Paola 9

Via Garibaldi. **Map** 7 B1. 🚌 44, 75.

Fontana dell'Acqua Paola

This monumental fountain
commemorates the
reopening in 1612 of an
aqueduct originally built by
Emperor Trajan in AD 109.
The aqueduct was renamed
"dell'Acqua Paola" after Paul
V, the Borghese pope who
ordered its restoration. When
it was first built, the fountain
had five small basins, but in
1690 Carlo Fontana altered the
design, adding the huge basin
you can see today. Despite
many laws intended to deter
them, generations of Romans
used this convenient pool of
fresh water for bathing and
washing their vegetables.

Bramante's round chapel, the Tempietto

Villa Farnesina ➊

THE WEALTHY SIENESE BANKER Agostino Chigi, who had established the headquarters of his far-flung financial empire in Rome, commissioned the villa in 1508 from his compatriot Baldassarre Peruzzi. The simple, harmonious design, with a central block and projecting wings, made this one of the earliest true Renaissance villas. The decoration was carried out between 1510 and 1519 and this has recently been restored. Peruzzi frescoed some of the interiors himself. Later, Sebastiano del Piombo, Raphael and his pupils added more elaborate works. The frescoes illustrate Classical myths, and the vault of the main hall, the Sala di Galatea, is adorned with astrological scenes showing the position of the stars at the time of Chigi's birth. Artists, poets, cardinals, princes and the pope himself were entertained here in magnificent style by their wealthy and influential host. In 1577 the villa was bought by Cardinal Alessandro Farnese. Since then, it has been known as the Villa Farnesina.

North Façade
The Loggia of Cupid and Psyche looks out on formal gardens that were used for parties and putting on plays.

Entrance

The Wedding of Alexander and Roxanne by Sodoma
Cherubs are shown helping the bride Roxanne to prepare for her marriage.

★ **Triumph of Galatea by Raphael**
The beautiful sea nymph Galatea was one of the 50 daughters of the god Nereus.

The Gabinetto delle Stampe sometimes holds exhibitions of rare prints.

Frescoes in the Room of Galatea
Perseus beheads Medusa in a scene from one of Peruzzi's series of mythological frescoes.

THE ARCHITECT

Baldassarre Peruzzi, painter and architect, arrived in Rome from Siena in 1503 aged 20 and became Bramante's chief assistant. Although his architectural designs were typical of Classicism, his painting owes more to Gothic influences, as his figurework is very highly stylized. On Raphael's death, he became Head of Works at St Peter's, but was captured in the Sack of Rome (*see p31*), exiled to Siena until 1535, and died in 1536.

Baldassarre Peruzzi

★ Salone delle Prospettive

Peruzzi's frescoes create the illusion of looking out at views of 16th-century Rome through a marble colonnade.

VISITORS' CHECKLIST

Via della Lungara 230. **Map** 4 D5 & 11 A5. 🚌 *23, 280 to Lungotevere Farnesina.* 📞 *06-6802 7268.* **Open** *9am–1pm Mon–Sat.* 🚫 🅿 ♿ **Adm charge**. **Gabinetto delle Stampe** *(rare print collection)* 📞 *06-69 98 0313.* **Open** *only by appt. Letter of introduction needed.* 🚫

Fresco from the Salone delle Prospettive
This scene shows the Torre delle Milizie (see p90) as it looked in the 1500s.

★ Loggia of Cupid and Psyche

The model for the figure on the left in Raphael's painting of The Three Graces *was Agostino Chigi's mistress, the courtesan Imperia.*

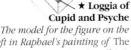

Lunette in the Room of Galatea
This giant monochrome head by Peruzzi was once attributed to Michelangelo.

STAR FEATURES

★ **Triumph of Galatea by Raphael**

★ **Salone delle Prospettive**

★ **Loggia of Cupid and Psyche**

VATICAN

AS THE SITE where St Peter was martyred and buried, the Vatican became the residence of the popes who succeeded him. Decisions taken here have shaped the destiny of Europe, and the great basilica of St Peter's draws pilgrims from all over the Christian world. The papal palaces beside St Peter's house the Vatican Museums. With the added attractions of Michelangelo's Sistine Chapel and the Raphael Rooms, their wonderful

Nuns in St Peter's Square

collections of Classical sculpture make them the finest museums in Rome. The Vatican's position as a state within a state was guaranteed by the Lateran Treaty of 1929, marked by the building of a new road, the Via della Conciliazione. This leads from St Peter's to Castel Sant' Angelo, a monument to a far grimmer past. Built originally as the Emperor Hadrian's mausoleum, this papal fortress and prison has witnessed many fierce battles for control of the city.

SIGHTS AT A GLANCE

Churches and Temples
St Peter's pp230–33 ❶
Santo Spirito in Sassia ❹
Santa Maria in Traspontina ❾

Museums and Galleries
Vatican Museums pp234–47 ❷

Historic Buildings
Hospital of Santo Spirito ❺
Palazzo del Commendatore ❻
Palazzo dei Convertendi ❼
Palazzo dei Penitenzieri ❽

Palazzo Torlonia ⓬
Castel Sant'Angelo pp248–9 ⓭
Palazzo di Giustizia ⓮

Gates
Porta Santo Spirito ❸

Historic Streets and Piazzas
The Borgo ❿
Vatican Corridor ⓫

GETTING THERE
The quickest way to reach the area is by Metro line A to Ottaviano S. Pietro. The 40 and 64 buses run regularly from Piazza dei Cinquecento, in front of Termini station, although the 62 is the only bus which runs along Via della Conciliazione. Other routes that serve the area include the 81 and 492, which stop in Piazza del Risorgimento.

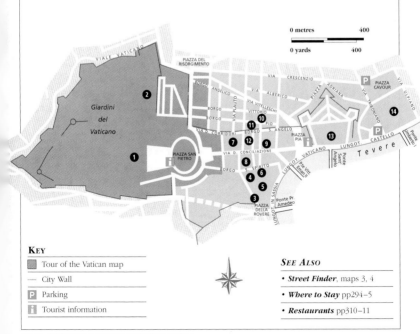

| 0 metres | 400 |
| 0 yards | 400 |

KEY

▨	Tour of the Vatican map
—	City Wall
🅿	Parking
ℹ	Tourist information

SEE ALSO

Dome of St Peter's dominating the Vatican skyline

A Tour of the Vatican

THE VATICAN, a centre of power for Catholics all over the world and a sovereign state since February 1929, is ruled by the pope. About 1,000 people live here, staffing the Vatican's facilities. There are a post office and shops, Vatican radio, broadcasting to the world in over 20 languages, a daily newspaper (*l'Osservatore Romano*), Vatican offices and a publishing house.

The Madonna of Guadalupe shows the miraculous image of the Madonna which appeared on the cloak of a Mexican Indian in 1531.

Papal heliport

The Grotto of Lourdes is a replica of the grotto in the southwest of France, where in 1858 the Virgin appeared to St Bernadette.

The Vatican Railway Station, opened in 1930, connects with the line from Rome to Viterbo, but is now used only for freight.

Radio Vatican is broadcast from this tower, part of the Leonine Wall built in 847.

The Papal Audience Chamber, by Pier Luigi Nervi, was opened in 1971. It seats up to 12,000.

The information office gives details of tours of the Vatican Gardens.

★ **St Peter's**
The Chapel of St Peter is in the Grottoes under the basilica. The rich marble decoration was added by Clement VIII at the end of the 16th century ❶

Piazza San Pietro was laid out by Bernini between 1656 and 1667. The narrow space in front of the church opens out into an enormous ellipse flanked by colonnades.

The obelisk was erected here in 1586 with the help of 150 horses and 47 winches.

STAR SIGHTS

★ **St Peter's**

★ **Vatican Museums**

The Eagle Fountain was built to celebrate the arrival of water from the Acqua Paola aqueduct at the Vatican. The eagle is the Borghese crest.

LOCATOR MAP
See Central Rome Map pp12–13

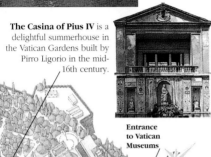

The Casina of Pius IV is a delightful summerhouse in the Vatican Gardens built by Pirro Ligorio in the mid-16th century.

Entrance to Vatican Museums

★ **Vatican Museums**
Raphael's Madonna of Foligno *(1513) is just one of the Vatican's many Renaissance masterpieces* ❷

The Galleon Fountain is a perfect scale model of a 17th-century ship in lead, brass and copper. It was made by a Flemish artist for Pope Paul V.

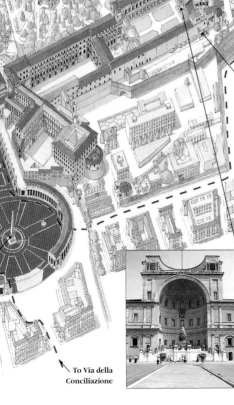

The Cortile della Pigna is mostly the work of Bramante. The niche for the pine cone, once a Roman fountain, was added by Pirro Ligorio in 1562.

KEY

– – – Suggested route

0 metres 75

0 yards 75

To Via della Conciliazione

St Peter's ❶

See pp230–33.

Vatican Museums ❷

See pp234–47.

Porta Santo Spirito ❸

Via dei Penitenzieri. **Map** 3 C3. 🚌
23, 34, 46, 62, 64, 98, 870, 881, 982.

THIS GATE stands at what was the southern limit of the "Leonine City", the area enclosed within walls by Pope Leo IV as a defence against the Saracens who had sacked Rome in AD 845. The walls measure 3 km (2 miles) in circumference.

Work on the walls started in AD 846. Pope Leo supervised the huge army of labourers personally, and thanks to his encouragement, the job was completed in 4 years. He then led a solemn procession to consecrate his massive feat of construction.

Since the time of Pope Leo the walls have needed much reinforcement and repair. The gateway visible today at Porta Santo Spirito was built by the architect Antonio da Sangallo the Younger in 1543–4. It is framed by two huge bastions that were added in 1564 by

Pope Pius IV Medici. Sadly, Sangallo's design for a monumental entrance to the Vatican was never completed; the principal columns come to an end somewhat abruptly in a modern covering of cement.

Santo Spirito in Sassia ❹

Via dei Penitenzieri 12. **Map** 3 C3.
📞 06-687 9310. 🚌 *23, 34, 46, 62, 64, 98, 870, 881, 982.* **Open** *7am–noon, 3–7.30pm daily.* ✝ ♿

Nave of Santo Spirito in Sassia

BUILT ON THE SITE of a church erected by King Ine of Wessex, who died in Rome in the 8th century, the church is the work of Antonio da Sangallo the Younger. It was rebuilt (1538–44) after the

Sack of Rome had left it in ruins in 1527. The façade was added under Pope Sixtus V (1585–90). The nave and side chapels are decorated with a series of light, lively frescoes. The pretty bell tower, is earlier, dating from the reign of Sixtus IV (1471–84). It was probably the work of the pope's architect, Baccio Pontelli, who also built the Hospital of Santo Spirito, **Sixtus V's arms over door of Santo Spirito** and the Ponte Sisto *(see p210)* further down the River Tiber.

Hospital of Santo Spirito ❺

Borgo Santo Spirito 2. **Map** 3 C3.
🚌 *23, 34 46, 62, 64, 98, 870, 881, 982.* **Octagonal chapel open** *8.30am–2pm daily.*

THE OLDEST HOSPITAL in Rome, this is said to have been founded as a result of a nightmare experienced by Pope Innocent III (1198–1216). In the dream, an angel showed him the bodies of Rome's unwanted babies dredged up from the Tiber River in fishing nets. As a result, the pope hastened to build a hospice for sick paupers.

Fresco of an angel in the octagonal chapel of the Hospital of Santo Spirito

In 1475 the hospital was reorganized by Pope Sixtus IV to care for the poor pilgrims expected for the Holy Year. Sixtus's hospital was a radical building. Cloisters divided the different types of patients; one area is still reserved for orphans and their nurses.

Unwanted infants were passed through a revolving barrel-like contraption called the *rota,* still visible to the left of the central entrance in Borgo Santo Spirito, to guarantee anonymity. Martin Luther, who visited in 1511, was shocked by the number of abandoned children he saw, believing them to be "the sons of the pope himself".

In the centre, under the hospital's conspicuous drum, is an octagonal chapel, where mass was said for patients. This room can be visited while the rest of the building still functions as a hospital.

Rusticated doorway of the Palazzo dei Convertendi

The *rota* of Santo Spirito, where mothers left unwanted babies

Palazzo del Commendatore 6

Borgo Santo Spirito 3. **Map** 3 C3.
23, 34, 46, 62, 64, 98, 881, 982.
Courtyard only open to the public.

AS DIRECTOR of the Hospital of Santo Spirito, the Commendatore not only ran the hospital, he was also responsible for its estates and revenues. This important post was originally given to members of the pope's family.

The palazzo, built next door to the hospital, has a spacious 16th-century frescoed loggia appropriate to the dignity and sobriety of its owners. The frescoes represent the story of the founding of the Hospital of Santo Spirito. To the left of the entrance is the Spezieria, or Pharmacy. This still has the wheel used for grinding the bark of the cinchona tree to produce the drug quinine, first introduced here in 1632 by Jesuits from Peru as a cure for malaria.

Above the courtyard is a splendid clock (1827). The dial is divided into six; it was not until 1846 that the familiar division of the day into two periods of 12 hours was introduced in Rome by Pope Pius IX.

Palazzo dei Convertendi 7

Via della Conciliazione 43.
Map 3 C3. 23, 34, 62, 64.
Not open to the public.

WITH THE BUILDING of Via della Conciliazione in the 1930s, Palazzo dei Convertendi was taken down and later moved to this new site nearby. The house, which is partly attributed to the architect Bramante, is where the artist Raphael died in 1520.

Della Rovere arms

Palazzo dei Penitenzieri 8

Via della Conciliazione 33.
Map 3 C3. 06-682 8121.
23, 34, 62, 64. **Open** for visits 3.30–6.30pm Mon, Thu (fax to 06-6880 2298). **Adm charge** for groups. See **Where to Stay** p295.

THE PALAZZO owes its name to the fact that the place was once home to the confessors *(penitenzieri)* of St Peter's. Now the Hotel Columbus, it was originally built by Cardinal Domenico della Rovere in 1480. The palazzo still bears the family's coat of arms, the oak tree *(rovere* means oak), on its graceful courtyard well-head. On the cardinal's death, the palazzo was acquired by Cardinal Francesco Alidosi, Pope Julius II della Rovere's favourite. Suspected of treason, the cardinal was murdered in 1511 by the pope's nephew, the Duke of Urbino, who took over the palazzo. A few of the rooms still contain beautiful frescoes.

View of the Tiber and the Borgo between Castel Sant'Angelo and St Peter's by Gaspare Vanvitelli (1653–1736)

Santa Maria in Traspontina ❾

Via della Conciliazione 14. **Map** 3 C3.
C 06-6880 6451.
🚌 23, 34, 62, 64.
Open 7am–noon, 4–7pm daily.
🕍 ♿

The façade of the Carmelite church of Santa Maria in Traspontina

THE CHURCH occupies the site of an ancient Roman pyramid, believed in the Middle Ages to have been the Tomb of Romulus. The pyramid was destroyed by Pope Alexander VI Borgia, but representations of it survive in the bronze doors at the entrance to St Peter's and in a Giotto triptych in the Vatican Pinacoteca *(see p240)*.

The present church was begun in 1566 to replace an earlier one which had been in the line of fire of the cannons defending Castel Sant'Angelo during the Sack of Rome in 1527. The papal artillery officers insisted that the dome of the new church should be as low as possible, so it was built without a supporting drum. The first chapel to the right is dedicated to the gunners' patron saint, Santa Barbara, and is decorated with warlike motifs. In the third chapel on the left are two columns, said to be those to which St Peter and Paul were bound before martyrdom.

The Borgo ❿

Map 3 C3. 🚌 23, 34, 40, 62.

THE WORD BORGO derives from the German *burg*, meaning town. Rome's Borgo is where the first pilgrims to St Peter's were housed in hostels and hospices, often for quite lengthy periods. The first of these foreign colonies, called "schools," was founded in AD 725 by a Saxon, King Ine of Wessex, who wished to live a life of penance and to be buried near the Tomb of St Peter. These days hotels and hostels have made the Borgo a colony of international pilgrims once again. Much of the area's character was destroyed by redevelopment in the 1930s, but it is still enjoyable to explore the old narrow streets on either side of Via della Conciliazione.

Vatican Corridor ⓫

Castel Sant'Angelo to the Vatican.
Map 3 C3. 🚌 23, 34, 40, 62.

Clement VII, who used the Vatican Corridor to evade capture in 1527

LOCALLY KNOWN as the Passetto (small corridor), this long passageway was built into the fortifications during medieval times. Meant to link the Vatican with the fortress of Castel Sant'Angelo, it constituted a fortified escape route which could also be used to control the strategic Borgo area. Arrows and other missiles could be fired from its bastions on to the streets and houses below. The corridor was used in 1494 by Pope Alexander VI Borgia when Rome was invaded by King Charles VIII of France. In 1527 it enabled Pope Clement VII to take refuge in Castel Sant'Angelo, as the troops commanded by the Constable of Bourbon began the Sack of Rome.

Palazzo Torlonia ⓬

Via della Conciliazione 30.
Map 3 C3. 🚌 23, 34, 40, 62, 64.
Not open to the public.

THE PALAZZO was built in the late 15th century by the wealthy Cardinal Adriano Castellesi, in a style closely resembling Palazzo della Cancelleria (see p149). The cardinal was a much-travelled rogue, who collected vast revenues from the bishopric of Bath and Wells which he was given

Pope Leo X

by his friend King Henry VII of England. In return he gave Henry his palazzo for use as the seat of the English ambassador to the Holy See. Castellesi was finally stripped of his cardinalate by Pope Leo X Medici and disappeared from history.

Since then the palazzo has had many owners and tenants. In the 17th century it was rented for a time by Queen Christina of Sweden. The Torlonia family, who acquired the building in 1820, owed its fortune to the financial genius of shopkeeper-turned-banker Giovanni Torlonia. He lent money to the impoverished Roman nobility and bought up their property during the Napoleonic Wars.

Palazzo Torlonia (1496), unaffected by changes to the surrounding area

Castel Sant'Angelo ⓭

See pp248–9.

Palazzo di Giustizia ⓮

Piazza Cavour. **Map** 4 E3. 🚌 34, 49, 70, 87, 186, 280, 492, 913, 926, 990. **Not open** to the public.

THE MONUMENTAL Palazzo di Giustizia (Palace of Justice) was built between 1889 and 1910 to house the national

law courts. Its riverside façade is crowned with a bronze chariot and fronted by giant statues of the great men of Italian law.

The building was supposed to embody the new order replacing the injustices of papal rule, but it has never endeared itself to the Romans. It was soon dubbed the Palazzaccio (roughly, "the ugly old palazzo") both for its appearance and for the nature of its business. By the 1970s the building was collapsing under its own weight, but it has now been restored.

The ornate travertine façade of the Palazzo di Giustizia

St Peter's ❶

THE CENTRE of the Roman Catholic faith, St Peter's draws pilgrims from all over the world. Few are disappointed when they enter the sumptuously decorated basilica beneath Michelangelo's vast dome.

A shrine was erected on the site of St Peter's tomb in the 2nd century and the first great basilica, ordered by the Emperor Constantine, was completed around AD 349. By the 15th century it was falling down, so in 1506 Pope Julius II laid the first stone of a new church. It took more than a century to build and all the great architects of the Roman Renaissance and Baroque had a hand in its design.

★ Dome of St Peter's
Designed by Michelangelo, though not finished in his lifetime, the spectacular cupola, 136.5 m (448 ft) high, gives unity to the majestic interior of the basilica.

The nave's total length is 218 m (715 ft).

Papal Altar
The present altar dates from the reign of Clement VIII (1592–1605). The plain slab of marble found in the Forum of Nerva stands under Bernini's baldacchino, overlooking the well of the confessio, the crypt where St Peter's body is reputedly buried.

Baldacchino
This magnificent canopy of gilded bronze, supported on spiral columns 20 m (66 ft) high, was designed by Bernini in the 17th century.

TIMELINE

AD 61 Burial of St Peter		1506 Julius II lays first stone	1547 Michelangelo named as chief architect of St Peter's		1626 New basilica of St Peter's consecrated
324 Constantine builds basilica	1452 Nicholas V plans restoration			1593 Dome completed	

AD 60	800	1500		1550	1600
200 Altar built marking grave of St Peter	1503 Pope Julius II chooses Bramante as architect for new basilica		1538 Antonio da Sangallo the Younger made director of works	1606 Carlo Maderno extends basilica	1614 Maderno finishes the façade
800 Charlemagne crowned Holy Roman Emperor in St Peter's			1514 Raphael director of works	1564 Death of Michelangelo	

★ View from the Dome
The superb symmetry of Bernini's colonnade can be appreciated from the dome.

The two minor cupolas at the corners of the transept are by Vignola.

Pope Urban VIII's Keys
At the base of the columns of the baldacchino, the coat of arms of Pope Urban VIII features the keys to the Kingdom of Heaven.

Façade by Carlo Maderno (1614)

Stairs to the dome

Filarete Door
Finished in 1445, Antonio Averulino's bronze door came from the original basilica.

Entrances

STAR FEATURES

★ **Dome of St Peter's**

★ **View from the Dome**

Piazza San Pietro
On Sundays and re-ligious occasions the Pope blesses the crowds from his balcony above the square.

A Guided Tour of St Peter's

THE VAST BASILICA'S 187-m (615-ft) long, marble-encrusted interior contains 11 chapels and 45 altars in addition to a wealth of precious works of art. Some were salvaged from the original basilica and others commissioned from late Renaissance and Baroque artists, but much of the elaborate decoration is owed to Bernini's work in the mid-17th century. The two side aisles are 76 m (250 ft) long and converge under Michelangelo's enormous dome. The central focus of the building is the Papal Altar beneath Bernini's great baldacchino, filling the space between four massive piers which support the dome. From the basilica you can visit the Grottoes, the Treasury and St Peter's Sacristy, or climb up to the terrace for panoramic views.

⑤ **Baldacchino by Bernini**
Commissioned by Pope Urban VIII in 1624, the extravagant Baroque canopy dominates the nave and crowns the Papal Altar, at which only the pope may celebrate mass.

Bernini's Monument to Urban VIII

④ **Throne of St Peter in Glory**
In the domed apse, look up to the window above Bernini's Baroque sculpture of 1656–65. It lights the image of the Holy Spirit, shown as a dove amid clouds, rays of sunlight and flights of angels.

Entrance to Treasury and Sacristy

HISTORICAL PLAN OF THE BASILICA OF ST PETER'S

St Peter was buried c.AD 64 in a necropolis near his crucifixion site at the Circus of Nero. Constantine built a basilica on the burial site in AD 324. In the 15th century the old church was found to be unsafe and had to be demolished. It was rebuilt in the 16th and 17th centuries. By 1614 the façade was ready, and in 1626 the new church was consecrated.

Entrance to Necropolis

KEY

▨	Circus of Nero
▨	Constantinian
▨	Renaissance
▨	Baroque

③ **Monument to Pope Alexander VII**
Bernini's last work was finished in 1678 and is in an alcove on the left of the transept. The pope sits among the figures of Truth, Justice, Charity and Prudence.

② **Monument to Leo XI**
On the left beneath the aisle arch is Alessandro Algardi's white marble 1650 monument to Leo XI, whose reign as pope lasted only 27 days.

KEY

- - - - Tour route

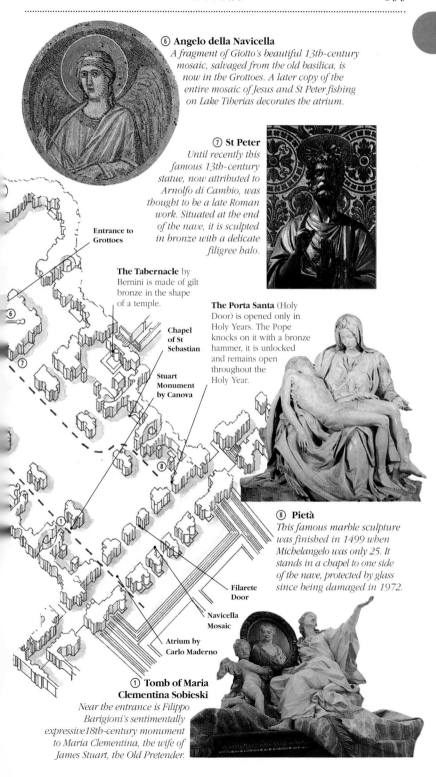

⑥ **Angelo della Navicella**
A fragment of Giotto's beautiful 13th-century mosaic, salvaged from the old basilica, is now in the Grottoes. A later copy of the entire mosaic of Jesus and St Peter fishing on Lake Tiberias decorates the atrium.

⑦ **St Peter**
Until recently this famous 13th-century statue, now attributed to Arnolfo di Cambio, was thought to be a late Roman work. Situated at the end of the nave, it is sculpted in bronze with a delicate filigree halo.

Entrance to Grottoes

The Tabernacle by Bernini is made of gilt bronze in the shape of a temple.

Chapel of St Sebastian

Stuart Monument by Canova

The Porta Santa (Holy Door) is opened only in Holy Years. The Pope knocks on it with a bronze hammer, it is unlocked and remains open throughout the Holy Year.

⑧ **Pietà**
This famous marble sculpture was finished in 1499 when Michelangelo was only 25. It stands in a chapel to one side of the nave, protected by glass since being damaged in 1972.

Filarete Door

Navicella Mosaic

Atrium by Carlo Maderno

① **Tomb of Maria Clementina Sobieski**
Near the entrance is Filippo Barigioni's sentimentally expressive 18th-century monument to Maria Clementina, the wife of James Stuart, the Old Pretender.

Vatican Museums ❷

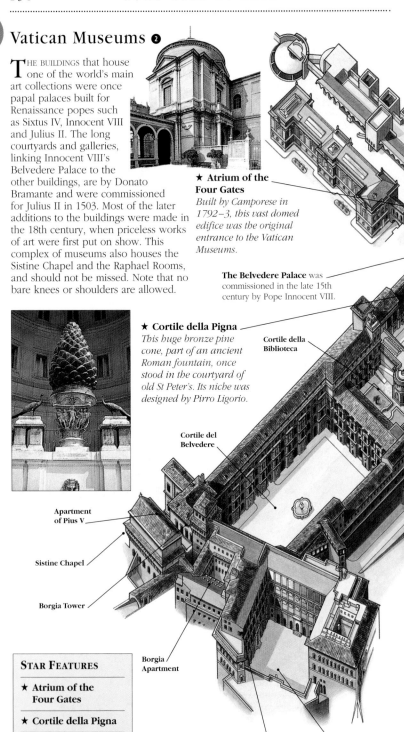

THE BUILDINGS that house one of the world's main art collections were once papal palaces built for Renaissance popes such as Sixtus IV, Innocent VIII and Julius II. The long courtyards and galleries, linking Innocent VIII's Belvedere Palace to the other buildings, are by Donato Bramante and were commissioned for Julius II in 1503. Most of the later additions to the buildings were made in the 18th century, when priceless works of art were first put on show. This complex of museums also houses the Sistine Chapel and the Raphael Rooms, and should not be missed. Note that no bare knees or shoulders are allowed.

★ **Atrium of the Four Gates**
Built by Camporese in 1792–3, this vast domed edifice was the original entrance to the Vatican Museums.

The Belvedere Palace was commissioned in the late 15th century by Pope Innocent VIII.

★ **Cortile della Pigna**
This huge bronze pine cone, part of an ancient Roman fountain, once stood in the courtyard of old St Peter's. Its niche was designed by Pirro Ligorio.

Cortile della Biblioteca

Cortile del Belvedere

Apartment of Pius V

Sistine Chapel

Borgia Tower

Borgia Apartment

Raphael Loggia

Cortile di San Damaso

STAR FEATURES

★ **Atrium of the Four Gates**

★ **Cortile della Pigna**

★ **Bramante Stairway**

Spiral Ramp
*The spectacular stair-
way leading down
from the museums
to the street was
designed by Giuseppe
Momo in 1932.*

Entrance

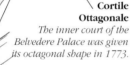

VISITORS' CHECKLIST

Città del Vaticano. Entrance in Viale
Vaticano. **Map** 3 B2. ☏ 06-6988
3860. 🚌 49 to entrance, 23, 81,
492, 990 to Piazza del Risorgimento
or 62 to St Peter's. Ⓜ Cipro Musei
Vaticani, Ottaviano S. Pietro. **Open**
8.45am–4.45pm (last adm: 3.20pm)
Mon–Fri (Nov–Feb: to 1.45pm, last
adm: 12.20pm); 8.45am–1.45pm
(last adm: 12.20pm) Sat and last
Sun of each month. **Closed** public
& relig hols. Special permit needed
for Raphael Loggia, Vatican Library,
Lapidary Gallery & Vatican Archives.
Adm charge, free last Sun of
month. ♿ special routes. ⬛
Temporary exhibitions, lectures.
🍴 ▢ ⬛ 🛒 Vatican Gardens:
06-6988 4676. 🌐 www.vatican.va

Simonetti Stairway
*Built in the 1780s with a
vaulted ceiling, the stairs
were part of the conversion of
the Belvedere Palace into the
Pio-Clementine Museum.*

**Cortile
Ottagonale**
*The inner court of the
Belvedere Palace was given
its octagonal shape in 1773.*

★ Bramante Stairway
*Pope Julius II built the spiral
staircase within a square
tower as an entrance to the
palace. The staircase could
be ridden up on horseback
in case of emergency.*

**Braccio
Nuovo**

TIMELINE

1000	1500	1600	1700	1800
1198 Innocent III creates papal palace	**1503** Bramante lays out Belvedere Courtyard	**1655** Bernini designs Scala Regia	**1756** Foundation of Christian Museum	**1800–23** Chiaramonti Museum founded
	1509 Raphael begins work on Rooms			**1837** Etruscan Museum founded
1473 Pope Sixtus IV builds Sistine Chapel			**1758** Museum of Pagan Antiquities founded	**1822** Braccio Nuovo is opened
	1503–13 Pope Julius II starts Classical sculpture collection	*Bramante (1444–1514)*	**1776–84** Pius VI enlarges museum	**1970** Pope Paul VI opens Gregorian Museum of Pagan Antiquities

Exploring the Vatican Museums

FOUR CENTURIES of papal patronage and connoisseurship have resulted in one of the world's great collections of Classical and Renaissance art. The Vatican houses many of the great archaeological finds of central Italy including the *Laocoön* group, discovered in 1506 on the Esquiline, the *Apollo del Belvedere* and the Etruscan bronze known as the *Mars of Todi*. During the Renaissance, parts of the museums were decorated with wonderful frescoes commissioned for the Sistine Chapel, the Raphael Rooms and the Borgia Apartment.

Mars of Todi

Gallery of the Candelabra
Once an open loggia, this gallery of Greek and Roman sculpture has a fine view of the Vatican Gardens.

Room of the Biga

Gallery of Tapestries

Etruscan Museum

Siege of Malta
The Gallery of Maps is an important record of 16th-century history and cartography.

Upper floor

Modern Religious Art

Raphael Loggia

Sistine Chapel

Raphael Rooms

GALLERY GUIDE
Visitors have to follow a one-way system. It is best to concentrate on a single collection or to choose one of the four suggested itineraries. These are colour-coded so that you can follow them throughout the museums. They vary in length from 90 minutes to 5 hours. If you are planning a long visit, make sure you allow plenty of time for resting. Conserve your stamina for the Sistine Chapel and the Raphael Rooms; they are 20–30 minutes' walk from the entrance, without allowing for any viewing time along the way.

Sala dei Misteri
This is one of the rooms of the Borgia Apartment, richly decorated with Pinturicchio frescoes.

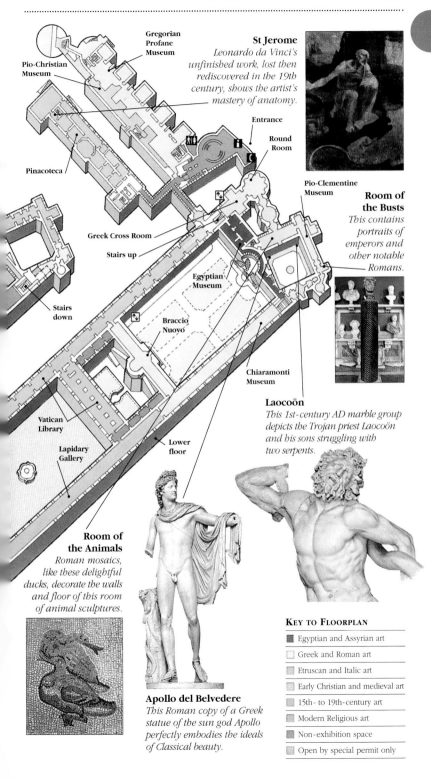

Gregorian
Profane
Museum

Pio-Christian
Museum

St Jerome
*Leonardo da Vinci's
unfinished work, lost then
rediscovered in the 19th
century, shows the artist's
mastery of anatomy.*

Entrance

Round
Room

Pinacoteca

Pio-Clementine
Museum

**Room of
the Busts**
*This contains
portraits of
emperors and
other notable
Romans.*

Greek Cross Room

Stairs up

Egyptian
Museum

Stairs
down

Braccio
Nuovo

Chiaramonti
Museum

Laocoön
*This 1st-century AD marble group
depicts the Trojan priest Laocoön
and his sons struggling with
two serpents.*

Vatican
Library

Lapidary
Gallery

Lower
floor

**Room of
the Animals**
*Roman mosaics,
like these delightful
ducks, decorate the walls
and floor of this room
of animal sculptures.*

Apollo del Belvedere
*This Roman copy of a Greek
statue of the sun god Apollo
perfectly embodies the ideals
of Classical beauty.*

KEY TO FLOORPLAN

■	Egyptian and Assyrian art
☐	Greek and Roman art
▨	Etruscan and Italic art
▨	Early Christian and medieval art
▨	15th- to 19th-century art
▨	Modern Religious art
■	Non-exhibition space
☐	Open by special permit only

Exploring the Vatican's Collections

T HE VATICAN'S GREATEST TREASURES are its Greek and
Roman antiquities. These have been on display
since the 18th century. The 19th century saw the
addition of exciting discoveries from Etruscan tombs
and excavations in Egypt. In the Pinacoteca (art gallery)
there is a small, choice collection of paintings, including
works by Raphael, Titian and Leonardo. Works by great
painters and sculptors are also on view throughout the
older parts of the museums in the form of sumptuous
decorations commissioned by the Renaissance popes.

Coloured bas-relief from an Egyptian tomb (c2400 BC)

EGYPTIAN AND ASSYRIAN ART

T HE EGYPTIAN COLLECTION
contains finds from 19th-
and 20th-century excavations
in Egypt and statues which
were brought to Rome in
Imperial times. There are also
Roman imitations of Egyptian
art from Hadrian's Villa *(see
p269)* and from the Campus
Martius district of ancient
Rome. Egyptian-style statuary
from Hadrian's Villa was used
to decorate the Greek Cross
Room, the entrance to the
new wing built in 1780 by
Michelangelo Simonetti.

The genuine Egyptian works,
exhibited on the lower floor of
the Belvedere Palace, include
statues, mummies, mummy
cases and funerary artifacts.
There is also a large collection
of documents written on
papyrus, the paper the ancient
Egyptians made from reeds.
Among the main treasures is
a colossal granite statue of
Queen Tuia, the mother of
Rameses II, found on the site
of the Horti Sallustiani gardens

(see p251) in 1714. The statue,
which dates from the 13th
century BC, may have been
brought to Rome by the
Emperor Caligula (reigned
AD 37–41), who had an
unhealthy interest in
pharaohs and in his own
mother, Agrippina.

Also noteworthy are the
head of a statue of
Montuhotep IV (21st
century BC), the
beautiful mummy
case of Queen
Hetep-heret-es,
and the tomb of
Iri, the guardian
of the Pyramid of
Cheops (22nd
century BC).

The Assyrian
Stairway is
decorated with
fragments of
reliefs from
the palaces of
the Kings of
Nineveh (8th century BC).
These depict the military
exploits of King Sennacherib
and his son Sargon II, and
show scenes from Assyrian
and Chaldean mythology.

ETRUSCAN AND OTHER PRE-ROMAN ART

T HIS COLLECTION comprises
artifacts from pre-Roman
civilizations in Etruria and
Latium, from Neolithic times
to the 1st century BC, when
these ancient populations were
assimilated into the Roman
state. Pride of place in the
Gregorian Etruscan Museum
goes to the objects found in
the Regolini-Galassi tomb,
excavated in 1836 at the
necropolis of Cerveteri *(see
p271)*. The tomb was found
intact and yielded numerous
everyday household objects,
plus a throne, a bed and a
funeral cart, all cast in bronze,
dating from the 7th century
BC. Beautiful black vases,
delightful terracotta figurines
and bronze statues such as
the famous *Mars of Todi*,
displayed in the Room of the
Bronzes, show the Etruscans
to have been a highly civilized,
sophisticated people.

A number of Greek vases
that were found in Etruscan
tombs are on display in the
Vase Collection. The Room of
the Italiot Vases contains only
vases produced locally in the
Greek cities of Southern Italy
and in Etruria itself. These
date from the 3rd to the 1st
century BC.

**Etruscan
gold clasp
(fibula)
from the 7th
century BC**

Head of an athlete in mosaic from the Baths of Caracalla

GREEK AND ROMAN ART

THE GREATER PART of the Vatican Museums is dedicated to Greek and Roman art. Exhibits line connecting corridors and vestibules; walls and floors display fine mosaics; and famous sculptures decorate the main courtyards.

The first serious organization of the collection took place in the reign of Julius II (1503–13) around Bramante's Belvedere Courtyard. The prize pieces form the nucleus of the 18th-century Pio-Clementine Museum. In the pavilions of the Octagonal Courtyard and in the surrounding rooms are sculptures considered among the greatest achievements of Western art. The *Apoxyomenos* (an athlete wiping his body after a race) and the *Apollo del Belvedere* are high-quality Roman copies of Greek originals of about 320 BC. The magnificent *Laocoön*, sculpted by three artists from Rhodes, had long been known to exist from a description by Pliny the Elder. It was rediscovered near the ruins of the Domus Aurea *(see p175)* in 1506. Classical works such as these had a profound influence on Michelangelo and other Renaissance artists.

The much smaller Chiaramonti Museum, named after Pope Pius

VII Chiaramonti, was laid out by Canova in the early 19th century. It includes a striking colossal head of the goddess Athene. The Braccio Nuovo, an extension of the Chiaramonti, decorated with Roman floor mosaics, contains a statue of Augustus from the villa of his wife Livia at Prima Porta. Its pose is based on the famous *Doryphoros* by the Greek sculptor Polyclitus, of which there is a Roman copy on display opposite.

Exhibits in the Vase Rooms range from the Greek geometric style (8th century BC) to black-figure vases from Corinth, such as the famous vase by Exekias, with Achilles and Ajax playing a game similar to draughts (530 BC), and the later red-figure type, such as the *kylix* (a wide shallow cup) with Oedipus and the Sphinx from the 5th century BC. A stairway links this section to the Gallery of the Candelabra and the Room of the Biga (a two-horse chariot). The horses and harness were added in the 18th century.

The Gregorian Profane Museum, housed in a new wing, charts the evolution of Roman art from dependence upon Greek models to a recognizably Roman style.

The *Doryphoros* or spear-carrier, a Roman copy in marble of an original Greek bronze

Original Greek works include large marble fragments from the Parthenon in Athens. There is also a Roman copy of *Athene and Marsyas* by Myron, which was part of the decoration of the Parthenon. Totally Roman in character are two reliefs known as the Rilievi della Cancelleria, because they were discovered beneath the Palazzo della Cancelleria *(see p149)* in the 1930s. They show military parades of the Emperor Vespasian and his son Domitian. This section also has fine Roman floor mosaics. There are two from the Baths of Caracalla *(see p197)*, depicting athletes and referees. They date from the 3rd century AD. Most striking of all is a mosaic that creates the impression of an unswept floor, covered with debris after a meal. Away from the main Classical collections, in one of the rooms of the Vatican Library, is the *Aldobrandini Wedding*, a beautiful Roman fresco of a bride being prepared for her marriage, dating from the 1st century AD.

Marble relief of the Emperor Vespasian

Floor mosaic from the Baths of Otricoli in Umbria, in the Chiaramonti Museum

Detail from Giotto's *Stefaneschi Triptych*

EARLY CHRISTIAN AND MEDIEVAL ART

THE MAIN COLLECTION of early Christian antiquities is in the Pio-Christian Museum, founded in the last century by Pope Pius IX and formerly housed in the Lateran Palace. It contains inscriptions and sculpture from catacombs and early Christian basilicas. The sculpture consists chiefly of reliefs decorating sarcophagi, though the most striking work is a free-standing 4th-century statue of the *Good Shepherd*. The sculpture's chief interest lies in the way it blends Biblical episodes with pagan mythology. Christianity adopted Classical images so that its doctrines could be understood in clear visual terms. The idealized pastoral figure of the shepherd, for example, became Christ himself, while bearded philosophers turned into the Apostles. At the same time, Christianity laid claim to be the spiritual and cultural heir of the Roman Empire.

The first two rooms of the Pinacoteca are dedicated to late medieval art, mostly tempera-painted wooden panels which served as altarpieces. The outstanding work is Giotto's altarpiece dating from about 1300, known as the *Stefaneschi Triptych*. It expresses much the same theme as the early Christian works: the continuity between the Classical world of the Roman Empire and the new order of Christian Europe. The crucifixion of St Peter takes place between two landmarks of ancient Rome, the Pyramid of Caius Cestius *(see p205)*, and the pyramid known in the Middle Ages as the Tomb of Romulus, which stood near the Vatican. The triptych, which decorated the main altar of old St Peter's, includes portraits of Pope St Celestine V (reigned 1294), and of the donor, Cardinal Jacopo Stefaneschi, shown offering the triptych to St Peter.

The Vatican Library has a number of medieval treasures exhibited rather haphazardly in showcases; these include woven and embroidered cloths, reliquaries, enamels and icons. One of the aims of the 18th-century reorganization of the Vatican collections was to glorify Christian works by contrasting them with earlier pagan creations. In the long Lapidary Gallery over 3,000 stone tablets with Christian and pagan inscriptions are displayed on opposite walls. The world's greatest collection of its kind, it may be visited only with special permission.

15TH- TO 19TH-CENTURY ART

THE RENAISSANCE POPES, many of whom were cultured connoisseurs of the arts, considered it their duty to sponsor the leading painters, sculptors and goldsmiths of

Pietà **by the Venetian artist Giovanni Bellini (1430–1516)**

RAPHAEL'S LAST PAINTING

When Raphael died in 1520, the *Transfiguration* was found in his studio, almost complete. The wonderful luminous work was placed at the head of the bier where the great artist's body lay. It depicts the episode in the Gospels in which Christ took three of the Apostles to the top of a mountain, where He appeared to them in divine glory. In the detail shown here Christ floats above the ground in a halo of ethereal light.

MODERN RELIGIOUS ART

MODERN ARTISTS exhibited in the Vatican Museums face daunting competition from the great works of the past. Few modern works are displayed conspicuously, the exceptions being Momo's spiral staircase of 1932, which greets visitors as they enter the museums, and Giò Pomodoro's abstract sculpture in the centre of the Cortile della Pigna.

In 1973 a contemporary art collection was inaugurated by Pope Paul VI. Housed in the Borgia Apartment, it includes over 800 exhibits by modern artists from all over the world, donated by collectors or the artists themselves. Works in a great variety of media show many contrasting approaches to religious subjects. There are paintings, drawings, engravings and sculpture by 19th- and 20th-century artists, as well as mosaics, stained glass, ceramics and tapestries. Well-known modern painters such as Georges Braque, Paul Klee, Edvard Munch and Graham Sutherland are all represented. There are also drawings by Henry Moore, ceramics by Picasso and stained glass by Fernand Léger. Projects for modern church ornaments include Matisse's decorations for the church of St Paul de Vence, Luigi Fontana's models for the bronze doors of Milan cathedral, and Emilio Greco's panels for the doors of Orvieto cathedral.

the age. The galleries around the Cortile del Belvedere were all decorated by great artists between the 16th and the 19th centuries. The Gallery of Tapestries is hung with tapestries woven in Brussels to designs by students of Raphael; the Apartment of Pope Pius V has beautiful 15th-century Flemish tapestries; and the Gallery of Maps is frescoed with 16th-century maps of ancient and contemporary Italy. When you go to visit the Raphael Rooms *(see pp242–3)*, you should not overlook the nearby Room of the Chiaroscuri and Pope Nicholas V's tiny private chapel, frescoed by Fra Angelico between 1447 and 1451. Similarly, before reaching the Sistine Chapel *(see pp244–7)*, visit the Borgia Apartment, frescoed in a decorative, flowery style by Pinturicchio and his students in the 1490s. The contrast with Michelangelo's Sistine Chapel ceiling, begun in 1508, could hardly be greater. Another set of fascinating frescoes decorates the Loggia of Raphael, but this requires special permission to visit.

Many important works by Renaissance masters are on show in the Pinacoteca (art gallery). Highlights among the works by 15th-century painters are a fine *Pietà* by the Venetian Giovanni Bellini and Leonardo da Vinci's unfinished *St Jerome*. Of the

great 16th-century works, do not miss the fine altarpiece by Titian, the *Crucifixion of St Peter* by Guido Reni, the *Deposition* by Caravaggio and the *Communion of St Jerome* by Domenichino. Raphael has a whole room dedicated to his work. It contains the beautiful *Madonna of Foligno* and the *Transfiguration* as well as eight tapestries made to his designs.

Lunette of the *Adoration of the Magi* by Pinturicchio in the Room of the Mysteries in the Borgia Apartment

***Town with Gothic Cathedral* by Paul Klee (1879–1940)**

Raphael Rooms

P OPE JULIUS II'S PRIVATE APARTMENTS were built above those of his hated predecessor, Alexander VI, one of the Borgias, who died in 1503. Julius was impressed with Raphael's work and chose him to redecorate the four

Detail from *The Expulsion of Heliodorus from the Temple*, showing Pope Julius II watching the scene from his litter

rooms *(stanze)*. Raphael and his pupils began the task in 1508, replacing existing works by several better-known artists, including Raphael's own teacher, Perugino. The work took over 16 years and Raphael himself died before its completion. The frescoes express the religious and philosophical ideals of the Renaissance. They quickly established Raphael's reputation as an artist in Rome, putting him on a par with Michelangelo, then working on the ceiling of the Sistine Chapel.

Cortile del Belvedere

HALL OF CONSTANTINE ①

T HE FRESCOES in this room were started in 1517, 3 years before Raphael's death, but Raphael himself probably had little hand in their execution. As a result they are not held in the same high regard as those in the other rooms. The work was completed in 1525 in the reign of Pope Clement VII by Giulio Romano and two other former pupils of Raphael, Giovanni Francesco Penni and Raffaellino del Colle.

The theme of the decoration is the triumph of Christianity over paganism. The four major frescoes show scenes from the life of Constantine and include his *Vision of the Cross* and his victory over his rival Maxentius at *The Battle of the Milvian Bridge*, for which Raphael had provided a preparatory sketch. In both *The Baptism of Constantine* and *The Donation of Constantine*, the figure of Pope Sylvester *(see p170)* was given the features of Clement VII.

ROOM OF HELIODORUS ②

T HIS PRIVATE antechamber was decorated by Raphael between 1512 and 1514. The main frescoes show the miraculous protection granted to all the Church's ministers, doctrines and property. The room's name refers to the fresco on the right, *The Expulsion of Heliodorus from the Temple*. This shows a story from Jewish history, in which a thief called Heliodorus is felled

Swiss guards waiting with papal chair in *The Mass at Bolsena*

by a horseman as he tries to make off with the treasure from the Temple of Jerusalem. The scene is witnessed by the pope, borne on a litter by courtiers. The incident is also a thinly veiled reference to Julius II's success in driving foreign armies out of Italy. In *The Meeting of Leo I and Attila* Raphael pays a similar compliment to the pope's political skill. Pope Leo was originally given the face of Julius II, but after his death, Raphael substituted the features of Julius's successor, Leo X.

The Mass at Bolsena depicts a miracle that occurred in 1263. A priest

***The Battle of the Milvian Bridge*, completed by one of Raphael's assistants**

The Liberation of St Peter, a three-part composition, shows the saint asleep in his cell in the middle section, led out of prison by an angel on the right, while, on the left, the prison guards cower in terror.

following their master's own plans. The most famous, *The Fire in the Borgo*, was painted from Raphael's designs and reflects his maturity as an artist. It celebrates the miracle that took place in 847, when Pope Leo IV extinguished a fire raging in the Borgo *(see p228)* by making the sign of the cross. The incident is likened to the flight of Aeneas from Troy described by Virgil. The figure of Aeneas appears in the foreground carrying his father on his back. This borrowing of an event from Classical legend shows a new willingness to experiment on the part of Raphael. Sadly, his pupils did not always follow his designs faithfully and this, combined with some poor restoration, has spoilt the work.

who doubted that the bread and wine really were the body and blood of Christ suddenly saw the host bleed while he was celebrating mass. Julius II appears in this fresco, accompanied by a colourful group of Swiss guards.

Julius appears yet again as St Peter in *The Liberation of St Peter*. This fresco is remarkable for its dramatic lighting effects, achieved despite the painting's awkward shape and its position above a window.

ROOM OF THE SEGNATURA ③

THE NAME is derived from a special council which met in this room to sign official documents. The frescoes here were completed between 1508 and 1511. The scheme Raphael followed was dictated by Pope Julius II. It reflects the Humanist belief that there could be perfect harmony between Classical culture and Christianity in their mutual search for truth.

The Dispute over the Holy Sacrament, the first fresco completed by Raphael for Pope Julius, represents the triumph of religion and spiritual truth. The consecrated host is shown at the centre of the painting. This links the group of learned scholars, who discuss its significance, to the Holy Trinity and the saints floating on clouds up above.

On the opposite wall, *The School of Athens (see p30)* is a bustling scene

centred around the debate on the search for truth between Greek philosophers Plato and Aristotle. It also features portraits of many of Raphael's contemporaries, including Leonardo da Vinci, Bramante and Michelangelo. The other works include a portrait of the bearded Pope Julius II, who in 1511 vowed not to shave until he managed to rid Italy of all usurpers.

ROOM OF *THE FIRE IN THE BORGO* ④

THIS WAS ORIGINALLY the dining room, but when the decoration was completed under Pope Leo X, it became a music room. All the frescoes exalt the reigning pope by depicting events in the lives of his namesakes, the 9th-century popes Leo III and IV. The main frescoes were finished by two of Raphael's assistants between 1514 and 1517,

Detail from *The Fire in the Borgo*, showing Aeneas, the Trojan hero, with his father on his back, fleeing from the fire

The Dispute over the Holy Sacrament, the first fresco completed in the Rooms

Sistine Chapel: The Walls

THE MASSIVE WALLS of the Sistine Chapel, the main chapel in the Vatican Palace, were frescoed by some of the finest artists of the 15th and 16th centuries. The 12 paintings on the side walls, by artists including Perugino, Ghirlandaio, Botticelli and Signorelli, show parallel episodes from the life of Moses and of Christ. The decoration of the chapel walls was completed between 1534 and 1541 by Michelangelo, who added the great altar wall fresco, *The Last Judgment*.

KEY TO THE FRESCOES: ARTISTS AND SUBJECTS

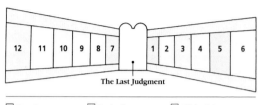

The Last Judgment

☐ Perugino ☐ Botticelli ☐ Ghirlandaio

☐ Rosselli ☐ Signorelli ☐ Michelangelo

1 Baptism of Christ in the Jordan
2 Temptations of Christ
3 Calling of St Peter and St Andrew
4 Sermon on the Mount
5 Handing over the Keys to St Peter
6 Last Supper
7 Moses's Journey into Egypt
8 Moses Receiving the Call
9 Crossing of the Red Sea
10 Adoration of the Golden Calf
11 Punishment of the Rebels
12 Last Days of Moses

THE LAST JUDGMENT BY MICHELANGELO

REVEALED IN 1993 after a year's restoration, *The Last Judgment* is considered to be the masterpiece of Michelangelo's mature years. It was commissioned by Pope Paul III Farnese, and required the removal of some earlier frescoes and two windows over the altar. A new wall was erected which slanted inwards to stop dust settling on it. Michelangelo worked alone on the fresco for seven years, until its completion in 1541.

The painting depicts the souls of the dead rising up to face the wrath of God, a subject that is rarely used for an altar decoration. The pope chose it as a warning to Catholics to adhere to their faith in the turmoil of the Reformation. In fact the work conveys the artist's own tormented attitude to his faith. It offers neither the certainties of Christian orthodoxy, nor the ordered view of Classicism.

In a dynamic, emotional composition, the figures are caught in a vortex of motion. The dead are torn from their graves and hauled up to face Christ the Judge, whose athletic, muscular figure is the focus of all the painting's movement.

Christ shows little sympathy for the agitated saints around him, clutching the instruments of their martyrdom. Neither is any pity shown for the damned, hurled down to the demons in hell. Here Charon, pushing people off his boat into the depths of Hades, and the infernal judge Minos, are taken from Dante's *Inferno*. Minos has ass's ears, and is a portrait of courtier Biagio da Cesena, who had objected to the nude figures in the fresco. Michelangelo's self-portrait is on the skin held by the martyr St Bartholomew.

Souls meeting the wrath of Christ in Michelangelo's *Last Judgment*

WALL FRESCOES

Detail from Botticelli's fresco
Temptations of Christ

WHEN THE Sistine Chapel was built, the papacy was a strong political power with vast accumulated wealth. In 1475 Pope Sixtus IV was able to summon some of the greatest painters of his day to decorate the chapel. Among the artists employed were Perugino, who was Raphael's master and is often credited with overseeing the project, Sandro Botticelli, Domenico Ghirlandaio, Cosimo Rosselli and Luca Signorelli. Their work on the chapel's frescoes took from 1481 to 1483.

Although frequently overlooked by visitors who concentrate on Michelangelo's work, the frescoes along the side walls of the chapel include some of the finest works of 15th-century Italian art. The two cycles of frescoes represent scenes from the lives of Moses and Christ. Above them in the spaces between the windows are portraits of the earliest popes, painted by various artists, including Botticelli.

The fresco cycles start at the altar end of the chapel, with the story of Christ on the right-hand wall and that of Moses on the left. Originally there were two paintings, *The Birth of Christ* and *The Finding of Moses*, on the wall behind the altar, but these were both destroyed to make way for Michelangelo's *Last Judgment*.

The final paintings of the two cycles are also lost. They were on the entrance wall, which collapsed during the 16th century. When the wall was restored, they were replaced with poor substitutes.

As was customary at the time, each fresco contains a series of scenes, linked thematically to the central episode. Hidden meanings and symbols connect each painting with its counterpart on the opposite wall, and there are also many allusions to contemporary events.

The elaborate architectural details in the frescoes include familiar Roman monuments. The Arch of Constantine *(see p91)* provides the backdrop for the *Punishment of the Rebels* by Botticelli, the fifth panel in the cycle of Moses, in which the artist himself appears as the last figure but one on the right. Two similar arches appear in the painting opposite, Perugino's *Handing over the Keys to St Peter*.

Moses was both spiritual and temporal leader of his people. He called down the wrath of God on those who challenged his decisions, thus

The crowd of onlookers in the *Calling of St Peter and St Andrew* by Ghirlandaio

setting a precedent for the power exercised by the pope. In *Handing over the Keys to St Peter*, Christ confers spiritual and temporal authority on St Peter by giving him the keys to the Kingdoms of Heaven and Earth. The golden-domed building in the centre of the vast piazza represents both the Temple of Jerusalem and the Church, as founded by Peter, the first pope. The fifth figure on the right is thought to be a self-portrait by Perugino.

Botticelli's *Temptations of Christ* includes a view of the

The central episode in Botticelli's *Punishment of the Rebels*

Hospital of Santo Spirito, rebuilt in 1475 by Sixtus IV *(see p226)*. Here the devil is disguised in the habit of a Franciscan monk. Portraits of both Botticelli and Filippino Lippi are visible in the left hand corner. A portrait of the pope's nephew, Girolamo Riario, appears in the painting of the *Crossing of the Red Sea* by Rosselli, in which the sea is literally red. This painting also commemorates the papal victory at Campomorto in 1482.

Perugino's *Handing over the Keys to St Peter*

Sistine Chapel: The Ceiling

MICHELANGELO FRESCOED the ceiling for Pope Julius II between 1508 and 1512, working on specially designed scaffolding. The main panels, which chart the Creation of the World and Fall of Man, are surrounded by subjects from the Old and New Testaments – except for the Classical Sibyls who are said to have foreseen the birth of Christ. In the 1980s the ceiling was restored revealing colours of an unsuspected vibrancy.

Libyan Sibyl
The pagan prophetess reaches for the Book of Knowledge. Like most female figures Michelangelo painted, the beautiful Libyan Sibyl was probably modelled on a man.

Illusionistic architecture

30	19	10	26	12	21	14	28	16	23	32
18	1	2	3	4	5	6	7	8	9	24
31	25	11	20	13	27	15	22	17	29	33

Creation of the Sun and Moon
Michelangelo depicts God as a dynamic but terrifying figure commanding the sun to shed light on the earth.

KEY TO CEILING PANELS

☐ **GENESIS: 1** God Dividing Light from Darkness; **2** Creation of the Sun and Moon; **3** Separating Waters from Land; **4** Creation of Adam; **5** Creation of Eve; **6** Original Sin; **7** Sacrifice of Noah; **8** The Deluge; **9** Drunkenness of Noah.

☐ **ANCESTORS OF CHRIST: 10** Solomon with his Mother; **11** Parents of Jesse; **12** Rehoboam with Mother; **13** Asa with Parents; **14** Uzziah with Parents; **15** Hezekiah with Parents; **16** Zerubbabel with Parents; **17** Josiah with Parents.

☐ **PROPHETS: 18** Jonah; **19** Jeremiah; **20** Daniel; **21** Ezekiel; **22** Isaiah; **23** Joel; **24** Zechariah.

☐ **SIBYLS: 25** Libyan Sibyl; **26** Persian Sibyl; **27** Cumaean Sibyl; **28** Erythrean Sibyl; **29** Delphic Sibyl.

☐ **OLD TESTAMENT SCENES OF SALVATION: 30** Punishment of Haman; **31** Moses and the Brazen Serpent; **32** David and Goliath; **33** Judith and Holofernes.

Original Sin

This shows Adam and Eve tasting the forbidden fruit from the Tree of Knowledge, and their expulsion from Paradise. Michelangelo represents Satan as a snake with the body of a woman.

The Ignudi are athletic male nudes whose significance is uncertain.

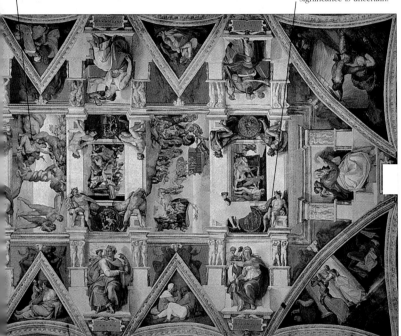

The lunettes are devoted to frescoes of the ancestors of Christ, like Hezekiah.

RESTORATION OF THE SISTINE CEILING

Restorers used computers, photography and spectrum analysis to inspect the fresco before cleaning began. They were therefore able to detect and remove the changes previous restorers had made to Michelangelo's original work. Analysis showed that the ceiling had been cleaned with materials ranging from bread to retsina wine. The restoration then revealed the familiarly dusky, eggshell-cracked figures to have creamy skins, lustrous hair and to be dressed in brightly coloured, luscious robes: "a Benetton Michelangelo" mocked one critic, claiming that a layer of varnish which he had added to darken the colours had been removed. However, after examining the work, most experts agreed that the new colours probably matched those painted by Michelangelo.

A restorer cleaning the Libyan Sibyl

Castel Sant'Angelo ⑬

THE MASSIVE FORTRESS of Castel Sant'Angelo takes its name from the vision that Pope Gregory the Great had of the Archangel Michael on this site. It began life in AD 139 as Emperor Hadrian's mausoleum. Since then it has had many roles: as part of Emperor Aurelian's city wall, as a medieval citadel and prison, and as the residence of the popes in times of political unrest. From the dank cells in the lower levels to the fine apartments of the Renaissance popes above, a 58-room museum covers all aspects of the castle's history.

Mausoleum of Hadrian
This artist's impression shows the tomb before Aurelian fortified its walls in AD 270–75.

Courtyard of Honour
Heaps of stone cannonballs decorate the courtyard, once the castle's ammunition store.

The Treasury was probably the original site of Hadrian's burial chamber.

Hall of the Columns

Loggia of Paul III

Hall of the Library

PROTECTING THE POPE
The Vatican Corridor leads from the Vatican Palace to Castel Sant'Angelo. It was built in 1277 to provide an escape route when the pope was in danger. The pentagonal ramparts built around the castle during the 17th century improved its defences in times of siege.

The Rooms of Clement VIII are inscribed with the family crest of the Aldobrandini pope (1592–1605).

The Hall of Justice is decorated with a fresco of *The Angel of Justice* by Domenico Zaga (1545).

The spiral ramp was the entrance to the mausoleum.

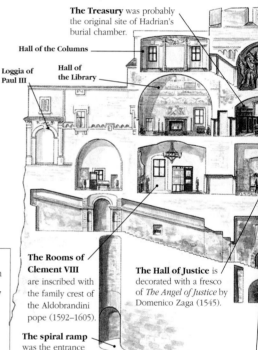

■ Walls and fortifications
□ Vatican Corridor

★ View from Terrace
The castle's terrace, scene of the last act of Puccini's Tosca, *offers splendid views in every direction.*

The Chamber of the Urns housed the ashes of members of Hadrian's family.

STAR FEATURES

★ **View from Terrace**

★ **Sala Paolina**

★ **Staircase of Alexander VI**

Bronze Angel
The gigantic statue of the Archangel Michael is by the 18th-century Flemish sculptor Pieter Verschaffelt.

VISITORS' CHECKLIST

Lungotevere Castello 50 (entrance through gardens to the right of building). **Map** 4 D3 & 11 A1. 06-3996 7600. 23, 34, 62 to Lungotevere Vaticano; 34, 49, 87, 280, 492, 926, 990 to Piazza Cavour. **Open** 9am–8pm (last admission 7pm) Tue–Sun. **Closed** 1 Jan, 25 Dec. **Adm charge.** Exhibitions.

The Round Hall houses the original model from which Verschaffelt's angel was cast.

★ **Sala Paolina**
The illusionistic frescoes by Perin del Vaga and Pellegrino Tibaldi (1546–8) include one of a courtier entering the room through a painted door.

Hall of Apollo
The room is frescoed with scenes from mythology attributed to the pupils of Perin del Vaga (1548).

Ventilation shaft

★ **Staircase of Alexander VI**
This staircase cuts right through the heart of the building.

Bridge

TIMELINE

AD 139 Mauseoleum completed by Antoninus Pius	**590** Legendary date of appearance of Archangel Michael above the castle	**1493** Pope Alexander VI restores Vatican Corridor	*Façade of Castel Sant'Angelo*
		1390 Pope Boniface IX remodels the castle	

AD 100	500	1000	1500	

271 Tomb is incorporated into Aurelian Wall and fortified		**1527** Castle withstands siege during Sack of Rome	**1557** Ramparts built to protect the castle
AD 130 Hadrian begins family mausoleum	*Cannonballs in the Courtyard of Honour*	**1542–9** Sala Paolina and apartments built for Pope Paul III	**1870** Castle used as barracks and military prison

VIA VENETO

IN IMPERIAL ROME, this was a suburb where rich families owned luxurious villas and gardens. Ruins from this era can be seen in the excavations in Piazza Sallustio, named after the most extensive gardens in the area, the Horti Sallustiani. After the Sack of Rome in the 5th century, the area reverted to open countryside. Not until the 17th century did it recover its lost splendour, with the building of Palazzo Barberini and the now-vanished Villa Ludovisi.

Film director Federico Fellini

When Rome became capital of Italy in 1870, the Ludovisi sold their land for development. They kept a plot for a new house, but tax on the profits from the sale was so high, they had to sell that too. By 1900, Via Veneto had become a street of smart modern hotels and cafés. It featured prominently in Fellini's 1960 film *La Dolce Vita*, a scathing satire on the lives of film stars and idle rich, but since then has lost its position as the meeting place of the famous.

SIGHTS AT A GLANCE

Churches and Temples
Santa Maria della Concezione ❸
Santa Susanna ❼
Santa Maria della Vittoria ❽

Historic Buildings
Casino dell'Aurora ❷
Palazzo Barberini ❻

Famous Streets
Via Veneto ❶

Fountains
Fontana delle Api ❹
Fontana del Tritone ❺

SEE ALSO

• *Street Finder*, map 5
• *Where to Stay* pp294–5
• *Restaurants* pp310–11

0 metres   200

0 yards   200

GETTING THERE
This is one of the easiest parts of Rome to reach by public transport. Barberini and Repubblica Metro stations on line A are very handy, and Stazione Termini is only 10–15 minutes' walk away. The Via Veneto itself starts at Piazza Barberini, well served by buses from all parts of the city. The 95 goes the whole length of Via Veneto to Porta Pinciana. Other useful routes include the 52, 53, 63, 80, 116 and 119.

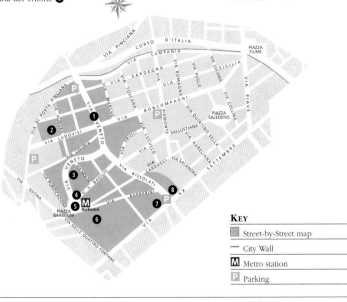

KEY

▨	Street-by-Street map
―	City Wall
Ⓜ	Metro station
Ⓟ	Parking

The onset of autumn in Via Veneto

Street-by-Street: Via Veneto

THE STREETS AROUND VIA VENETO, though within the walls of ancient Rome, contain little dating from before the unification of Italy in 1870. With its hotels, restaurants, bars and travel agencies, the area is the centre of 20th-century tourism in the way that Piazza di Spagna was the hub of the tourist trade in the Rome of the 18th-century Grand Tour. However, glimpses of the old city can be seen among the modern streets. These include Santa Maria della Concezione, the church of the Capuchin friars, whose convent once stood in its own gardens. In the 17th century Palazzo Barberini was built here for the powerful papal family. Bernini's Fontana del Tritone and Fontana delle Api have stood in Piazza Barberini since it was the meeting place of cart tracks entering the city from surrounding vineyards.

Casino dell'Aurora
A pavilion is all that remains of the great Ludovisi estate that once occupied most of this quarter of Rome ❷

Santa Maria della Concezione
This church is best known for the macabre collection of bones in its crypt ❸

Fontana delle Api
Bernini's drinking fountain is decorated with bees, emblem of his Barberini patrons ❹

Fontana del Tritone
Bernini's muscular sea god has been spouting water skywards for 350 years ❺

VIA VENETO

PIAZZA BARBERINI

VIA DI SAN BASILIO

VIA DI SAN NICOLA DA TOLENTINO

VIA BARBERINI

★ **Palazzo Barberini**
Pietro da Cortona worked on his spectacular ceiling fresco The Triumph of Divine Providence *between 1633 and 1639* ❻

VIA XX SETTEMBRE

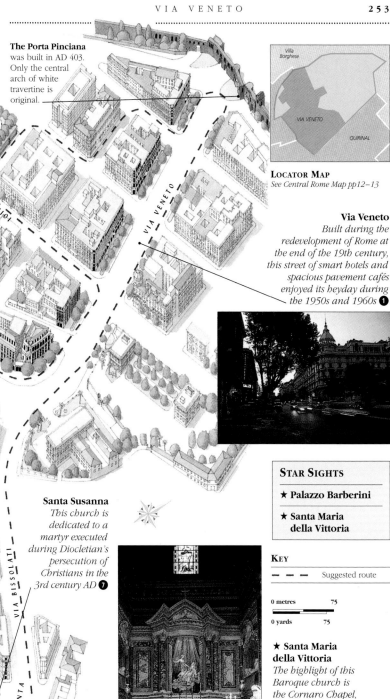

The Porta Pinciana was built in AD 403. Only the central arch of white travertine is original.

LOCATOR MAP
See Central Rome Map pp12–13

Via Veneto
Built during the redevelopment of Rome at the end of the 19th century, this street of smart hotels and spacious pavement cafés enjoyed its heyday during the 1950s and 1960s **1**

Santa Susanna
This church is dedicated to a martyr executed during Diocletian's persecution of Christians in the 3rd century AD **7**

STAR SIGHTS

★ **Palazzo Barberini**

★ **Santa Maria della Vittoria**

KEY

– – – Suggested route

| 0 metres | 75 |
| 0 yards | 75 |

★ **Santa Maria della Vittoria**
The highlight of this Baroque church is the Cornaro Chapel, designed to resemble a theatre. The centre of the stage is occupied by Bernini's thrilling sculpture of The Ecstasy of St Teresa **8**

Pavement café in Via Veneto

Via Veneto ❶

Map 5 B1. 🚌 52, 53, 63, 80, 95, 116, 119 and many routes to Piazza Barberini. Ⓜ Barberini.

VIA VENETO descends in a lazy curve from the Porta Pinciana to Piazza Barberini, lined in its upper reaches with exuberant late 19th-century hotels and canopied pavement cafés. It was laid out in 1879 over a large estate sold by the Ludovisi family in the great building boom of Rome's first years as capital of Italy. Palazzo Margherita, intended to be the new Ludovisi family palazzo, was completed in 1890. It now houses the American embassy.

In the 1960s this was the most glamorous street in Rome, its cafés patronized by film stars and plagued by the paparazzi. Most of the people drinking in the cafés today are tourists, as film stars now seem to prefer the livelier bohemian atmosphere of Trastevere.

Palazzo Margherita, the US embassy

Casino dell'Aurora ❷

Via Lombardia 46. **Map** 5 B2. 📞 06-48 39 42. 🖷 06-4201 0745. 🚌 52, 53, 63, 80, 95, 116, 119. Ⓜ Barberini. **Open** by appt only. Ring above number, then fax.

THE CASINO (a stately country residence) was a summer-house on the grounds of the Ludovisi palace. It was built by Cardinal Ludovisi in the 17th century, and frescoed by Guercino. The ceiling fresco creates the impression that the Casino has no roof, but lies open to a cloudy sky, across which horses pull the carriage of Aurora, the goddess of dawn, from the darkness of night towards the light of day.

Santa Maria della Concezione ❸

Via Veneto 27. **Map** 5 B2. 📞 06-487 1185. 🚌 52, 53, 61, 62, 63, 80, 95, 116, 119, 175. Ⓜ Barberini. **Open** 7am–noon, 3–7pm daily. **Crypt open** 9am–noon, 3–6pm Fri–Wed. **Donation** expected. 🔼

POPE URBAN VIII's brother, Antonio Barberini was a cardinal and a Capuchin friar. In 1626 he founded this plain, unassuming church at what is now the foot of the Via Veneto. When he died he was buried not, like most cardinals, in a grand marble sarcophagus, but below a simple flag-stone near the altar, with the bleak epitaph in Latin: "Here lies dust, ashes, nothing".

The grim reality of death is illustrated even more graphically in the crypt beneath the church, where generations of Capuchin friars decorated the walls of the five vaulted chapels with the bones and skulls of their departed brethren. In all, some 4,000 skeletons were used over about 100 years to create this macabre *memento mori* started in the late 17th century. Some of the bones are wired together to form Christian symbols such as crowns of thorns, sacred hearts and crucifixes. There are also some complete skeletons, including one of a Barberini princess who died as a child. At the exit, an inscription in Latin reads: "What you are, we used to be. What we are, you will be."

Pope Urban VIII

Fontana delle Api ❹

Piazza Barberini. **Map** 5 B2. 🚌 52, 53, 61, 62, 63, 80, 95, 116, 119, 175. Ⓜ Barberini.

THE FOUNTAIN of the bees – *api* are bees, symbol of the Barberini family – is one of Bernini's more modest works. Tucked away in a corner of Piazza Barberini, it is quite easy to miss. Dating from 1644, it pays homage to Pope Urban VIII Barberini, and features rather crab-like bees which appear to be sipping the water as it dribbles down into the basin. A Latin inscription informs us that the water is for the use of the public and their animals.

Bernini's Fontana delle Api

Fontana del Tritone ❺

Piazza Barberini. **Map** 5 B3. 🚌 52, 53, 61, 62, 63, 80, 95, 116, 175. Ⓜ Barberini.

IN THE CENTRE of busy Piazza Barberini is one of Bernini's liveliest creations, the Triton Fountain. It was created for Pope Urban VIII Barberini in 1642, shortly after the completion of his palace on the ridge above. Acrobatic dolphins stand on their heads, twisting their tails together to support a huge scallop shell on which the sea god Triton kneels, blowing a spindly column of water up into the air through a conch shell. Entwined artistically among the dolphins' tails are the papal tiara, the keys of St Peter and the Barberini coat of arms.

The Triton and his conch shell in Bernini's Fontana del Tritone

Palazzo Barberini ❻

Via delle Quattro Fontane 13. **Map** 5 B3. 📞 06-328 10. 🚌 52, 53, 61, 62, 63, 80, 95, 116, 175, 492, 590. Ⓜ Barberini. **Open** 8.30am–7.30pm Tue–Sat (last adm 30 mins before closing). **Closed** public hols. **Adm charge.** 📷 🚻 📶 🔼 ♿ ⏃ 🅦 www.galleriaborghese.it

WHEN MAFFEI Barberini became Pope Urban VIII in 1623 he decided to build a grand palace for his family on the fringes of the city, over-looking a ruined temple. The architect, Carlo Maderno, designed it as a typical rural villa, with wings extending into the surrounding gardens. Maderno died in 1629 and Bernini took over, assisted by Borromini. The peculiar pediments on some of the top floor windows, and the oval staircase inside, are almost certainly by Borromini.

Of the many sumptuously decorated rooms, the most striking is the Gran Salone, with a dazzling illusionistic ceiling fresco by Pietro da Cortona. The palazzo also houses paintings from the 13th to the 16th centuries, part of the Galleria Nazionale d'Arte

Antica, with important works by Filippo Lippi, El Greco and Caravaggio. There is also a Holbein portrait of King Henry VIII of England dressed for his wedding to Anne of Cleves. Of greater local significance are Guido Reni's *Beatrice Cenci*, the young woman executed for planning her father's murder *(see p152)*, and *La Fornarina*, tradition-ally identified as a portrait of Raphael's mistress, although not necessarily painted by him.

Santa Susanna ❼

Via XX Settembre 14. **Map** 5 C2. 📞 06-4201 4554. 🚌 60, 61, 62, 84, 175, 492, 910. Ⓜ Repubblica. **Open** 9am–noon, 4–7pm daily. ⏃

Façade of Santa Susanna

SANTA SUSANNA'S most striking feature is its vigorous Baroque facade by Carlo Maderno, finished in 1603. Christians have worshipped on the site since at least the 4th century. In the nave, there are four huge frescoes by Baldassarre Croce (1558–1628), painted to resemble tapestries. These depict scenes from the life of Susanna, an obscure Roman saint who was martyred here, and the rather better-known life of the Old Testament Susanna, who was spotted bathing in her husband's garden by two lecherous judges.

Santa Susanna is the Catholic church for Americans in Rome and holds services in English every day.

Santa Maria della Vittoria ❽

Via XX Settembre 17. **Map** 5 C2. 📞 06-4274 0571. 🚌 60, 61, 62, 84, 175, 492, 910. Ⓜ Repubblica. **Open** 8.30–11am, 3.30–6pm Mon–Sat, 8.45–10am, 3.30–6pm Sun. ⏃ ⏃

SANTA MARIA della Vittoria is an intimate Baroque church with a lavishly decorated candlelit interior. It contains one of Bernini's most ambitious sculptural works, *The Ecstasy of St Teresa* (1646), centrepiece of the Cornaro Chapel, built to resemble a miniature theatre. It even has an audience: sculptures of the chapel's benefactor, Cardinal Federico Cornaro, and his ancestors sit in boxes, as if watching and discussing the scene occurring in front of them.

Visitors may be shocked or thrilled by the apparently physical nature of St Teresa's ecstasy. She lies on a cloud, her mouth half open and her eyelids closed, with rippling drapery covering her body. Looking over her with a smile, which from different angles can appear either tender or cruel, is a curly-haired angel holding an arrow with which he is about to pierce the saint's body for a second time. The marble figures are framed and illuminated by rays of divine light materialized in bronze.

Bernini's astonishing *Ecstasy of St Teresa*

FURTHER AFIELD

HE MORE INQUISITIVE visitor to Rome may wish to try a few excursions to the large parks and some of the more isolated churches on the outskirts of the city. With a day to spare, you can explore the villas of Tivoli and the ruins of the ancient Roman port of Ostia. Traditional haunts of

Dish (3rd century BC) in Villa Giulia

the Grand Tour *(see p130)*, such as the catacombs and the ruined aqueducts of Parco Appio Claudio, still offer glimpses of the rapidly vanishing Campagna, the country-side around Rome. More modern sights include the suburb of EUR, built in the Fascist era, and the memo-rial at the Fosse Ardeatine.

SIGHTS AT A GLANCE

Towns and Areas
EUR ⓴
Tivoli ⓲

Historic Roads
Via Appia Antica ⓼

Churches
Santa Costanza ⓹
Sant'Agnese fuori le Mura ⓺
San Lorenzo fuori le Mura ⓻
San Paolo fuori le Mura ⓯

Museums and Galleries
Museo e Galleria Borghese pp260–61 ⓶
Villa Giulia pp262–3 ⓷
Museo di Arte Contemporanea di Roma ⓸
Centrale Montemartini ⓰

Ancient Sites
Hadrian's Villa ㉑
Ostia Antica ㉒

Parks and Gardens
Villa Borghese ⓵
Villa Doria Pamphilj ⓱
Villa d'Este ⓳
Villa Gregoriana ⓴

Tombs and Catacombs
Catacombs of San Callisto ⓽
Catacombs of San Sebastiano ⓾
Catacombs of Domitilla ⑪
Fosse Ardeatine ⑫
Tomb of Cecilia Metella ⑬

SIGHTS OUTSIDE ROME

KEY

Main sightseeing areas

Motorway

0 kilometres   2

0 miles   1

SIGHTS OUTSIDE THE CENTRE

Caryatids beside the canal of the Canopus at Hadrian's Villa

Villa Borghese **❶**

Map 2 E5. 🚌 *52, 53, 88, 95, 116, 490, 495.* 🚊 *3, 19.* **Park open** *dawn to sunset.* **Bioparco** Viale del Giardino Zoologico. **Map** 2 E4. 🛈 *06-360 8211.* 🚌 *52.* 🚊 *3, 19.* **Open** *daily end Mar–Oct: 9.30am–6pm; Nov–end Mar: 9.30am–5pm (last adm 1hr before closing).* **Closed** *25 Dec.* 🚽 🏛 🖥 🛈 **W** www.bioparco.it

Galleria Nazionale d'Arte Moderna Viale delle Belle Arti 131. **Map** 2 D4. 🛈 *06-32 29 81.* 🚊 *3, 19.* **Open** *8.30am–7.30pm Tue–Sun.* **Closed** *1 May.* 🚽 🖥 🏛 🖥 🛈

British School at Rome, designed by Edwin Lutyens in 1911

T HE VILLA and its park were designed in 1605 for Cardinal Scipione Borghese, nephew of Pope Paul V. The park was the first of its kind in Rome. It contained 400 newly-planted pine trees, garden sculpture by Bernini's father, Pietro, and dramatic waterworks built by Giovanni Fontana. The layout of the formal gardens was imitated by other prominent Roman families at Villa Ludovisi and Villa Doria Pamphilj, but the cardinal's 18th-century successors preferred a more natural-looking park.

In the early 19th century Prince Camillo Borghese assembled the family's magnificent art collection in the Casino Borghese, now the home of the Galleria and Museo Borghese.

In 1901 the park became the property of the Italian state. Within its 6-km (4-mile) circumference there are now museums and galleries, foreign academies and schools of archaeology, a zoo, a riding school, a grassy amphitheatre, an artificial lake, an aviary and an array of summerhouses, fountains, Neo-Classical statuary and exotic follies.

There are several ways into the park, including a monumental entrance on Piazzale Flaminio, built for Prince Camillo Borghese in 1825 by Luigi Canina. Other conveniently-sited entrances are at Porta Pinciana at the end of Via Veneto and from the Pincio Gardens *(see p136).* The main attraction of Italian gardens in hot weather is shade, so the long avenues are lined with hedges and trees. Piazza di Siena, a pleasantly open, grass-covered amphitheatre surrounded by tall umbrella pines, was the inspiration for Ottorino Respighi's famous symphonic poem *The Pines of Rome,* written in 1924. Near Piazza di Siena are the so-called Casina di Raffaello, said to have been owned by Raphael, and the

Statue of the English poet Byron by Thorvaldsen

18th-century Palazzetto dell'Orologio. These were summerhouses from which people enjoyed the beautiful vistas across the park. Many buildings in the park were originally surrounded by formal gardens: the Casino Borghese and the nearby 17th-century Casino della Meridiana and its aviary *(uccelliera)* have both kept their geometrical flowerbeds. Throughout the park the intersections of paths and avenues are marked by fountains and statues. West of Piazza di Siena is the Fontana dei Cavalli Marini (the Fountain of the Seahorses) added during the villa's 18th-century remodelling. Walking through the park you will encounter statues of Byron, Goethe and Victor Hugo, and a gloomy equestrian King Umberto I.

Dotted about the park are picturesque temples made to look like ruins, including a circular Temple of Diana between Piazza di Siena and Porta Pinciana, and a Temple of Faustina, wife of Emperor Antoninus Pius, on the hill north of Piazza di Siena. The nearby medieval-looking Fortezzuola by Canina contains the works of the sculptor Pietro Canonica, who lived in the building and died there in 1959. In the garden stands Canonica's *Monument to the Alpino and his Mule,* which honours the humblest

Neo-Classical Temple of Diana

Ionic temple dedicated to Aesculapius, built on the lake island

protagonists in Italy's alpine battles against Austria in World War I.

In the centre of the park is the Giardino del Lago, its main entrance marked by an 18th-century copy of the Arch of Septimius Severus.

The garden has an artificial lake complete with an Ionic Temple to Aesculapius, the god of health, by the 18th-century architect Antonio Asprucci. Rowing boats and ducks make the lake a favourite with children, banana trees and bamboo grow around the shore, and clearings are studded with sculptures.

Surrounded by flowerbeds south of the lake is the Art Nouveau Fontana dei Fauni, one of the garden's prettiest sculptures. In a clearing close to the entrance on Viale Pietro Canonica are the original Tritons of the Fontana del Moro in Piazza Navona *(see p120)* – they were moved here and replaced by copies in the 19th century.

From the northwest the park is entered by the Viale delle Belle Arti, where the Galleria Nazionale d'Arte Moderna houses a good collection of 19th- and 20th-century paintings. The Art Nouveau character of the area dates from the International Exhibition held here in 1911, for which pavilions were built by many nations, the most impressive being the British School at Rome,

by Edwin Lutyens, with a façade adapted from the upper west portico of St Paul's Cathedral in London. Originally a School of Archaeology, it is now a research institute for classical studies, history and the visual arts. Nearby statues include one of Simon Bolivar and other liberators of Latin America, and the Persian poet, Firdusi.

In the northeastern corner of the park lie the Museo Zoologico and a small re-developed Zoo, the Bioparco, where the emphasis is on conservation. Nearby, the pretty 16th-century Villa Giulia houses a world-famous collection of Etruscan and

Bioparco symbol

other pre-Roman remains. Another Renaissance building of importance is the Palazzina of Pius IV, close to the Via Flaminia entrance. Designed by the architect Vignola in 1552, it later became an elegant apartment for Pius IV's nephew Carlo Borromeo. It now houses the Italian Embassy to the Holy See.

Museo e Galleria Borghese ❷

See pp260–61.

Villa Giulia ❸

See pp262–3.

A stone lion guarding the ornate entrance to the Zoo

Museo e Galleria Borghese ❷

THE VILLA AND PARK were laid out by Cardinal Scipione Borghese, favourite nephew of Paul V, who had the house designed for pleasure and entertainment. The hedonistic cardinal was also an extravagant patron of the arts and he commissioned sculptures from the young Bernini which now rank among his most famous works. Scipione also opened his pleasure park to the public. Today the villa houses the superb private Borghese collection of sculptures and paintings in the Museo and Galleria Borghese.

Façade of the Villa Borghese
This painting (1613) by the villa's Flemish architect Jan van Santen shows the highly ornate façade of the original design.

MUSEUM GUIDE

The museum is divided into two sections: the sculpture collection (Museo Borghese) occupies the entire ground floor and the picture gallery (Galleria Borghese) is on the upper floor. The Galleria Borghese has reopened to the public after extensive restoration work.

★ Rape of Proserpine
One of Bernini's finest works shows Pluto (Hades) abducting his bride. The sculptor's amazing skill with marble can be seen clearly in the twisting figures.

Sleeping Hermaphrodite
Dated around 150 BC, this is a bronze Roman copy of the Greek original by Polycles. The head and mattress were added by Andrea Bergondi in the 17th century.

The Egyptian Room
Frescoes show episodes in Egyptian history and Egyptian motifs.

TIMELINE

1613 15-year-old Bernini sculpts *Aeneas and Anchises*	**Early 1800s** Statues and reliefs are considered too ornate and stripped from the villa's façade	**1809** Much of the collection is sold by Prince Camillo Borghese to France and goes to Louvre
1621–5 Bernini sculpts *Pluto and Persephone*		**1902** Villa, grounds and collection bought by the state

1625	**1725**	**1825**

1622–5 Bernini sculpts *Apollo and Daphne*		**1805** Canova sculpts the semi-nude, reclining Pauline Borghese
1613–15 The Flemish architect Jan van Santen designs and builds Villa Borghese	*Daphne's fingers turning into leaves*	**Early 1900s** Balustrade round the forecourt is bought by Lord Astor for the Cliveden estate in England

Rear entrance

★ **Apollo and Daphne**
Bernini's most famous masterpiece depicts the nymph Daphne fleeing the sun god Apollo at the moment of Daphne's dramatic transformation into a tree.

David is captured the moment before he slays Goliath in the sculpture by Bernini, who modelled his face on his own.

★ **Galleria Borghese**
The gallery has old master paintings, such as Titian's Sacred and Profane Love (detail) dating from 1514.

★ **Pauline Borghese**
Napoleon's sister Pauline posed as Venus for this sculpture. Once the statue was finished, her husband locked it away, even from its sculptor Canova.

Front entrance

Gladiator Mosaic
The floor is decorated with the fragments of a 4th-century AD mosaic from a villa in Torrenova.

VISITORS' CHECKLIST

Villa Borghese, Piazzale Scipione Borghese 5. Map 2 F5.
C 06-328 10 (reservations).
FAX 06-3265 1329. 52, 53, 116, 910 to Via Pinciana.
3, 19 to Viale delle Belle Arti.
Open 9am–7.30pm Tue–Sun.
Closed 1 Jan, 1 May, 25 Dec.
Adm charge. Advance booking recommended weekdays and obligatory Sat & Sun.
w www.galleriaborghese.it

STAR SCULPTURES

★ **Rape of Proserpine by Bernini**

★ **Apollo and Daphne by Bernini**

★ **Galleria Borghese**

★ **Pauline Borghese by Canova**

KEY TO FLOORPLAN

☐ Exhibition space

▨ Non-exhibition space

Villa Giulia ❸

THIS VILLA was built as a country retreat for Pope Julius III, and was designed for entertaining rather than as a permanent home. It once housed an impressive collection of statues – 160 boatloads were sent to the Vatican after the pope died in 1555. The villa, gardens, pavilions and fountains were designed by exceptional architects: Vignola (designer of the Gesù), Vasari and the sculptor Ammannati. Michelangelo also contributed. The villa's main features are its façade, the court-yard and garden and the *nymphaeum*. Since 1889 Villa Giulia has housed the Museo Nazionale Etrusco, with its outstanding collection of pre-Roman antiquities from central Italy.

★ Ficoroni Cist
Engraved and beautifully illustrated, this fine bronze marriage coffer dates from the 4th century BC.

Chigi Oinochoe
Battle and hunting scenes adorn this Corinthian vase from the 6th century BC.

★ Husband and Wife Sarcophagus
This 6th-century BC masterpiece, from Cerveteri, shows a dead couple at the eternal banquet.

MUSEUM GUIDE
This is the most important Etruscan museum in Italy, housing artifacts from most of the major excavations in Tuscany and Lazio. Rooms 1–10 and 23–34 are arranged by site and include Vulci, Todi, Veio and Cerveteri, while private collections are in rooms 11–22.

Votive Offering
The religious Etruscans made artifacts, such as this model of a boy feeding a bird, in their gods' honour.

TIMELINE

1550	1650	1750	1850	1950

1550 Work begins on Villa Giulia under Pope Julius III

1655 Queen Christina of Sweden stays in villa as Vatican guest

1889 Etruscan museum founded

Late 1700s First large-scale studies of Etruscan artifacts

1919 Castellani private collection donated to museum

Late 1500s First, chance finds of Etruscan artifacts raise some scholastic interest

1555 Villa completed

1908 Barberini private collection bought by the state

1972 Pesciotti private collection bought by the state

Corner decoration of bronze chariot used to burn incense

Façade
The villa's façade dates from 1552–3. The entrance is designed in the form of a triumphal arch.

VISITORS' CHECKLIST

Piazzale di Villa Giulia 9.
Map 1 C4.
06-322 6571.
52, 926 to Viale Bruno Buozzi, 88, 95, 490, 495 to Viale Washington.
3, 19 to Piazza Thorwaldsen.
Open 8.30am–7.30pm Tue–Sun (last entry 30 mins before closing time). **Closed** 1 Jan, 1 May, 25 Dec. **Adm charge.**
with seven days' notice.
Concerts in the courtyard in July.

★ **Reconstruction of an Etruscan Temple**
Count Adolfo Cozza built the Temple of Alatri here in 1891. He based his design on the accounts of Vitruvius and 19th-century excavations.

Nymphaeum
Literally, the "area dedicated to the nymphs", this is a sunken courtyard decorated with Classical mosaics, statues and fountains.

STAR EXHIBITS

★ **Husband and Wife Sarcophagus**

★ **Ficoroni Cist**

★ **Reconstruction of an Etruscan Temple**

Main entrance

Faliscan Crater of the Dawn
This ornate vase, painted in the free style of the 4th century BC, shows Dawn rising in a chariot.

KEY TO FLOORPLAN

☐ Ground floor
☐ First floor
☐ Non-exhibition space

Museo di Arte Contemporanea di Roma ❹

Via Reggio Emilia 54. **Map** 6 E1.
📞 06-6710 7900. 🚌 36, 60, 84, 90. **Open** 9am–7pm Tue–Sat, 10am–2pm Sun. **Adm charge.** 📷
💻 Ⓦ www.macro.roma.museum

Part of the 4th-century mosaic in the ambulatory of Santa Costanza

THE HISTORIC Peroni beer factory on Via Reggio Emilia is now home to MACRO, the city's gallery of contemporary art. Apart from a permanent collection of late 20th-century art, featuring artists such as Carla Accardi, Achille Perilli and Mario Schifano, there are interesting exhibitions showcasing the latest developments on the local and national scene.

Interior of Santa Costanza

Santa Costanza ❺

Via Nomentana 349. 📞 06-861 0840.
🚌 36, 60, 84, 90. **Open** 9am–noon, 4–6pm Tue–Sat, 4–6pm Sun, 9am–noon Mon. **Adm charge.** ♿ 📷

THE ROUND CHURCH of Santa Costanza was first built as a mausoleum for Emperor Constantine's daughters Constantia and Helena, in the early 4th century. The dome and its drum are supported by a circular arcade resting on 12 magnificent pairs of granite columns. The ambulatory that runs around the outside of the central arcade has a barrel-vaulted ceiling decorated with wonderful 4th-century mosaics of flora and fauna and charming scenes of a Roman grape harvest. In a niche on the far side of the church from the entrance is a replica of Constantia's ornately carved porphyry sarcophagus. The original was moved to the Vatican Museums in 1790.

Constantia's sanctity is debatable – she was described by the historian Marcellinus as a fury incarnate, constantly goading her equally unpleasant husband Hannibalianus to violence. Her canonization was probably the result of some confusion with a saintly nun of the same name.

Sant'Agnese fuori le Mura ❻

Via Nomentana 349. 📞 06-861 0840.
🚌 36, 60, 84, 90. **Open** 9am–noon, 4–6pm Tue–Sat, 4–6pm Sun, 9am–noon Mon. **Adm charge** to catacombs. ♿ 📷

THE CHURCH OF Sant'Agnese stands among a group of early Christian buildings which includes the ruins of a covered cemetery, some extensive catacombs and the crypt where the 13-year-old martyr St Agnes was buried in AD 304. Agnes was exposed naked by order of Emperor Diocletian, furious that she should have rejected the advances of a young man at his court, but her hair miraculously grew to protect her modesty *(see p121)*.

The church is said to have been built at the request of the Emperor Constantine's daughter, Constantia, after she had prayed at the Tomb of St Agnes for delivery from leprosy.

Though much altered over the centuries, the form and much of the structure of the 4th-century basilica remain intact. In the 7th-century apse mosaic St Agnes appears as a bejewelled Byzantine empress in a stole of gold and a violet robe. According to tradition she appeared like this 8 days after her death holding a white lamb. Every year on 21 January two lambs are blessed on the church altar and a vestment called the *pallium* is woven from their wool. Every newly appointed archbishop is sent a *pallium* by the pope.

Apse mosaic in Sant'Agnese, showing the saint flanked by two popes

Cloister, San Lorenzo fuori le Mura

San Lorenzo fuori le Mura 𝟕

Piazzale del Verano 3. 📞 06-49 15 11. 🚌 71, 492. 🚃 3, 19. **Open** 7.30am–12.30pm, 3–7pm (7.30pm in summer) daily. ♿

JUST OUTSIDE the eastern wall of the city stands the church of San Lorenzo. Roasted slowly to death in AD 258, San Lorenzo was one of the most revered of Rome's early Christian martyrs. The first basilica erected over his burial place by Constantine was largely rebuilt in 576 by Pope Pelagius II. Close by stood a 5th-century church dedicated to the Virgin Mary. The intriguing two-level church we see today is the result of these two churches being knocked into one. This process, started in the 8th century, was completed in the 13th century by Pope Honorius III, when the nave, the portico and much of the decoration were added. The remains of San Lorenzo are in the choir of the 6th-century church (beneath the 13th-century high altar).

Romanesque bell tower of San Lorenzo

Via Appia Antica 𝟖

🚌 118, 218, 660. See **Walks** pp284–5.

THE FIRST PART of the Via Appia was built in 312 BC by the Censor Appius Claudius Caecus. When it was extended to the ports of Benevento, Taranto and Brindisi in 190 BC, the road became Rome's link with its expanding empire in the East. It was the route taken by the funeral processions of the dictator Sulla (78 BC) and Emperor Augustus (AD 14) and it was along this road that St Paul was led a prisoner to Rome in AD 56.

Gradually abandoned during the Middle Ages, the road was restored by Pope Pius IV in the mid-16th century. It is lined with ruined family tombs and collective burial places known as columbaria. Beneath the fields on either side lies a vast maze of catacombs. Today the road starts at Porta San Sebastiano (see p196). Major Christian sights include the church of Domine Quo Vadis?, built where St Peter is said to have met Christ while fleeing from Rome, and the Catacombs of San Callisto and San Sebastiano. The tombs lining the road include those of Cecilia Metella (see p266) and Romulus (son of Emperor Maxentius) who died in 309. The ancient Villa dei Quintili is nearby, at Via Appia Nuova 1092 (phone 06-481 5576).

Catacombs of San Callisto 𝟗

Via Appia Antica 126. 📞 06-513 0151. 🚌 118, 218, 660. **Open** 8.30am–noon, 2.30–5.30pm (Oct–Mar: 5pm) Thu–Tue. **Closed** Feb; 1 Jan, Easter Sun & 25 Dec. **Adm charge.** 🚻 🚫 ♿ 🅿 📷 W www.catacombe.roma.it

IN BURYING their dead in underground cemeteries outside the city walls, the early Christians were obeying the laws of the time: it was not because of persecution. So many saints were buried that the catacombs became shrines and places of pilgrimage.

The vast Catacombs of San Callisto are on four different levels and only partly explored.

The rooms and connecting passageways are hewn out of volcanic tufa. The dead were placed in niches, known as *loculi*, which held two or three bodies. The most important rooms were decorated with stucco and frescoes. The area that can be visited includes the Crypt of the Popes, where many of the early popes were buried, and the Crypt of Santa Cecilia, where the saint's body was discovered in 820 before being moved to her church in Trastevere (see p211).

Catacombs of San Sebastiano 𝟏𝟎

Via Appia Antica 136. 📞 06-788 7035. 🚌 118, 218, 660. **Open** 8.30am–noon, 2.30–5.30pm (Oct–Mar: 5pm) Mon–Sat. **Closed** Mid-Nov–mid-Dec, 1 Jan, Easter Sun, 25 Dec. **Adm charge.** 🚻 ♿ 📷 W www.catacombe.roma.it

THE 17TH-CENTURY church of San Sebastiano, above the catacombs, occupies the site of a basilica. Preserved at the entrance to the catacombs is the *triclia*, a building that once stood above ground and was used by mourners for taking funeral refreshments. Its walls are covered with graffiti invoking St Peter and St Paul, whose remains may have been moved here during one of the periods of persecution.

Cypresses lining part of the Roman Via Appia Antica

Catacombs of Domitilla ⓫

Via delle Sette Chiese 282. 📞 *06-511 0342*. 🚌 *218, 716*. **Open** *8.30am–noon, 2.30pm–5.30pm (Oct–Mar: 5pm) Wed–Mon*. **Closed** *Jan, Easter Sun, 25 Dec*. **Adm charge**. 🚫 ✔

This network of catacombs is the largest in Rome. Many of the tombs from the 1st and 2nd centuries AD have no Christian connection. In the burial chambers there are frescoes of both Classical and Christian scenes, including one of the earliest depictions of Christ as the *Good Shepherd*. Above the catacombs stands the basilica of Santi Nereo e Achilleo. After rebuilding and restoration, little remains of the original 4th-century church.

Bronze entrance gates to the Fosse Ardeatine by Mirko Basaldella

Fosse Ardeatine ⓬

Via Ardeatina 174. 📞 *06-513 6742*. 🚌 *218, 716*. **Open** *8.15am–5pm daily*. **Closed** *public hols*.

On the evening of 24 March 1944, Nazi forces took 335 prisoners to this abandoned quarry south of Rome and shot them at point blank range. The execution was in reprisal for a bomb attack that had killed 32 German soldiers. The victims included various political prisoners, 73 Jews and ten other civilians, among them a priest and a 14-year-old boy. The Germans blew up the tunnels where the massacre had taken place, but a local peasant had witnessed the scene and later helped find the corpses. The site is

now a memorial to the values of the Resistance against the Nazi occupation, which gave birth to the modern Italian Republic *(see p185)*. A forbidding bunker-like monument houses the rows of identical tombs containing the victims.

Beside it is a museum of the Resistance. Interesting works of modern sculpture include *The Martyrs*, by Francesco Coccia, and the gates shaped like a wall of thorns by Mirko Basaldella.

Tomb of Cecilia Metella ⓭

Via Appia Antica, km 3. 📞 *06-3996 7700*. 🚌 *118, 660*. **Open** *9am–1 hr before sunset Tue–Sun*.

One of the most famous landmarks on the Via Appia Antica is the huge drum-shaped tomb built for the noblewoman Cecilia Metella. Her father and husband were rich patricians and successful generals of late Republican Rome, but hardly anything is known about the woman herself. Byron muses over her unknown destiny in his poem *Childe Harold*.

In 1302 Pope Boniface VIII donated the tomb to his family, the Caetani. They incorporated it in a fortified castle that blocked the Via Appia, allowing them to control the traffic on the road and exact high tolls.

The marble facing of the tomb was pillaged by another pope, Sixtus V, at the end of the 16th century.

Fragments of marble relief on the Tomb of Cecilia Metella

EUR's Palazzo della Civiltà del Lavoro, the "Square Colosseum"

EUR ⓮

🚌 *170, 671, 714 and other routes .* Ⓜ *EUR Fermi, EUR Palasport*. **Museo della Civiltà Romana** *Piazza G. Agnelli 10*. 📞 *06-592 6041*. **Open** *9am–6.15pm Tue–Sat, 9am–1.30pm Sun and public hols*. **Closed** *1 Jan, 1 May, 25 Dec*. **Adm charge**.

The esposizione Universale di Roma (EUR), a suburb south of the city, was built for an international exhibition, a kind of "Work Olympics", that was planned for 1942, but never took place because of the war. The architecture was intended to glorify Fascism and the style of the public buildings is very overblown and rhetorical. The eerie shape of the Palazzo della Civiltà del Lavoro (The Palace of the Civilization of Work) is an unmistakable landmark for people arriving from Fiumicino airport.

The scheme was completed in the 1950s. In terms of town planning, EUR has been quite successful and people are still keen to live here. The great marble halls house several government offices and museums.

The Museo della Civiltà Romana displays a vast scale model of Rome at the time of Constantine and casts of the reliefs on Trajan's Column. These are highly recommended and make the museum well worth a visit.

To the south is a lake and park, and the huge domed Palazzo dello Sport built for the 1960 Olympics.

San Paolo fuori le Mura ⓯

Via Ostiense 186. 📞 06-541 0341.
🚌 23, 128, 170, 670, 707, 761,
769. Ⓜ San Paolo.
Open 7am–7pm daily (summer),
7am–6.30pm daily (winter). **Cloister
closed** 1–3pm daily. 🔲 ♿ 🔲

T ODAY'S CHURCH IS a faithful
reconstruction of the great
4th-century basilica destroyed
by fire on 15 July 1823.
Few fragments of the
original church survived. The
triumphal arch over the nave
is decorated on one side with
restored 5th-century mosaics.
On the other side are mosaics
by Pietro Cavallini, originally
on the façade. The splendid
Venetian apse mosaics (1220)
depict the figures of Christ
with St Peter, St Andrew,
St Paul and St Luke.

The fine marble canopy
over the high altar is signed
by the sculptor Arnolfo di
Cambio (1285) "together
with his partner Pietro",
who may have been Pietro
Cavallini. Below the altar is
the *confessio*, the tomb of
St Paul. To the right is an
impressive Paschal candlestick
by Nicolò di Angelo and
Pietro Vassalletto.

The cloister of San Paolo,

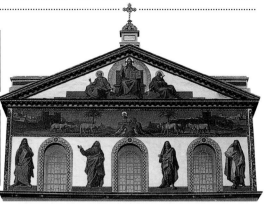

19th-century mosaic on façade of San Paolo fuori le Mura

with its pairs of colourful
inlaid columns supporting the
arcade, was spared completely
by the fire. Completed around
1214, it is considered one of
the most beautiful in Rome.

Centrale Montemartini ⓰

Via Ostiense 106. 📞 06-574 8042.
🚌 769, 23. **Open** 9.30am–7pm
Tue–Sun. **Closed** public hols.
Adm charge. 🔲 ♿ 🔲 ✓

A N ENORMOUS old industrial
site has been restored to
house the ACEA art centre.
Originally, the building was
used as Rome's first power

station and its two huge
generators still occupy the
central machine room
creating quite an intriguing
contrast to the exhibitions.
On display are Roman statues
and artifacts belonging to the
Capitoline Museums *(see
pp70–73)*. Many of the statues
were discovered during
excavations in the late 19th
and early 20th centuries but
were kept in storage until
fairly recently.

Casino del Bel Respiro, summer
residence in Villa Doria Pamphilj

Villa Doria Pamphilj ⓱

Via di San Pancrazio. 🚌 31, 44,
75, 710, 870. **Park** open dawn–
dusk daily.

O NE OF ROME'S largest public
parks, the Villa Doria
Pamphilj was laid out in the
mid-17th century for Prince
Camillo Pamphilj. His uncle,
Pope Innocent X, paid for
the magnificent summer
residence, the Casino del Bel
Respiro, and the fountains
and summerhouses, some of
which still survive.

Statue in Centrale Montemartini, former power plant turned art centre

Day Trips around Rome

Tivoli, a favourite place to escape the heat of the Roman summer

Tivoli ⑱

Town is 31 km (20 miles) northeast of Rome. **FS** *from Tiburtina.* 🚌 *COTRAL from Ponte Mammolo (on Metro line B).*

TIVOLI HAS BEEN a popular summer resort since the days of the Roman Republic. Among the famous men who owned villas here were the poets Catullus and Horace, Caesar's assassins Brutus and Cassius, and the Emperors Trajan and Hadrian. Tivoli's main attractions were its clean air and beautiful situation on the slopes of the Tiburtini hills, its healthy sulphur springs and the waterfalls of the Aniene – the Emperor Augustus said these had cured him of insomnia. The Romans' luxurious lifestyle was revived in Renaissance times by the owners of the Villa d'Este, the town's most famous sight.

Detail of Fontana dell'Organo at Villa d'Este

In the Middle Ages Tivoli suffered frequent invasions as its position made it an ideal base for an advance on Rome. In 1461 Pope Pius II built a fortress here, the Rocca Pia, declaring: "It is easier to regain Rome while possessing Tivoli, than to regain Tivoli while possessing Rome."

After suffering heavy bomb-damage in 1944, Tivoli's main buildings and churches were speedily restored. The town's cobbled streets are still lined with medieval houses. The Duomo (cathedral) houses a beautiful 13th-century life-size wooden group representing the *Deposition from the Cross.*

Villa d'Este ⑲

Piazza Trento 1, Tivoli. 📞 *0774-31 2070.* 🚌 *COTRAL from Ponte Mammolo (on Metro line B).* **Open** *8.30am–1 hr before sunset Tue–Sun.* **Closed** *1 Jan, 1 May, 25 Dec.* **Adm charge.** ▣

THE VILLA OCCUPIES the site of an old Benedictine convent. In the 16th century the estate was developed by Cardinal Ippolito d'Este, son of Lucrezia Borgia. A palace was designed by Pirro Ligorio to make the most of its hilltop situation, but the villa's fame rests more on the terraced gardens and fountains laid out by Ligorio and Giacomo della Porta.

The gardens have suffered neglect in the past, but the grottoes and fountains still give a vivid impression of the great luxury which the princes of the church enjoyed. From the great loggia of the palace you descend through the privet-lined paths to the Grotto of Diana and Bernini's Fontana del Bicchierone. Below to the right is the Rometta (little Rome), a model of Tiber Island with allegorical figures and the legendary she-wolf. The Rometta is at one end of the Viale delle Cento Fontane, 100 fountains in the shapes of grotesques, obelisks, ships and the eagles of the d'Este coat of arms. Other fountains are now being restored to their former glory. The Fontana dell'Organo is a water-organ, in which the force of the water pumps air through the pipes. The garden's lowest level has flower beds and fountains as well as some splendid views out over the plain below.

Terrace of 100 Fountains in the gardens of Villa d'Este

Villa Gregoriana ⑳

Largo Massimo, Tivoli. **FS** 🚌 *Tivoli, then short walk.* **Closed** *for restoration.*

THE MAIN ATTRACTIONS of this steeply sloping wooded park are the waterfalls and grottoes created over the centuries by the River Aniene. The park is named after Pope Gregory XVI, who in the 1830s ordered the building of a tunnel to ward against flooding. When the tunnel was completed it created a new waterfall, called the Grande Cascata, which plunges 160 m (525 ft) into the valley behind the town.

The Canopus, extensively restored, with replicas of its original caryatids lining the bank of the canal

Hadrian's Villa ㉑

Villa Adriana, Via Tiburtina. Site is 6 km (4 miles) southwest of Tivoli. ☎ 0774-53 02 03. ⓕ Tivoli, then local bus No. 4. 🚌 COTRAL from Ponte Mammolo (on Metro line B). **Open** 9am–1 hr before sunset daily. **Closed** 1 Jan, 1 May, 25 Dec. **Adm charge**. 🖥 🚻 ♿

BUILT AS a private summer retreat between AD 118 and 134, Hadrian's Villa was a vast open-air museum of the finest architecture of the Roman world. The grounds of the Imperial palace covered an area of 120 hectares (300 acres) and were filled with full-scale reproductions of the emperor's favourite buildings from Greece and Egypt. Although excavations on this site began in the 16th century, many of the ruins lying scattered in the surrounding fields have yet to be identified with any certainty. The grounds of the villa make a very picturesque site for a picnic, with scattered fragments of columns lying among olive trees and cypresses.

For an idea of how the whole complex would have looked in its heyday, study the scale model in the building beside the car park. The most important buildings are signposted and several have been partially restored or reconstructed. One of the most impressive is the so-called Maritime Theatre. This is a round pool with an island in the middle, surrounded by columns. The island, reached by means of a swing bridge, was probably Hadrian's private studio, where he withdrew from the cares of the Empire to indulge in his two favourite pastimes, painting and architecture. There were also theatres, Greek and Latin libraries, two bathhouses, extensive housing for guests and the palace staff, and formal gardens with fountains, statues and pools.

Hadrian also loved Greek philosophy. One part of the gardens is thought to have been Hadrian's reproduction of the Grove of Academe,

Fragment of marble mosaic pavement in the Imperial palace

where Plato lectured to his students. He also had a replica made of the Stoà Poikile, a beautiful painted colonnade in Athens, from which the Stoic philosophers took their name. This copy enclosed a great piazza with a central pool. The so-called Hall of the Philosophers close to the Poikile was probably a library.

The most ambitious of Hadrian's replicas was the Canopus, a sanctuary of the god Serapis near Alexandria. For this a canal 119 metres (130 yards) long was dug and Egyptian statues were imported to decorate the temple and its grounds. This impressive piece of engineering has been restored and the banks of the canal are lined with caryatids.

Another picturesque spot in the grounds is the Vale of Tempe, the legendary haunt of the goddess Diana with a stream representing the river

Pair of Ionic columns in the vaulted baths of Hadrian's Villa

Peneios. Below ground the emperor even built a fanciful recreation of the underworld, Hades, reached through underground tunnels, of which there were many linking the various parts of the villa.

Plundered by barbarians who camped here in the 6th and 8th centuries, the villa fell into disrepair. Its marble was burnt to make lime for cement and Renaissance antiquarians contributed even further to its destruction. Statues unearthed in the grounds are on show in museums around Europe. The Vatican's Egyptian Collection (see p238) has many fine works that were found here.

Ostia Antica ㉒

Viale dei Romagnoli 717. Site is
25 km (16 miles) southwest of Rome.
[06-5635 8099. **FAX** 06-565 1500.
M *Piramide, then train from Porta
San Paolo station.*
Excavations and museum open
9am – 1 hour before sunset.
Closed *1 Jan, 1 May, 25 Dec.*
Adm charge. 🔲 🔲 🔲

Ruins of shops, offices and houses near Ostia's theatre

I N REPUBLICAN TIMES Ostia
was Rome's main com-
mercial port and a military
base defending the coastline
and the mouth of the Tiber.
The port continued to flourish
under the Empire, despite
the development of Portus,
a new port slightly to the
northwest, in the 2nd century
AD. Ostia's decline began in
the 4th century, when a
reduction in trade was combined with the gradual silting
up of the harbour. Then
malaria became endemic in
the area and the city, whose
population may have been
nearly 100,000 at its peak,
was totally abandoned.

Buried for centuries by
sand, the city is remarkably
well preserved. The site is
less spectacular than Pompeii
or Herculaneum because
Ostia died a gradual death,
but it gives a more complete
picture of life under the
Roman Empire. People of all
social classes and from all
over the Mediterranean lived
and worked here.

Visitors can understand the
layout of Ostia's streets almost
at a glance. The main road
through the town, the
Decumanus Maximus, would
have been filled with hurrying
slaves and citizens, avoiding
the jostling carriages and
carts, while tradesmen

pursued their business under
the porticoes lining the street.
The floorplans of the public
buildings along the road are
very clear. Many were bathhouses, such as the Baths of
the Cisiarii (carters) and the
grander Baths of Neptune,
named after their fine black-
and-white floor mosaics.
Beside the restored theatre,
three large masks, originally
part of the decoration of the
stage, have been mounted
on large blocks of tufa.
Beneath the great brick
arches that supported the
semicircular tiers of seats
were taverns and shops.
Classical plays are put on
here in the summer.

The Tiber's course has
changed considerably since
Ostia was the port of Rome. It
once flowed past just to the
north of Piazzale delle

**Mask decorating
the theatre**

Corporazioni, the square
behind the theatre. The
corporations were the guilds
of the various trades involved
in fitting out and
supplying ships:
tanners and rope-
makers, ship-
builders and
timber merchants,
ships' chandlers
and corn weighers.
There were some
60 or 70 offices
around the square.
Mosaics showing
scenes of everyday
life in the port and
the names and
symbols of the
corporations can
still be seen.

There were also offices used
by ship-owners and their
agents from places as far apart
as Tunisia and the south of
France, Sardinia and Egypt.
In one office, belonging to
a merchant from the town
of Sabratha in North Africa,
there is a delightful mosaic
of an elephant.

The main cargo coming into
Rome was grain from Africa.
Much of this was distributed
free to prevent social unrest.
Although only men received
this *annona* or corn dole,
at times over 300,000 were
eligible. In the centre of the
square was a temple, probably

Mural from Ostia of merchant ship being loaded with grain

dedicated to Ceres, goddess of the harvest. Among the buildings excavated are many large warehouses in which grain was stored before it was shipped on to Rome.

The Decumanus leads to the Forum and the city's principal temple, erected by Hadrian in the 2nd century AD and dedicated to Jove, Juno and Minerva. In this rather romantic, lonely spot, it is hard to imagine the Forum as a bustling centre, where justice was dispensed and officials

Floor mosaic of Nereid and sea monster in the House of the Dioscuri

met to discuss the city's affairs. In the 18th century it was used as a sheepfold.

Away from the main street are the buildings where Ostia's inhabitants lived. The great majority were housed in rented

Detail of floor mosaic in the Piazzale delle Corporazioni

apartments in blocks three or four storeys high known as *insulae*. These varied considerably in their comfort and decoration. The House of Diana was one of the smarter ones, with a balcony around the second floor, a private bathhouse and a central courtyard with a cistern where tenants came to collect their water. Around the ground floor of the block were shops, taverns and bars selling snacks and drinks. In the bar at the House of Diana you can see the marble counter used by customers buying their

sausages and hot wine sweetened with honey.

For the wealthy there were detached houses *(domus)* such as the House of the Dioscuri, which has fine mosaics, and the House of Cupid and Psyche, named after a statue there. This is now in the site's Museo Ostiense, near the Forum, along with other sculptures and reliefs found in Ostia.

Among the houses and shops there are other fascinating buildings including a laundry and the firemen's barracks. The religions practised in Ostia reflect the cosmopolitan nature of the port. There are also no fewer than 18 temples dedicated to the Persian god Mithras, as well as a Jewish Synagogue dating from the 1st century AD and a Christian basilica. A plaque records the death of St Augustine's mother in a hotel here in AD 387.

ALSO WORTH SEEING

Anagni FS *from Termini (c.50 min).*
Picturesque hill-town with papal palace and famous Romanesque cathedral.

Bracciano FS *from Termini or Tiburtina (c.90 min).* 🚌 *from Lepanto, on Metro line A (bus c.90 min).*
Volcanic lake with villages and wooded hills. Nice for walks or a visit to Orsini Castle. Swimming in summer.

Cerveteri FS *from Termini, Tiburtina or Ostiense to Cerveteri-Ladispoli, then local bus (c.70 min).* 🚌 *from Via Lepanto, on Metro line A (bus c.80 min).*
One of the greatest Etruscan cities. Necropolis with complete streets and houses.

Nemi 🚌 *from Anagnina, on Metro line A (bus c.60 min).*
Charming village at volcanic lake in the Castelli Romani. Famous for its wine and strawberries.

Palestrina 🚌 *from Anagnina, on Metro line A (bus c.70 min).*
Impressive Roman sanctuary to goddess Fortuna. Museum and the Mosaic of the Nile.

Pompeii FS *to Naples, then change to local train (c.170 min).* 🚌 *Special bus tours from tourist agents.*
Excavations of the wealthy and bustling Roman city where the busy daily life was put to a sudden end by the eruption of Vesuvius in AD 79.

Subiaco 🚌 *from Ponte Mammolo, on Metro line B (bus c.120 min).*
Birthplace of St Benedict. Two monasteries to visit.

Tarquinia FS *from Termini or Ostiense (c.180 min).* 🚌 *from Via Lepanto, on Metro line A. Change at Civitavecchia (c.150 min).*
Outstanding collection of Etruscan objects and frescoes from Tarquinia's necropolis.

Viterbo FS *from Ostiense (c.100 min) or train from Roma Nord, Piazzale Flaminio, on Metro line A (c.120 min).* 🚌 *from Saxa Rubra reached by the train above (bus c.90 min).*
Medieval quarter, papal palace and archaeological museum within 13th-century walls.

A Two-Hour Walk by the River Tiber

ROME OWES ITS VERY EXISTENCE to the Tiber; the city grew up around an easy fording point where a market place developed. The river could also be a hazard; shallow and torrent-like, it flooded the city every winter up to 1870, when work began on the massive Lungotevere embankments that run along both sides of the river. These provide many fine views from points along their avenues of plane trees. The walk also explores the neighbourhoods along the riverside, in particular the Jewish Ghetto and Trastevere, which have preserved much of their character from earlier periods in the colourful history of Rome.

From the old port of Rome to Via dei Funari

Starting from the church of Santa Maria in Cosmedin ① *(see p202)*, cross the piazza to the Temples of the Forum Boarium ② *(see p203)*. This was the cattle market that stood near the city's river port. The river here has preserved two less obvious structures from ancient Rome: the mouth of the Cloaca Maxima ③, the city's great sewer, and one arch of a ruined bridge, known as the Ponte Rotto ④. In Via Petroselli stands the rather extraordinary medieval Casa dei Crescenzi ⑤ *(see p203)*, decorated with fragments of Roman temples. Passing the modern Anagrafe (public records office) ⑥, built on the site of the old Roman port, you come to San Nicola in Carcere ⑦ *(see p151)*.

You are now in the Foro Olitorio, Rome's ancient vegetable market. To the east stand the ruins of a Roman portico and the medieval house of the Pierleoni family. Head for the massive Theatre

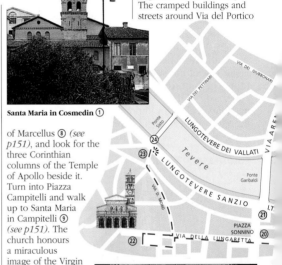

Santa Maria in Cosmedin ①

of Marcellus ⑧ *(see p151)*, and look for the three Corinthian columns of the Temple of Apollo beside it. Turn into Piazza Campitelli and walk up to Santa Maria in Campitelli ⑨ *(see p151)*. The church honours a miraculous image of the Virgin credited with halting the plague in 1656. The 16th-century piazza was the home of Flaminio Ponzio, its architect, who lived at No. 6. Take Via dei Delfini to Piazza Margana where you should look up at the 14th-century tower of the Margani family ⑩. Retrace your steps, then go up Via dei Funari (Street of the Ropemakers) to the 16th-century façade of Santa Caterina dei Funari ⑪.

The Ghetto

From Piazza Lovatelli take Via Sant'Angelo in Pescheria, which leads to the ruined Portico of Octavia ⑫ *(see p152)* in the Jewish Ghetto *(see p152)*. The Roman portico, once Rome's fish market, houses the church of Sant'Angelo in Pescheria. Find the marble plaque on the façade: fish longer than this slab were given to the city's *conservatori* (governors). Turn into the Ghetto: two column stumps belonging to the Portico stand in front of a patched-up doorway made of fragments of Roman sculpture. The cramped buildings and streets around Via del Portico

Arch of the Ponte Rotto ④

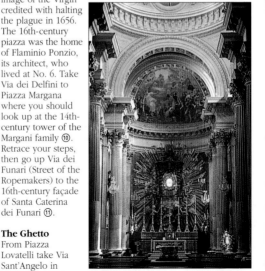

Main altar of Santa Maria in Campitelli ⑨

d'Ottavia are typical of old Rome: see the Casa di Lorenzo Manilio ⑬ *(see p152)*, and turn down Via del Progresso, past Palazzo Cenci ⑭ *(see p152)*, towards the river. On Lungotevere walk past the Synagogue ⑮ *(see p152)* to the small church of San Gregorio ⑯. Here stood the Ghetto's gates, which were locked at sundown.

Across the river to Trastevere

Crossing to Tiber Island *(see p153)* by Ponte Fabricio, with its two ancient

Classical relief of Medusa above the doorway of Palazzo Cenci ⑭

much of the spirit of old Trastevere. Walk up to the start of Viale di Trastevere at Piazza Belli. After crossing the road look back

Santa Maria in Trastevere, don't miss the old-fashioned chemist's shop at No. 7. The piazza itself, in front of the magnificent church of Santa Maria in Trastevere ㉒ *(see pp212–13)*, has a cheerful atmosphere, and the fountain steps are a favourite meeting place. Go back a little way to Via del Moro. This leads to Piazza Trilussa, dominated by the fountain of the Acqua Paola ㉓, where you emerge on to the bank of the river again. Note the lifelike statue, near the fountain, of Roman poet Trilussa, who wrote in the local dialect. From Ponte Sisto ㉔ *(see p210)*, look back to Tiber Island and, beyond it, to the medieval bell tower of Santa Maria in Cosmedin, set against the pine trees on the summit of the Palatine.

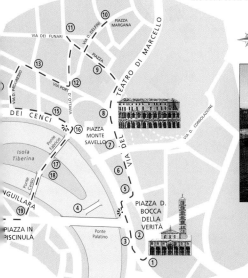

The western tip of Tiber Island

| 0 metres | 250 |
| 0 yards | 250 |

stone heads on the parapet, you can enjoy a good view of the river in both directions. On the island itself, you should not miss the Pierleoni Tower ⑰ or the church of San Bartolomeo all'Isola ⑱.

Trastevere

As you cross into Trastevere, you can see the medieval house of the powerful Mattei family ⑲, with its fragments of ancient sculpture. Beyond it, Piazza in Piscinula and the surrounding streets retain

KEY

- - Walk route

⚕ Good viewing point

at the medieval tower of the Anguillara ⑳ and the statue honouring the poet Gioacchino Belli ㉑ *(see p209)*. As you go down Via della Lungaretta to Piazza

Piazza in Piscinula, old Trastevere

TIPS FOR WALKERS

Starting point: *Piazza della Bocca della Verità.*

Length: *3.5 km (2 miles).*

Getting there: *The 23, 44, 81, 160, 280, 628, 715 and 716 buses stop near Santa Maria in Cosmedin.*

Best time for walk: *This walk can be very romantic in the evening but is enjoyable at any time.*

Stopping-off points: *Piazza Campitelli and Piazza Margana have typical Roman restaurants, and Via del Portico d'Ottavia has restaurants and a bakery. Tiber Island has a bar and the famous Sora Lella restaurant (see p314). In Viale Trastevere there are bars and pizzerias. Piazza Santa Maria in Trastevere has lively bars and restaurants with outdoor tables.*

A One-Hour Walk along Via Giulia

LAID OUT BY BRAMANTE for Pope Julius II in the early 16th century, Via Giulia was one of the first Renaissance streets to slice through Rome's jumble of medieval alleys. The original plan included new law courts in a central piazza, but this project was abandoned for lack of cash. The street now is dominated by antiques shops and furniture restorers. On summer evenings, hundreds of oil lamps light the street while cloisters and courtyards provide romantic settings for a special season of concerts.

Baroque capital on the façade of Sant'Eligio degli Orefici ⑦

From Lungotevere to Largo della Moretta

Starting from Lungotevere dei Tebaldi ① at the eastern end of Via Giulia, you will see ahead of you an archway ② spanning the road. This was the start of Michelangelo's unrealized project linking Palazzo Farnese and its gardens *(see p147)* with the Villa Farnesina *(see pp220–21)* on the other side of the river.

Just before you reach the archway, you will see to your left the curious Fontana del Mascherone ③, in which an ancient grotesque mask and granite basin were combined to create a Baroque fountain.

Beyond the Farnese archway on the left is the lively Baroque façade of the church of Santa Maria dell'Orazione e Morte ④ *(see p147)*. A bit further along on the same side of the road stands Palazzo Falconieri ⑤, enlarged by Borromini in 1650. Note its two stone falcons glowering at each other across the width of the façade. On the other side of the road you pass the yellowish façade of Santa Caterina da Siena ⑥, church of the Sienese colony in Rome, which has pretty 18th-century reliefs. The figures of Romulus and Remus symbolize Rome

Relief of Romulus and Remus on Santa Caterina da Siena ⑥

and Siena – there is a legend that the city of Siena was founded by the less fortunate of the twins. After passing the short street that leads down to Sant'Eligio degli Orefici ⑦ *(see p148)* and the façade of Palazzo Ricci ⑧ *(see p149)*, you come to an area of half-demolished buildings around the ruined church of San Filippo Neri ⑨, called Vicolo della Moretta. If you look to the left down to the river, you

Fontana del Mascherone ③

can see Ponte Mazzini and the huge prison of Regina Coeli on the other side of the Tiber. At this point you may like to make a small detour to the right to the beginning of Via del Pellegrino, where there is an inscription ⑩, defining the *pomerium*, or boundary, of the city in the time of the Emperor Claudius.

From Largo della Moretta to the Sofas of Via Giulia

Further on, facing the narrow Vicolo del Malpasso are the imposing prisons, the Carceri Nuove ⑪, built by Pope Innocent X Pamphilj in 1655. When first opened, they were a model of humane treatment of prisoners, but were replaced by the Regina Coeli prison across the river at the end of the 19th century. The buildings now house offices of the Ministry of Justice and a small Museum of Crime.

At the corner of Via del Gonfalone, a small side street running down to the river,

KEY

-- Walk route

½ Good viewing point

0 metres	250
0 yards	250

Farnese archway across Via Giulia, built to a design by Michelangelo ②

the traditional distribution of bread to the poor that took place on the saint's feast day.

On the corner there are more travertine blocks belonging to the foundations of Julius II's projected law courts, known because of their curious shape as the "Sofas of Via Giulia".

The Florentine Quarter

Your next stop should be the imposing Palazzo Sacchetti at No. 66 ⑮. Originally this was the house of Antonio da Sangallo the Younger, the architect of Palazzo Farnese, but it was greatly enlarged by later owners. The porticoed courtyard houses a 15th-century Madonna and a striking Roman relief of the 3rd century AD. Just opposite Palazzo Sacchetti, note the beautiful late Renaissance portal of Palazzo Donarelli ⑯. The 16th-century house at No. 93 is richly decorated with stuccoes and coats of arms ⑰. No. 85 is another typical Renaissance palazzo with a heavily rusticated ground floor ⑱. There is a tradition

Plaque honouring Antonio da Sangallo on Palazzo Sacchetti ⑮

that, like many houses of the period, it once belonged to Raphael. Palazzo Clarelli ⑲ was built by Antonio da Sangallo the Younger as his own house. The inscription above the doorway bears the name of Duke Cosimo II de' Medici, whose family later bought the palazzo.

This whole area used to be inhabited by a flourishing Florentine colony, which had its own water-mills built on pontoons along the Tiber. Their national church is San Giovanni dei Fiorentini ⑳ (see p153), the final great landmark at the end of Via Giulia. Many Florentine artists and architects had a hand in its design, including Sangallo and Jacopo Sansovino.

Coat of arms of Pope Paul III Farnese on the façade of Via Giulia No. 93 ⑰

you can see part of the foundations of Julius II's planned law courts. Just down the street stands the small Oratorio di Santa Lucia del Gonfalone ⑫, which is often used for concerts.

The next interesting façade is Carlo Rainaldi's 17th-century Santa Maria del Suffragio ⑬ on the left. On the same side is San Biagio degli Armeni ⑭, the Armenian church in Rome. It is often referred to by local people as San Biagio della Pagnotta (of the loaf of bread). The nickname originates from

Detail on the side of the door of Santa Maria del Suffragio ⑬

TIPS FOR WALKERS

Starting point: Lungotevere dei Tebaldi, by Ponte Sisto.

Length: 1 km (1,100 yds).

Getting there: The 116 goes to and along Via Giulia, or you can take 46, 62 or 64 to Corso Vittorio Emanuele II, then walk down Via dei Pettinari, or take a 23 or 280 along Lungotevere.

Best time for walk: On summer evenings oil lamps light the street. At Christmas, there are cribs on display in many shop windows.

Stopping-off points: There are bars in Via Giulia, at Nos. 21 and 84. Campo de' Fiori has better bars, with outdoor tables, and a wide choice of places to eat. These include a fried fish restaurant in Piazza Santa Barbara dei Librai (closed Sun).

A 90-Minute Tour of Rome's Triumphal Arches

Rome's greatest gift to architecture was the arch, and the Roman people's highest tribute to its victorious generals was the triumphal arch. In Imperial times, arches were erected to honour an emperor's campaign victories almost as a matter of course, promoting his personal cult and ensuring his subsequent deification. Spectacular processions passed through these arches. Conquering generals, cheered by rapturous crowds, rode in their chariots to the Capitol, accompanied by their legions bearing spoils from their campaigns.

Part of the Via Sacra, once spanned by the Arch of Augustus ③

Arches of the Forum

This walk through the Forum and around the base of the Palatine takes in Rome's three great surviving triumphal arches and two arches of more

Relief of barbarian captives on the Arch of Septimius Severus ①

humble design that were used simply as places of business. It starts from the Arch of

Tips for Walkers

Starting point: The Roman Forum, entrance Largo Romolo e Remo, on Via dei Fori Imperiali.
Length: 2.5 km (1.5 miles).
Getting there: The nearest Metro station is Colosseo on line B. Buses 84, 85, 87, 117, 175, 186, 810, 850 stop in Via dei Fori Imperiali, near Forum entrance.
Best time for walk: Any time of day during Forum opening hours (see p82) is suitable.
Stopping-off points: Several bars and restaurants overlook the Colosseum. There is a small bar in Via dei Cerchi and a smarter one behind San Giorgio in Velabro, in Piazza San Giovanni Decollato (closed Sun). For a meal, try Alvaro al Circo Massimo (closed Mon) in Via di San Teodoro.

Emperor Septimius Severus ① and his sons Geta and Caracalla *(see p83)* in the Forum. Erected in AD 203, it celebrates a successful campaign in the Middle East. Eight years later, when Caracalla had his brother killed, all mention of Geta was removed from the inscription.

Look up at the reliefs showing phases of the campaigns. Set in tiers, they are probably the sculptural counterparts of the paintings illustrating the general's feats that were borne aloft in the triumphal procession. On the right, the inhabitants of a fortified city surrender to the Romans' siege machines. Below are smaller friezes showing the triumphal procession itself.

Heading east, make your way through the Forum to the ruins of the Temple of Julius Caesar ②. The temple was built by Augustus in 29 BC, on the site where Caesar's body was cremated after Mark Antony's famous funerary oration. A nearby sign marks the ruins of one of the arches dedicated to Augustus ③, spanning the Via Sacra between the Temple of Castor and Pollux ④ *(see p84)* and the Temple of Caesar. This arch, erected after Augustus had defeated Mark Antony and Cleopatra, was finally demolished in 1545, and its

Capital from Temple of Castor and Pollux ④

materials were used in the new St Peter's. From here, proceed uphill towards the elegant Arch of Titus ⑤ *(see p87)*. Compared with Septimius Severus's arch, it shows an earlier, simpler style. Look up at the beautiful lettering of the inscription before

KEY

▬	Walk route
✹	Good viewing point
M	Metro station

0 metres   250
0 yards   250

Arch of Titus in a 19th-century watercolour by the English artist Thomas Hartley Cromek ⑤

Arches of Domitian's extension to the Claudian Aqueduct ⑨

excavated in the 18th and 19th centuries. Many of the carts that passed through the arch would have been carrying building materials quarried from the Forum's many ruined monuments.

Arch of Constantine

Leave the Forum by heading down the hill towards the Colosseum ⑥ *(see pp92–5)* and the nearby Arch of Constantine ⑦ *(see p91)*. This arch, hastily built to commemorate the emperor's victory over his rival Maxentius in AD 312, is a patchwork of reliefs from different periods. Stand on the Via di San Gregorio side and compare you examine the inner bas-reliefs. These show Roman legionaries carrying the spoils looted from the conquest of Jerusalem, heralds holding plaques with the names of vanquished peoples and cities, and Titus riding in triumph in his chariot.

The medieval Frangipane family turned the Colosseum into a vast impregnable stronghold and incorporated the Arch of Titus into their fortifications. Notice the wheelmarks scratched on the inside walls of the arch by generations of carts; they indicate the steady rise in the level of the Forum floor before it was eventually the earlier panels at the top (AD 180–193) with the hectic battle scenes just above the smaller arches, sculpted in AD 315. In the curious dwarf-like soldiers, you can see the transition from Classicism to a cruder medieval style of sculpture.

Now take Via di San Gregorio, which runs the length of the valley between the Palatine and Celian hills. This was the ancient route taken by most triumphal processions. Passing the entrance to the Palatine ⑧ and the well-preserved arches of the Claudian Aqueduct ⑨ on the right, you come to Piazza di Porta Capena ⑩, named after the gate that stood here to mark the beginning of the Via Appia *(see p284)*. After rounding the back of the Palatine, follow Via dei Cerchi, which runs alongside the grassy area that preserves, in an oval outline, all that remains of the Circus Maximus ⑪ *(see p205)*.

Arches of the Forum Boarium

When you reach the church of Sant'Anastasia ⑫, turn right up Via di San Teodoro, then first left down Via del Velabro. Straddling the street is the four-sided Arch of Janus ⑬ *(see p202)*, erected in the 3rd century AD. This is not a triumphal arch but a covered area where merchants could take shelter from the sun or rain when discussing business. Like the Arch of Titus, it became part of a fortress built by the Frangipane family during the Middle Ages.

Tucked away beside the nearby church of San Giorgio in Velabro ⑭ *(see p202)* is what looks like a large rectangular doorway. This is the Arco degli Argentari, or Moneychangers' Arch ⑮. Look up at the inscription, which says that it was erected by local silversmiths in honour of Septimius Severus and his family in AD 204. As in the emperor's triumphal arch, the name of Geta has been obliterated by his brother and murderer, Caracalla. Geta's figure has also been removed from among the portraits on the panels inside the arch. Triumph in Imperial Rome could be very short-lived.

Four-sided Arch of Janus in the Forum Boarium ⑬

A Three-Hour Tour of Rome's Best Mosaics

IN IMITATION of the audience chambers of Imperial palaces, Rome's early Christian churches were decorated with colourful mosaics. These were pieced together from cubes of marble, coloured stone and fragments of glass. To create a golden background, gold leaf was placed between pieces of glass. These were then heated so that they fused. The glorious colours and subjects portrayed gave the faithful a glimpse of the heavenly court of the King of Kings. This walk concentrates on a few of the churches decorated in this wonderful medium.

Apse mosaic in the Chapel of Santa Rufina ③

San Giovanni

Start from Piazza di Porta San Giovanni, where you can visit the heavily restored mosaic of the Triclinio Leoniano (see p179). Originally in the banqueting hall of Pope Leo III (795–816) ①, it shows Christ among the Apostles. On the left are Pope Sylvester and the Emperor Constantine, on the right, Pope Leo and Charlemagne just before he

Obelisk and side façade of San Giovanni in Laterano ②

was crowned Holy Roman Emperor in AD 800. Inside the basilica of San Giovanni in Laterano ② (see pp182–3), the 13th-century apse mosaic shows Christ as he appeared miraculously during the consecration of the church. In the panels by the windows, look for the small figures of two Franciscan friars; these are the artists Jacopo Torriti (left) and Jacopo de Camerino

(right). Leave by the exit on the right near the splendid 16th-century organ and head for the octagonal Baptistry of San Giovanni ③, where the Chapel of Santa Rufina has a beautiful apse mosaic, dating from the 5th century. In the neighbouring Chapel of San Venanzio, there are golden 7th-century mosaics, showing the strong influence of the Eastern Church at this time.

Santo Stefano Rotondo to San Clemente

Leave the piazza by the narrow road that leads to the round church of Santo Stefano Rotondo ④ (see p185). One of its chapels contains a 7th-century Byzantine mosaic honouring two martyrs buried here. Further on, in Piazza della Navicella, is the church of Santa Maria in Domnica ⑤ (see p193). It houses the superb mosaics commissioned by Pope Paschal I, who gave new impetus to Rome's mosaic production in the 9th century. He is represented kneeling beside the Virgin. On leaving the church, notice the façade of San Tommaso in Formis ⑥, which has a charming mosaic of Christ flanked by two freed slaves, one black and one white, dating from the 13th

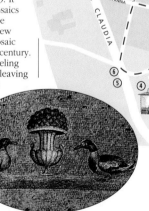

Ceiling mosaic, Baptistry of San Giovanni ③

Interior of Baptistry of San Giovanni ③

acanthus leaves. San Clemente also has a fine 12th-century Cosmatesque mosaic floor.

The Colle Oppio
Passing the old entrance to the church, cross Via Labicana and walk up the hill to the small Colle Oppio park ⑨. This has fine views of the Colosseum and contains the ruins of the Domus Aurea ⑩ *(see p175)* and the Baths of

century. From here, head up the steep hill, past the forbidding apse of Santi Quattro Coronati ⑦ *(see p185)*, to the fascinating church of San Clemente ⑧ *(see pp186–7)*. Its 12th-century apse mosaic shows the cross set in a swirling pattern of

Trajan ⑪. Across the park lie San Martino ai Monti ⑫ *(see p170)*, which has a 6th-century mosaic portrait of Pope St Sylvester near the crypt, and Santa Prassede ⑬ *(see p171)*. Here the Chapel of St Zeno contains the most important Byzantine mosaics in Rome, reminiscent of the fabulous mosaics of Ravenna. Pope Paschal I erected the chapel as a mausoleum for his

14th-century façade mosaics by Filippo Rusuti. Inside, the 5th-century mosaics in the nave depict Old Testament stories, while the triumphal arch has scenes relating to the birth of Christ, including one of the Magi wearing striped stockings. In the apse there is a *Coronation of the Virgin* by Jacopo Torriti (1295).

On leaving Santa Maria, pass the obelisk ⑮ in the piazza behind the church and go downhill to Via Urbana and Santa Pudenziana ⑯ *(see p171)*. The figures in the apse mosaic, one of the oldest in Rome (AD 390), are remarkable for their naturalism. The two women with crowns are traditionally identified as Santa Prassede and Santa Pudenziana.

Mosaic saint in Santa Prassede ⑬

When you leave the church, you can either retrace your steps to Santa Maria Maggiore or walk down Via Urbana to Via Cavour Metro station.

11th-century frieze above the doorway of Santa Pudenziana ⑯

mother Theodora. The apse and triumphal arch of the church itself also have fine mosaics. When you move on to Santa Maria Maggiore ⑭ *(see pp172–3)*, go to the column in the centre of the piazza in front of the church to see the beautiful

PIAZZA DI S. GIOVANNI IN LATERANO

PIAZZA DI PORTA S. GIOVANNI

San Giovanni Ⓜ

KEY

- ▬ ▪ Walk route
- ▬ City Wall
- ☀ Good viewing point
- Ⓜ Metro station

0 metres 250
0 yards 250

TIPS FOR WALKERS

Starting point: Piazza di Porta San Giovanni.
Length: 3.5 km (2 miles).
Getting there: The nearest Metro station is San Giovanni, on line A, in Piazzale Appio, just outside Porta San Giovanni. The 16, 81, 85, 87, 650 and 850 buses and the 3 tram stop in front of San Giovanni in Laterano, while 117 and 218 stop around the corner on Piazza San Giovanni in Laterano.
Best time for walk: Go in the morning, in order to appreciate the mosaics in the best light.
Stopping-off points: The bars and restaurants in Piazza del Colosseo are popular with tourists. In the Parco del Colle Oppio there is a café kiosk with tables. There are several bars around Santa Maria Maggiore, some with outdoor tables.

A Two-Hour Walk around Bernini's Rome

GIAN LORENZO BERNINI (1598–1680) is the artist who probably left the strongest personal mark on the appearance of the city of Rome. Favourite architect, sculptor and town planner to three successive popes, he turned Rome into a uniquely Baroque city. This walk traces his enormous influence on the development and appearance of the centre of Rome. It starts from the busy Largo di Santa Susanna just north of Termini station, at the church of Santa Maria della Vittoria.

Façade of Santa Maria in Via ⑬

Quirinale. The long wing of the Palazzo del Quirinale ⑦ *(see p158)*, nicknamed the Manica Lunga (long sleeve), is by Bernini. On the other side of the road is the façade of Sant'Andrea al Quirinale ⑧ *(see p161)*, one of Bernini's greatest churches. When you reach the Piazza del Quirinale ⑨, note the doorway of the palazzo, attributed to Bernini. From the piazza, go down the

composer Donizetti lived at No. 77 and turn into Via di Santa Maria in Via, where the church ⑬ has a fine Baroque

Bernini's Fontana del Tritone ②

Through Piazza Barberini

Santa Maria della Vittoria ① *(see p255)* houses the Cornaro Chapel, the setting for one of Bernini's most revolutionary and controversial sculptures, *The Ecstasy of St Teresa* (1646). From here take Via Barberini to Piazza Barberini. In its centre is Bernini's dramatic Fontana del Tritone ② *(see p254)* and at one side stands the more modest Fontana delle Api ③ *(see p254)*. As you go up Via delle Quattro Fontane, you catch a glimpse of Palazzo Barberini ④ *(see p255)* built by Bernini and several other artists for Pope Urban VIII. The gateway and cornices are decorated with the bees that made up part of the Barberini family crest. Next make your way to the crossroads, decorated by Le Quattro Fontane ⑤ *(see p162)*, to enjoy the splendid views in all four directions.

Passing the diminutive San Carlo alle Quattro Fontane ⑥ *(see p161)*, built by Bernini's rival Borromini, take Via del

stairs to Via della Dataria, and into Vicolo Scanderbeg which leads to a small piazza with the same name ⑩. Scanderbeg was the nickname of the Albanian prince Giorgio Castriota (1403–68), the "Terror of the Turks". His portrait is preserved on the house where he lived.

The Trevi Fountain

Go along the narrow Vicolo dei Modelli ⑪, where male models waited to be chosen by artists, then turn towards the Trevi Fountain ⑫ *(see p159)*. Its energy is clearly inspired by Bernini's work, a tribute to his lasting influence on Roman taste. Leave the piazza along Via delle Muratte where the

Neptune Fountain at the north end of Piazza Navona ⑱

façade by Bernini's follower Carlo Rainaldi. At the top of this street, turn left down to Via del Corso. On the other side of the road, you will see the towering Column of Marcus Aurelius ⑭ *(see p113)* in Piazza Colonna. Beyond this is Palazzo Montecitorio ⑮, begun in 1650 by Bernini and now the home of the Italian parliament *(see p112)*.

Pantheon to Piazza Navona

Via in Aquiro leads you to the Pantheon ⑯ *(see pp110–11)*. Refusing Pope Urban VIII's request for him to redecorate

Statue of the river Nile from the Fontana dei Quattro Fiumi

Quattro Fiumi *(see p120)*, was by Bernini, though the figures symbolic of the four rivers were sculpted by other artists. The central figure in the Fontana del Moro, however, is by Bernini himself. Bernini's contemporaries were fascinated by the innovative use of shells, rocks and other natural forms in his fountains, and his expert handling of water to create constant movement.

An extended walk

More energetic walkers may like to head towards the river to see the Ponte Sant'Angelo and its Bernini angels, and then on to St Peter's *(see pp230–33)* where they can admire Bernini's great colonnaded piazza in front of the church, the papal tombs, his altar decorations and the bronze baldacchino.

the dome, Bernini said that although St Peter's had a hundred defects, the Pantheon did not have any. From the Pantheon, make a small detour to Piazza della Minerva where you can see the bizarre Bernini obelisk, supported by a small elephant, by the church of Santa Maria sopra Minerva ⑰ *(see p108)*. Then retrace your steps and take Salita dei Crescenzi to

Angel on Ponte Sant'Angelo

reach the fabulous Piazza Navona ⑱ *(see p120)* which was remodelled by Bernini for Pope Innocent X Pamphilj. The design for the central fountain, the Fontana dei

KEY

— Walk route

☀ Good viewing point

Ⓜ Metro station

0 metres	250
0 yards	250

TIPS FOR WALKERS

Starting point: Largo di Santa Susanna.

Length: 3.5 km (2 miles).

Getting there: Take Metro line A to Repubblica or any bus to Termini, then walk. Buses 61, 62, 175 and 492 stop in Via Barberini.

Best time for walk: Go either between 9am and noon for good lighting conditions in the churches, or between 4pm and 7pm.

Stopping-off points: The Piazza Barberini and Fontana di Trevi areas have lots of bars and pizzerias. The many elegant cafés en route include the famous Caffè Giolitti (see p109) and outdoor cafés and restaurants are plentiful around Piazza della Rotonda and Piazza Navona.

A 90-Minute Walk along the Via Appia Antica

L INED WITH CYPRESSES AND PINES as it was when the
ancient Romans came here by torchlight to bury
their dead, the Via Appia is wonderfully atmospheric.
The fields are strewn with ruined tombs set against the
picturesque background of the Alban hills to the south.
Although the marble or travertine stone facings of most
tombs have been plundered, a few statues and reliefs
survive or have been replaced by copies.

**Tomb of Sixtus Pompeus
the Righteous** ⑨

Capo di Bove

Start from the
Tomb of Cecilia
Metella ① *(see
p266).* In the
Middle Ages this
area acquired the
name Capo di
Bove (ox head)
from the frieze of
festoons and ox
heads still visible
on the tomb. On

**Gothic windows in the church
of San Nicola** ②

the other side of
the road you can see the
ruined Gothic church of San
Nicola ②, which, like the
Tomb of Cecilia Metella, was
part of the medieval fortress
of the Caetani family.

Proceed to the crossroads ③,
where there are still many
original Roman paving slabs,
huge blocks of extremely
durable volcanic basalt. Just

on both sides of
the Appia, are
other tombs, some
still capped with the
remains of the medieval
towers that were built over
them. On the right after
passing some private villas,
you come to a military zone
around the Forte Appio ⑤,
one of a series of forts built
around the city in the
19th century. On the
left, a little further on,
stand the ruins of
the Tomb of Marcus
Servilius ⑥, showing
fragments of reliefs
excavated in 1808 by
the Neo-Classical
sculptor Antonio
Canova. He was one
of the first to work
on the principle that
excavated tombs and
their inscriptions and reliefs
should be allowed to remain
in situ. On the other side of
the road stands a tomb with a
relief of a man, naked except
for a short cape, known as the

"Heroic
Relief" ⑦.
On the left of
the road are the
ruins of the so-
called Tomb of
Seneca ⑧. The great
moralist Seneca owned
a villa near here, where
he committed suicide in
AD 65 on the orders of Nero.

The next major tomb is that
of the family of Sixtus
Pompeus the Righteous, a
freed slave of the 1st century
AD ⑨. The verse inscription
records the father's sadness at
having to bury his own
children, who died young.

The ruined church of San Nicola ②

past the next turning (Via
Capo di Bove), you will see
on your left the nucleus of a
great mausoleum overgrown
with ivy, known as the Torre
di Capo di Bove ④. Beyond it,

Artist's impression of how the mausoleums and tombs lining the Via Appia looked in the 2nd century AD

Section of the Via Appia Antica, showing original Roman paving stones

From Via dei Lugari to Via di Tor Carbone

Just past Via dei Lugari on the right, screened by trees, is the Tomb of Pope St Urban (reigned 222–230) ⑩. Set back from the road on the left stands a large ruined podium, probably part of a Temple of Jupiter ⑪. The next stretch was excavated by the architect Luigi Canina early in the 19th century. On the right is the Tomb of Caius Licinius ⑫, followed by a smaller Doric tomb ⑬ and the imposing Tomb of Hilarius Fuscus ⑭, with five portrait busts in relief of members of his family. Next comes the Tomb of Tiberius Claudius Secondinus ⑮, where a group of freedmen of the Imperial household were buried in the 2nd century AD.

Passing a large ruined columbarium, you reach the Tomb of Quintus Apuleius ⑯ and the reconstructed Tomb of the Rabirii freed slaves (1st century BC) ⑰. This has a frieze of three half-length figures above an inscription.

The figure on the right is a priestess of Isis. Behind her you can see the outline of a *sistrum*, the metal rattle used at ceremonies of the cult.

The majority of the tombs are little more than shapeless stacks of eroded brickwork. Two exceptions in the last stretch of this walk are the Tomb of the Festoons ⑱, with its reconstructed frieze of festive putti, and the Tomb of the Frontispiece ⑲, which has a copy of a relief with four portraits. The two central figures are holding hands.

When you reach Via di Tor Carbone, the Via Appia still stretches out ahead of you in a straight line and, if you wish to extend your walk, there are many more tombs and ruined villas to visit along the way.

KEY

– – Walk route

🔆 Good viewing point

0 metres	250
0 yards	250

Figure on the Tomb of the Heroic Relief ⑦

TIPS FOR WALKERS

Starting point: Tomb of Cecilia Metella.

Length: 3 km (2 miles).

Getting there: Taking a taxi is the easiest way to reach the tomb. Alternatively, take the 118 from Piazzale Ostiense or the 660 from Colli Albani on Metro Line A.

Best time for walk: Go fairly early, before it becomes too hot.

Stopping-off points: There is a bar near the church of Domine Quo Vadis?, before the start of the walk, but it is advisable to take your own refreshment. There are also several well-established restaurants on the first stretch of the Appia, including the Cecilia Metella, Via Appia Antica 129, tel 06-513 6743 (closed Mon).

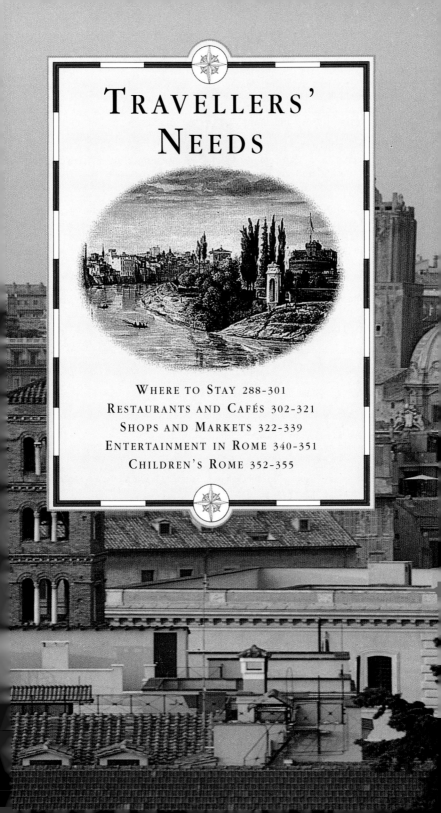

TRAVELLERS' NEEDS

WHERE TO STAY

ROME HAS BEEN a major tourist centre since the Middle Ages, when pilgrims from all over Europe came to visit the home of Catholicism and its relic-packed churches. The nostalgic can still sleep in a 15th-century hotel, or stay around the Campo de' Fiori market, where visiting ecclesiastics were entertained by courtesans in the Renaissance era. Those who prefer their history a little less raffish could opt for an ex-monastery or convent, or stay in a still-functioning religious house. Romantics could sleep in the house once occupied by Keats, while stargazers could stay

Porter at the Majestic Hotel

in former palaces graced by celebrities of the past and present. Rome can offer the full range of accommodation, mostly in historical buildings, very little purpose-built. *Pensione* (guesthouse) is no longer an official category, but in practice many retain the name and more personal character that has made them so popular with travellers. Other possibilities include hostels, residential hotels and self-catering accommodation.

The 72 hotels we have selected are organized in the *Choosing a Hotel* chart *(pp294–5)* and in the listings *(pp296–301)* according to their price category and area.

WHERE TO LOOK

AROUND the Spanish Steps and Piazza di Spagna lies the traditional heartland of foreign visitors, with some of the most exclusive smaller hotels. Similar places can be found all over the centre, to the west of Via del Corso.

While moderately priced accommodation is rare in central Rome, the advantages of staying right on the doorstep of the city's many ancient sights cannot be over-estimated; you can walk to the major areas of interest and easily return at midday for a shower and siesta. If the

less expensive hotels we have recommended in the centre are full, try the Borgo – close to the Vatican – or the lively quarter of Trastevere.

Those in search of glamour should head for Via Veneto, which has many grand and luxurious hotels.

If you're looking for a peaceful retreat, try the area around the Aventine, or one of the high-class hotels next to the Villa Borghese park.

Although many of the streets immediately around Termini station are rather seedy, the area is nonetheless a convenient stopover for travellers and there's a

concentration of cheap hotels, with some decent (if basic) ones among them. The hotels recommended lie in a fairly safe area on the east side of the station. The approach to the centre from Termini has a number of good hotels that are particularly suitable for the business traveller.

HOTEL PRICES

ALTHOUGH ROME MAY still offer less expensive accommodation than other large cities like London or New York, rates for comparable establishments have caught up. Prices are set by the state, and hotels are supposed to display the official rate on the door of each room. VAT (*IVA* in Italian) is usually included, and has been taken into account in the price categories on page 291.

Hotels in Rome generally have low and high season rates, so it is often advisable to double-check when booking, as you may be quoted the higher rate, even in the winter months before and after Christmas, when competition is less strong. Discounts for long-stay visitors and groups are often negotiable.

Rooms without a bathroom can cost about 30 per cent less. Single travellers are badly

The Verdi Room in Via Veneto's Majestic Hotel *(see p301)*

The Plaza Minerva *(see p296)*

catered for, and though it is possible to find a single room for 60 per cent of the price of a double, on average you'll pay as much as 70 per cent, and occasionally even 90 per cent.

HIDDEN EXTRAS

EVEN IF the price of your room includes service, you are often still expected to give a tip for room service and for bellboys.

Hotels will often add hefty surcharges to international phone calls, and may charge extra for parking and air conditioning. The cost of drinks in minibars can be high – you can buy a cheaper supply from local shops.

FACILITIES

HOTEL STANDARDS have improved of late – you can expect air conditioning and some bathrooms with hair dryers in middle-range establishments and direct-dial phones in middle to lower price rooms, although budget travellers staying in cheaper hotels shouldn't expect much more than a clean room.

Because most hotels occupy historic buildings, room sizes can vary dramatically even within the same establishment (and this is often reflected in the

pricing), so don't be afraid to ask to see your room before you check in. For the same reason, swimming pools are few and far between, but roof terraces or gardens are common across the range.

Top-class hotels will usually have some soundproofing; otherwise noise levels can be dreadful, in which case ask for a room facing away from the road. The chart on pages 294–5 indicates which hotels have a quiet location – this covers both peaceful neighbourhoods and certain quiet streets in busy areas which don't have a constant stream of traffic.

Parking in central Rome is a problem, though a few hotels have a limited number of parking spaces of their own.

Business visitors to the capital are well catered for, with hotel facilities ranging from internet access to meeting rooms *(see pp294–5)*.

HOW TO BOOK

THE ITALIAN postal service tends to be unreliable, so it is safer to book by phone, fax or through the hotel website. You should do this at least two months in advance if you want a particular hotel in May, June, September or October; Easter and Christmas are also busy.

If a deposit is required you can usually pay by credit card. Under Italian law a booking is valid as soon as the deposit is paid, so you're likely to lose money if you pull out. If you arrive by train, touts may descend on you at the station with offers of accommodation. They can be of some use if you are looking for a budget hotel, but you should exercise the usual caution. A better bet if you have not booked anywhere in advance is to head for one of the tourist board offices. Here, staff will reserve you a room within the price range you specify.

Villa San Pio garden *(see p299)*

CHECKING IN AND OUT

ITALIAN HOTELIERS are legally obliged to register you with the police, which is the reason they always ask for your passport. They usually hold on to it for a while, but you need it if you are going to change money. Everyone in Italy is supposed to carry with them some sort of identification.

In some of Rome's cheaper *pensioni*, do not be surprised if you are asked to pay in advance. To speed up the checking out process, mention in advance if you intend to pay by credit card.

The Locarno *(see p297)*

TOURIST BOARDS

PROVINCIAL and state tourist boards can provide advice on accommodation. There is also a free booking service.

Rome Provincial Tourist Board (APT)
Via Parigi 5, 00185.
C 06-48 89 91.
Open 9am–7pm Mon–Sat.

Leonardo da Vinci Airport, Fiumicino.
C 06-48 89 91.
Open 8.15am–7pm daily.

Termini Station, Piazza dei Cinquecento, 00185. **C** 06-4890 6300. **Open** 8am–9pm daily.

Hotel Reservation
C 06-699 1000.
Open 7am–10pm daily.

The Portoghesi Hotel *(see p297)*

The reception area of the Regina Hotel Baglioni *(see p301)*

DISABLED TRAVELLERS

PROVISION for disabled travellers is very poor. Small hotels that occupy parts of buildings sometimes only start their rooms up several flights of stairs, whereas certain establishments can accommodate disabled guests on the ground floor, or only have a couple of rooms which are appropriate. Ramps, wide doorways and bathroom handrails are rare.

Our entries for wheelchair access in the listings below rely on the establishments' own assessments; any specific requirements should be checked before booking.

There is a private organization, CO.IN, at Via E. Giglioli, which advises disabled travellers. They can be contacted on 06-712 9011 (www.coinsociale.it).

TRAVELLING WITH CHILDREN

ITALIANS LOVE CHILDREN and they are usually welcome across the range of hotels. Facilities, however, tend to be unimpressive on paper. Most hotels can provide cots or small beds, but high chairs, children's meals and baby-sitting services are rare. In practice, though, many establishments – especially smaller, family-run ones – go out of their way to be helpful.

Many hotels do not have any special rates for children, especially in high season, and charge a standard rate if you require an extra bed in a room, whether for a baby or an adult, which can add anything from a few euros to 40 per cent on to the price of a double room. For a family with older children, two-room suites are sometimes to be found. For hotels providing children's facilities, see Choosing a Hotel *(pp294–5)*.

BED & BREAKFAST

A FAIRLY NEW option for visitors to Rome is bed & breakfast accommodation. Roman hosts offer their spare rooms to visitors, generally for a lower price than an equivalent hotel room. Contact the **Bed & Breakfast Association of Rome** for a good selection of rooms and apartments, or **Rome Bed & Breakfast**, based in the US.

Bed & Breakfast Association of Rome
Via A. Pacinotti 73.
(06-5530 2248. FAX 06-5530 2259.
@ inquiry@b-b.rm.it
W www.b-b.rm.it

Rome Bed & Breakfast
(1-800-872-2632.
FAX 1-619-531 1686.
W www.romebandb.com

RESIDENTIAL HOTELS

IF YOU WANT the comfort and privacy of your own apartment coupled with the services of a hotel, you could opt to stay in a *residenza*. Prices range from around €250 to over €3,000 for a week in a two-bedded room, though some *residenze* are only available for fortnightly or monthly lets. A full list is available from tourist board offices *(see p289)*. These are some of the most central:

Residence Babuino
Via del Babuino 172, 00187.
(06-361 1663. FAX 06-679 2185.

Di Ripetta
Via di Ripetta 231, 00186.
(06-323 1144.
FAX 06-320 3959.
@ info@ripetta.it
W www.ripetta.it

In Trastevere
Vicolo Moroni 35–36, 00153.
(06-581 2768. FAX 06-679 2185.

Vittoria
Via Vittoria 60-64, 00187.
(06-679 7533. FAX 06-679 2185.

RELIGIOUS INSTITUTIONS

IF YOU DO NOT MIND an early curfew, quite a few religious institutions take in paying guests. You do not have to be a practising Catholic to stay in one of these, but be sure to book well in advance as all of the following places cater for groups of students and pilgrims. **Domus Mariae** and **Istituto Madri Pie** are near the Vatican; **Congregazione Suore dello Spirito Santo** is further out of town, 6 km (4 miles) west of the centre. Prices are in the same range as the cheapest hotels.

Domus Mariae
Via Aurelia 481, 00165.
(06-662 3138.

The Gregoriana *(see p297)*

Residenza Madri Pie
Via A. de Gasperi 4, 00165. 📞 *06-63 19 67*. 🌐 *www.residenzamadripie.it*

Congregazione Suore dello Spirito Santo
Via della Pineta Sacchetti 227, 00168. 📞 & FAX *06-305 3101*.

Facade of the Excelsior *(see p301)*

BUDGET ACCOMMODATION

EVEN IF YOU ARE TRAVELLING on a shoestring, it is possible to find a clean, decent room in Rome. Dormitory accommodation can be found at rock-bottom prices in simple establishments, such as the **Ottaviano.** Youth hostels are a good option – and not just for the young. At the **Ostello del Foro Italico** bed, breakfast and shower can all be had at a very reasonable price.

Women can get single, double or triple rooms at the **Young Women's Christian Association** (YWCA). Its location near Termini is convenient but insalubrious, so those arriving at night should take care. Those wishing to book budget

accommodation are advised to contact the organisation in advance. Advance bookings are not always accepted.

HOSTEL AND DORMITORY ADDRESSES

Ottaviano
Via Ottaviano 6, 00192.
📞 *06-3973 7253*.
@ *info@pensioneottaviano.com*
🌐 *www.pensioneottaviano.com*

Associazione Italiana Alberghi per la Gioventù
(Youth Hostels Association)
Via Cavour 44, 00184.
📞 *06-487 1152*.
FAX *06-488 0492*.
🌐 *www.ostellionline.org*

Ostello del Foro Italico
Viale delle Olimpiadi 61, 00194.
📞 *06-323 6267*.
FAX *06-324 2613*.
🌐 *www.hostels-aig.org*

YWCA
Via C. Balbo 4, 00184.
📞 *06-488 3917*.
FAX *06-487 1028*.

CAMPING

MOST CAMPSITES are located quite far out of town – suitable for an occasional excursion into Rome – with the exception of **Flaminio Village**, near the Olympic Village, which is only 6 km (4 miles) north of the centre.

Flaminio Village
Via Flaminia Nuova 821, 00191.
📞 *06-333 2604*.
FAX *06-333 0653*.
🌐 *www.villageflaminio.com*

The pool in the Aldrovandi Palace garden *(see p301)*

Rome's Best: Hotels

Roman hotels range from frescoed palaces and *fin-de-siècle* bastions of faded glamour to family-run guesthouses. Most are within easy reach of restaurants, shops and transport. Whatever the price level, all the hotels shown on this map have something special to offer, whether it is a chic location, or a roof terrace with soaring views across the city. The only drawback is that these places and the others listed on pages 294–301 are exceptions to the many unremarkable hotels in the city, so you should book well in advance. The hotels shown here are the best in their particular style or price range.

Hotel Raphaël

Sole al Pantheon
The writers Jean Paul Sartre and Simone de Beauvoir stayed in this superbly located – and recently refurbished – 15th-century palazzo. (See p296.)

0 metres   500

0 yards   500

Raphael
Full of antiques and art, the Raphael offers a central location. (See p297.)

Vatican

Piazza di Spagna

Piazza del Rotonda

Piazza Navona

Campo de' Fiori

Janiculum

Trastevere

Campo de' Fiori
Central Rome's best bargain offers small, well-furnished rooms and terrific views from the sixth-floor roof terrace. (See p298.)

Grand Hotel de la Minerve
Smart, post-modern interiors grace this international standard hotel. (See p296.)

Sant'Anselmo
To be sure of getting a room you need to book well in advance at this peacefully located Roman villa. An added bonus is the lovely secluded garden. (See p299.)

Hassler
Luxurious suites and an air of faded grandeur remind visitors of the Hassler's heyday. The roof-top restaurant is Rome's most famous. (See p298.)

Hotel Eden
One of the oldest and most exclusive hotels in Rome, the Eden offers elegant decor and truly innovative cuisine. (See p301.)

Carriage
The serene atmosphere makes this city-centre hotel a special haven. (See p297.)

Via Veneto

Quirinal

St Regis Grand
Good service and extensive facilities are the main features of this old-fashioned, luxury hotel. (See p299.)

apitol

Esquiline

Forum

Palatine

Lateran

Caracalla

ntine

Scalinata di Spagna
The prized location at the top of the Spanish Steps, and a large private terrace, make this hotel a popular choice with visitors. (See p298.)

Inghilterra
Sip a cocktail in the Inghilterra's club-like bar, once frequented by Ernest Hemingway. (See p298.)

Choosing a Hotel

THE 72 HOTELS listed in the following pages have all been inspected and assessed. This chart shows some of the features which may affect your hotel choice. The hotels are listed alphabetically within their price category. For more detailed information, see pages 296–301.

	Price	Number of Rooms	Large Rooms	Business Facilities	Hotel Parking	Recommended Restaurant	Close to Shops and Restaurants	Quiet Location	24-Hour Room Service
FORUM (see p296)									
Lancelot	€€€€	60				●		■	
Forum	€€€€€	78		■					●
PIAZZA DELLA ROTONDA (see p296)									
Mimosa	€€€	11					●	■	
Abruzzi	€€€€	25					●		
Santa Chiara	€€€€	98		■			●		
Colonna Palace	€€€€€	110	●				●		
Grand Hotel de la Minerve	€€€€€	134	●	■		■	●	■	
Nazionale	€€€€€	80	●	■			●		
Sole al Pantheon	€€€€€	25					●		
PIAZZA NAVONA (see p296)									
Genio	€€€	60					●		
Navona	€€€	21					●	■	
Due Torri	€€€€	26					●	■	
Portoghesi	€€€€	27					●	■	
Raphael	€€€€€	59					●	■	
PIAZZA DI SPAGNA (see p297)									
Jonella	€	3					●		
Gregoriana	€€€	20					●	■	●
Manfredi	€€€	18		■			●	■	●
Margutta	€€€	24					●	■	
Piazza di Spagna	€€€	17	●				●		
Suisse	€€€	12	●				●	■	
Carriage	€€€€	24	●				●		
Condotti	€€€€	16	●				●		
Homs	€€€€	48					●	■	
Locarno	€€€€	48		■	●		●		
Valadier	€€€€	60		■		■	●	■	●
Dei Borgognoni	€€€€€	51		■	●		●	■	
Hassler	€€€€€	102	●	■	●	■	●		
Hotel de Russie	€€€€€	130		■		■	●		●
D'Inghilterra	€€€€€	98		■			●	■	●
Mozart	€€€€€	56					●	■	
Scalinata di Spagna	€€€€€	16					●		●
CAMPO DE' FIORI (see p298)									
Della Lunetta	€	35					●	■	
Pomezia	€€	24					●		
Campo de' Fiori	€€€	27					●		
In Parione	€€€	16					●		
Smeraldo	€€€	50					●		
Sole	€€€	59		■	●		●		
Teatro di Pompeo	€€€	13		■	●		●	■	

Price categories for a double room per night, including breakfast, tax and service:
€ under €65
€€ €65–€99
€€€ €100–€149
€€€€ €150–€200
€€€€€ over €200

HOTEL PARKING
Car parking facilities attached to the hotel or in the hotel complex.

CLOSE TO SHOPS AND RESTAURANTS
Within a 5-minute walk of a good area for shops, bars, cafés and restaurants.

BUSINESS FACILITIES
Message-taking service, fax machine for guest use, desk and telephone in each room and a meeting room which is available within the hotel.

		NUMBER OF ROOMS	LARGE ROOMS	BUSINESS FACILITIES	HOTEL PARKING	RECOMMENDED RESTAURANT	CLOSE TO SHOPS AND RESTAURANTS	QUIET LOCATION	24-HOUR ROOM SERVICE
QUIRINAL (see p299)									
Hotel des Artistes	€€€	32	●				●	●	
Residenza Cellini	€€€€	6	●	●	●			●	●
St Regis Grand	€€€€€	161	●	●		●			●
TERMINI (see p299)									
Cervia	€	28							
Katty	€	17							
Giuliana	€€	11	●				●		
Restivo	€€	6							
Canada	€€€	70	●	●					
Venezia	€€€€€	61	●				●		
AVENTINE (see p299)									
Aventino	€€	21	●	●				●	
Sant'Anselmo	€€	45		●				●	
Villa San Pio	€€€	78	●	●	●			●	
Domus Aventina	€€€€€	26	●	●				●	●
TRASTEVERE (see p300)									
Carmel	€€	11							
San Francesco	€€€€	24	●	●			●		
VATICAN (see p300)									
Amalia	€€	30					●		
Alimandi	€€€€	35		●				●	
Columbus	€€€€	92		●	●				
Atlante Star	€€€€€	62	●	●	●	●	●		●
Hotel dei Mellini	€€€€€	80		●	●			●	●
VIA VENETO (see p300)									
Oxford	€€€€	56		●					
La Residenza	€€€€	26	●		●		●		
Alexandra	€€€€€	45					●		
Barocco	€€€€€	28		●			●		
Bernini Bristol	€€€€€	127	●	●			●		●
Eden	€€€€€	121	●	●		●	●	●	●
Excelsior	€€€€€	327	●	●	●		●		●
Imperiale	€€€€€	95		●			●		●
Majestic	€€€€€	100			●	●	●		●
Regina Hotel Baglioni	€€€€€	151	●	●	●		●		
Victoria	€€€€€	113		●			●	●	●
VILLA BORGHESE (see p301)									
Villa Borghese	€€€€	32			●				●
Aldrovandi Palace	€€€€€	119		●	●	●		●	●
Lord Byron	€€€€€	34		●				●	●

FORUM

Lancelot

Via Capo d'Africa 47, 00184. **Map** 9 A1. 📞 06-7045 0615. 📠 06-7045 0640. 🌐 www.lancelothotel.com

Rooms: 60.
AE, DC, JCB, MC, V. €€€€

In a quiet street close to the Colosseum, this family-run hotel offers tastefully furnished rooms, some with terraces and views. Public rooms have a comfortably retro feel, while special features include a cool courtyard bar and a restaurant with vegetarian dishes.

Forum

Via Tor de' Conti 25, 00184. **Map** 5 B5. 📞 06-679 2446. 📠 06-678 6479. 🌐 www.hotelforumrome.com

Rooms: 78. 🛏 1 24 TV
AE, DC, JCB, MC, V. €€€€€

Occupying a palace built out of materials from the ruins of the nearby Imperial Fora, the Forum is an old-fashioned hotel, with mellow, wood-panelled public rooms, and a sunny roof-terrace restaurant giving wonderful views over the archaeological centre.

PIAZZA DELLA ROTONDA

Mimosa

Via di Santa Chiara 61, 00186. **Map** 4 F4 & 12 D3. 📞 06-6880 1753. 📠 06-683 3557. 🌐 www.hotel mimosa.net *Rooms*: 11. 🛏 10.
1 €€€

The Mimosa is a clean, if slightly basic, family-run hotel close to the Pantheon. Rooms are cool and the five communal bathrooms immaculate. The hotel is popular with visiting students, so book ahead.

Abruzzi

Piazza della Rotonda 69, 00186. **Map** 4 F4 & 12 D3. 📞 06-679 2021. 📠 06-6978 8076. 🌐 www.hotel abruzzi.it *Rooms*: 25. 1 €€€€

The Abruzzi provides clean, basic rooms with terracotta-tiled floors in an ochre-coloured palazzo overlooking the Pantheon. The rooms at the back are not the best, but quiet.

Santa Chiara

Via di Santa Chiara 21, 00186. **Map** 4 F4 & 12 D3. 📞 06-687 2979. 📠 06-687 3144.
🌐 www.albergosantachiara.com

Rooms: 96. 🛏 1 TV
AE, DC, JCB, MC, V. €€€€

Conveniently located in the historic centre, the Santa Chiara occupies an apricot-washed palazzo. Public rooms are cool, particularly the marble reception area. Bedrooms are carpeted and well furnished.

Colonna Palace

Piazza di Montecitorio 12, 00186. **Map** 4 F3 & 12 E2. 📞 06-67 51 91. 📠 06-679 4496. 🌐 www. itihotels.it *Rooms*: 104. 🛏 1 TV
AE, DC, MC, V. €€€€€

The Colonna Palace stands on the same piazza as Italy's Chamber of Deputies, and so attracts politicians as well as tourists. Bedrooms are spacious, though the bathrooms are small. Breakfast is served in a basement room livened up by frescoes. There are lovely views from the impressive roof garden where a Jacuzzi has been installed.

Grand Hotel de la Minerve

Piazza della Minerva 69, 00186. **Map** 4 F4 & 12 D3. 📞 06-69 52 01. 📠 06-679 4165. 🌐 www.hotel-invest.com

Rooms: 134. 🛏 1 TV
AE, DC, JCB, MC, V. €€€€€

Occupying Palazzo Fonseca behind the Pantheon, this is one of Rome's newest luxury hotels. The interior was designed by Post-Modern architect Portoghesi, and its centrepiece is the lounge, canopied in semi-translucent Venetian glass, and presided over by a statue of Minerva. The large bedrooms are decorated in shades of beige and coral. Views from the roof terrace are magnificent, stretching over the Pantheon, St Peter's and the Janiculum hill.

Nazionale

Piazza di Montecitorio 131, 00186. **Map** 4 F3 & 12 E2. 📞 06-69 50 01. 📠 06-678 6677. 🌐 www. nazionaleroma.it *Rooms*: 80. 🛏
1 TV
AE, DC, MC, V. €€€€

Home to Robert de Niro while making *Godfather II*, the Nazionale is usually frequented by tourists, businessmen and politicians – it stands right on the corner of the Chamber of Deputies. Public rooms are comfortable, particularly the lounge, with its brocade sofas and flower arrangements. Some of the rooms are huge, and most are partially furnished with French and Italian antiques.

Sole al Pantheon

Piazza della Rotonda 63, 00186. **Map** 4 F4 & 12 D3. 📞 06-678 0441. 📠 06-6994 0689. 🌐 www.hotel solealpantheon.com *Rooms*: 25.
🛏 1 TV
AE, DC, MC, V. €€€€€

A hotel since 1467, the Sole's illustrious list of former guests ranges from Renaissance writer Ariosto to Jean-Paul Sartre and Simone de Beauvoir. It is easy to explain its attraction: its location opposite the Pantheon is unbeatable, and though it has been modernized (60 per cent of the rooms now have Jacuzzis) there are still bedrooms with painted, panelled ceilings.

PIAZZA NAVONA

Genio

Via Zanardelli 28, 00186. **Map** 4 E3 & 11 C2. 📞 06-683 3781. 📠 06-6830 7246. @ leonardi@ travel.it *Rooms*: 60. 🛏 1
TV
AE, DC, JCB, MC, V. €€€

On a fairly busy road behind Piazza Navona, the Genio's bedrooms are ordinary, though comfortable. It has a roof terrace where you can bring your picnic.

Navona

Via dei Sediari 8, 00186. **Map** 4 F4 & 12 D3. 📞 06-686 4203. 📠 06-6880 3802. 🌐 www.hotel navona.com *Rooms*: 21.
🛏 15. 1 €€€

Run largely by the owners' Australian son-in-law, the Navona has fairly comfortable bedrooms, most of which have bathrooms. The superb location – across the road from Piazza Navona and 5 minutes' stroll from the Pantheon – means you may have to book well in advance.

Due Torri

Vicolo del Leonetto 23, 00186. **Map** 4 E3 & 11 C1. 📞 06-687 6983. 📠 06-686 5442. 🌐 www.hotel duetorriroma.com *Rooms*: 26. 1
TV
AE, DC, MC, V. €€€€

This amiable hotel is a short walk from Piazza Navona, tucked into an alleyway in the artisans' district of the old town. Bedrooms vary: some are stylish, others plain. The lounge is both elegant and homely, with swept-back drapes, statuettes, an immense gilt-framed mirror and pink velvet sofas.

Portoghesi

Via dei Portoghesi 1, 00186.
Map 4 E3 & 11 C2. [06-686 4231.
FAX 06-687 6976. [w] www. hotel
portoghesiroma.com **Rooms**: 27.
🛏 1 ⊞ TV 🍽 🔃 🔇 🥾 MC, V.
€€€€

Ideally located on a cobbled street
a couple of minutes' walk from
Piazza Navona, the Portoghesi is
a fairly simple hotel, with slightly
dated bedrooms. The public
rooms, however, are elegant and
there is a roof terrace looking on
to the dome of the Portuguese
community's church next door.

Raphael

Largo Febo 2, 00186. **Map** 4 E3
& 11 C2. [06-68 28 31. FAX 06-
687 8993. [w] www.raphaelhotel.com
Rooms: 59. 🛏 1 TV 🍸 ❄ 🍽
🔃 🍴 🖧 🗞 🔇 🥾 AE, DC, JCB,
MC, V. €€€€€

The Raphael, just off Piazza
Navona, is curtained with ivy.
The big reception lounge has
the air of an exhibition hall –
full of antique statues, modern
sculpture and even a painted
sled. There is a restaurant in the
basement where pride of place
goes to an ornate wine cabinet.
Bedrooms have parquet floors,
marbled walls and 18th-century-
style furniture. The top-floor
rooms have terrific views.

PIAZZA DI SPAGNA

Jonella

Via della Croce 41, 00187.
Map 4 F2. [06-679 7966.
FAX 06-446 2368. **Rooms**: 3.
1 ⊞ 🔇 **Closed** Feb, Mar, Dec.

The Jonella B&B occupies an
orange-coloured palazzo on one of
the most attractive shopping streets
in the Piazza di Spagna area. The
decor is somewhat down-at-heel,
but the location and low prices
make it worth considering. The
owner occasionally pops out to
shop, so it's best to phone with
the precise time of your arrival.

Gregoriana

Via Gregoriana 18, 00187.
Map 5 A2 & 12 F1. [06-679 4269.
FAX 06-678 4258. **Rooms**: 20.
🛏 1 📅 TV 🍽 🖧 🔃
🍴 🍴 🔇 €€€€

The Gregoriana is a stylish hotel,
situated close to the Spanish Steps
in a tree-lined, quiet street of
elegant palazzi. The rooms are
all the same: black lacquer

---

doors, terracotta-coloured carpets,
flowery wallpaper and 1920s
drawings on the walls. There are
no public rooms, so breakfast and
drinks are served in the bedrooms.

Manfredi

Via Margutta 61, 00187. **Map** 5 A2.
[06-320 7676. FAX 06-320 7736.
[w] www.hotelmanfredi.com **Rooms**:
18. 🛏 1 ⊞ TV 🍸 🍽 🖧 🔃
🍸 🍴 🔇 AE, JCB, MC, V. €€€

This pretty hotel is excellently
located, just off Piazza di Spagna,
in a cobbled street of art galleries
and antique shops. The reception
area and bar-breakfast room are
paved with marble and decorated
in soft pastels. The comfortable
bedrooms are all soundproofed,
with pale fabric wall coverings and
co-ordinated furnishings.

Margutta

Via Laurina 34, 00187. **Map** 4 F1.
[06-322 3674. FAX 06-320 0395.
Rooms: 24. 🛏 📅 🔃 🔇 AE, DC,
MC, V. €€€

The Margutta sits on a quiet
cobbled street just below the
Piazza del Popolo. The scruffy
façade and slightly grubby seats in
the lobby are forgotten as soon as
you get into your room, which has
white walls and green wrought-
iron bedsteads and candle-holders.
The three attic rooms that share
a pretty roof terrace have to be
booked well in advance.

Piazza di Spagna

Via Mario de' Fiori 61, 00187. **Map** 5
A2 & 12 F1. [06-679 6412. FAX 06-
679 0654. [w] www.hotelpiazzadi
spagna.it **Rooms**: 17. 🛏 1 📅
TV 🍸 🍽 🖧 🔃 🔇 AE, MC, V.
€€€

Close to the designer boutiques of
Via Condotti, this attractive, small
hotel has simple, but good-sized
rooms, with tiled floors and a
couple of bathrooms with jacuzzis.
The breakfast room and bar are
tiny, so most residents decide to
take breakfast in their own rooms.

Suisse

Via Gregoriana 54–56, 00187.
Map 5 A2 & 12 F1. [06-678 3649.
FAX 06-678 1258. [w] www.hotel
suisserome.com **Rooms**: 12.
🛏 12. 1 📅 🔃 €€€

Occupying the third floor of a
dusty palazzo, the Suisse is a
small, pleasant hotel with friendly
staff. Chinese prints hang along
the corridors and in the rooms.
These also have polished floors,
moulded ceilings and marble-
topped dressers and tables.

Carriage

Via delle Carrozze 36, 00187. **Map**
5 A2. [06-699 0124. FAX 06-678
8279. [w] www.hotelcarriage.net
Rooms: 24. 🛏 1 TV 🍸 🍽 🔇 🥾
🔇 AE, DC, JCB, MC, V. €€€€

Situated in a street where noblemen used to park their carriages,
this hotel's elegance is immediately evident in the reception area,
with its panelling, candelabra and
gilt-framed mirrors. The rooms live
up to expectations, decorated in a
serene shade of blue, with some
antique furniture. Two rooms open
on to the leafy, terracotta-tiled
terrace for all residents while two
have their own private terrace.

Condotti

Via Mario de' Fiori 37, 00187.
Map 5 A2 & 12 F1. [06-679 4661.
FAX 06-679 0457. [w] www.hotel
condotti.com **Rooms**: 16. 🛏 1 TV
🍸 🍽 🥾 🔃 🍴 🔇 AE, DC, JCB,
MC, V. €€€€

Close to Piazza di Spagna and
in the heart of the designer
shopping district, the Condotti
is a comfortable, welcoming
hotel with an ambience and style
all of its own. Rooms are medium
to large and well decorated. One
room has its own small terrace
and three others share one.

Homs

Via della Vite 71–72, 00187.
Map 5 A3 & 12 F1. [06-679 2976.
FAX 06-678 0482. **Rooms**: 48.
🛏 1 📅 TV 🍸 🍽 🔇
🔇 AE, DC, MC, V. €€€€

On one of the quieter, less preten-
tious shopping streets in the Piazza
di Spagna area, the Homs has basic
rooms with dark-green carpets,
white walls and white bathrooms.
The breakfast room opens out on
to a pleasant terrace.

Locarno

Via della Penna 22, 00186. **Map** 4 F1.
[06-361 0841. FAX 06-321 5249.
[w] www.hotellocarno.com
Rooms: 68. 🛏 📅 TV 🍸 🍽
🥾 🍴 🔃 P 🔇 🍸 🍴
🔇 AE, DC, MC, V. €€€€

Situated on a small, busy side-
street near the Tiber, a brief
walk from Piazza del Popolo,
the Locarno is an attractive 1920s
hotel with an Art Nouveau door
and swags of lilac growing across
its façade. Old-fashioned touches
remain, such as a grandfather
clock and a marble-topped bar
of polished wood. Outside,
there is a patio packed with
greenery and kept cool by a
tiny fountain.

Valadier

Via della Fontanella 15, 00187. **Map** 4 F1. 📞 06-361 1998. 📠 06-320 1558. 🌐 www.hotelvaladier.com **Rooms**: 60. 🛏 1 ⬛ 24 📺 📶 🍴 🔌 🏃 🔒 📶 🍴 🔌 🏃 *AE, DC, JCB, MC, V.* €€€€€

Slickly decorated with shiny wood and marble, the Valadier also boasts a roof garden and styles itself as an intimate hideaway for those on a romantic visit to Rome. Public rooms are tailor-made for seduction, with low sofas, marble floors and oriental rugs.

Dei Borgognoni

Via del Bufalo 126, 00187. **Map** 5 A3 & 12 F1. 📞 06-6994 1505. 📠 06-6994 1501. 🌐 www.hotel borgognoni.it **Rooms**: 51. 🛏 1 ⬛ 📺 📶 🍴 🔌 🏃 📶 🅿 🔌 📶 *AE, DC, JCB, MC, V.* €€€€€

This elegant hotel is just off Piazza San Silvestro, five minutes from the Spanish Steps. In the public rooms, modern style is coupled with traditional oil paintings. The bedrooms, some with terraces, are exquisitely understated.

Hassler

Piazza Trinità dei Monti 6, 00187. **Map** 5 A2. 📞 06-69 93 40. 📠 06-678 9991. 🌐 www.hotelhasslerroma.com **Rooms**: 102. 🛏 1 ⬛ 📺 📶 ✳ 📶 🏃 🔌 📶 🅿 🔌 📶 🍴 🔌 📶 🏃 📶 *AE, DC, JCB, MC, V.* €€€€€

At the top of the Spanish Steps, with magnificent views of Rome from its roof terrace, suites and restaurant (*see p313*), the Hassler also boasts a VIP area frequented by royalty and European and American glitterati. Its *dolce vita* days continue, the lounges and bedrooms lit by Venetian glass chandeliers, the wood-panelled bar and marble bathrooms retaining the air of a more extravagant era.

Hotel de Russie

Via del Babuino 9, 00187. **Map** 4 F1. 📞 06-32 88 81. 📠 06-3288 8888. 🌐 www.roccofortehotels.com **Rooms**: 130. 🛏 1 ⬛ 24 📺 📶 🍴 🔌 🏃 📶 🍴 *AE, DC, JCB, MC, V.* €€€€€

A recent addition to Rocco Forte's empire, this historic hotel, once frequented by Cocteau and Picasso, has reopened on its original site. Apart from the breathtaking views, understated luxury is the keynote here, with muted colours and unobtrusive efficiency. The facilities include terrace cafés, a great restaurant and access to a garden on the slopes of the Pincio Hill.

D'Inghilterra

Via Bocca di Leone 14, 00187. **Map** 5 A2. 📞 06-69 9811. 📠 06-6992 2243. 🌐 www.hotel dinghilterraroma.it **Rooms**: 98. 🛏 1 ⬛ 24 📺 📶 🍴 🔌 🏃 📶 🍴 🔌 📶 *AE, DC, MC, V.* €€€€€

Liszt and Hemingway are among the writers, artists and musicians who have stayed here. In Rome's designer shopping area and close to the Spanish Steps, it is a desirable place to stay. The bedrooms are all individually decorated and furnished. The bar could have been lifted straight from a gentlemen's club, and the restaurant walls, painted with views of gardens and the sky-frescoed ceiling, create the illusion of dining in the open.

Mozart

Via dei Greci 23b, 00187. **Map** 4 F2. 📞 06-3600 1915. 📠 06-3600 1735. 🌐 www.hotelmozart.com **Rooms**: 56. 🛏 1 📺 📶 🍴 🔌 📶 🍴 *AE, DC, JCB, MC, V.* €€€€€

Located in a cobbled street between Piazza del Popolo and Piazza di Spagna, the Mozart is immediately appealing. Decor is attractively worn and includes a Venetian mirror. There is a breakfast room, as well as a bar-café, which opens off the stone-flagged reception. Rooms have ceramic-tiled or parquet floors, and bathrooms are small, most having only a shower.

Scalinata di Spagna

Piazza Trinità dei Monti 17, 00187. **Map** 5 A2. 📞 06-679 3006. 📠 06-6994 0598. 🌐 www. hotelscalinata.com **Rooms**: 16. 🛏 1 ⬛ 24 📺 📶 ✳ 🍴 🔌 📶 *AE, DC, MC, V.* €€€€€

This hotel occupies a small 18th-century villa at the top of the Spanish Steps. Breakfast is at a communal table under the gaze of a parrot. Some rooms retain their panelled ceilings. Book well ahead if you want to stay in one of the rooms that open out on to the large terrace.

CAMPO DE' FIORI

Della Lunetta

Piazza del Paradiso 68, 00186. **Map** 4 E4 & 11 C4. 📞 06-686 1080. 📠 06-689 2028. **Rooms**: 35. 🛏 25. 1 📶 🔌 €

Located on a tiny, crumbling piazza, this little hotel offers neat,

simple rooms and a courtyard. It is popular with large groups of American students and can be very noisy. No breakfast is served.

Pomezia

Via dei Chiavari 12, 00186. **Map** 4 E4 & 12 D4. 📞 📠 06-686 1371. 📧 h.pomezia@libero.it **Rooms**: 24. 🛏 14. 1 ⬛ 📶 🔌 *AE, DC, MC, V.* €€

In the heart of the lively Campo de' Fiori district, the Pomezia has spotless, simply decorated rooms and a bar in the reception area to welcome weary arrivals.

Campo de' Fiori

Via del Biscione 6, 00186. **Map** 4 E4 & 11 C4. 📞 06-6880 6865. 📠 06-687 6003. 🌐 www.hotelcampode fiori.com **Rooms**: 27. 🛏 12. ⬛ ✳ 🔌 🔌 *MC, V.* €€€

This mid-range hotel occupies a well-kept house, just off the noisy Campo de' Fiori market square. You enter the tiny reception area along a passageway, in which mirrors repeat a series of columns into an illusory suggestion of infinity. The small bedrooms have beams and paisley furnishings, or sky-painted ceilings, lacy walls and frilly bedcovers. On the sixth floor a split-level roof garden affords vertiginous but aesthetically rewarding views over such landmarks as the Pantheon, the Victor Emmanuel monument and St Peter's.

In Parione

Via dei Chiavari 32, 00186. **Map** 4 E4 & 11 C4. 📞 06-6880 2560. 📠 06-683 4094. 🌐 www.inparione.com **Rooms**: 16. 🛏 16. 1 ⬛ 🔌 📶 📺 📶 🍴 🔌 *AE, DC, JCB, MC, V.* €€€

This small hotel has been smartly refurbished and offers pleasant, air-conditioned rooms with soothing, predominantly rustic, dark wood décor. A great bonus, apart from its central location, is the hotel's roof terrace, which offers excellent views of Rome.

Smeraldo

Vicolo dei Chiodaroli 9, 00186. **Map** 4 F5 & 12 D4. 📞 06-687 5929. 📠 06-6880 5495. 🌐 www.smeraldo roma.com **Rooms**: 50. 🛏 46. 1 📺 📶 🔌 📶 🍴 🔌 *AE, MC, V.* €€€

Situated in the heart of the bustling Campo de' Fiori quarter, the Smeraldo offers an oasis of serenity, with clean, simple rooms in an ochre-washed building with shutters over the windows.

Sole

Via del Biscione 76, 00186. **Map**
4 E4 & 11 C4. **06-6880 6873.**
FAX 06-689 3787. **W** www.sole
albiscione.it **Rooms**: 59.

Possibly the oldest hotel in Rome,
this establishment is in a palazzo
just off the central Campo de' Fiori.
Rooms are furnished in a haphazard
way, but with some character. There
are small sitting areas and a sunny
terrace with a drinks and snack
machine. No breakfast is served.

Teatro di Pompeo

Largo del Pallaro 8, 00186. **Map** 4 E4
& 11 C4. **06-6830 0170.** **FAX** 06-
6880 5531. **W** www.hotelteatrodi
pompeo.it **Rooms**: 13.

This small hotel sits over the ruins
of the first permanent theatre in
the city, which was completed
in 55 BC. You can eat breakfast
among the original theatre arches,
and the bar has a terracotta floor
and marble tables.

QUIRINAL

Hotel des Artistes

Via Villafranca 20, 00185. **Map** 6 D3.
06-445 4365. **FAX** 06-446 2368.
W www.hoteldesartistes.com
Rooms: 32.

On a quiet side street close to
shops and tourist attractions, this
hotel has been recently renovated.
Its rooms are comfortable and
reasonably priced and the staff
are friendly and helpful.

Residenza Cellini

Via Modena 5, 00184. **Map** 5 C3.
06-4782 5204. **FAX** 06-4788 1806.
W www.residenzacellini.it **Rooms**: 6.

This delightful small hotel has
recently been created in a 19th-
century building, just a short walk
from Termini station. It is family run
and the welcome is warm. Bedrooms are spacious and elegant, and
attractively furnished with antiques
and hypoallergenic materials; junior
suites have jacuzzis.

St Regis Grand

Via V. E. Orlando 3, 00185. **Map** 5 C2.
06-47 091. **FAX** 06-474 7307.
W www.stregis.com/grandrome

Rooms: 161.

To step into the Grand is to
enter another world. Cherubs
cavort over the reception area
and rich pastel rugs lie on the
parquet floor. Facilities include
a sauna, beauty salon, hairdresser
and a restaurant renowned as
one of the most beautiful in the
country. The standard of bedrooms
is variable, but you might find
yourself sleeping in an antique
bed, reading by the light of a
genuine Venetian lamp.

TERMINI

Cervia

Via Palestro 55, 00185. **Map** 6 E2.
06-49 10 57. **FAX** 06-49 10 56.
W www.hotelcervia.com **Rooms**:
28.

The Cervia is housed in the same
palazzo as the Restivo. Some of
the rooms have been refurbished
with sponge-painted walls and
private bathrooms, and these
are excellent value. The rest are a
bit more basic. The public areas
are immaculate, and there is a
pleasant bar-breakfast room.

Katty

Via Palestro 35, 00185. **Map** 6 E2.
& FAX 06-444 1216. **Rooms**: 17.

The Katty has clean, basic rooms,
some with an occasional piece of
antique furniture. It is very popular
with British and American students,
so either book in advance or turn
up early, ideally between 8am
and 9am. No breakfast is served.

Giuliana

Via Agostino Depretis 70, 00185. **Map**
5 C3. **06-488 0795.** **FAX** 06-482
4287. **W** www.hotelgiuliana.com
Rooms: 11.

The Santacroce husband and
English wife team run this small,
welcoming hotel close to the bustle
of the Via Nazionale and the
Basilica of Santa Maria Maggiore.
Rooms are simple but spacious.

Restivo

Via Palestro 55, 00185. **Map** 6 E2.
06-446 2172. **FAX** 06-445 2629.
Rooms: 6.

The Restivo has six immaculately
maintained bedrooms. The owner
has a hall full of gifts and postcards from grateful guests who
often return again and again.

Canada

Via Vicenza 58, 00185. **Map** 6 E2.
06-445 7770. **FAX** 06-445 0749.
W www.hotelcanadaroma.com
Rooms: 70.

Behind Termini station, the Canada
is an above-average, mid-range
hotel. Rooms are very comfortable,
and there is a pleasant lounge-bar
with squashy sofas and attractive
cane seats. The service is courteous.

Venezia

Via Varese 18, 00185. **Map** 6 E2.
06-445 7101. **FAX** 06-495 7687.
W www.hotelvenezia.com **Rooms**: 61.

One of the nicer mid-size hotels
near Termini station, the Venezia
is pleasantly decorated with antique
furniture and Murano glass chandeliers in the common areas. The
bedrooms are light and airy with
smart bathrooms.

AVENTINE

Aventino

Via San Domenico 10, 00153. **Map**
8 D2. **06-574 5232.** **FAX** 06-574
1112. **W** www.aventinohotels.com
Rooms: 21.

Run by the owners of Villa San Pio
and Sant'Anselmo, the Aventino is
more modest, with large but fairly
simple rooms. However, its lush,
garden location is gorgeous, and
the breakfast room has a magnificent armoire and stained glass.

Sant'Anselmo

Piazza di Sant'Anselmo 2, 00153.
Map 8 D2. **06-574 5174.** **FAX** 06-
578 3604. **W** www.aventinohotels.
com **Rooms**: 45.

This pretty villa, in the gardens
of the peaceful Aventine, is quite
near the Colosseum. The entrance
hall ceiling is stencilled with
flowers; there are chandeliers
and corridors with floors of inlaid
marble. The lounge looks on to
the hotel's garden. Book well
in advance.

Villa San Pio

Via di San Melania 19, 00153. **Map**
8 E3. **06-574 5231.** **FAX** 06-574
1112. **W** www.aventinohotels.com
Rooms: 78.

The Villa San Pio is set in a garden graced with statues. The entrance hall is furnished with velvet and brocade chairs and 18th-century Venetian tapestry. Some rooms have flower-stencilled furniture.

Domus Aventina

Via di Santa Prisca 11B, 00153. **Map** 8 E2. 06-574 6135. FAX 06-5730 0044. w www.domus-aventina.com *Rooms*: 26.
AE, DC, JCB, MC, V.
€€€€€

This immaculate hotel occupies a 14th-century convent at the foot of the Aventine hill. Rooms are large, and simply decorated in pastel tones. There are wonderful views of the Celian hill from many of the rooms and from the huge terrace.

TRASTEVERE

Carmel

Via Mameli 11, 00153. **Map** 7 C2. 06-580 9921. FAX 06 581 8853. w www.hotelcarmel.it
Rooms: 11. €€

The Carmel's most appealing feature is a terrace with its leafy canopy. A couple of rooms open off the terrace. All the rooms are spotless, and most have bathrooms. It is essential to book in advance.

San Francesco

Via Jacopa de' Settesoli 7, 00193. **Map** 4 E2. 06-5830 0051. FAX 06-5833 3413. w www. hotelsanfrancesco.net *Rooms*: 24.
AE, DC, JCB, MC, V.
€€€€

The rooms here are furnished with traditional Roman elegance. Special attractions include rooftop terrace views and a chance to linger over coffee looking out onto a small 15th-century cloister.

VATICAN

Amalia

Via Germanico 66, 00192. **Map** 3 C2. 06-3972 3356. FAX 06-3972 3365. w www.hotelamalia.com
Rooms: 30.
AE, DC, JCB, MC, V. €€

Situated between the Ottaviano Metro station and the Vatican, the Amalia attracts mainly Italian guests. It has spotless rooms ranged on three floors and a lounge with bar.

Alimandi

Via Tunisi 8, 00192. **Map** 3 B2. 06-3972 6300. FAX 06-3972 3943. w www.alimandi.org *Rooms*: 35.
AE, DC, MC, V. €€€€

On a quietish street just below the entrance to the Vatican Museums, the Alimandi is a three-star hotel at the cheaper end of its price band. It is quite popular with younger travellers. Rooms are clean and adequate. Its outstanding feature is the lovely large roof terrace. A courtesy bus service to and from Fiumicino airport is available.

Columbus

Via della Conciliazione 33, 00193. **Map** 3 C3. 06-686 5435. FAX 06-686 4874. w www.hotelcolumbus.net
Rooms: 92. AE, DC, JCB, MC, V. €€€€

Perfect for anyone wishing to stay near the Vatican, the Columbus occupies an austere former monastery. Heavy wrought-iron light fittings hang in the reception hall; the magnificent upper lounge has a beamed ceiling and terra-cotta floor; the function room (the old refectory) has kept its frescoes, and there is a walled terrace garden.

Atlante Star

Via Vitelleschi 34, 00193. **Map** 3 C2. 06-687 3233. FAX 06-687 2300. w www.atlantehotels.com *Rooms*: 62. AE, DC, JCB, MC, V. €€€€€

This hotel is a good option for business travellers needing on-site office facilities. The rooftop restaurant has views of St Peter's. Service is generally attentive and there is a good range of facilities. Double rooms are modest in size and singles can be cramped, some of them with only a shower. Street-facing rooms can be noisy.

Hotel dei Mellini

Via Muzio Clementi 81, 00193. **Map** 4 E2. 06-32 47 71. FAX 06-3247 7801. w www. hotelmellini.com
Rooms: 80. AE, DC, MC, V. €€€€€

Opened in 1996 in a converted late 19th-century building, this hotel has all the modern comforts you could wish for. It is located in a quiet residential area near Castel Sant'Angelo and only a short walk across the river from Via Condotti. The reception staff are very helpful, and there is an attractive bar in the lobby and a roof terrace.

VIA VENETO

Oxford

Via Boncompagni 89, 00187. **Map** 5 C1. 06-420 3601. FAX 06-4281 5349. w www.hoteloxford.com
Rooms: 56. AE, DC, JCB, MC, V. €€€€

On a quiet road off Piazza Fiume, about ten minutes' walk from Via Veneto, the Oxford has stylish public rooms: squashy sofas and modern pictures in the reception area; striped sofas and abstract art in the bar. The bedrooms are more dated, with hessian-covered walls and candlewick bedspreads.

La Residenza

Via Emilia 22–24, 00187. **Map** 5 B2. 06-488 0789. FAX 06-48 57 21. w www.thegiannettihotelsgroup. com *Rooms*: 26. AE, MC, V. €€€€

La Residenza is an elegant hotel that occupies a villa in a quiet road off Via Veneto. There is a canopied terrace with pine furniture, and a terracotta-tiled roof garden with potted plants. The bedrooms are comfortable and well-equipped.

Alexandra

Via Veneto 18, 00187. **Map** 5 B2. 06-488 1943. FAX 06-487 1804. @ alexandra@venere.it *Rooms*: 45. AE, DC, JCB, MC, V. €€€€€

One of the less expensive hotels on the up-market Via Veneto, the Alexandra has a pleasant conservatory-style breakfast room and a lounge decorated with chintz and brocade. All the bedrooms are different; some furnished with antiques, some with splash-painted walls. Traffic noise is audible in some rooms.

Barocco

Via della Purificazione 4, 00187. **Map** 5 B3. 06-487 2001. FAX 06-48 59 94. w www.hotelbarocco.it
Rooms: 28. AE, DC, JCB, MC, V. €€€€€

On the site of a restored palazzo at the bottom of Via Veneto, the Barocco is ideal for anyone who prefers a small hotel. Bedrooms are pleasant with unobtrusive decor, and some have a working area. Public areas include two small lounges (one with a bar) and a restaurant.

Bernini Bristol

Piazza Barberini 23, 00187. **Map** 5 B3. ☎ 06-488 3051. 📠 06-482 4266. 🆆 www.berninibristol.com
Rooms: 127. 🛏 ① ♨ 24 TV 🍸 🌺 🗏 🛗 🚶 ♨ 🐾 📶 🍸 🍴 ♨ AE, DC, JCB, MC, V. €€€€€

This unprepossessing brick building overlooks a busy piazza that has Bernini's Triton fountain as its centrepiece. The marble-laden hotel is comfortable, with a roof garden, but the decor is uninspiring and the atmosphere more conducive to work than pleasure. The central location and secretarial facilities ensure a steady stream of business visitors.

Eden

Via Ludovisi 49, 00187. **Map** 5 B2. ☎ 06-47 81 21. 📠 06-482 1584. 🆆 www.hotel-eden.it **Rooms**: 121. 🛏 ① ♨ 24 TV 🍸 🗏 🚶 🐾 ♨ 🍸 🍴 📶 ♨ AE, DC, JCB, MC, V. €€€€€

Historically one of Rome's most illustrious hotels, the Eden has recently been restored to pristine condition. The roof garden is stunning, giving every justification for the hotel's name. La Terrazza restaurant *(see p317)* nestles on the roof like a beacon of refinement.

Excelsior

Via Veneto 125, 00187. **Map** 5 B1. ☎ 06-47 081. 📠 06-482 6205. 🆆 www.westin.com/excelsiorrome
Rooms: 327. 🛏 ① ♨ 24 TV 🍸 🗏 🚶 🐾 ♨ 📶 🍸 🍴 📶 ♨ AE, DC, JCB, MC, V. €€€€€

Exotically sculpted balconies supported by statues set the tone for this extravagant hotel, which houses boutiques, saunas, a restaurant and a famous piano bar. Public rooms are sumptuous, with marble walls and floors, rich carpets and brocade furnishings, and the corridors are panelled with silk or imitation marble. The bedrooms are elegant and spacious with chandeliers, painted and gilded wooden panelling and ornate, marble bathrooms.

Imperiale

Via Veneto 24, 00187. **Map** 5 B2. ☎ 06-482 6351. 📠 06-474 2583. 🆆 www.hotelimperialeroma.it
Rooms: 95. 🛏 ① ♨ 24 TV 🍸 🗏 🚶 🐾 ♨ 🍸 🍴 📶 ♨ AE, DC, MC, V. €€€€€

One of the more reasonably priced Via Veneto hotels, the Imperiale lacks the panache of its more glamorous neighbours, but the friendly staff make for a relaxed atmosphere. The bar is quite pleasant and the bedrooms are well decorated, with pretty co-ordinating furnishings and small marble bathrooms.

Majestic

Via Veneto 50, 00187. **Map** 5 B2. ☎ 06-42 14 41. 📠 06-488 0984. 🆆 www.hotelmajestic.com
Rooms: 100. 🛏 ① ♨ TV 🍸 🗏 🐾 📶 ♨ 🍸 🍴 🚶 24 ♨ AE, DC, JCB, MC, V. €€€€€

Founded in 1889, the Majestic is the oldest of Via Veneto's hotels. Since its five-year refurbishment it has played host to international stars such as Pavarotti and Sylvester Stallone. Most of the furniture and much of the decor in the public rooms are original, down to the startling lime-green and gilt lounge. Bedrooms and corridors are decorated in a bold, bright style, particularly on the fifth floor, where carpets with a zig-zag pattern provide the background to chintz and brocade.

Regina Hotel Baglioni

Via Veneto 72, 00187. **Map** 5 B2. ☎ 06-42 11 11. 📠 06-4201 2130. 🆆 www.baglionihotels.com **Rooms**: 151. 🛏 ① ♨ TV 🍸 🌺 🗏 🚶 🐾 📶 🍸 🍴 📶 ♨ AE, DC, MC, V. €€€€€

The exuberance of the Baglioni's exterior – it is painted vanilla and strawberry pink and decorated with grimacing masks – continues in the reception area where a wrought-iron staircase is guarded by the statue of a sea god. The bedrooms are painted in vivid shades of coral, aqua and blue, and many are very spacious. Double glazing in the rooms overlooking Via Veneto cuts down on some of the traffic noise.

Victoria

Via Campania 41, 00187. **Map** 5 B1. ☎ 06-47 39 31. 📠 06-487 1890. 🆆 www.hotelvictoriaroma.com
Rooms: 113. 🛏 ① ♨ 24 TV 🍸 🌺 🗏 🚶 🐾 ♨ ♨ 🍸 🍴 📶 ♨ AE, DC, MC, V. €€€€€

Situated on a quiet road at the top of Via Veneto and overlooking the walls abutting the Porta Pinciana, the Victoria prides itself on being a "hotel for individuals", keeping its personal touch by refusing large group bookings. It is renowned for good service. There are stylish public rooms and an attractive roof terrace, but the bedrooms are rather small and uninspired.

Villa Borghese

Via Pinciana 31, 00198. **Map** 2 F5. ☎ 06-854 9648. 📠 06-841 4100. 🆆 www.hotelvillaborghese.it
Rooms: 32. 🛏 ① ♨ 24 TV 🍸 🌺 📶 ♨ 🚶 AE, DC, JCB, MC, V. €€€€€

This immediately likeable hotel occupies a villa close to Villa Borghese. Although the hotel is situated on a rather busy main road, the atmosphere is pleasant: more that of a private home than a hotel. Public rooms include an intimate, old-fashioned bar and a lounge with comfortable sofas. There is also a courtyard sheltered by a pretty ivy-covered pergola. The rooms are on the small side but they are tastefully decorated.

Aldrovandi Palace

Via Aldrovandi 15, 00197. **Map** 2 E4. ☎ 06-322 3993. 📠 06-322 1435. 🆆 www.aldrovandi.com **Rooms**: 119. 🛏 ① ♨ 🗏 🚶 🐾 📶 ♨ 🚶 🍸 🍴 📶 🌺 ♨ 24 AE, DC, JCB, MC, V. €€€€€

Among the most restful luxury hotels in the city, the Aldrovandi is situated just outside the centre of Rome on a fairly busy road overlooking Villa Borghese. The reception lounge is elegant and decorated with rich soft furnishings, carpets and chandeliers. The real highlight of the hotel, however, is the sunny garden with its attractive swimming pool, which is overlooked by an airy restaurant.

Lord Byron

Via de Notaris 5, 00197. **Map** 2 D4. ☎ 06-322 0404. 📠 06-322 0405. 🆆 www.lordbyronhotel.com
Rooms: 34. 🛏 ① ♨ 24 TV 🍸 🗏 🚶 🐾 ♨ 🍸 🍴 📶 ♨ AE, DC, MC, V. €€€€€

This small, refined hotel is housed in a dazzling white building in the residential district of Parioli. Although it was originally a monastery, there is nothing ascetic about its rooms today. The lounge is lavishly furnished with antiques and tapestry-seated chairs and the tiny sitting room has capacious sofas and old-fashioned portraits. The restaurant is decorated with plenty of chintz and fresh flowers and serves some of the best food in Rome. All the bedrooms have tapestry and floral soft furnishings with marble coffee tables. Each room is also provided with a full decanter of port, which comes with the compliments of the management.

For key to symbols *see p291*

What to Drink in Rome

Roman mosaic showing bird and vines

ITALY IS ONE OF Europe's most significant wine-producing countries, keeping up a tradition started in the hills around Rome over 2,000 years ago. Today, wine is usually drunk with meals as a matter of course, and knowing the difference between *rosso* (red) and *bianco* (white) may be all the vocabulary you need to get by. Beer is widely available too, as well as good ranges of apéritifs and digestifs. Rome's drinking water, another debt to the ancient Romans, is particularly good, fresh and sweet, and in abundant supply.

The vineyards of Frascati, southeast of Rome

WHITE WINE

VINES THRIVE in the warm climate of Lazio, the region around Rome, producing abundant supplies of inexpensive dry white wine for the city's cafés and restaurants. It is usually sold by the carafe. Of local bottled wines, Frascati is the best-known, but Castelli Romani, Marino, Colli Albani and Velletri are very similar in style. All are made from one grape variety, the Trebbiano, though better quality versions contain a dash of Malvasia for perfume and flavour. Other central Italian whites worth trying are Orvieto and Verdicchio. Quality white wines from all over Italy, including fine whites from Friuli in the northeast, are widely available in Rome.

Orvieto **Frascati**

Calcaia comes from Barberani, a reliable producer of Orvieto.

Bigi produce good quality Orvieto, especially the single-vineyard Torricella.

Casal Pilozzo is an easy-drinking white wine from Frascati producers, Colli di Catone. Choose the youngest vintage.

Colle Gaio, with its rich, fruity flavour, stands out among the dry white Frascatis.

WINE TYPE	GOOD VINTAGES	GOOD PRODUCERS
WHITE WINE		
Friuli (Pinot Bianco, Chardonnay, Pinot Grigio, Sauvignon)	The most recent	Gravner, Jermann, Puiatti, Schiopetto, Volpe Pasini
Orvieto/ Orvieto Classico	The most recent	Antinori, Barberani, Bigi, Il Palazzone
RED WINE		
Chianti/ Chianti Classico/ Chianti Rufina	95, 90, 88, 85	Antinori, Castello di Ama, Castello di Cacchiano, Castello di Volpaia, Felsina Berardenga, Fontodi, Frescobaldi, Isole e Olena, Il Palazzino, Riecine, Rocca delle Macie, Ruffino, Vecchie Terre di Montefili, Villa Cafaggio
Brunello di Montalcino/ Vino Nobile di Montepulciano	95, 90, 88, 85	Altesino, Avignonesi, Biondi Santi, Caparzo, Case Basse, Lisini, Il Poggione, Poliziano, Villa Banfi
Barolo/ Barbaresco	95, 90, 89, 88, 85, 82, 78	Aldo Conterno, Altare, Ceretto, Clerico, Gaja, Giacomo Conterno, Giacosa, Mascarello, Ratti, Voerzio

Tuscan table wine   Barolo

RED WINE

THOUGH SOME local red wine is made, most of the bottled red wine in Rome comes from other parts of Italy. Regions like Tuscany and Piedmont produce very good everyday drinking as well as top-class wines like Barolo. Price should reflect quality – try Dolcetto, Rosso di Montalcino or Montepulciano for good-value reds.

READING THE LABEL

ITALY has a two-tier system for labelling quality wine. DOC *(denominazione di origine controllata)* means you can be sure the wine is from the region declared on the label and is made from designated grape varieties. A higher classification – DOCG *(denominazione di origine controllata e garantita)* – is given to top wines such as the reds Barolo, Barbaresco, Chianti Classico and Brunello di Montalcino.

Chianti Classico

Montepulciano d'Abruzzo, a rich and juicy red wine, is always good value. It is produced in the Abruzzi region east of Rome.

Chianti Classico Riserva is older and stronger than a normal Chianti Classico.

Torre Ercolana is produced in small quantities and is generally regarded as one of Lazio's best red wines. It is made from Cesanese and Cabernet grapes and requires at least five years' ageing.

APÉRITIFS AND OTHER DRINKS

BITTER, herb-flavoured drinks like Martini, Campari or Aperol are the most popular apéritifs. (Ask for an *analcolico* if you prefer a non-alcoholic one.) Italians drink their apéritifs neat or with ice and soda. Strong, herby after-dinner drinks, known as *digestivi* or *amari*, are worth trying if you need to settle your stomach. Italian brandy and grappa can be very fiery. Italian beer, popular with pizza, is made in lager style.

Campari

SOFT DRINKS

ITALIAN FRUIT juices are good and most bars squeeze fresh orange juice *(spremuta di arancia)* on the spot. Iced coffee and fruit-flavoured tea, such as peach, are popular.

Refrigerated storage for wine and beer

DRINKING WATER

Unlike many Mediterranean cities, Rome benefits from a constant supply of fresh drinking water, piped down from the hills through a system of pipes and aqueducts which has changed little from ancient Roman times. Only if there is a sign saying *acqua non potabile* is the water not safe to drink.

One of Rome's many fresh water drinking fountains

Coffee is almost more important to Roman life than wine. Take espresso for neat strong black coffee at any time of day, milky cappuccino for breakfast or mid-afternoon, caffelatte for extra milk.

Espresso

Cappuccino

Caffelatte

Rome's Best: Restaurants and Cafés

Rome is not particularly known for luxury restaurants, but more for atmospheric places where the focus is on the social side of dining and on regional cooking. An amazing variety can be found. Many places specialize, priding themselves on being the best of their kind – whether they offer superb espresso, or traditional foods like deep-fried salted cod (*baccalà*). Other restaurants can offer beautiful settings or are the best places to see and be seen. This selection shows some of the many highlights of a city where eating is taken very seriously.

Caffè Giolitti
This historic ice cream shop serves a variety of flavours, to eat in or take away. (See p320.)

Camponeschi
This stylish restaurant offers elegantly prepared dishes and outdoor tables on Piazza Farnese. (See p314.)

Filetti di Baccalà
This small, crowded place serves tasty fried fillets of cod – one of Rome's most traditional dishes – and offers a truly Roman experience. (See p320.)

Alberto Ciarla
Fish dominate the exquisite dishes as well as the decor in this elegant restaurant. (See p316.)

Vatican

Campo de' Fiori

Piazza Navona

Janiculum

Trastevere

Piperno
For over a century, traditional Roman Jewish cooking has been the speciality of Piperno, in the heart of the Jewish Ghetto. (See p314.)

Babington's Tea Rooms
This old-fashioned, genteel establishment at the foot of the Spanish Steps serves English tea and cakes. (See p320.)

La Terrazza
Gloriously situated in the roof garden of Hotel Eden, La Terrazza offers some of the finest cuisine in Rome, with views to match. (See p317.)

Caffè Greco
Famous as the haunt of writers, artists and intellectuals in the 19th century, this café still retains the faded grandeur shown in this painting. (See p320.)

Via Veneto

Quirinal

Capitol

Esquiline

Forum

Palatine

Caracalla   Lateran

Aventine

0 metres   500

0 yards   500

Sora Lella
This Roman trattoria is famous for its setting on the Isola Tiberina and for the fashionable crowd which it attracts. (See p314.)

Tazza d'Oro
This figure graces the façade of Tazza d'Oro, where you will find some of the best espresso in Rome. (See p320.)

Choosing a Restaurant

THE RESTAURANTS in this guide have been selected for their good value or exceptional food. This chart highlights some of the factors which may influence your choice. Entries are alphabetical within each price category. For more details on the restaurants, see pages 312–17. Information on cafés and wine bars is on pages 318–21.

	FIXED PRICE MENU	VEGETARIAN DISHES	TABLES OUTSIDE	SEAFOOD SPECIALTIES	LATE OPENING	AIR-CONDITIONING	ATTRACTIVE SETTING
PIAZZA DELLA ROTONDA (see p312)							
Il Buco €				●	●	■	
Da Gino €							
Il Bacaro €€	●			●	■	●	■
Alle Due Colonne €€	●	■			■	●	■
Myosotis €€			■	●		■	
Vecchia Locanda €€	●	■	●		●	■	●
Enoteca Capranica €€€	●	■		■			●
Sangallo €€€	●					■	
El Toulà €€€€€	●	■		■		■	
La Rosetta ★ €€€€€				●	■	●	
PIAZZA NAVONA (see p312)							
La Campana €€							
Osteria dell'Antiquario €€			●			■	●
La Taverna €€	●		●		●	■	●
Il Passetto €€€			■		●	■	
Il Convivio ★ €€€€€	●			■		■	
PIAZZA DI SPAGNA (see p313)							
Birreria Viennese €	●		●		●	■	
Al 34 €€	●	■	●	■		■	
Mario alle Vite €€			●			■	
Nino €€							
Porto di Ripetta €€	●			■		■	
Hassler Roof Restaurant €€€€€						■	●
CAMPO DE' FIORI (see p313)							
Il Drappo €€	●		●		●	■	
Monserrato €€			●			■	
Dal Pompiere €€						■	
Piperno €€€	●	■	●	■		■	
Sora Lella €€€	●					■	
Vecchia Roma €€€		■	●	■	●	■	●
Camponeschi €€€€€			●	■	●	■	●
QUIRINAL (see p314)							
Colline Emiliane €€						■	
Hasekura €€	●	■				■	
Il Posto Accanto €€			■		■	■	
Quadrifoglio €€					●	■	
Al Moro €€€			●	■	●	■	
TERMINI (see p314)							
Coriolano €€€		■		■		■	
ESQUILINE (see p315)							
La Gallina Bianca €			●			■	
Trattoria Monti €€						■	
Cicilardone €€€					●	■	
Agata e Romeo ★ €€€€€	●					■	

Price categories for a three-course meal for one, half a bottle of house wine, and all unavoidable extra charges such as cover, service, tax:
€ up to €25
€€ €25–€44
€€€ €45–€64
€€€€ €65–€80
€€€€€ over €80.

★ Means highly recommended.

FIXED PRICE MENU
Restaurant offering *menu turistico* (tourist menu): usually three or four courses without wine or coffee, for a set price.

VEGETARIAN DISHES
Restaurant with a good selection of vegetarian dishes.

LATE OPENING
Last orders on or after 11.30pm.

ATTRACTIVE SETTING
Restaurant set in a pretty piazza or with a garden terrace, or with a lovely view.

	Price	Fixed Price Menu	Vegetarian Dishes	Tables Outside	Seafood Specialities	Late Opening	Air-Conditioning	Attractive Setting
LATERAN *(see p315)*								
Alfredo a Via Gabi	€€		●				●	
Cannavota	€€				●		●	
Charly's Saucière	€€					●	●	
AVENTINE *(see p315)*								
Court Delicati	€		●					
Luna Piena	€		●	●			●	
Perilli a Testaccio	€€						●	
Checchino dal 1887 ★	€€€				●	●	●	
TRASTEVERE *(see p316)*								
Asinocotto	€€		●		●			
La Cornucopia	€€	●		●	●		●	●
Da Lucia	€€				●			
Romolo nel Giardino della Fornarina	€€				●	●		●
Da Paris	€€€				●	●	●	●
Alberto Ciarla ★	€€€€€	●		●	●	●	●	
JANICULUM *(see p316)*								
Antico Arco ★	€€€					●	●	
VATICAN *(see p316)*								
Romolo	€€			●			●	
Taverna Angelica	€€						●	
Les Etoiles	€€€€			●	●			●
VIA VENETO *(see p317)*								
Andrea	€€€		●		●		●	
Giovanni	€€€				●		●	
Girarrosto Fiorentino	€€€						●	
Tullio	€€€					●	●	
George's	€€€€				●	●	●	●
La Terrazza ★	€€€€€		●	●	●	●	●	●
VILLA BORGHESE *(see p317)*								
Al Ceppo	€€€		●	●	●		●	
Relais la Piscine ★	€€€€	●		●	●		●	●
Relais le Jardin	€€€€€				●		●	

PIAZZA DELLA ROTONDA

Il Buco

Via di Sant'Ignazio 8 (Piazza Collegio Romano). **Map** 4 F4 & 12 E3. **(** 06-679 3298, 06-678 4467. **Open** 12.30–4pm, 7pm–midnight Tue–Sun. **Closed** Aug & Christmas. 🛠 🎭 👫 *AE, DC, MC, V.* €

Much has happened since the tiny *buco* (hole) opened in 1891 – the small *osteria* has become a large restaurant, yet the calm atmosphere, unfailing courtesy and formidable Tuscan menu remain. From the traditional *crostini* (liver pâté canapés), robust *ribollita* (thick vegetable soup) and huge Florentine steaks, to the final *tozzetti* (almond biscuits) with *vin santo* (dessert wine), this is a truly Tuscan experience.

Da Gino

Vicolo Rosini 4 (Piazza del Parlamento). **Map** 4 F3 & 12 D1. **(** 06-687 3434. **Open** 1–3pm, 8–10.30pm Mon–Sat. **Closed** Aug. 👫 €

Journalists, politicians and the initiated scramble for a seat under the kitsch, frescoed pergola of this ancient, ultra-Roman trattoria to feast upon traditional daily dishes: *gnocchi* and *osso buco* (Thursdays), *baccalà* (Fridays), tripe (Saturdays), plus classic sturdy soups and delectable homemade *tiramisù*.

Il Bacaro

Via degli Spagnoli 27. **Map** 12 D2. **(** 06-686 4110. **Open** 12.30–2.30pm, 8–11.30pm Mon–Fri, 8–11.30pm Sat. **Closed** 3 wks Jan. 🎭 👤 🍴 🗐 *DC, JCB, MC, V.* €€

Located in the historic centre of the city, near the Pantheon, this tiny restaurant serves meals cooked in a minute kitchen. The menu is based on meat and fish dishes and includes such main courses as fillet steak in a red wine sauce. The superb desserts include an excellent chocolate mousse.

Alle Due Colonne

Via del Seminario 122. **Map** 4 F4 & 12 D3. **(** 06-678 1449. **Open** 11.30am–3.30-pm, 6.30–11.30pm daily. 🌱 👫 🍴 🗐 *AE, DC, JCB, MC, V.* €€

Evocative of ancient Rome, the decor of this restaurant includes two imperial columns, from which it gets its name, and an ancient fountain. The cuisine is rich in Mediterranean flavours with most dishes cooked on the spot. Dishes such as *spigolla alla griglia* (grilled sea bass) and grilled buffalo *mozzarella con radicchio* (red chicory) are particularly good.

Myosotis

Vicolo della Vaccarella 3–5. **Map** 12 D2. **(** 06-686 5554. **Open** 7.30–11.30pm Mon, 12.30–3pm, 7.30–11.30pm Tue–Sat. **Closed** 1 wk Jan, 2 wks Aug. 🛠 🗐 🎭 🌱 🌱 👫 👤 🗐 *AE, DC, MC, V.* €€

Situated in a tiny street near the Pantheon, Myosotis has emerged as a foodie temple for those who want to keep an eye on their pockets. An imaginative approach and the freshest ingredients mean that whatever choice you make is a good one, from the house *antipasti* (mozzarella, ricotta and stuffed pimentos) to the *frittura di paranza* (lightly fried fish and seafood).

Vecchia Locanda

Vicolo Sinibaldi 2. **Map** 4 F4 & 12 D3. **(** 06-6880 2831. **Open** 12.30–3pm, 7–11.30pm Mon–Sat. **Closed** 1 wk mid-Aug, Christmas. 🌱 🎭 👤 🍴 🗐 *AE, DC, MC, V.* €€

Visit this small, family-run restaurant in summer, when tables line the secluded arched street. Everything shows extreme care – including the impeccable service. An imaginative combination of herbs and vegetables characterizes the menu: risotto with courgette flowers, *porcini* mushroom crêpes, stuffed truffled rabbit and lots of fresh fish. There is a good selection of French and regional wines.

Enoteca Capranica

Piazza Capranica 99–100. **Map** 12 D2. **(** 06-6994 0992. **Open** 7.30–11pm daily. **Closed** possibly Aug (check). 🍴 🗐 🌱 👫 🗐 *AE, DC, JBC, V.* €€€

Housed in part of the impressive 15th-century Palazzo Capranica (see p113), the Enoteca Capranica offers an extensive menu, mostly based around seafood and vegetable dishes. Starters include lobster and mango salad, while the exotic main courses include *risotto con zucca e tartufo* (risotto with pumpkin and truffles) and *spigola al sale* (sea bass in a salt crust).

Sangallo

Vicolo della Vaccarella 11. **Map** 4 F3 & 12 D2. **(** 06-686 5549. **Open** 7.30–11pm Mon–Sat. **Closed** Aug. 👫 🍴 🗐 *AE, DC, MC, V.* €€€

This elegant fish restaurant has an interesting menu complemented by an impressive wine list. Antipasti include *crostini con calamaretti al radicchio* (baby squid and radicchio on toast). First courses such as *fettucelle con gamberi, pomodori e pecorino* (pasta with shrimps, tomatoes and pecorino cheese) are prepared delicately and simply. Ask about the speciality of the day.

El Toulà

Via della Lupa 29B. **Map** 4 F3 & 12 D1. **(** 06-687 3498. **Open** 1–3pm, 8–11pm Mon–Fri, 8–11pm Sat. **Closed** Aug, Christmas. 🍴 🌱 👤 👫 🗐 *AE, DC, JCB, MC, V.* €€€€€

El Toulà is justly renowned as one of the most exclusive, traditional and luxurious restaurants in Rome. The Venetian-inspired cooking is serious and professional, with forays into the realms of the best classic international cuisine. In dignified, sober surroundings the service is exemplary and the selection of wines superb.

La Rosetta

Via della Rosetta 9. **Map** 4 F4 & 12 D2. **(** 06-6830 8841. **Open** 7.30–11.15pm Mon–Sat, 12.45–2.45pm Mon–Fri. **Closed** 3 wks Aug, Christmas. 👤 🎭 👫 ★ 🗐 *AE, DC, JCB, MC, V.* €€€€€

Despite the exorbitant prices, people flock nightly (having booked in advance) for a seat in this elegant restaurant. Fresh fish and seafood, brought in daily from Sicily and cooked in the simplest ways, achieve close to culinary perfection. The enthusiastic service and top-quality wines, particularly the Sicilian whites, do justice to the cuisine.

PIAZZA NAVONA

La Campana

Vicolo della Campana 18. **Map** 12 D1. **(** 06-686 7820. **Open** 12.30–3pm, 7.30–11.30pm Tue–Sun. **Closed** Aug. 🌱 👫 🗐 *AE, DC, MC, V.* €€

The Campana, reputedly Rome's oldest restaurant, was already in business when Michelangelo was a lad. There is something timeless about the brisk, friendly service provided by experienced waiters. Specialities on the extensive menu include pasta with fresh anchovies, *vignarola* (traditional vegetable and bean soup), *frittura mista* (fried cheese, vegetables and brains) and, for die-hard Roman cuisine lovers, *coda alla vaccinara* (stewed ox-tail).

Osteria dell'Antiquario

Piazzetta San Simeone 27. **Map** 4 E3 & 11 B2. 06-687 9694. FAX 06-6880 5381. **Open** 12.30–2.30pm, 8–11pm Tue–Sat, 8–11pm Mon. **Closed** 2 wks Aug & 2 wks Jan. AE, DC, MC, V. €€

In the comfort of the elegantly restructured rooms of an old antique shop, Giorgio Nisti offers an unusual menu dictated by the whims of the chef and the daily market. The largely traditional dishes are creatively adapted to contemporary health-conscious tastes. There is an impressive choice of regional, French and Californian wines.

La Taverna

Via del Banco di Santo Spirito 58. **Map** 4 D3 & 11 A2. 06-686 4116. FAX 06-686 4116. **Open** noon–3pm, 7–11pm Tue–Sun. AE, DC, JCB, MC, V. €€

Tourists and local residents mingle in Giovanni's crowded Roman trattoria to enjoy the family atmosphere and traditional regional cooking. Particularly appreciated are the *rigatoni all'amatriciana, coda alla vaccinara* and, on Thursday, Friday and Saturday respectively, *gnocchi, baccalà* and tripe.

Il Passetto

Via Zanardelli 14. **Map** 4 F4 & 12 D3. 06-6880 3696. **Open** noon–3pm, 7–11.30pm daily. AE, JCB, MC, V €€€

Haunt of Charlie Chaplin and Leonardo di Caprio, this restaurant seems to belong to another age. The décor is authentically retro, and the menu is fiercely traditional. Lentil soup or *cannelloni al funghi* (with mushrooms) are worthy starters, with dishes like *osso buco* and *saltimbocca* making a classic follow-up. The home-made desserts, such as *mousse al cioccolato bianco e nero* (white and dark chocolate mousse), deserve special attention.

Il Convivio

Vicolo dei Soldati 28. **Map** 4 E3 & 11 C2. 06-686 9432. **Open** 1–2.30pm, 8–10.30pm Tue–Sat, 8–10.30pm Mon. **Closed** 1 week Aug. ★ AE, DC, JCB, MC, V. €€€€€

An air of sophisticated tranquility pervades this intimate restaurant, one of the very best specializing in modern creative cookery. Its young chef, one of the three Troiani brother-owners from the

Marches, creates both subtle and unusual combinations of flavours, and the highly personalized menu evolves with the seasons. The wine list is extensive and the service discreet.

PIAZZA DI SPAGNA

Birreria Viennese

Via della Croce 21. **Map** 5 A2. 06-679 5569. **Open** 10am–midnight daily. AE, DC, MC, V. €

The stained-glass entrance leads to a long, crowded room where, for more than 60 years, traditional beers and Austrian specialities have been sampled. Try sausages, goulash, *Wienerschnitzel*, sauerkraut, or the massive *piatto di legno della Transilvania* (wooden platter heaped with delights, for two). Wine is available, and the service is helpful and courteous.

Al 34

Via Mario de' Fiori 34. **Map** 5 A2. 06-679 5091. **Open** 12.30–3pm, 7–11pm Tue–Sun. **Closed** 3 wks Aug. AE, DC, MC, V. €€

This busy, bustling restaurant is a good option if you're in a hurry, as the service is speedy and efficient. Predominantly featuring southern Italian cooking, the extensive menu offers an esoteric choice, particularly where vegetables and herbs are allied with pasta, meat and fish. Given its location, the prices are affordable.

Mario alla Vite

Via della Vite 55. **Map** 5 A3 & 12 E1. 06-678 3818. **Open** noon–3pm, 7–11pm Mon–Sat. **Closed** Aug. AE, DC, MC, V. €€

Despite an exclusive address, Mario has kept prices reasonable, and his food is still simple Tuscan fare. Elbow-to-elbow dining, haphazard service and noisy confusion seem inevitable. Nevertheless, the food is usually worth it – traditional *fagioli al fiasco* (cannellini beans in oil), *ribollita* (thick vegetable soup), Florentine steaks and delicious pastries are the attractions, along with a wide selection of wines.

Nino

Via Borgognona 11. **Map** 5 A2 & 12 E1. 06-679 5676. **Open** 12.30–3pm, 7.30–11pm Mon–Sat. AE, DC, JCB, MC, V. €€

A reliable restaurant, located among the fancy shops around Piazza di Spagna, Nino has been popular since it opened in 1934. The menu features mostly Tuscan food, so there is always a hearty soup as well as game and other standards, such as *bistecca alla fiorentina* (grilled T-bone steak). The desserts are all homemade.

Porto di Ripetta

Via di Ripetta 250. **Map** 4 F2. 06-361 2376. **Open** 7.30–11pm Mon, 12.45–2.30pm, 7.30–11pm Tue–Sat. **Closed** 2 wks Aug. AE, DC, JCB, MC, V. €€

The fame of this restaurant depends largely on the genius of chef Antonio Zaccaria. With the fish that arrives daily from nearby Anzio he creates inspired combinations such as fish and broad bean soup or giant prawns with artichokes. It is expensive, but worth it; the fixed price menu is much cheaper. There's a selection of excellent wines.

Hassler Roof Restaurant

Piazza Trinità dei Monti 6. **Map** 5 A2. 06-6993 4726. **Open** 7.30–11am, 12.30–2.30pm (to 3pm Sun), 7.30–10.30pm daily. AE, DC, JCB, MC, V. €€€€€

Perched on the sixth floor of the Hotel Hassler, overlooking the Spanish Steps, the roof restaurant commands a breathtaking view of Rome. Come for the gargantuan and pricey Sunday brunch. The wine list is excellent and the hovering waiter service timely and discreet. In the evening, when prices are higher, there is piano music.

CAMPO DE' FIORI

Il Drappo

Vicolo del Malpasso 9. **Map** 4 D4 & 11 B3. 06-687 7365. **Open** 12.30–3pm, 7.30–11.30pm Mon–Sat. **Closed** 1 Jan, 3 wks Aug. AE, DC, JCB, MC, V. €€

A small, intimate restaurant, with ceiling drapes (hence the name), plants and candlelight, Il Drappo provides an authentic taste of Sardinia – traditional dishes imbued with flashes of culinary creativity. Everything is evocative of the island, particularly the *seada* (sweet cheese-filled ravioli) for dessert. Try the *mirto* liqueur at the end.

For key to symbols *see p303*

Monserrato

Via Monserrato 96. **Map** 4 D4.
(06-687 3386. **Open** 12.30–3pm,
7.30–11pm Tue–Sun. **Closed** 2 wks
Aug. 🍴 🌿 AE, DC, MC, V. €€€

Monserrato is one of the safest
bets in the city centre. It serves
reliably good food throughout
the year cooked with imaginative
touches. The *gnocchi alle vongole
veraci* (gnocchi with clams) is a
good starter, and the *rombo al
forno con patate* (oven-cooked
turbot with potatoes) is an
excellent main course. Various fish
dishes are served, with ingredients
depending on the season.

Dal Pompiere

Via S. M. dei Calderari 38.
Map 4 F5 & 12 D5. **(** 06-686
8377. **Open** 12.30–3pm, 7.30–
11pm Mon–Sat. **Closed** Aug.
🟡 🚹 🌿 AE, MC, V. €€€

Dal Pompiere occupies the first
floor of the 16th-century Palazzo
Cenci-Bolognetti in the Jewish
Ghetto. Under its frescoed and
open-beamed ceilings, in an
authentically retro atmosphere,
all the classic dishes of Roman
cuisine are expertly served:
among them fried courgette
flowers with anchovies, *rigatoni
con la pajata*, and spring lamb.

Piperno

Via Monte de' Cenci 9. **Map** 4 F5
& 12 D5. **(** 06-686 1113. **Open**
12.45–2.30pm, 8–10.30pm Tue–
Sat, 12.30–3pm Sun. **Closed** Aug,
Christmas, Easter. 🟡 🔥 🍴
🍴 🌿 AE, DC, MC, V. €€€€

Piperno, at the heart of the Jewish
Ghetto, has been famed for over
a century for its traditional
Jewish/Roman dishes. Despite
the competition, the restaurant
is still unbeaten for lightly fried
courgette flowers, vegetable *fritto
misto, carciofi alla giudia*, tripe
and superb fish, served in plain
surroundings. Service is familiarly
attentive and timely. The house
wine is excellent Frascati. Book
well in advance.

Sora Lella

Via Ponte Quattro Capi 16, Isola
Tiberina. **Map** 8 D1. **(** 06-686 1601.
Open 1–2.30pm, 8–11pm Mon–Sat.
Closed Aug. 🌿 🟡 🌿 AE, DC, MC,
V. €€€

Founded by the exuberant Roman
actress Sora Lella, this small,
bright trattoria is a well-known
place to people-watch. Sora Lella
is now run by Lella's son Aldo.
Dishes are based on traditional
Roman cuisine, but there are

pleasant surprises too, such as
the excellent range of vegetables
and side dishes. Go also for the
beautiful location on the Isola
Tiberina, the often glamorous
clientele, and the good service.

Vecchia Roma

Piazza Campitelli 18. **Map** 4 F5 & 12
E5. **(** 06-686 4604. **Open** 1–3pm,
8–11pm Thu–Tue. **Closed** 2 weeks
Aug. 🟡 🔥 🍴 🟡 🌿 AE, DC.
€€€

Set in a quiet, atmospheric piazza,
this is one of the best places for a
summer evening. Reliable Roman
cooking is on offer, with tempting
antipasto, simply-cooked fish and
grilled meats, and a connoisseur's
wine list. Specialities are summer
salads and, in winter, numerous
variations on polenta. Added
pleasures are the 18th-century
interior and the excellent service.

Camponeschi

Piazza Farnese 50. **Map** 4 E5 &
11 C4. **(** 06-687 4927. **Open**
8pm–12.30am Mon–Sat. **Closed**
10 days Aug. 🍴 🟡 🌿 AE, DC,
MC, V. €€€€€

Camponeschi is set in one of the
most attractive piazzas in Rome,
especially beautiful in summer, and
booking in advance is necessary.
The extensive menu includes
modern and regional Italian
cooking, creative Mediterranean
fish and meat dishes, soufflés
and French specialities.

QUIRINAL

Colline Emiliane

Via degli Avignonesi 22. **Map** 5 B3. **(**
06-481 7538. **Open** 12.45–2.45pm,
7.45–10.45pm Sat–Thu. **Closed**
Aug. 🌿 🌿 JCB, MC, V. €€€

Regional dishes are the hallmarks
of this small family trattoria: one
unpretentious room presenting a
haven from the nearby bustle of Via
del Tritone. Enjoy food typical of
the province of Emilia Romagna –
salami and cold meats, homemade
pastas (*tagliatelle, tortellini*),
boiled meats with *salsa verde*
(spinach, onion and anchovy
sauce) and Emilian wines.

Hasekura

Via dei Serpenti 27. **Map** 5 B4.
(06-48 36 48. **Open** noon–2pm,
7–10.30pm Mon–Sat. **Closed** Aug.
🍴 ☰ 🟡 🌿 AE, DC, JCB, MC, V.
€€

While Hasekura is not the most
typical Japanese restaurant in
Rome as far as decor goes, it is the

one that expatriates recommend.
The lunch menu is good value
(with delicious, melt-in-the-mouth
tempura) and Ito, the master chef,
makes excellent *sushi* and *sashimi*
(slices of raw fish). Fine sake and
Japanese beer, and friendly
service. Booking advisable.

Il Posto Accanto

Via del Boschetto 36 A. **Map** 5 B4.
(06-474 3002. **Open** 1– 3pm
Mon–Fri, 8–11pm Mon–Sat. **Closed**
Aug. 🟡 🚹 🌿 AE, DC, MC, V.
€€

Tiny, intimate and pleasant, this
family-run restaurant owes its
success to a short, carefully chosen
menu revolving around homemade
pasta (excellent *tagliolini con
asparagi* and *ravioli con zenzero*
– ginger), simply prepared fish
and meat, top-quality vegetables
and familiar desserts (*tiramisù*),
often prepared within sight of the
lucky diners. There is a range of
wines, as well as good *grappas*.

Quadrifoglio

Via del Boschetto 19. **Map** 5 B4.
(06-482 6096. **Open** 7–11pm
Mon–Sat. **Closed** Aug. 🚹 🌿
🌿 AE, DC, JCB, MC, V. €€

Chef Pino Forlenza prepares
authentic dishes from Naples,
Campania and the tip of Africa,
tailored to modern tastes by the
carefully selected raw ingredients.
These are delivered with
courteous service. Excellent
Neapolitan desserts; most of the
wines are from Campania, too.

Al Moro

Vicolo delle Bollette 13. **Map** 5 A3
& 12 F2. **(** 06-678 3495. **Open**
1–3pm, 8–11.30pm Mon–Sat.
Closed Aug. 🍴 🌿 V. €€€

Franco Romagnoli's trattoria is
a reliable choice for traditional
Roman cooking, using fresh local
ingredients. Noisy and crowded,
its closely packed tables do not
encourage intimate dining. Classic
dishes are served: *bucatini
all'amatriciana, spaghetti alla
Moro* (special *carbonara*), fried
vegetables, excellent *baccalà alla
Moro* (salt cod), tripe, *abbacchio*
(lamb). There is a vast wine list.

TERMINI

Coriolano

Via Ancona 14. **Map** 6 D1. **(** 06-
4424 9863. **Open** 12.30–3pm,
7.30–11pm daily. **Closed** 3 wks
Aug. 🟡 🟡 🌿 AE, DC, MC, V.
€€€

This small restaurant aims at perfection with its lacy tablecloths and crystal glasses. The Italian menu changes with the seasons and uses only the freshest of raw materials, including fish. Specialities include the home-made *ravioli di ricotta e spinaci*, *capretto* (kid) and creamy chocolate *zuppa del contadino*.

ESQUILINE

La Gallina Bianca

Via Antonio Rosmini 9. **Map** 6 D4.
☎ 06-474 3777. **Open** noon–3pm 6pm–midnight daily. 🏥 🚼 🛠   📋 🚻 **V** AE, DC, MC, V. €

For all its ersatz rustic atmosphere, this popular restaurant-pizzeria is renowned for its wide-ranging menu which offers everything from large salads to various pasta dishes and deep-fried fare. However, the best option is to imitate local aficionados and to order a pizza (cooked in a wood-fired oven) or a platter of grilled meats with vegetables.

Trattoria Monti

Via di San Vito 19. **Map** 6 D4.
☎ 06-446 6573. **Open** 12.30–3pm, 7.30–11pm Tue–Sat, 12.30–3pm Sun. **Closed** Easter, Aug & 2 wks Dec–Jan. & **V** 🛠 DC, MC, V. €€

This small, unpretentious trattoria serves delicate, creative regional dishes from the Marches. Franca Camerucci cooks, while her husband Mario is an attentive waiter and expert *sommelier*. Their specialities include fried stuffed olives, artichokes and *ciauscolo* (salami); *tortello al rosso d'uova* (fresh pasta stuffed with ricotta cheese, spinach and tomato); and *tacchino all'aceto balsamico* (turkey braised in balsamic vinegar). There is a good Verdicchio house wine and a commendable wine list.

Cicilardone

Via Farini 12. **Map** 6 D4. ☎ 06-48 35 49. **Open** noon–3pm Tue–Sat, 8pm–midnight Mon–Sat. **Closed** 3 wks Aug. 🍴 🚻 AE, DC, MC, V. €€€

Ring at Cicilardone's door and your host – Domenico Lucia – will greet you like an old friend and converse about the gastronomic delights from the region of Basilicata. Try the *menu di assaggini* – a selection of dishes to give you an idea of the regional taste, including traditional pastas and hot chocolate profiteroles. There are some unusual southern wines available.

Agata e Romeo

Via Carlo Alberto 45. **Map** 6 D4. ☎ 06-446 6115. **Open** 1–3pm, 8–11pm Mon–Fri. **Closed** 2 wks Jan & 2 wks Aug. 🍴 🚻 🛠 🚻 ★ 🚻 AE, DC, JCB, MC, V. €€€€€

One of the newer trattorie-turned-restaurants, its increasing prices sadly reflect recent popular acclaim. Nevertheless, Agata's skill in creating a changing menu of predominantly Roman and southern Italian dishes, and Romeo's impeccable service and range of carefully chosen wines, are hard to beat. Well-spaced, elegantly set tables are ideal for tranquil eating. The set *menu degustazione* is recommended.

LATERAN

Alfredo a Via Gabi

Via Gabi 36. **Map** 10 D3.
☎ 06-7720 6792. **Open** 12.30–3pm, 7.30–11pm, except Sun. **Closed** Aug. 🚻 🚻 AE, DC, MC, V. €€

This is a spacious local trattoria with a pavement pergola for outdoor eating. Regional specialities – served in ample portions – include *tonnarelli ai sapori di bosco* (pasta with mushrooms), excellent *porcini* mushrooms (in season), *coniglio con tartufo* (rabbit with truffles), and *panna cotta* (rich crème caramel) with fruit or chocolate. Service is cheerful and friendly.

Cannavota

Piazza San Giovanni in Laterano 20. **Map** 9 C1. ☎ 06-7720 5007. **Open** 12.30–3pm, 7.45–11pm Thu–Tue. **Closed** 1–20 Aug. 🚻 AE, DC, MC, V. €€

Join the enthusiastic regulars who crowd this friendly restaurant if you are feeling especially hungry. Portions are generous, the cooking is traditional Italian and the service is swift. Seafood – prawns, in particular – is excellent, but meat also features on the menu.

Charly's Saucière

Via San Giovanni in Laterano 270. **Map** 9 B1. ☎ 06-7049 5666. **Open** 12.45–2.15pm, 7.45–11.15pm Tue–Fri, 8pm–midnight Mon & Sat. **Closed** 2 wks Aug. & 🚻 AE, DC, JCB, MC, V. €€

An old-style, unsurprising and well-established French restaurant, this has scarcely altered over the years and is especially warm and intimate on a winter evening. Diners choose from reassuring

French and Swiss fare: pâtés, onion soup, cheese soufflé, fondues, *rösti*, steaks in a variety of sauces and crêpes, accompanied by a small but careful selection of wines. Service is professional and attentive.

AVENTINE

Court Delicati

Viale Aventino 39. **Map** 8 E3. ☎ 06-574 6108. **Open** noon–2.45pm, 7.30–11pm Tue–Sun. **Closed** Aug. & **V** AE, DC, MC, V. €

This excellent Chinese restaurant has gained in popularity owing to the various Indonesian and Thai specialities it offers alongside the more traditional fare of pancake rolls and steamed dumplings. Thus the more adventurous can try out *nasi-goreng*, or the incredibly hot *tomyam* soup. The restaurant is much patronised by workers from the nearby UN Food and Agriculture Organisation building, and the reasonable mark-ups on beer and wine add to the wallet-friendly experience.

Luna Piena

Via Luca della Robbia 15–17.
Map 8 D3. ☎ 06-575 0279.
Open 12.30–3pm, 7.30–11pm Mon, Thu–Sun, 7.30–11pm Tue. **Closed** mid-Jun–mid-Jul. & 📋 🚻 🛠 **V** 🚻 AE, DC, JCB, MC, V. €

The success of Luna Piena derives from its simple Mediterranean classics made from ingredients bought at the local Testaccio market. The menu varies according to the season, with the day's specials chalked up on a board at the door. This is the place for a traditional *pasta alla carbonara* and *saltimbocca alla Romana* (veal and Parma ham cooked with sage and wine).

Perilli a Testaccio

Via Marmorata 39. **Map** 8 D3.
☎ 06-574 2415. **Open** 12.30–3pm, 7.30–11pm Thu–Tue. **Closed** Aug. & 🚻 AE, DC, MC, V. €€

In the heart of Testaccio, this archetypal Roman trattoria is always packed with hungry regulars (and the occasional famous face). On offer are giant-size quantities of robust traditional fare – *rigatoni alla pajata* (pasta with veal intestines), *spaghetti alla carbonara* (served in king-size bowls), *coda alla vaccinara* and *carciofi alla romana* – helpfully and efficiently served. Ignore the noise and hideous murals – tuck in and enjoy yourself.

SHOPS AND MARKETS

ROME HAS BEEN a thriving centre for design and cosmopolitan shopping since ancient times. In the heyday of the Empire the finest craftsmen were drawn to Rome, and artifacts and produce of all kinds, including gold, furs, wine and slaves, were imported from far-flung corners of the Empire to service the needs of the wealthy Roman population. Shopping in Rome today in many ways reflects this diverse tradition. Italian designers

Stylish window display

have an international reputation for their luxuriously chic style in fashion, knitwear and leather goods (especially shoes and handbags) as well as in interior design, fabrics, ceramics and glass. The artisan-craftsman tradition is strong and the love of good design filters through into the smallest items. Rome is not a city for bargains (although it is often better value than Florence or Milan), but the joys of window shopping here will offer plenty of compensation.

BEST BUYS

LEATHER GOODS of all kinds, including shoes and bags, are a strong point. Ready-to-wear Italian designer clothes are not cheap, but they are certainly less expensive than in other countries. Armani jeans are a good example *(see p327)*. You are also likely to find designer lighting fixtures, for example, at lower prices here. Both modern and traditional Italian ceramics and handicrafts can be very beautifully made and, if you have time to wander around the back streets, really unusual and individual gifts can often be found.

SALES

SALE TIME *(saldi)* is from mid-July to mid-September and the period from just before Christmas to the first week in March. Top designers

(see p326) slash prices by half, but their clothes are still very expensive even then. Good bargains can be found in the young designer-wear shops *(see p327)* and good-quality large shoe sizes are sold off very cheaply (most Italians have small feet). Both of the Cesari shops *(see p327 and p333)* are well known for their sales. In general, though, sales in Rome do not offer huge discounts.

Both the original and the sale price should be quoted on each reduced item. *Liquidazioni* (closing-down sales) are usually genuine and can sometimes be worth investigating. However, other signs in shop windows such as *vendite promozionali* (special introductory prices) and *sconti* (discounts) are often only lures to get you into the shop. The sign on the door saying *entrata libera* means "browsers welcome".

Antiques at Acanto *(see p336)*

WHEN TO SHOP

SHOPS ARE GENERALLY open from 9am to 1pm and from 3.30pm to 7.30pm (4pm to 8pm in the summer months). Some of the shops in the centre stay open all day from 10am to 7.30pm.

Most shops are closed on Sunday (except immediately before Christmas). Shops are also closed on Monday morning, apart from most food stores, which close on Thursday afternoons in winter and Saturday afternoons in high summer.

August brings the city to a virtual standstill as Roman families escape the heat to the sea or the mountains, but this is gradually changing, with Romans taking shorter summer holidays. Most shops close for at least 2 weeks around 15 August, the national holiday.

Flower stalls in Piazza Campo de' Fiori *(see p338)*

SHOPPING ETIQUETTE

APART FROM a few department stores, most Roman shops are small, specializing in just one field. Browsing at leisure may at first seem daunting if you are used to large shopping centres. Customers will almost always receive better attention if they dress smartly – the emphasis on *fare una bella figura* (making a good impression) is taken seriously.

Sizes are not always uniform, so it is wise to try clothes on if possible before buying, since refunds and exchanges are not always given.

Stylish leather gloves on display

HOW TO PAY

MOST SHOPS now accept all the major credit cards, whose signs are displayed on the shop window. Some will also accept foreign currency, though the exchange rate may not be good. When you make a purchase you are bound by Italian law to leave the shop with a *scontrino fiscale* (receipt). You can try asking for a discount if paying cash and you may be lucky, though many shops have a *prezzi fissi* (fixed prices) sign.

VAT EXEMPTION

VALUE ADDED TAX – VAT (IVA in Italy) – ranges from 12 per cent on clothing to 35 per cent on luxury items such as jewellery and furs. Marked or advertised prices normally include the IVA. It is possible for non-European Union

One of many designer shops around Piazza di Spagna

residents to obtain an IVA refund for individual purchases that exceed about 160 euros, but be prepared for a long and bureaucratic process. The simplest method is to shop at a place displaying the "Euro Free Tax" sign.

Present your passport when you make your purchase, and fill in a form from the shop; the shop then deducts the IVA, gives you a copy of the form, and sends their copy to the Euro Free Tax Organization in Milan which will then deal with the paperwork.

If you wish to buy something from a shop which is not part of the "Euro Free Tax" scheme, you must get the Italian customs to stamp the vendor's receipt at your departure, showing them the purchased article, and then post the stamped receipt back to the shop, who should then send you a refund.

Mercato delle Stampe *(see p338)*

DEPARTMENT STORES AND SHOPPING CENTRES

DEPARTMENT STORES, known as *grandi magazzini*, are few and far between in Rome, but they tend to have longer opening hours than smaller shops. **La Rinascente** and **Coin** are good for ready-to-wear clothes, both for men and women, household linens and haberdashery, and have well-stocked perfume counters. The **Oviesse** and **Upim** chain stores offer moderately priced medium-quality clothes and a variety of household goods.

Another alternative for the zealous shopper is to head for one of Rome's shopping malls. **Cinecittà Due Centro Commerciale**, built in 1988, offers around 100 shops plus bars, banks

Bargains in Via Sannio *(see p339)*

and restaurants within easy reach of the centre by Metro (line A to Cinecittà).

Cinecittà Due Centro Commerciale
Viale Palmiro Togliatti 2.
☎ 06-722 09 10.

Coin
Piazzale Appio 7. **Map** 10 D2.
☎ 06-708 00 20.

Via Cola di Rienzo 173.
Map 3 C2.
☎ 06-3600 4298.

La Rinascente
Via del Corso 189.
Map 5 A3 & 12 E2.
☎ 06-679 76 91.

Piazza Fiume.
Map 6 D1.
☎ 06-884 12 31.

Oviesse
Viale Trastevere 62.
Map 7 C2.
☎ 06-5833 3633.

Via Appia Nuova 181–5.
Map 10 D2.
☎ 06-702 32 14.

Upim
Via del Tritone 172.
Map 5 A3.
☎ 06-678 33 36.

Termini Station.
Map 6 D3.
☎ 06-4782 5909.

Piazza Santa Maria Maggiore.
Map 6 D4.
☎ 06-446 55 79.

Rome's Best: Shopping Streets and Markets

T HE MOST INTERESTING shops in Rome are in the old centre, so shopping is easy to combine with sightseeing. The shops are often housed in medieval or Renaissance buildings and their window displays can be exquisite. Just like shopkeepers in past centuries, traders tend to specialize in one type of merchandise. Street names often refer to the old tradesmen: locksmiths in Via dei Chiavari, leather jerkin makers in Via dei Giubbonari and chairs in Via dei Sediari. Today, antique merchants have taken over from the rosary sellers on Via dei Coronari. The top names in fashion and modern design dominate the Via Condotti area, and the artisan-craftsman tradition is still strong around Campo de' Fiori and Piazza Navona.

Via dei Coronari
Art Nouveau and antiques enthusiasts will love browsing in the shops that line this charming street just northwest of Piazza Navona. But be prepared for high prices as most of the items are imported.

Via Cola di Rienzo
Situated close to the Vatican Museums, this long wide street has the finest food shops and is also good for clothes, books and gifts.

Via del Pellegrino
Book and art shops abound here next to working artisans in the historic centre. Do not miss the mirror-lined alley near Campo de' Fiori.

Via dei Cappellari
This narrow, medieval street is a great place for watching furniture restorers and other artisans plying their crafts in the open air.

Porta Portese
You can buy anything from antiques to a tin whistle at Trastevere's Sunday morning flea market. (See p339.)

Vatican

Janiculum

Piazza Navona

Campo de' Fiori

Trastevere

Via Margutta
Up-market antique shops mix with genteel restaurants on this peaceful, cobbled street.

Via del Babuino
This street is renowned for designer furniture, lighting and glass, as well as interesting antique and fashion shops.

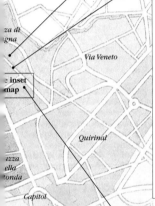

DESIGNER SHOPPING

All the well-known stars of the Italian fashion scene, plus exclusive jewellers, gift shops, shoe designers and tailors, are concentrated in this cluster of chic and stylish shopping streets by the Spanish Steps *(see pp326–31).* Romans love to stroll here in the early evening.

MISSONI
GIORGIO ARMANI
TRUSSARDI
VIA CONDOTTI
PRADA
GUCCI
D&G
valentino
VIA BORGOGNONA
PIAZZA DI SPAGNA
VIA DEL CORSO
FENDI
VIA FRATTINA
MaxMara

Via Borgognona
Crowds flock here to buy, or just gaze at, high-fashion clothes, shoes, leather bags and other accessories.

| 0 metres | 500 |
| 0 yards | 500 |

Testaccio Market
A visual feast of fruit and vegetables greets the eye in this lively market. (See p338.)

Shoes and Accessories

ITALY'S LEATHER INDUSTRY is renowned all over the world, and shoes, bags and belts are a good buy in Rome. Accessories in general are not just an afterthought but an integral part of an outfit for the well-dressed Roman. The choice of stylish jewellery, scarves, ties and other accessories is excellent.

SHOES

ROME IS FULL of shoe shops, ranging from high-quality stores in the Via Condotti area (where prices tend to start at €155) to the more economical shops around the Trevi fountain, and every big market has its bargain shoe stalls on its fringes.

Probably the best-known shop is **Ferragamo** – one of the world's top shoe shops. It stocks classic yet fashion-conscious shoes, as well as women's clothing and leather goods – the silk signature scarves are quite a feature.

Fratelli Rossetti is a close contender for the number one position. Founded by brothers Renzo and Renato 40 years ago, this company produces classic men's shoes and beautiful, dressy low-heeled shoes for women that reflect the most up-to-the-minute trends. Along with **Campanile** in Via Condotti it represents the epitome of elegance. Its prices, of course, are sky-high but why not buy something small, and at least you'll have the bag!

Bruno Magli, Bologna's well-known star, has dressy patent-leather pumps and other classic styles. **Barrilà** near Piazza di Spagna sells more affordable women's shoes.

Rome's own **Raphael Salato** has three extremely elegant, high-priced shops: his shoes are genuine master-pieces of craftsmanship, and many are made of intricately embroidered leather.

Carlotto Rio is one of the more long-lived shoe shops in Rome, having been in business for over a decade, but it can't compete with **Domus**, which opened in 1938. Carlotto Rio sells made-to-measure footwear for both men and women, particularly shoes for special occasions, and also makes bags to customers' specifications. Domus sells a selection of high-quality footwear, specializing in classic shoes for women. They also stock a limited range of bags. **De Bach** has colourful shoe styles for women.

Via Frattina has several more great shoe shops such as **Pollini**, which makes boots and bags for both men and women in trendy and imaginative styles. Native deigner **Fausto Santini** stocks original, stylish, colourful designs for younger people. More moderate prices can be found at **Cervone**, which specializes in highly colourful women's shoes.

Borini stocks simple and elegant, low-heeled designs. The **Mr Boots** chain of shops stocks a wide range of trendy boots and casual shoes for men and women, while **Dominici** sells witty, smart and affordable footwear for women.

LEATHER BAGS AND ACCESSORIES

THE MOST FAMOUS of Rome's leather shops is the super-trendy **Gucci**, a dandy's paradise selling shoes, suit-cases, handbags, wallets, belts and other accessories. It has a fashion boutique for men and women and is well-known for its silk ties and scarves. **Fendi** also has exqui-site leather goods as well as some lower-priced lines in synthetic materials and a range of gift items. Although their famous "stripe" line of leather-finished synthetic hand-bags cost €130 (and their all-leather ones start at €155), they are at least cheaper to buy here than abroad. **Skin**, situated around the Via Sistina area, is also quite pricey. Located a short walk to the south of Skin and Ginocchi, near the Trevi Fountain, is **La Sella**. It sells all things leather, including a range of shoes, bags, purses and belts.

Mandarina Duck's brightly coloured fabric bags and range of luggage are very much in fashion and make an attractive (and vegetarian) alternative to the more traditional leather styles. For sleek, utterly fashionable handbags try **Furla** or go for one of **Alviero Martini**'s famous "map" bags.

For a more unusual men's present, try **La Cravatta** in Trastevere. In addition to their selection of classy hand-made ties, they also manufacture ties to meet customers' spe-cifications. You can choose the design, material, length and shape of the tie to create the perfect gift.

CLASSIC JEWELLERY

WHAT CARTIER is to Paris, Tiffany & Co is to New York and Asprey's is to London, **Bulgari** is to Rome. This internationally revered jeweller's has passers-by glued to the windows gazing at its large fat gemstones. These "windows" are rather curious small boxes inserted into a wall with one or two pieces of jewellery in each of them, which adds to the feeling of looking at precious items in a case at a museum. Bulgari's watches, especially the men's, are popular and very elegant, as are the famous mesh necklaces. It specializes in large, colourful stones in High Renaissance-style settings but also produces a selection of contemporary designs. This was one of Andy Warhol's favourite shops, and it is definitely the most palatial shop on Via Condotti. Inside, the shop's atmosphere is one of almost religious awe and contemplation.

Buccellati is an offshoot of the famous Florentine dynasty, which was begun by Mario Buccellati in the 1920s and patronized by the poet Gabriele D'Annunzio.

Its delicately engraved designs are inspired by the Italian Renaissance, and are real classics, displaying superb craftsmanship.

Ansuini designs are fashionable yet classic with strong, imaginative themes being introduced for each new collection. **Massoni**, founded in 1790, is one of Rome's oldest jewellery houses. Its refined one-offs and brooches are quite outstanding.

At **Moroni Gioielli** you will also find imaginative, unique pieces of the highest-quality workmanship. **Petochi**, which was jeweller to the former Italian monarchy (1861–1946), the House of Savoy, has both traditional and contemporary styles on display.

Peroso is an old-fashioned shop which has been going since 1891 and specializes in antique jewellery and silver-ware. **Boncompagni Sturni** sells traditional designs with the emphasis on quality and craftsmanship. You have to ring the bell to be admitted to both of these shops, and they are extremely expensive.

COSTUME JEWELLERY

FOR LESS conventional tastes, there are several shops selling innovative, avant-garde pieces, often using semi-precious metals and stones. **Via dei Coronari 193** is worth trying.

Tempi Moderni has an interesting collection of Art Deco and Liberty period jewellery. You can also find some nice pieces from the 1920s and 1930s in Cose Così (*see p336*).

Bozart is the place for trendy, flashy costume jewellery. **Siragusa** puts beautiful 3rd- and 4th-century BC beads and coins into handmade gold chains, in a museum-like shop just off the Piazza di Spagna.

TRADITIONAL GOLDSMITHS AND SILVERSMITHS

THE MAINSTAY of Rome's jewellery industry is still the traditional artisan goldsmith and silversmith, working to order in tiny studio workshops. These are concentrated in the old Jewish Ghetto area by the Tiber river, Campo de' Fiori, Ponte Sisto near Via Giulia, and in Montepietà (which is also where the pawnbrokers live).

Artisan jewellery can also be found in Via dei Coronari, Via dell'Orso and Via del Pellegrino. The jewellers create individual pieces to their own designs and have often learned their profession from their parents and grand-parents. They will also do repair work, or take old gold jewellery, melt it down and make it into something to suit you especially.

Gioie d'Arte produces some traditional artisan jewellery and always works to customers' commissions.

GLOVES, HATS AND HOSIERY

IF YOU'RE LOOKING for top quality, you will find an expensive line of gloves at **Di Cori** and **Sermoneta**, which stock every imaginable kind.

To find smart leather gloves to match your new shoes and handbags, whatever their colour, make a visit to **Settimio Mieli** which is sure to have something suitable, and at a reasonable price. **Catello d'Auria** specializes in gloves and hosiery. **Borsalino** is a good place to go for all sorts of hats, including its namesake.

Calza e Calze has the best range of hosiery in Rome – the friendly staff will serve you with almost any colour or pattern of tights and stockings that you could wish for.

SIZE CHART

For Australian sizes follow British and American convention.

Children's clothing

Italian	2-3	4-5	6-7	8-9	10-11	12	14	14+ (years)
British	2-3	4-5	6-7	8-9	10-11	12	14	14+ (years)
American	2-3	4-5	6-6x	7-8	10		12	14	16 (size)

Children's shoes

Italian	24	25½	27	28	29	30	32	33	34
British	7	8	9	10	11	12	13	1	2
American	7½	8½	9½	10½	11½	12½	13½	1½	2½

Women's dresses, coats and skirts

Italian	38	40	42	44	46	48	50
British	8	10	12	14	16	18	20
American	6	8	10	12	14	16	18

Women's blouses and sweaters

Italian	81	84	87	90	93	96	99 (cms)
British	31	32	34	36	38	40	42 (inches)
American	6	8	10	12	14	16	18 (size)

Women's shoes

Italian	36	37	38	39	40	41
British	3	4	5	6	7	8
American	5	6	7	8	9	10

Men's suits

Italian	44	46	48	50	52	54	56	58 (size)
British	34	36	38	40	42	44	46	48 (inches)
American	34	36	38	40	42	44	46	48 (inches)

Men's shirts (collar size)

Italian	36	38	39	41	42	43	44	45 (cms)
British	14	15	15½	16	16½	17	17½	18 (inches)
American	14	15	15½	16	16½	17	17½	18 (inches)

Men's shoes

Italian	39	40	41	42	43	44	45	46
British	6	7	7½	8	9	10	11	12
American	7	7½	8	8½	9½	10½	11	11½

DIRECTORY

WOMEN'S HIGH FASHION

Dolce & Gabbana
Piazza di Spagna 93.
Map 5 A2.
06-6938 0870.

Fendi
Via Borgognona 36–39.
Map 5 A2.
06-69 66 61.

Gente
Via del Babuino 80.
Map 4 F1.
06-320 7671.
Also: Via Frattina 70.
Map 5 A2.
06-678 9132.

Gianni Versace
Via Bocca di Leone 27.
Map 5 A2.
06-678 0521.

Giorgio Armani
Via Condotti 76.
Map 5 A2.
06-699 1461.
Also: Via del Babuino 139.
Map 4 F1.
06-3600 2197.

Laura Biagiotti
Via Borgognona 43–44.
Map 5 A2.
06-679 1205.

Max & Co
Via Condotti 46.
Map 5 A2.
06-678 7946.

MaxMara
Via Frattina 28. **Map** 5 A2.
06-679 3638.

Prada
Via Condotti 92–95.
Map 5 A2.
06-679 0897.

Renato Balestra
Via Sistina 67.
Map 5 A2.
06-679 5537.

Roberto Capucci
Via Gregoriana 56.
Map 5 A2.
06-679 5180.

Roberto Cavalli
Via Borgognona 7A.
Map 5 A2.
06-6938 0130.

Salvatore Ferragamo
Via Condotti 73–74.
Map 5 A2.
06-679 1565.

Sorelle Fontana
Salita S. Sebastianello 5.
Map 5 A2.
06-6992 2156.

Trussardi
Via Condotti 49–50. **Map** 5 A2. 06-679 2151.

Valentino
Via Condotti 13. **Map** 5 A2.
06-673 9420.

MEN'S TAILORS AND DESIGNER WEAR

Battistoni
Via Condotti 61A. **Map** 5 A2. 06-697 6111.

Brioni
Via Condotti 21A.
Map 5 A2.
06-678 3635.

Davide Cenci
Via Campo Marzio 1–7.
Map 4 F3 & 12 D2.
06-699 0681.

Degli Effetti
Piazza Capranica 79.
Map 4 F3 & 12 D2.
06-679 0202.

Enzo Ceci
Via della Vite 52. **Map** 5 A3 & 12 E1. 06-679 8882.

Ermenegildo Zegna
Via Borgognona 7 E. **Map** 5 A2. 06-678 9143.

Etro
Via del Babuino 102.
Map 5 A2.
06-678 8257.

Gianfranco Ferrè
Via Borgognona 6.
Map 5 A2.
06-679 7445.

Gianni Versace
Via Borgognona 24–25.
Map 5 A2.
06-679 5037.

Gucci
Via Condotti 8. **Map** 5 A2.
06-678 3940.

Testa
Via Borgognona 13.
Map 5 A2.
06-679 6174.
Also: Via Frattina 104.
Map 5 A2.
06-679 1296.

Trussardi
See Women's High Fashion.

Valentino
Via Bocca di Leone 16.
Map 5 A2.
06-678 3656.

YOUNG DESIGNER WEAR

Aria
Via Nazionale 239.
Map 5 C3.
06-48 44 21.

Arsenale
Via del Governo Vecchio 64. **Map** 4 E4 & 11 B3.
06-686 1380.

Diesel
Via del Corso 186.
Map 4 F3 & 12 E1.
06-678 3933.

Emporio Armani
Via del Babuino 139.
Map 4 F1.
06-3600 2197.

Energie
Via del Corso 486–487.
Map 4 F2.
06-322 7046.

Eventi
Via del Serpenti 134.
Map 5 B4.
06-48 49 60.

Luna e L'Altra
Via del Governo Vecchio 105. **Map** 4 E4 & 11 B3.
06-6880 4995.

Maga Morgana
Via del Governo Vecchio 27.
Map 4 E4 & 11 C3.
06-687 9995.

Max & Co
Via Nazionale 56.
Map 5 C3.
06-481 7524.
Also: Via Appia Nuova 201–203.
Map 10 D2.
06-701 4413.

Prada Casual
Via del Babuino 91. **Map** 4 F1. 06-361 0596.

SBU
Via S. Pantaleo 68.
Map 11 C3.
06-6880 2547.

Timberland
Via del Corso 488. **Map** 4 F2. 06-322 7266.

T'Store
Via del Corso 477. **Map** 4 F2. 06-322 6057.

Valentino Sport
Via del Babuino 61.
Map 4 F1.
06-3600 1906.

HIGH STREET FASHION

Benetton
Via Cesare Battisti 129.
Map 5 A4 & 12 F3.
06-6992 4010.

Discount dell'Alta Moda
Via di Gesù e Maria
14 & 16A. **Map** 4 F2.
06-361 3796.

Emporio Armani
See Young Designer Wear.

Max & Co
See Young Designer Wear.

Onyx
Via del Corso 142.
Map 4 F2.
06-699 321.

KNITWEAR

Choses de Cachemire
Via del Babuino 105.
Map 4 F1.
06-679 8488.

Laura Biagiotti
See Women's High Fashion.

Liz
Via Appia Nuova 90.
Map 10 D2.
06-700 3609.

Luisa Spagnoli
Via del Tritone 30.
Map 5 A3 & B3 & 12F1.
06-6992 2769.

Also: Via Vittorio
Veneto 130. **Map** 5 B1.
[06-4201 1281.
Also: Via Frattina 84B.
Map 5 A2.
[06-699 1706.

Missoni
Piazza di Spagna 78.
Map 5 A2.
[06-679 2555.

LINGERIE

Brighenti
Via Frattina 7–8. **Map** 5 A2.
[06-679 1484.
Also: Via Borgognona 27.
Map 5 A2.
[06-678 3898.

Cesari
Via del Babuino 195.
Map 5 B3.
[06-361 3451.

Liberti
Via del Tritone 101.
Map 12 F1.
[06-488 2246.

Schostal
Via del Corso 158.
Map 4 F3 & 12 E1.
[06-679 1240.

SECOND-HAND CLOTHES

Le Gallinelle
Via del Boschetto 76.
Map 5 B4.
[06-488 1017.

Mado
Via del Governo Vecchio
89A. **Map** 4 E4 & 11 B3.
[06-687 5028.

SHOES

Barrilà
Via del Babuino 33A.
Map 4 F1.
[06-3600 1726.

Borini
Via dei Pettinari 86–87.
Map 4 E5 & 11 C5.
[06-687 5670.

Bruno Magli
Via Condotti 6. **Map** 5
A2. [06-679 3587.

Campanile
Via Condotti 58. **Map** 5 A2.
[06-678 3041.

Carlotto Rio
Via dell'Arco della
Ciambella 8.
Map 12 D3.
[06-687 2308.

Cervone
Via del Corso 99.
Map 4 F2.
[06-678 3522.

De Bach
Via del Babuino 123.
Map 4 F1.
[06-678 3384.

Dominici
Via del Corso 14.
Map 12 E1.
[06-361 0591.

Domus
Via Belsiana 52.
Map 4 F2.
[06-678 9083.

Fausto Santini
Via Frattina 120.
Map 5 A2.
[06-678 4114.

Ferragamo
Via Condotti 73–74.
Map 5 A2.
[06-679 1565.
Also: Via Condotti 66.
Map 5 A2.
[06-678 1130.

Fratelli Rossetti
Via Borgognona 5A.
Map 5 A2.
[06-678 2676.

Mr Boots
Piazza Re di Roma 10.
Map 10 D3.
[06-7720 8672.
Also: Via A Brunetti 2.
Map 4 F1.
[06-321 5733.

Pollini
Via Frattina 22–24.
Map 5 A2 & 12 E1.
[06-679 8360.

Raphael Salato
Via Veneto 149.
Map 5 B1.
[06-482 1816.

LEATHER GOODS

Alviero Martini
Via Borgognona 4G.
Map 5 A2.
[06-6992 3381.

Furla
Via del Corso 481. **Map** 4
F3. [06-3600 3619.

Gucci
Via Borgognona 7D. **Map**
5 A2. [06-6920 2077.

Mandarina Duck
Via di Propaganda 1.
Map 5 A2.
[06-6994 0320.

La Sella
Via del Lavatore 56.
Map 5 A3 & 12 F2.
[06-679 6654.

Skin
Via Capo le Case 41.
Map 5 A3 & 12 F1.
[06-678 5531.

CLASSIC JEWELLERY

Ansuini
Via del Babuino 150 D.
Map 4 F1.
[06-3600 2219.

Boncompagni
Via del Babuino 115.
Map 4 F1.
[06-678 3239.

Buccellati
Via Condotti 31. **Map**
5 A2. [06-679 0329.

Bulgari
Via Condotti 10. **Map**
5 A2. [06-679 3876.

Massoni
Largo Carlo Goldoni 48.
Map 4 F2 & 12 E1.
[06-678 2679.

Moroni Gioielli
Via Belsiana 32A. **Map**
4 F2. [06-678 0466.

Peroso
Via Sistina 29A. **Map** 5 B3.
[06-474 7952.

Petochi
Piazza di Spagna 23.
Map 5 A2.
[06-679 1128.

COSTUME JEWELLERY

Bozart
Via Bocca di Leone 4.
Map 5 A2.
[06-678 1026.

Siragusa
Via delle Carrozze 64.
Map 5 A2.
[06-679 7085.

Tempi Moderni
Via del Governo
Vecchio 108.
Map 4 E4 & 11 B3.
[06-687 7007.

**Via dei Coronari
193**
Via dei Coronari 193.
Map 4 E3 & 11 B2.
[06-6880 1503.

TRADITIONAL GOLDSMITHS AND SILVERSMITHS

Gioie d'Arte
Via de' Gigli d'Oro 10.
Map 4 E3 & 11 C2.
[06-687 7524.

GLOVES, HATS AND HOSIERY

Borsalino
Piazza del Popolo 20.
Map 4 F1.
[06-3265 0838.

Calza e Calze
Via della Croce 78.
Map 4 F2.
[06-678 4281.

Catello d'Auria
Via dei Due Macelli 55.
Map 5 A2 & 12 F1.
[06-679 3364.

Di Cori
Piazza di Spagna 53.
Map 5 A2.
[06-678 4439.

La Cravatta
Via di Santa Cecilia 12.
Map 8 D1.
[06-581 6676.

Fendi
See Women's High Fashion.

Sermoneta
Piazza di Spagna 61.
Map 5 A2.
[06-679 1960.

Settimio Mieli
Via San Claudio 70.
Map 5 A3 & 12 E2.
[06-678 5979.

Interior Design

ITALIAN DESIGN belongs to a long-established tradition based on the skills of the master craftsman, and some firms have a history going back hundreds of years. Rome's stylish interior design shops are worth seeking out, even if it is only to look around and enjoy the ambience. You might well pick up some design ideas for your home, or find some interesting or unusual things to buy. They are an excellent place to buy souvenirs and presents to take home.

FURNITURE

ALTHOUGH THERE is no distinct area of Rome that is renowned for its furniture shops, most of the top stores are located to the north of the city centre.

Take a look at **Studio Punto Tre** if you want something different: it's packed with strangely painted chests of drawers, Egyptian-style artifacts and small items that would make good presents.

Myricae dazzles with its sensible prices and its covetable Tuscan wrought iron and Venetian painted furniture in sun-drenched or delicate hues.

Spazio Sette, near Largo Argentina, is worth visiting for the building itself. The store has a spectacular showroom on three levels in the Palazzo Lazzaroni, a former cardinal's palace. It is one of Rome's premier home furnishing stores and, as well as furniture, it stocks plenty of items that would make interesting gifts. The furniture – modern, laminated, stack-up chairs and so forth, vases, glass, bowls, and kitchen equipment – is jumbled together in a fascinating display.

Nearby, on Via dei Chiavari, stands **Paola Agostara**, another shop that stocks an impressive cornucopia of household objects. Items ranging from hand-painted furniture to glassware from Eastern Europe are on sale here, along with a collection of designer fabrics and furniture by Paola Agostara herself.

Benedetti, which occupies a line of shops on the Via Marmorata, offers a range of fine modern wood furniture.

LIGHTING FIXTURES

LIGHTING FIXTURES are one of the most popular and more easily transportable items, and there are several superb showrooms in Rome that are worth a visit.

Flos is a merger of two design houses whose Roman showroom displays its lights as if they were museum exhibits. The design style is chic and minimalist, with plenty of black and white, chrome and steel.

Nearby **Artemide** is, like Flos, a design house in its own right, and is similarly well-known abroad. Its showroom in Rome is elegant, with expensive, hi-tech lighting design. **Borghini** sells less famous names, and so is more economical.

Paolo Marj is a sculptor working in mixed media such as glass, wood and plastics to create lamps that are original works of art in themselves. Also on sale is a variety of original sculptures by the artist.

Italian lighting and other electrical equipment is designed for 220–240 volts. If you are going to use it in countries with lower voltage always ask the shop whether the product needs a transformer, as this can depend on the model.

Lighting fixtures generally take screw-bulbs, although some designer models can be ordered with fittings for bayonet-bulbs.

KITCHENS AND BATHROOMS

ALTHOUGH YOU won't be able to take one home with you, you may like to take a look at the ultra-modern hi-tech kitchen designs in Rome.

For an overview of the latest smart, steel designs, visit **Arclinea**, near Ponte Garibaldi, for its select display of state-of-the-art kitchens. Equally inspiring are the kitchens on display at **Emporio Cucina**, just off Piazza Navona.

Italian bathroom shops concentrate almost exclusively on modern designs, some of which are luxuriously decadent. **Ravasini** has very decorative floral fixtures with some matching accessories. **Andreucci** is another bathroom shop that sells all the latest styles.

TILES

THE ITALIAN ceramic tile tradition is an ancient one. A great variety of tiles is displayed in kitchen and bathroom showrooms, but there are also a number of specialist shops.

The most beautiful, and the most expensive, of these is **Farnese**, looking ancient Roman in style with its mosaic tables. Di Donato uses old-fashioned methods to design and produce the tiles – hence the cost. He is influenced by Roman as well as Pompeian art but also produces modern, one-off designs.

Ceramiche Musa specializes in modern tiles with decorative floral and ancient Roman motifs, which are popular, especially with foreign visitors.

GLASS

DECORATIVE GLASS objects are a popular buy in Rome. **Murano Più**, just behind Piazza Navona, sells Murano and other glass items at reasonable prices. This shop is one of the few that opens on Sundays – which can be useful for visitors on short trips to Rome.

Archimede Seguso also specializes in Murano glass

but includes smaller pieces and also offers a range of gift-sized items.

Arteque is a very beautiful shop which has a more traditional flavour.

For less expensive gifts, try **Stilvetro**. It is the ideal place for pasta bowls, glass and ceramics.

An added advantage is that shipment abroad can usually be arranged at any of these glass establishments so you can make your purchase without worrying about transporting it home.

FABRICS

BEAUTIFUL FABRICS and wallpapers to order are offered by **Il Sigillo** who has a rich assortment of samples.

At **Emporio Triestino** you can find all manner of beautiful fabrics, including those by the most famous designer names.

If you are looking for worthwhile bargains, take a walk round the old Jewish quarter, Il Ghetto, that runs from Largo Argentina down to the Tiber; the area contains numerous cheaper fabric shops such as **Paganini**. During sale times, remnants of fabrics *(scampoli)* are always sold cheaply, and you could find just the right fabric for just the right price.

HOUSEHOLD LINEN AND KITCHENWARE

A SELECTION of lovely sheets can be found at **Frette**. If you enjoy designer kitchenware, don't miss **C.u.c.i.n.a.** tucked away in No. 65 Via Mario de' Fiori. It stocks kitchen utensils from all over the world, as well as pots and pans in both rustic and hi-tech styles and countless space-saving accessories.

Culti specializes in stainless steel designs and other minimalist lines for bathroom and kitchen fittings and furnishings.

The Roman pizzeria **'Gusto** *(see p320)* also offers an interesting range of kitchen utensils and essentials in its ground-floor shop.

Finally, for the budget conscious, there is also **Salvoni**, whose basement is well stocked with cut-price gift ideas. Here, you'll find an extraordinary array of household and kitchenware, including silver, china and crystal items.

DIRECTORY

FURNITURE

Benedetti
Via Marmorata 141.
Map 8 D3.
06-574 6610.

Myricae
Piazza del Parlamento 38–39. 06-687 3742.
Also: Via Campo Marzio 11. **Map** 4 F3 & 12 D1.
06-689 2485.

Paola Agostara
Via dei Chiavari 8.
Map 4 E4 & 11 C4.
06-689 3777.

Spazio Sette
Via dei Barbieri 7.
Map 4 F5 & 12 D4.
06-6880 4261.

Studio Punto Tre
Via Giulia 145.
Map 4 E4 & 11 B4.
06-686 4321.

LIGHTING FIXTURES

Artemide
Via Margutta 107–108.
Map 4 F1.
06-3600 1802.

Borghini
Via Belsiana 87-89.
Map 4 F2.
06-679 0629.

Flos
Via del Babuino 84.
Map 5 A2.
06-320 7631.

Paolo Marj
Piazza del Fico 21a.
Map 11 B3.
06-6880 7707.

KITCHENS AND BATHROOMS

Andreucci
Via Po 39.
Map 2 F5.
06-855 0265.

Arclinea
Lungotevere
dei Cenci 4b.
Map 4 F5 & 12 D5.
06-686 5104.

Emporio Cucina
Piazza delle Cinque Lune 74. **Map** 11 C2.
06-6880 3685.

Ravasini
Via di Ripetta 71.
Map 4 F2.
06-322 7096.

TILES

Ceramiche Musa
Via Campo Marzio 39.
Map 4 F3 & 12 D1.
06-687 1242.

Farnese
Piazza Farnese 52.
Map 4 E5 & 11 C4.
06-687 4792.

GLASS

Archimede Seguso
Via dei Due Macelli 56.
Map 5 A2.
06-679 1781.

Arteque
Via Giulia 13. **Map** 4 D4 & 11 A3. 06-687 7388.

Murano Più
Corso Rinascimento 43.
Map 4 E3.
06-6880 8038.

Stilvetro
Via Frattina 56. **Map** 5 A2.
06-679 0258.

FABRICS

Emporio Triestino
Corso Vittorio Emanuele 9.
Map 12 D4.
06-679 2773.

Paganini
Via delle Botteghe Oscure 50.
Map 4 F5 & 12 E4.
06-678 6831.

Il Sigillo
Via Laurina 15.
Map 4 F1.
06-361 3247.

HOUSEHOLD AND KITCHENWARE

C.u.c.i.n.a.
Via Mario de' Fiori 65.
Map 5 A2.
06-679 1275.

Culti
Via Francesco Crispi 45–47.
Map 5 B2.
06-679 0272.

Frette
Piazza di Spagna 10.
Map 5 A2.
06-679 0673.

'Gusto
Piazza Augusto Imperatore 9.
Map 4 F2.

Salvoni
Via Arenula 38.
Map 4 F5.
06-6880 6770.

Books and Gifts

Rome OFFERS HUGE SCOPE for gift buying. You will find products from all over Italy as well as locally produced artisan wares. Seeking out the smaller shops can be an adventure in itself, as many are in attractive parts of the city that you might not otherwise visit.

Some of the artisan ceramics are very unusual; there are beautiful books on Italian art and architecture, and wonderful paper products. Foodie gifts and drinks are always welcome – especially if it is something really special such as a 20-year-old balsamic vinegar. As well as the usual souvenirs, there is an abundance of religious artifacts – for obvious reasons – and Michelangelo masterpieces are the number one icon for T-shirts, statuettes and postcards.

BOOKSHOPS

Rome IS RICH in bookshops, from the encyclopedic to the very specialized. Italian books, both hardback and softback, are generally very attractive but also tend to be quite expensive.

Feltrinelli, one of Rome's largest bookshops, has a wide selection on art and cookery among other subjects, and many books in English and other foreign languages. There are four branches in the capital. The most central are situated in Largo Argentina and the Galleria Alberto Sordi.

There is also an excellent **Feltrinelli International** bookshop in Via Emanuele Orlando, which sells foreign books and magazines.

Milanese **Franco Maria Ricci** offers very beautiful art books, as well as its own glossy magazine *FMR*. **Libreria Godel** is good for browsing – it has a lot of books on Rome, great postcards, art calendars and some second-hand art books.

Remainder has half-price bargains and sells games for children too. There are lots of cut-price bargains as well as second-hand book stalls in Via delle Terme di Diocleziano and in Largo della Fontanella di Borghese.

MULTIMEDIA AND MUSIC

Rome's BIGGEST music store is **Ricordi**. As well as records, cassettes and CDs, it sells musical instruments and musical scores in its four central outlets. By contrast, **Discoteca Frattina** is quite a small, handy music shop that also sells video cassettes.

STATIONERY AND PAPER CRAFTS

A WIDE SELECTION of pretty marbled notebooks, writing papers, and files and boxes in various sizes are on offer at **Laboratorio Scatole**. **Pineider**, stationery suppliers to the Roman gentry, will print sets of exquisite visiting cards for you. For excellent paper articles and gifts, try also **Fabriano**. Just as classy, though less traditional, **Vertecchi** is filled with original paper gifts. These include boxes of every size and shape, paper napkins and tablecloths, wrapping paper and a dazzling range of Christmas decorations.

ARTISAN HANDICRAFTS AND DESIGN

Domenico and Lavinia Sarti's **Bottega Artigiana** nearby is a small shop with ceramics made by the couple in their Anzio studio. You can buy vases and urns in unglazed terracotta and some attractive terracotta wall-light fittings. **Studio Arti e Mestieri** is the workshop of a friendly mother and daughter who make original articles in wood and terracotta.

If you are more interested in contemporary design, visit the **Palazzo delle Esposizioni** *(see p164)* where a wide range of objects by famous designers is available.

For a really original gift, try **Buendia Mosaici**, a workshop that reproduces ancient Roman and Pompeian mosaics, where they will recreate any design you choose to order.

SOUVENIRS AND RELIGIOUS ARTIFACTS

Most OF the tobacconists in central Rome sell postcards, stamps and a variety of souvenirs, and many cheap and sometimes appealingly kitsch souvenirs are sold by the mobile stalls around the major tourist attractions.

Bookshops near the main basilicas, such as **Libreria Belardetti**, sell souvenirs and religious mementos. Other shops specialize in religious articles for both the clergy and the layman. Facing the Vatican gates in Via di Porta Angelica there are several shops, such as **Al Pellegrino Cattolico**, selling mementos to visiting pilgrims.

FOOD

One OF THE unusual things about shopping in Rome is the absence of large-scale supermarkets in the centre. It has been local government policy to keep them out in order to protect the little *alimentari* or delicatessens. There are hundreds of these, not on the main shopping streets, but in small side streets running off them or in the "village" districts such as Monti, Trastevere, the Ghetto, Borgo and Campo de' Fiori. They are often crammed from floor to ceiling with all the irresistible delicacies that are typical of Italy.

Here you can buy, the day before your departure, your supply of parmesan and pecorino romano cheese *(see p305)*, Parma ham or prosciutto di montagna, attractive bottles of dark-green, extra-virgin unfiltered olive oil, dried porcini mushrooms and sun-dried tomatoes to take home (but check customs restrictions first). Food is by no means cheap, and most of the above are considered luxury items.

Pietro Franchi is without doubt the most exclusive delicatessen in the city, and its windows are a visual feast of seafood platters, pâtés, cheeses and cold meats. Next door is the famous coffee shop **Castroni**, which has Rome's largest selection of imported products from all over the world. It also stocks Italian olive oils, balsamic vinegars, honeys and preserves, and of course coffee.

Via della Croce deserves a special mention for its good selection of well-stocked *alimentari* like **Fratelli Fabbi**, while over in Testaccio, **Volpetti** sells an

excellent range of regional hams, cheeses, breads, pies and pasta.

Cheese-lovers can find plenty of Italian varieties in any of the many small *alimentari* dotted around the city. However, it is also well worth trying the local cow, sheep and buffalo milk cheeses that are sold at the **Cisternino Cooperativa fra Produttori di Latte di Lazio**. There are several branches, but the most central is situated near Piazza Campo de' Fiori.

Boxes of chocolates and traditional confectionery and cakes such as *torrone* and *panettone* can generally be bought from good-quality bars. **L'Albero del Pane** sells wonderful wholemeal and rye flour breads and other health foods.

WINE

WINE IS GENERALLY sold in *alimentari* and supermarkets, but there are also specialist shops called *enoteca*. These invariably have a bar where they serve wine and light snacks or canapés. Two of the best are **Enoteca Buccone**, housed in an old coachhouse, and **Antica Enoteca**, which has an old-world feeling to it. **Enoteca del Corso** is more modern, with a good selection of Italian *grappa* and jars of marinated fruits. **Enoteca Corsi** in Via del Gesù is also worth a visit, as is **Enoteca Costantini** in Piazza Cavour. **Enoteca Guerrini** in Via San Vincenzo has a perfect location close to the Trevi Fountain.

DIRECTORY

BOOKSHOPS

Feltrinelli
Largo Argentina 5A. **Map** 4 F4. ☎ 06-6880 3248.
Also: Galleria Alberto Sordi 31–35. **Map** 12 E2. ☎ 06-6975 5001.

Feltrinelli International
Via E. Orlando 84–86. **Map** 5 C3. ☎ 06-482 7878.

Franco Maria Ricci
Via del Babuino 49. **Map** 4 F2. ☎ 06-320 7126.

Libreria Godel
Via Poli 45. **Map** 5 A3 & 12 F2. ☎ 06-679 0264.

Remainders
Piazza San Silvestro 28. **Map** 5 A3 & 12 E1. ☎ 06-679 2824.

MULTIMEDIA AND MUSIC

Discoteca Frattina
Via Frattina 50–51. **Map** 5 A2. ☎ 06-679 1493.

Ricordi
Via del Corso 506. **Map** 4 F2 & 12 E1. ☎ 06-361 2370.
Also: Forum Termini, Piazza dei Cinquecento. **Map** 6 D3. ☎ 06-8740 6113.

STATIONERY AND PAPERCRAFT

Fabriano
Via del Babuino 173. **Map** 4 F2. ☎ 06-3260 0361.

Laboratorio Scatole
Via della Stelletta 27. ☎ 06-6880 2053.

Pineider
Via dei Due Macelli 68. **Map** 5 A2 & 12 F1. ☎ 06-679 5884.

Vertecchi
Via della Croce 70. **Map** 4 F2. ☎ 06-678 3110

ARTISAN HANDICRAFTS AND DESIGN

Bottega Artigiana
Via Santa Dorotea 21. **Map** 4 D5 & 11 B5. ☎ 06-588 2079.

Buendia Mosaici
Vicolo della Palomba 1a. **Map** 4 E3 & 11 C2. ☎ 06-6880 2762.

Palazzo delle Esposizioni
Via Milano 9. **Map** 5 B4. ☎ 06-482 8540.

Studio Arti e Mestieri
Via dei Baullari 146. **Map** 4 E4 & 11 C4. ☎ 06-687 2467.

SOUVENIRS AND RELIGIOUS ARTIFACTS

Al Pellegrino Cattolico
Via di Porta Angelica 83. **Map** 3 C2. ☎ 06-6880 2351.

Libreria Belardetti
Via della Conciliazione 4B. **Map** 3 C3. ☎ 06-686 5502.

FOOD

L'Albero del Pane
Via Santa Maria del Pianto 19–20. **Map** 4 F5 & 12 D5. ☎ 06-686 5016.

Castroni
Via Cola di Rienzo 196. **Map** 4 D2. ☎ 06-687 4383.

Cisternino Cooperativa fra Produttori di Latte di Lazio
Vicolo del Gallo 18–19. **Map** 4 E5 & 11 C4. ☎ 06-687 2875.

Fratelli Fabbi
Via della Croce 28. **Map** 5 A2. ☎ 06-679 0612.

Pietro Franchi
Via Cola di Rienzo 200. **Map** 4 D2. ☎ 06-686 4576.

Volpetti
Via Marmorata 47. **Map** 8 D3. ☎ 06-574 2352.

WINE

Antica Enoteca
Via della Croce 76B. **Map** 5 A2. ☎ 06-679 0896.

Enoteca Buccone
Via di Ripetta 19. **Map** 4 F1. ☎ 06-361 2154.

Enoteca Corsi
Via del Gesù 88–89. **Map** 4 F4 & 12 E3. ☎ 06-679 0821.

Enoteca del Corso
Corso Vittorio Emanuele II 293–295. **Map** 4 D4 & 11 A3. ☎ 06-6880 1594.

Enoteca Costantini
Piazza Cavour 16. **Map** 4 E2. ☎ 06-320 3575.

Enoteca Guerrini
Via San Vincenzo 15/16. **Map** 5 A3 & 12 F2. ☎ 06-679 3320.

Art and Antiques

Rome's art and antique shops range from exclusive establishments to contemporary art galleries. In response to a fashion for collecting early-20th-century artifacts, new dealers and galleries are springing up throughout Rome – Venini's Murano glass is popular, as are lighting and furniture. Many more sell general bric-a-brac and jewellery. Copies of antique prints can be picked up for a fraction of the original's price. Rome is not good for antique bargains, but it is worth looking in shops along Via dei Cappellari and Via del Pellegrino or going to the Porta Portese Sunday market *(see p339)*.

ANTIQUES AND OLD MASTER PAINTINGS

There are antique shops dotted all over the centre of Rome, though the cream tend to be concentrated in distinct areas. Discreet haggling in the shops is accepted practice, but even if you get a reduction in price, make sure the dealer provides you with the relevant export documents.

The famous Via del Babuino, and to a lesser extent Via Margutta, which is better known for its art galleries, are home to around 30 of Rome's grandest showrooms for antique furniture, Old Master paintings and *objets d'art*.

Giulio Lampronti is owned by top dealer Cesare Lampronti. Aided and complemented by his partner Carlo Peruzzi, he sells 16th- to 18th-century European paintings, with an emphasis on Roman and Italian works in general.

Amedeo di Castro, apparently no relation to the other four di Castros on this street, is a fourth-generation dealer in bas-relief sculptures and exquisite furniture from the 18th and early 19th centuries.

Via Giulia *(see p153)* has over 20 high-quality antique shops to choose from. Definitely worth a visit is **Antichità Cipriani**, which is a temple to owner Paola Cipriani's love of simply elegant Neo-Classical furniture and paintings. She also sells the occasional modern piece. Another shop not to miss on Via Giulia is **Antiquariato Valligiano**.

This is the only place in Rome where you can find 19th-century Italian country furniture, a rustic antidote for those overpowered by the grandiose Baroque.

Via Monserrato, running parallel, is worth scouring for slightly lower-quality pieces at more attainable prices.

The area just to the north of Via Giulia is also a good potential hunting ground. **Mario Prilli**, on Via Banchi Nuovi, is tiny, but don't let that deter you. With every inch of space occupied by a wide variety of antiques, this fascinating shop is worth a look even if you are only browsing.

Via dei Coronari is almost exclusively devoted to antiques, with over 40 shops lining both sides of this picturesque street. Quality is very high – as are the prices. It is a good place for Baroque and Empire elaborate inlaid vases, secretaries and consoles. **Ad Antiqua Domus** is a treasure trove of antique Italian furniture. Pieces dating from ancient Rome through to the 19th century are on sale.

L'Art Nouveau specializes in high-quality Art Nouveau (usually called *Liberty* here). The **Art Deco Gallery** sells furniture and sculpture from that period.

Piero Taloni has a superb collection of lighting fixtures from the Baroque through to Art Deco periods. **Antichità Arredamenti** also specializes in Italian light fittings and candlesticks.

Slightly further away lies Via della Stelletta, which is home to a handful of unusual and fascinating shops.

Acanto is an inexpensively priced Aladdin's cave with an eclectic mix of *objets d'art*. It is the perfect place to search for religious memorabilia, Italian curiosities and prints.

Bilenchi is yet another specialist, this time in exquisite, early 20th-century lamps.

Another relatively undiscovered area is the one around Via del Boschetto and Via Panisperna. Shops around here tend to specialize in early-20th-century artifacts, with some English Victorian pieces thrown in.

Tad is a fairly good place to come and browse, with a large collection of weird and original design items from all around the world.

Of course there are many perennial favourites apart from these streets. The best way to discover them is through word of mouth or just by chance as you stroll along. **Antichità Carnovale**, on Via del Governo Vecchio, is a shop full of interesting 19th- and 20th-century canvases, while **Galleria dei Cosmati** is one of the oldest antique shops in Rome, and definitely one of the largest. It offers an impressive collection of European antiques.

Anticaja e Petrella has an eccentric collection of used junk and printed ephemera stored under Sant'Andrea della Valle *(see p123)*.

MODERN ART

Rome is rich in avant-garde galleries exhibiting paintings by recognized Modern Masters through to the up-and-coming generation of young, mainly Italian, artists.

Rome's art galleries are usually open 10am–1pm and 5pm–8pm Tue–Sat. Some open only in the afternoon; others also stay open on Monday afternoon. The best times to visit are afternoons and early evenings.

As with Rome's antique shops, the art galleries tend to be concentrated in a couple of distinct areas.

The largest of these covers the triangular area between Via del Babuino and Via di Ripetta and adjoining streets, known locally as the Trident.

The **Galleria Valentina Moncada** exhibits contemporary Italian and international art and also showcases 20th-century photography.

Sperone, under the owner-directorship of Gian Enzo Sperone, shows works by American artists such as Ray Smith, Jonathan Lasker and Julio Galan. Also on view are Italian artists like Gallo, Dessi, Bianchi, Paladino and Merzi.

One of this area's highlights is the Via Margutta art fair *(see p339)*, which usually takes place around Christmas and in springtime.

Via Giulia and its surroundings is the next area to investigate: **Galleria Giulia** is a gallery-cum-bookshop with works by artists such as Argeles, Boille, Cano, Cascella, Echaurren, Erba and Lionni, as well as by Bauhaus artists and German Expressionists.

Fabio Sargentini at **L'Attico** follows the latest trends in Italian art from Del Giudice to Corsini and Fabiani.

Other more innovative ventures in the city centre include: **Galleria Bonomo** (owned by Alessandra Bonomo) which spotlights Italian and foreign painters such as Schifano, Boetti, Twombly, Nunzio, Tremlett, LeWitt and Dokoupil.

In a stupendous villa situated quite a way out of Rome, **Mauro Vigneti** specializes in both Italian and international artists who are working in the city. Fortunately, he has also opened a showroom in the Monti District.

ANTIQUE PRINTS AND PHOTOGRAPHS

THE JUSTIFIABLY celebrated **Nardecchia**, named after its erudite owner Plinio, is the cream of Rome's print dealers. Look out for originals by the 18th-century engraver,

Piranesi, and views of the city and ancient Roman life.

Another Roman institution, **Casali**, has been trading for over 100 years. The family now runs two shops specializing in 16th- to 19th-century drawings and engravings of Roman scenes ranging from museum-standard Piranesi down to relatively inexpensive unknown and delightfully decorative floral scenes.

The Florence-based **Alinari** family is renowned for its old sepia photographs of Italy from 1890 onwards, including shots of Rome a century ago. At its Roman outlet, prices of photographs from the original plates start at around €16 and mounted prints at €260. Larger sizes can be mounted on wood or card.

Another place definitely worth heading for in search of that perfect print of old Rome and some enjoyable, relaxing and maybe persuasive browsing is the **Mercato delle Stampe** *(see p338)*.

DIRECTORY

ANTIQUES AND OLD MASTER PAINTINGS

Acanto
Via della Stelletta 10.
Map 4 F3 & 12 D2.
06-686 5481.

Ad Antiqua Domus
Via dei Coronari 39.
Map 4 E3 & 11 B2.
06-686 1186.

Amedeo di Castro
Via del Babuino 77–78.
Map 4 F1.
06-320 7650.

Anticaja e Petrella
Via Monte della Farina 62.
Map 4 F5 & 12D4.

Antichità Arredamenti
Via dei Coronari 219.
Map 4 E3.
06-6880 1254.

Antichità Carnovale
Via del Governo Vecchio.
Map 11 C3.
06-686 4850.

Antichità Cipriani
Via Giulia 122.
Map 4 D4 & 11 A3.
06-6830 8344.

Antiquariato Valligiano
Via Giulia 193.
Map 4 E5 & 11 B5.
06-686 9505.

Art Deco Gallery
Via dei Coronari 14.
Map 4 E3 & 11 C2.
06-686 5330.

L'Art Nouveau
Via dei Coronari 221.
Map 4 E3 & 11 C2.
06-6880 5230.

Bilenchi
Via della Stelletta 17.
Map 4 F3 & 12 D2.
06-687 5222.

Galleria dei Cosmati
Via Cavallini 8.
Map 4 E2.
06-361 1141.

Giulio Lampronti
Via del Babuino 67.
Map 4 F1.
06-323 0100.

Mario Prilli
Via dei Banchi Nuovi 42.
Map 4 D3 & 11 A2.
06-686 8816.

Piero Taloni
Via dei Coronari 135.
Map 4 E3 & 11 B2.
06-687 5450.

Tad
Via San Giacomo 5.
Map 4 F2.
06-3600 1679.
Also: Via del Babuino 155.
Map 4 F1.
06-3269 5131.

MODERN ART

L'Attico
Via del Paradiso 41.
Map 4 E4 & 11 C4.
06-686 9846.

Galleria Bonomo
Via del Gesù 62.
Map 12 E3.
06-6992 5858.

Galleria Giulia
Via Giulia 148.
Map 4 D4 & 11 B4.
06-6880 2061.

Galleria Valentina Moncada
Via Margutta 54. **Map** 5 A2. 06-320 7956.

Mauro Vigneti
Via Cimarra 12. **Map** 5 C4. 06-474 1804.

Sperone
Via di Pallacorda 15.
Map 4 F3 & 12 D1.
06-689 3525.

ANTIQUE PRINTS AND PHOTOGRAPHS

Alinari
Via Alibert 16 A.
Map 5 A2.
06-679 2923.

Casali
Piazza della Rotonda 81 A/82. **Map** 4 F4 & 12 D3. 06-678 3515.
Also: Via dei Coronari 115.
Map 11 B2.
06-687 3705.

Nardecchia
Piazza Navona 25.
Map 4 E4 & 11 C3.
06-686 9318.

Street Markets

ROME'S OPEN-AIR MARKETS are essential to visit if you are interested in soaking up the bubbling exuberance and earthiness for which Romans are renowned. They are wonderfully vivid experiences too, as Italian stallholders have raised the display of even the humblest vegetable to an art form.

The city is dotted with popular, small local food markets, and there are several fascinating well-established markets near the centre, along with the famous flea market over in Trastevere.

It is important to keep your wits about you in markets because pickpockets work with lightning speed in the bustling crowds. But this said, Roman markets provide a vibrant source of entertainment and it would be a shame to let such caveats deter you from joining in.

The street fairs that take place throughout the year are fun to go to, if they coincide with your visit, as they normally sell a good variety of local produce, handicrafts and clothes. Seasonal fairs also occur, especially around Christmas, when you can stock up on Italian specialities.

Campo de' Fiori

Piazza Campo de' Fiori. **Map** 4 E4 & 11 C4. 🚌 40, 46, 62, 64, 70, 81, 116, 492, 628. 🚋 8. **Open** 7am–1.30pm Mon–Sat. See p146.

Right in the heart of the old city, Rome's most picturesque market is also its most historical. Its name, Campo de' Fiori, which translates as field of flowers, sometimes misleads people into expecting a flower market. In fact the name is said to derive from Campus Florae (Flora's square) – Flora being the lover of the great Roman general Pompey. A market has actually been held in this beautiful piazza for many centuries.

Every morning, except Sunday, the piazza is transformed by an array of stalls selling fruit and vegetables, meat, poultry and fish. One or two stalls specialize in pulses, rice, dried fruit and nuts and there are also flower stalls situated near the fountain. But the huge open baskets of broccoli and spinach, chopped vegetables and freshly prepared green salad mixes are the main attraction for visitors. They provide a real visual display as well as an edible feast.

The excellent delicatessen shops on the square, and bread shops nearby, complement the market. They make it a great place to stock up for an impromptu picnic if the weather turns out fine and you are tempted to do some *alfresco* dining in one of Rome's many parks. The market gets extremely busy on Saturdays, so be prepared to fight your way through the crowds.

Mercato delle Stampe

Largo della Fontanella di Borghese. **Map** 4 F3 & 12 D1. 🚌 81, 116, 117, 492, 628. **Open** 7am–1pm Mon–Sat.

This market is a veritable haven for lovers of old prints, books (both genuine antiquarian and less-exalted second-hand), magazines and other printed ephemera. The quality varies, but it is a good deal more specialized than the *banche* or stalls near Termini station which are a more obvious tourist trap. Italian-speaking collectors can enjoy a field day leafing through back issues of specialist magazines. Other visitors might prefer the wonderful selection of illustrated art books and old prints of Rome. It is a good place to pick up that Piranesi print of your favourite Roman vista, ruin or church – but be prepared to bargain hard.

Mercato dei Fiori

Via Trionfale. **Map** 3 B1. Ⓜ Ottaviano S. Pietro. 🚌 23, 51, 70, 490. **Open** 10.30am–1pm Tue.

Essentially a trade market, the Flower Market, just north of Via Andrea Doria, is open to the public only on Tuesdays. Housed in a covered hall, it has two floors brimming over with cut flowers upstairs and all kinds of plants on the lower floor. Anyone who has an interest in flowers will enjoy this wonderful array of Mediterranean blooms, which are on sale at giveaway prices.

Mercato Andrea Doria

Via Andrea Doria. **Map** 3 B1. Ⓜ Ottaviano S. Pietro. 🚌 23, 70, 490. **Open** 7am–1.30pm Mon–Sat.

The market used to stretch the whole length of this wide avenue. It has now been reorganized on to a huge square of open ground between Via Santamaura and Via Tunisi. Apart from the magnificent displays of fruit and vegetables, it has numerous stalls selling meat, poultry, fish and groceries, as well as an interesting clothes and shoe section. Situated northwest of the Vatican Museums, it is a little off the normal beaten track and has remained very much a Roman market that caters for the needs of the large local population.

Nuovo Mercato Esquilino

Via Principe Amedeo. **Map** 6 E5. Ⓜ Vittorio Emanuele. 🚌 105. **Open** 7am–2pm Mon–Sat. See p174.

Bustling Piazza Vittorio was, until recently, perhaps the most Roman of the city's larger markets.

Now rechristened, it has moved to new covered premises, but it is still the place where bargain-hunting *popolari*, Rome's bustling shoppers, buy their food. Stallholders offer cheap prices if you buy by the kilo, but watch out for bad fruit.

Lately it has become more international and now features African and Asian food stalls which cater to the area's many ethnic groups. Definitely a place to go to to capture the atmosphere of a traditional but changing city.

Mercato di Testaccio

Piazza Testaccio. **Map** 8 D3. Ⓜ Piramide. 🚌 23, 75, 280. 🚋 3. **Open** 7.30am–1.30pm Mon–Sat.

The covered market at Testaccio occupies the central area of its eponymous piazza. The few cheap clothing and shoe stalls skirting the outside are unremarkable, but the inside is well worth a visit. Lined with butchers, grocers and fishmongers, the whole central area is given over to fruit and vegetables – a theatre-set array of seductive colours and textures. Very popular with local residents, it offers super-fresh, high-quality produce and reasonable prices. Much of this market's charm for visitors lies in its compact size and relaxed, friendly atmosphere.

Porta Portese

Via Portuense & Via Ippolito Nievo.
Map 7 C3. ▦ *H, 23, 44, 75.* ▦ *3, 8.*
Open 6.30am–2pm Sun.

The *mercato delle pulci* or flea market is a relatively new market in Roman terms. Established shortly after the end of World War II, it is said to have grown out of the thriving black market that operated at Tor di Nona opposite Castel Sant'Angelo during those lean years. Stallholders come from as far away as Naples and set up shop in the early hours of the morning – if you are strolling in that direction after a late night in Trastevere, it is well worth pausing just to watch them.

Anything and everything seems to be for sale, piled high on stalls in carefully arranged disorder – clothes, shoes, bags, luggage, camping equipment, linen, towels, pots, pans, kitchen utensils, plants, pets, spare parts, cassettes and CDs, old LPs and 78s.

Furniture stalls tend to be concentrated around Piazza Ippolito Nievo along with what they call "antiques", though you may have to sort through an awful lot of junk before finding a real one. And then you will have to bargain for it. The technique is to offer them half the asked price and then walk away. A lot of people go just for the fun of it and always end up buying something.

There are also second-hand clothes – leather or sheepskin coats and jackets go for €10 – with many of the Via Sannio stallholders relocating here for the Sunday trade. The stretch along Via Ippolito Nievo is often monopolized by "i Russi di Porta Portese", immigrant Russian stallholders selling lace, icons (authenticity uncertain), other ethnic handicrafts, old cameras and binoculars. A must if you have a Sunday morning to spare.

Mercato di Via Sannio

Via Sannio. **Map** 9 C2. Ⓜ *San Giovanni.* ▦ *16, 81, 87.* **Open** 8am–1pm Mon–Fri, 8am–6pm Sat.

In the 1960s and 1970s this used to be Italy's answer to Carnaby Street. Today, at first glance, it seems not to have anything very special to offer – random stalls selling inexpensive casual clothes, shoes, bags, belts, jewellery, toys, kitchen utensils and music cassettes. But towards the end of the street there is a large covered section which extends back to the Aurelian Wall *(see p196)* with many stalls piled high with second-hand clothes at very low prices for those who like to rummage. There is also a

section that sells military-style goods plus some camping and fishing equipment.

Some of these stalls move their wares to Porta Portese on a Sunday morning.

Local markets

Generally open 7am–1pm Mon–Sat.

Piazza delle Coppelle (map 4 F3 & 12 D2), near the Pantheon, is probably the most picturesque of the food markets sprinkled around the city. A tiny market devoted to food and fruit and flowers, it offers a charming splash of colour in the heart of the city.

Piazza San Cosimato (map 7 C1) in Trastevere hosts another lively local market with some tempting cheeses and salami.

There is a fairly big market on **Via Alessandria** (map 6 D1) in Nomentana, and other smaller ones in **Via della Pace** (map 4 E4 & 11 C3) near Piazza Navona, and in **Via Balbo** (map 5 C4) and **Via Milazzo** (map 6 E3) near Termini station.

All markets usually have at least one stall selling household goods and basic Italian kitchen gadgets.

STREET FAIRS

A special and interesting feature of shopping in Rome is the street fair:

The **Tevere Expo** exhibition starts each year between mid-June and mid-July on both sides of the river bank between the Sant'Angelo and Cavour bridges. Its stalls display Italian regional arts and crafts and also sell pasta, jam, olive oil, wines and liqueurs. Some items are cheaper than in the shops. The exhibition opens in the evening (6pm–1am). The entrance fee occasionally includes ferry transport across the Tiber.

There are two antiques fairs, both known as the **Fiera dell'Antiquariato**, that take place in Via dei Coronari. The first starts in the second half of May, 10am–1pm and 4–11pm daily. It makes a memorable event at night when lighted torches line the carpeted street. The second goes along Via dell'Orso as well and normally occurs in mid-October (but has also started in late September), Mon–Thu 3–11pm & Fri–Sun 10am–11pm. Stalls also sell leatherwork, jewellery and gifts.

The **Via Margutta Art Fair** usually takes place around Christmas and in springtime. Set in one of the most charming and exclusive streets of the city, this is an event not to be missed, although it is more for browsing as prices are very high.

The utterly glamorous **Spanish Steps Alta Moda Fashion Show** is a fairly new event and does not have a set date. The limited seating space is filled by invitation only. However, the public can squeeze in behind to enjoy this display of all-Italian designer fashion. So far it has been held mid- to late July.

The traditional **Christmas Fair** held in Piazza Navona from mid-December until 6 January is now rather down-at-heel, but still fascinating for those who have not seen it before or for children. Stalls selling clay statues for nativity scenes and sweets that look like pieces of coal are the main attraction.

Natale Oggi is a well-established event taking place once Christmas in the Fiera di Roma at EUR, and worth visiting to have a look at the special Italian Christmas treats.

Via Giulia hosts art fairs now and then, and open evenings when the antique and art galleries stay open late offering food and wine to all visitors.

Every year Trastevere hosts its very own carnival, the **Festa de Noantri**, in late July, when Viale Trastevere is overrun with the typical *porchetta* stalls *(see p341)*, party lights, gift stalls and people.

The details given here may change, so check the local listings, the tourist office or ring the tourist call centre *(see p359)*.

ENTERTAINMENT IN ROME

THERE'S A PARTICULAR excitement attached to Roman entertainment. Football and opera, for example, are both worth experiencing for sheer atmosphere alone, whether or not you are a fan. The jazz scene is especially good with international stars appearing alongside local talent. And concerts and films take on an added dimension when performances take place beneath the stars in the many open-air arenas

Gregory Peck and Audrey Hepburn in *Roman Holiday*

spread across the city. Unexpectedly, given the general shutdown among shops and restaurants, the summer remains Rome's liveliest time for live music and other cultural events. Rome's graceful Renaissance squares, vast parks, villa gardens, Classical ruins and other open spaces host various major arts festivals. If you prefer sport, or want to try out some Roman nightclubs, there's plenty on offer too.

PRACTICAL INFORMATION

A GOOD SOURCE of information about what's on is *Trovaroma,* the weekly Thursday supplement to *La Repubblica* newspaper. It has a day-by-day rundown of what's on and where, and covers music, exhibitions, theatre, cinemas,

Saxophonist at Alpheus (see p344)

guided tours, restaurants and children's entertainment. The weekly listings magazine *Roma c'è* has an English section and *Time Out Roma* makes occasional appearances. Daily newspapers like *Il Messaggero, Il Manifesto* and *La Repubblica* usually list that evening's entertainment.

The magazine *Wanted in Rome*, found at Via Veneto newsagents or English bookshops, provides less detailed listings in English. Also worth getting hold of is *L'Evento*, available from the APT *(see p359)*, which gives details in English of classical music, festivals, theatre and exhibitions in the city and surroundings. Up-to-date

information can also be found on various websites.

Punctuality is not what Italians are renowned for, so don't be surprised if events start later than advertised.

BOOKING TICKETS

B OOKING in advance is not part of Italian lifestyle, though this is slowly changing. Two ticket agencies that will book tickets for some performances for you (for a small fee) are **Orbis** and **Box Office**. Many theatres themselves do not accept telephone bookings – you have to visit the box office in person. They will charge you a *prevendita* supplement (about 10 per cent of the normal price) for any tickets sold in advance. The price of a theatre ticket can be anything between €8 and €52.

Tickets for classical concerts are usually sold on the spot, and are sometimes for that night only, an arrangement that favours the last-minute decision to

go. Opera is the exception. Tickets are sold months in advance, with just a few held back until two days before the performance.

Stage at Caffè Latino (see pp344-5)

It is usually easier (and also a bit cheaper) to get tickets for the open-air summer performances. The **Teatro dell'Opera** box office *(see p343)* handles sales for both summer and winter seasons, and they have a high-tech booking system, with a computer which colour-codes unsold seats.

Tickets for most big rock and jazz events can be bought at **Orbis** and at larger record shops such as **Ricordi**. Remember that if you are trying to get hold of a ticket for a particular performance that has already sold out, you are extremely unlikely to be able to obtain one from

Member of contemporary dance group Momix (see p343)

unofficial sources – there are very few ticket touts in Rome, except at major football matches such as important finals.

REDUCED-PRICE TICKETS

THEATRES AND concert venues tend not to offer discounts on tickets, even when left-over seats are in abundance.

Cinemas, however, offer people aged over 60 and disabled people a 30 per cent reduction on weekdays. Many cinemas also have cheaper ticket prices for weekday afternoon screenings and for all shows on Wednesdays.

Some clubs at the beach resorts such as Fregene offer reductions: look out for *due per uno* coupons in local bars that allow two people entrance for the price of one.

FACILITIES FOR THE DISABLED

FEW ROMAN venues provide easy access for people with restricted mobility, and any disabled visitors and their companions are likely to find the lack of provision for them very frustrating.

The situation does improve a little in summer, however, when a great many performances in the city are held at open-air venues. The classical concerts held in the beautiful gardens of Villa Giulia *(see pp262–3)* have wheelchair access.

For more general information on provision for the disabled, see page 359.

Summer night outdoor performance among Roman ruins

OPEN-AIR ENTERTAINMENT

OPEN-AIR OPERA, cinema, classical music and jazz concerts fill the calendar from late June until the end of September. These performances outdoors can be wonderful, with spectacular settings and enthusiastic audiences. Some of them are grand affairs, but small events may be just as evocative – a guitar recital in the cloisters of Santa Maria della Pace *(see p121),* for example, or jazz in the beautiful gardens of Villa Celimontana *(see p193).*

Singers performing the *Barber of Seville*

Some cinemas roll back their ceilings in summer for open-air screenings, or else move to outdoor arenas, and there are also annual open-air cinema festivals. The Cineporto along the Tiber and the Festival di Massenzio offer films, food and small exhibitions in July and August. Theatre, too, moves outside in summer. Greek and Roman plays are staged at Ostia Antica *(see p270)* and other shows take place at the Anfiteatro del Tasso *(see p347).*

Rome's most important autumn performing arts festival is RomaEuropa, with occasional performances in the grounds of the Villa Medici. There are other, smaller festivals too, but times and venues change from year to year, so it is best to consult listings in newspapers, magazines or websites *(see p340)* or watch for posters around the city for the most up-to-date information. More traditional is Trastevere's community festival, Festa de Noantri *(see p59),* with music, fireworks and processions. This religious festival begins on the Saturday after 16 July but celebrations continue into August. The Festa dell' Unità, run by the DS (the former Communist Party), but not limited to politics, is generally held in September. The programme includes games, stalls, food and drink.

Finally, if you like your entertainment less structured, you can always do as the Romans do and take part in the *passeggiata* (early evening stroll) – the city's favourite spots are Piazza Navona *(see p120)* and along Via del Corso.

TICKET AGENCIES

Box Office
Via del Corso 506 (inside Ricordi Record Shop). **Map** 4 F2 & 12 E1.
Tickets for classical music, rock, pop and jazz concerts and some sporting events.
📞 06-320 2790.

Orbis
Piazza dell'Esquilino 37.
Map 6 D4. 📞 06-482 7403.

USEFUL WEBSITES

W www.tkts.it
W www.romapreview.com
W www.romaturismo.it
W www.amitonline.it

The Teatro dell'Opera *(see p342)*

Classical Music and Dance

CLASSICAL CONCERTS take place in a surprising number of venues: tickets for opera premières may be hard to get, but soloists, groups or orchestras playing in gardens, churches, villas or ancient ruins are more accessible. World-renowned soloists and orchestras make appearances throughout the year; past visitors have included Luciano Pavarotti and Placido Domingo, the Berlin Philharmonic and prima ballerina Sylvie Guillem.

Programmes are generally international in scope but sometimes you will find a festival dedicated to one of Italy's own, like Palestrina, the great 16th-century master of polyphonic church music, or Arcangelo Corelli, inventor of the Baroque *concerto grosso*.

MUSIC IN CHURCHES

ONE OF ROME'S main attractions for classical music is the rich repertoire in the city's churches. Always sacred in theme (by decree of Pope John Paul II), music is mainly performed as concerts rather than during services.

Programmes are posted around the city and outside the churches. You will often find very good musicians playing in the main churches, while the smaller, out-of-the-way churches frequently have young musicians and amateur choirs as well.

St Peter's *(see p230)* hosts one major RAI (national broadcasting company) concert on 5 December attended by the Pope and free for the general public. It has two established choirs. The Coro della Cappella Giulia sing at the 10.30am mass and 5pm vespers on Sunday. The Coro della Cappella Sistina sing whenever the Pope celebrates mass here, as on 29 June (St Peter and St Paul's day).

Important choral masses also take place on 25 January in **San Paolo fuori le Mura** *(see p267)*, when the Pope attends, on 24 June in **San Giovanni in Laterano** *(p182)* and on 31 December at the **Gesù** *(pp114–5)* where the *Te Deum* is sung. The church of **Sant'Ignazio di Loyola** *(p106)* is another favourite venue for choral concerts.

Plain song and Gregorian chant can be heard in **Sant' Anselmo** *(p204)* every Sunday (Oct–Jul) at the 8.30am mass and 7.15pm vespers.

Easter and the Christmas festivities are a great time for cheap and chilly concerts.

ORCHESTRAL, CHAMBER AND CHORAL MUSIC

WITHOUT DOUBT, the arts event of the decade was the opening of the new Renzo Piano-designed **Parco della Musica** on the Via Flaminia in spring 2002. Up to then the Auditorium di Santa Cecilia and the **Teatro dell'Opera** had been Rome's two main auditoriums, with their own resident orchestras and choirs. The Orchestra e Coro dell'Accademia di Santa Cecilia is the top orchestra, but both offer interestingly varied seasons which include visiting groups and soloists from all over the world. It remains to be seen how the Santa Cecilia fares in its new home.

The season at the **Teatro Olimpico** usually offers good chamber music, some orchestral concerts and ballet with at least one concert a week.

Although a variety of classical concerts take place at the **Accademia Filarmonica Romana**, the emphasis is on chamber and choral music, with an internationally renowned series of concerts running from mid-October to mid-May. Performances take place in the Sala Casella, which seats around 180.

Ticket prices for classical concerts depend a lot on performers and venue. The **Auditorium del Foro Italico** sells tickets for most concerts for under €15; a ticket for the **Teatro Olimpico** costs

between €15–€25, but seats for an important concert at **Teatro dell'Opera** may cost as much as €80.

The Associazione Musicale Romana, dedicated to Renaissance and Baroque music, organizes three annual festivals in the **Palazzo della Cancelleria** *(see p149)*: the Festival Internazionale di Cembalo (harpsichord festival) in March; Musica al Palazzo in May; and the Festival Internazionale di Organo in September. Classical music fans should also watch out for performances by the Orchestra di Roma e del Lazio at **Teatro Argentina** or **Teatro Valle** *(see p347)*.

It is always worth checking which musicians are due to be playing at the **Teatro Ghione**, the **Oratorio del Gonfalone** and especially the **Aula Magna dell' Università La Sapienza**, which has one of the most innovative programmes of classical and contemporary music.

OPEN-AIR SUMMER CONCERTS

IN THE SUMMER music lovers can enjoy concerts in cloisters, palazzo courtyards and ancient ruins. Concerts can be one-offs or part of a festival programme, regular fixtures or impromptu. Do as the Romans do, wait until the last moment and keep an eye on the posters and listings pages *(see p340)*.

Open-air opera and dance once had their home in the Baths of Caracalla, but this venue is seldom used. Classical concerts are often part of festivals like Roma-Europa *(see p341)* but there are also open-air festivals and concert series dedicated to classical music. Among the more interesting is the Stagione Estiva dell'Orchestra dell'Accademia di Santa Cecilia held at the Ninfeo *(nympheum)* in the grounds of **Villa Giulia** *(see p263)*. Also listed as the Concerti a Villa Giulia, the concerts take place in July and tickets are around €12.

The Associazione Musicale Romana organizes Serenate in Chiostro – a lively and varied programme of concerts during July in the cloisters of **Santa Maria della Pace** *(see p121)* with tickets at reasonable prices. The Concerti del Tempietto are a real summer treat with concerts held almost every evening from July to September in the **Area Archeologica del Teatro di Marcello** *(see p151)* or in the park of the Villa Torlonia.

Festival Villa Pamphilj in Musica, in July, is a series of concerts in the gardens of **Villa Doria Pamphilj** *(see p267)*. Programmes range from comic opera to jazz and 20th-century classical music.

Brass bands can be heard in the **Pincio Gardens** *(see p136)* on Sunday mornings from the end of April until mid-July – they usually strike up at around 10.30am.

CONTEMPORARY MUSIC

THE **Parco della Musica** and the Accademia Filarmonica Romana (usually at the **Teatro Olimpico**) often include modern pieces in their programmes but these are less popular than the classical pieces and there is no set venue with a regular contemporary programme.

International names appear on festival programmes and at one-off concerts at the **Aula Magna dell'Università La Sapienza**. The most interesting contemporary music festival is organized by the Nuova Consonanza in the autumn. Modern Italian composers are performed in the Rassegna Nuova Musica Italiana concert series two or three times a year. Also worth keeping an eye out for are performances by scholars of the French Academy at **Villa Medici** *(see p135)*.

OPERA

ITALY AND OPERA are to many people synonymous. Critics will tell you (justifiably) that Rome's opera is not up to the standard of Milan's La Scala or Naples's San Carlo. But that doesn't mean it is not worth visiting – world-class singers do appear here *(see p38)*, mainly in premières or solo recitals. However you judge the quality of the performances, the surroundings in which they take place are often incomparable. In summer the visual spectacle of *Aida*, say, performed in the open air, is simply magnificent.

The season starts late at **Teatro dell'Opera**, between November and January. In recent years programmes have concentrated on the great popular operas, rather than staging experimental productions. Tickets range from €15 to €130.

Until recently the Teatro dell'Opera would move outdoors in July and August to stage opera and ballet in the ancient Baths of Caracalla. This celebrated tradition has now stopped as the vibrations were deemed to pose a threat to the structural integrity of the Baths.

BALLET AND DANCE

OPPORTUNITIES to watch ballet or contemporary dance are fairly limited in Rome. The opera house's resident company Corpo di Ballo del Teatro dell'Opera di Roma performs the great classics as well as Roland Petit-style modern choreographies. Performances are staged at **Teatro dell'Opera**.

Contemporary dance is best seen during summer festivals but foreign companies often perform at **Teatro Olimpico**. American modern dance groups of the Moses Pendleton school – Pilobolus, Momix, ISO and Daniel Ezralow – are popular visitors. **Teatro del Vascello** is another venue noted for its experimental dance performances.

In summer and autumn, entertaining outdoor performances are organized during the **RomaEuropa Festival**.

Cinema and Theatre

CINEMA-GOING IS A POPULAR pastime in Rome, with around 40 films on show on an average weekday, while theatre-goers have far less choice.

The great majority of Roman cinemas are *prima visione* (first run) and show the latest international films in dubbed version. The smaller art cinemas are more likely to show subtitled versions of foreign films.

Theatre productions are performed in Italian whether the plays are national classics or by foreign playwrights. The main theatres offer a selection by great Italian playwrights. There are also performances of traditional cabaret, avant-garde theatre and dance theatre. Theatre tickets cost between €8 and €50 and can generally only be booked in advance by visiting the theatre box office in person, or through agencies such as **Gesman** and **Box Office** *(see p341)*.

PRIMA VISIONE

THERE ARE OVER 80 *prima visione* cinemas in the city. The best cinemas for decor and comfort are the **Fiamma** (two screens) and **Barberini** (three screens).

Foreign films are usually dubbed. Films in the original language are shown at the **Metropolitan** (daily) and on Mondays at the **Nuovo Olimpia** and **Alcazar**.

Tickets for new films cost around €7, but a few cinemas listed as *prima visione* charge less, namely **Farnese** and **Augustus**. Over 60s and disabled people are normally entitled to a 30 per cent reduction on weekdays. Tickets are reduced in many cinemas on weekday afternoons and on Wednesdays. Check the newspaper or listings such as *Trovaroma* or *Roma c'è* for details *(see p340)*.

ART CINEMAS

THERE ARE TWO main types of art cinema in Rome: the *cine-clubs* and the *cinema d'essai*. Both are good if you're interested in catching older classics and new foreign films as well as films by contemporary Italian directors.

The *d'essai* cinemas now and then show films in the original language (indicated by *v.o.* for *versione originale* in the listings). Try the **Azzurro Scipioni** (one of the few to be open through-out summer), **Filmstudio** or

Nanni Moretti's **Nuovo Sacher**. Some of the smaller cinemas are called *cine-clubs* and require membership.

The **Palazzo delle Esposizioni** shows interesting series of international films in the Sala Rossellini (prior booking is advised).

Cartoons and children's favourites are shown at **Dei Piccoli**. The evening showings for adults, often in the original language, are listed as Dei Piccoli Sera.

The **Tibur** is a small cinema with a varied programme and one of the few places where students get a reduction.

ENGLISH-LANGUAGE FILMS

IN ADDITION TO occasional undubbed showings of British, American and Australasian films in art cinemas and the **Warner Village Moderno**, Rome has its own English-language cinema, the **Pasquino**, in Trastevere. Titles change every few days (tickets cost around €6).

SUMMER CINEMA

SOME ROMAN cinemas have roll-back ceilings which are in use during the summer, while the others close down. The **Nuovo Sacher** has an outdoor arena. Rome also has various summer cinema festivals: Cineporto and Massenzio to name but two. These show several films each night from 9pm until the small

hours, with food and drinks on sale and often live music during the intervals. Cineporto (nightly, Jul–Sep) takes place in the Parco della Farnesina, but Massenzio moves around (see listings).

Sci-fi enthusiasts should keep an eye out for the Fantafestival (early June), a science fiction, fantasy and horror film festival. The Venezia a Roma event in September gives film buffs the chance to see movies presented at the summer Venice Film Festival.

The listings pages *(see p340)* have details on retrospectives or avant-garde film seasons at the **Azzurro Scipioni** and the open-air arts festivals like RomaEuropa *(see p341)* and Festa dell'Unità *(see p341)*.

MAINSTREAM THEATRE

THE BACKBONE of Rome's theatrical repertoire are Luigi Pirandello's dramas and comedies by 18th-century Venetian Carlo Goldoni and 20th-century Neapolitan Eduardo de Filippo. Major foreign playwrights are also performed from time to time.

The best classic productions are staged at the **Teatro Argentina**, **Teatro Quirino**, **Teatro Valle**, **Teatro Eliseo** and **Teatro Piccolo Eliseo**. **Teatro Argentina** is state-owned and home of Rome's permanent theatre company. Its sister theatre, **Teatro India**, stages more innovative works. The **Quirino** and **Valle** host productions from other Italian cities. The latter shows both great Italian classics by famous companies and lesser known modernist works. Plays at the **Quirino** often feature famous Italian actors. The **Eliseo** and **Piccolo Eliseo** are among the best private theatres.

The newly re-vamped **Ambra Jovinelli** specializes in comedy, including the best in Italian stand-up, while **Teatro Vittoria** goes in for Noël Coward or Neil Simon. At **Teatro Sistina** you can see musicals by visiting foreign companies and shows by popular Italian actors.

CONTEMPORARY THEATRE

THE HOME OF contemporary theatre is the **Vascello**, **Politecnico**, **Ateneo** (situated inside the university) and in a host of small theatres, ingeniously rigged up in cellars, garages, small apartments or even tents.

The **Colosseo** hosts some alternative fringe-type productions (known here as *teatro off*) while the **Ateneo**, the **Vascello** and the **Politecnico** tend to stage works by contemporary authors and occasional avant-garde productions. Some of them, like the **Orologio**, also put on foreign-language productions.

FOLK, CABARET AND PUPPET THEATRE

ROMAN AND Neapolitan folk songs and cabaret can be enjoyed in Trastevere's lively tourist-trade restaurants, like **Fantasie di Trastevere** or **Meo Patacca**.

Puppet theatre is another Roman tradition. Shows take place early in the evening at weekends, and sometimes during the week, at **Teatro Verde**, **Teatro Mongiovino** and the **Puppet Theatre**, where recitals will be in English if there is enough demand. In summer, travelling Neapolitan and Sicilian marionette companies give one-off performances.

OPEN-AIR THEATRE

THE OPEN-AIR summer theatre season usually features Greek and Roman plays at **Ostia Antica** (*see pp270–71*).

The **Anfiteatro Quercia del Tasso** in the Janiculum park takes its name from the oak tree under which 16th-century poet Tasso used to sit. Comedy shows are staged here in July to September, when the weather permits. In winter the company performs at the **Teatro Anfitrione**.

Nearby is a Neapolitan street puppet theatre booth featuring *Pulcinella* (the Italian original of Punch). Shows are usually on in the afternoons, with morning shows on Sundays.

DIRECTORY

PRIMA VISIONE

Alcazar
Via Card. Merry del Val 14.
Map 7 C1.
06-588 0099.

Augustus
Corso V. Emanuele 203.
Map 11 B3.
06-687 5455.

Barberini
Piazza Barberini 52. **Map** 5 B3. 06-482 7707.

Farnese
Piazza Campo de' Fiori 56.
Map 4 E5.
06-686 4395.

Fiamma
Via Bissolati 47. **Map** 5 C2. 06-482 7100.

Metropolitan
Via del Corso 7. **Map** 4 F1. 06-3260 0500.

Nuovo Olimpia
Via in Lucina 16. **Map** 12 E1. 06-686 1068.

Warner Village Moderno
Piazza della Repubblica 45.
Map 5 C3.
06-4777 9201.

ART CINEMAS

Azzurro Scipioni
Via degli Scipioni 82. **Map** 3 C2. 06-3973 7161.

Dei Piccoli
Viale della Pineta 15.
Map 5 B1.
06-855 3485.

Filmstudio
Via degli Orti d'Alibert 1C.
Map 4 D4.
06-6819 2987.

Nuovo Sacher
Largo Ascianghi 1. **Map** 7 C2. 06-581 8116.

Palazzo delle Esposizioni
Via Nazionale 194. **Map** 5 B4. 06-474 5903.
www.palaexpo.com

Tibur
Via degli Etruschi 36.
06-495 7762.

ENGLISH-LANGUAGE

Pasquino
Piazza S. Egidio 10. **Map** 7 C1. 06-581 5208.

Warner Village Moderno
See left.

MAINSTREAM THEATRE

Ambra Jovinelli
Via G. Pepe 41. **Map** 6 E4. 06-4434 0262.

Teatro Argentina
Largo Argentina 56. **Map** 4 F4. 06-6880 4601.
www.teatrodiroma.it

Teatro Eliseo
Via Nazionale 183. **Map** 5 B4. 06-488 2114.
www.teatroeliseo.it

Teatro India
Lungotevere dei Papareschi.
Map 7 C5.
06-553 0089.

Teatro Piccolo Eliseo
Via Nazionale 183. **Map** 5 B4. 06-488 2114.

Teatro Quirino
Via delle Vergini 7.
Map 5 A4 & 12 F2.
06-679 4585.
www.teatroquirino.it

Teatro Sistina
Via Sistina 129. **Map** 5 B2. 06-420 0711.

Teatro Valle
Via del Teatro Valle 21.
Map 4 F4 & 12 D3.
06-6880 3794.
www.teatrovalle.it

Teatro Vittoria
Piazza S. Maria Liberatrice 8. **Map** 8 D3.
06-574 0170.

CONTEMPORARY THEATRE

Teatro Anfitrione
Via di San Saba 24. **Map** 8 E3. 06-575 0827.

Teatro Ateneo
Viale delle Scienze 3. **Map** 6 F3. 06-4991 4435.

Teatro Colosseo
Via Capo d'Africa 5 A. **Map** 9 A1. 06-700 4932.

Teatro dell'Orologio
Via dei Filippini 17A. **Map** 11 B3. 06-687 5550.

Teatro Politecnico
Via Tiepolo 13 A. **Map** 1 B3. 06-321 9891.

Teatro Vascello
Via G. Carini 72. **Map** 7 A2. 06-588 1021.

FOLK, CABARET, PUPPET THEATRE

Fantasie di Trastevere
Via S. Dorotea 6. **Map** 4 D5. 06-588 1671.

Meo Patacca
P. dei Mercanti 30. **Map** 8 D1. 06-581 6198.

Puppet Theatre
Piazza dei Satiri.
06-589 6201.

Teatro Mongiovino
Via Genocchi 15.
06-513 9405.

Teatro Verde
Circonvall. Gianicolense 10.
Map 7 B4.
06-588 2034.

OPEN-AIR THEATRE

Anfiteatro Quercia del Tasso
Passeggiata del Gianicolo.
Map 3 C5.
06-575 0827.

Nightclubs

THE CENTRE OF ROMAN NIGHT LIFE is no longer the Via Veneto area so effectively portrayed by Fellini in *La Dolce Vita*. The district still offers plenty of venues, but elsewhere more informal and less wallet-fleecing clubs have emerged, with a more vibrant atmosphere appealing to a younger and more diverse crowd.

With the new clubs come new areas. Venues are always springing up in the historic centre and Trastevere, while the once working-class districts of Testaccio and the Via Ostiense have also become new meccas for young Roman clubbers.

WHAT'S ON

AS IN ANY major city, Rome's nightlife is constantly changing. Roman club-goers are an extremely varied group and most clubs arrange different nights to appeal to different tastes – so it is essential to keep up-to-date on what's happening by checking listings magazines *(see p340)* that hit the newsstands every Thursday. Remember that most city clubs close from mid-June to mid-September, transferring to summer premises along the coast or to one of the open-air venues of the Roman Summer celebrations.

For a more direct source of information, head for the bars around the Via della Pace and Campo de' Fiori areas. At about 10.30pm the narrow streets and piazzas swarm with people and any interesting event will soon become common knowledge. *Buoni* (free or reduced price tickets) may be handed out.

PRACTICALITIES

PREFERRED CLUBBING nights are Friday and Saturday, when the cars and scooters of revellers block the streets of the city centre. Queues at the most popular places can be long at peak entrance time (around midnight) so get there an hour earlier.

Instead of an entrance fee, some clubs require a *tessera* (membership card) which you can buy on the spot. A ticket or *tessera* usually includes a free first drink, but your second could well be expensive – as much as €15.

In smarter places look is all important: for men a jacket and tie are a must and you might even need an invitation or a personal introduction. There is no problem getting into the more youth-oriented discos, with average dress codes ranging from smart casual to decidedly distressed. Beware: all-male groups are never welcome, and in some exclusive clubs neither are unaccompanied men.

CLUBS AND BARS

AN ELEGANT NIGHT OUT could start in one of the American-style bars on the Via Veneto or in smaller *centro storico* bars like **Tartarughino** and **Giulio Passami l'Olio**. If you prefer something more bohemian, go straight to **La Vineria** in Campo de' Fiori or **Bar del Fico** and the **Antico Caffè della Pace**, both a short walk from Piazza Navona.

To brush shoulders with parliamentary under-secretaries and TV starlets, make for **Gilda**, a favourite with the Roman jet set and hangers-on, with its glitzy dancefloor and restaurant. The famous Sixties nightclub, **Jackie O**, has been revamped in lavish style, with a lush interior and an expensive eatery. In a similar vein is the nearby **Club 84** where booking is "strongly advised".

Alien is a safe option for commercial music among Roman twenty-somethings, though **Heaven** is slightly funkier with its marked preference for house. The more traditional disco is at its best at **Piper**, which changes look each season and organizes imaginative floor shows and other happenings. **Blackout** is a huge disco south of S. Giovanni, with a large dance area dedicated to rave. There are some disco pubs worth noting too, like city-centre venue **Rock Castle** or the multi-level **Accademia 90** in Trastevere. More alternative, and a little further out, are **Brancaleone** and the **Circolo degli Artisti**, social centres with large dance floors and frequent live concerts.

Undoubtedly, the coolest clubs for the young and trendy are dotted around Monte Testaccio and along the nearby Via Ostiense. These include **Bush**, a temple to house and dance, the excellent **Ex-Bocciodromo**, the trendy **On the Rocks** and **Bliss**, which offers commercial hits and slick nostalgia. **Alpheus** has four separate dance floors with a different beat in each, while the ultra-hip **Goa** serves up everything from trip-hop to bhangra. In the same area, the **Ex-Magazzini** is worth going to if you enjoy indie and breakbeat. Another venue for seeing and being seen is **Radio Londra Caffè**, designed to look like a WW2 bunker, where dj-skills and free entrance attract the crowds until the small hours. The Testaccio-Ostiense area offers something for most tastes, with a host of venues which open, have a moment of glory and then decline swiftly, awaiting rebirth.

GAY SCENE

THERE ARE A NUMBER of bars and clubs for gay men in Rome. Apart from the justly-famous **Alibi** disco, with its explosive mix of house and Seventies hits, there are also city-centre bars like the legendary **Hangar** or newcomer **Side**, situated on what has been christened Rome's Gay Street. Look out too for the various gay one-nighters, the best being Tuesday's **Gorgeous Goa** night or Friday's Mucca Assassina

(Killer Cow) event at the **Qube**, organized by the city's **Mario Mieli** centre. This is one of the few mixed evenings in Rome, though younger lesbians may also enjoy the women-only bash on the last Sunday of the month at **Goa**. Pride week at the end of June/early July is a time when gay Romans hit the streets for seven days' partying.

JAZZ, SALSA AND AFRICAN SOUNDS

THERE ARE plenty of venues for jazz, from trad and swing to modern fusion *(see p344)*. Many jazz and Latin American clubs combine live music with dancing – and eating and drinking. For South American style music,

Fonclea and **Arriba Arriba** *(see p345)* or **Alpheus** all pay homage to Latin American and world music, though **Caffè Latino** is probably the best place to visit at the weekend.

CLUBBING IN SUMMER

IN SUMMER when everything closes down in the city, head for the various open-air Roman summer events or don your designer casuals and get down to the nearby seaside resort of Fregene where many of the nightclubs transfer for the June-September period. Take your swimwear too, as much of the fun takes place in and around the pools. Beach venues include **Gilda on the Beach** (now with its

world music offspring Mary'y'Sol) and **Miraggio**, popular with the younger, weekend crowd. Most seaside clubs also have their own fish and seafood restaurants.

AFTER HOURS

MOST ROMAN clubs stay open until 2am or 3am. However, night-owls may find one or two dance havens that see in the dawn, especially during the beach-party season. Before heading off to bed, join other die-hard clubbers (and an exceptionally varied fauna) for a final drink at one of the city's 24-hour bars – or else make for one of the early-morning bakers and feast on sweet breakfast *cornetti* straight from the oven.

DIRECTORY

Accademia 90
Vicolo della Renella 90.
Map 7 C1.
06-589 6321.

Alibi
Via di Monte Testaccio 40.
Map 8 D4.
06-574 3448.

Alien
Via Velletri 13.
Map 6 D1.
06-841 2212.

Alpheus
Via del Commercio 36/8.
Map 8 D5.
06-574 7826.

Antico Caffè della Pace
Via della Pace 3–7.
Map 4 E4 & 11 C2.
06-686 116.

Bar del Fico
Piazza del Fico 26/8.
Map 11 B2.
06-686 5205.

Blackout
Via Saturnia 18.
Map 9 C3.
06-7049 6791.

Bliss
Via Ostiense 131h (south of Mercati Generali).
06-578 3146.

Brancaleone
Via Levanna 11 (north of the city centre).
06-8200 0959.

Bush
Via Galvani 44.
Map 8 D4.
06-5728 8691.

Caffè Latino
Via di Monte Testaccio 96.
Map 8 D4.
06-5728 8556.

Circolo degli Artisti
Via Casilina Vecchia 42.
Map 10 F1.
06-7030 5684.

Circolo Mario Mieli di Cultura Omosessuale
Via Corinto 5 (off Via Ostiense south of Basilica San Paolo).
06-541 3985.

Club 84
Via Emilia 84.
Map 5 B2.
06-482 7538.

Ex-Bocciodromo
Via di Monte Testaccio 23.
Map 8 D4.
06-439 3512.

Ex-Magazzini
Via dei Magazzini Generali 8 bis. **Map** 8 D5.
06-575 8040.

Gilda
Via Mario de' Fiori 97.
Map 5 A2 & 12 F1.
06-678 4838.

Giulio Passami l'Olio
Via di Monte Giordano 28.
Map 11 B2.
06-6880 3288.

Goa
Via Libetta 13 (to the south of Stazione Ostiense).
06-574 8277.

Hangar
Via in Selci 69. **Map** 5 C5.
06-488 1397.

Heaven
Viale di Porta Ardeatina 118A. **Map** 9 B5.
06-574 3772.

Jackie O
Via Boncompagni 11.
Map 5 B2.
06-4288 5457.

La Vineria
Campo de' Fiori 15.
Map 4 E4 & 11 C4.
06-6880 3268.

On the Rocks
Via Galvani 54. **Map** 8 D4.
06-574 6013.

Piper
Via Tagliamento 9 (north of the city centre).
06-855 5398.

Qube
Via di Portonaccio 212 (north of the city centre).
06-438 5445.

Radio Londra Caffè
Via di Monte Testaccio 67.
Map 8 D4.
06-575 0044.

Rock Castle Café
Via B Cenci 8.
Map 12 D5.
06-6880 7999.

Side
Via Verri 1. **Map** 9 B1.
348 692 9472.

Tartarughino
Via della Scrofa 1.
Map 4 F3 & 12 D2.
06-686 4131.

Villaggio Globale
Ex-Mattatoio Lungotevere Testaccio 2.
Map 8 D4.
06-575 7233.

SUMMER CLUBS

Gilda on the Beach
Lungomare di Ponente 11.
Fregene.
06-6656 0649.

Miraggio
Lungomare di Ponente 93.
06-6656 0369.

Sport

Do NOT BE SURPRISED if the peace of a Sunday afternoon in Rome is interrupted by the honking of cars and people shouting. It simply means that one of the home football teams has won at the stadium and the whole city will vibrate with the excitement.

Football is Italy's national sport but other sports also attract a large following and Roman sports fans are never at a loss for varied events and activities.

You will find times and venues for most spectator sports listed in *Trovaroma* or *Roma c'è (see p340)*, as well as the local sections of *La Gazzetta dello Sport* or *Corriere dello Sport*.

FOOTBALL

AN ITALIAN SOCCER MATCH is an experience not to be missed for the quality of the play and the fun atmosphere, though hooliganism has begun to raise its ugly head.

Rome has two teams, Roma and Lazio, and they take it in turns to play at the **Stadio Olimpico** on a Sunday afternoon at 3pm, in the Campionato Italiano (Italian championship league).

Seats can be scarce, so get tickets in advance from the stadium (€22 to €78). The cheapest tickets are in the Le Curve stand; the middle-range and most expensive are in Le Gradinate and La Tribuna respectively.

On Wednesday evenings there may be international competitions – the UEFA cup or the Coppa dei Campioni (European Championship Cup). In between these, teams battle it out for the national Coppa Italia.

TENNIS

A MAJOR EVENT, the International Championships go on at **Foro Italico** for two weeks in May. The world's top tennis stars thrash it out on clay courts at 1pm and 8.30pm from Tuesday to Friday, and at 1pm only at weekends. Buy tickets in advance either directly from the Foro Italico or from a ticket agency.

If you wish to play yourself, there are now more than 350 tennis clubs in Rome. It is often essential to book at least a week in advance and

there is usually a moderate court fee.

Clubs where membership is not required include **Tennis Lazio** and the **Circolo Tennis Stampa** in northern Rome and the **Oasi di Pace**, just off the Via Appia Antica. The big hotels offer tennis for a reasonable price. The **Crowne Plaza** requires a small annual membership fee on top of the court price, which includes the gym and the pool (in the summer).

HORSE-RACING, TROTTING AND LEISURE-RIDING

IMPORTANT RACES include the Derby in May and the Premio Roma in November. There are trotting races at the **Ippodromo di Tor di Valle** and both flat races and steeple-chases at the **Ippodromo delle Capannelle**.

The International Horse Show is held in May in Piazza di Siena, Villa Borghese *(see p258)*. It is organized by the Federazione Italiana Sport Equestri (**FISE**) and is one of the most important social and sporting events in the calendar. The setting makes it a great attraction.

Through the FISE, it may be possible to find a riding club that will take you on a hack in the countryside around Rome, but most do not accept short-term members.

GOLF

EVEN THE MOST ELITE golf clubs will accept a touring golfer with a home membership and handicap. Most clubs are shut on Mondays and at the

weekend when they host competitions, and when guests cannot play. Prices range from €25–€65.

The **Olgiata Golf Club** is open to everybody from Tuesday to Sunday, though it is best to phone first if you want to play at the weekend. **Country Club Castel Gandolfo** is the newest club and **Circolo del Golf di Roma** the oldest and most prestigious. Within the city ring road is the course at the **Sheraton Golf Hotel** (closed Tuesdays).

One of the many important competitions on the various golf courses around Rome is the Circolo Golf Roma Coppa d'Oro (Gold Cup) in April.

CAR AND MOTORBIKE RACING

FORMULA 1 and Formula 3 races take place on Sundays at **Vallelunga**; be prepared for some expensive entrance fees. Frequently on Saturdays official trials are open to spectators, and on some non-racing Sundays Italy's car designers show new models.

RUGBY

RUGBY has taken off in Italy recently, particularly since Italy joined the Six Nations tournament. This means that in winter (usually Feb–Mar) there are a couple of inter-national matches in Rome. The home team is drawn against two other member "nations" each year: France, England, Scotland, Ireland or Wales.

ROWING

IN MID-JUNE an Oxbridge crew challenges the historic Aniene crew to a race taking place alternately on the Thames and the Tiber. The best place to view this from is between the Margherita and the Sant'Angelo bridges. The race usually starts at around 6pm. Another event is the battle between the Roma and Lazio crews, from Ponte Duca d'Aosta to Ponte Risorgimento, on the same variable date as the Roma-Lazio football Derby.

SWIMMING

SWIMMING POOLS are few and definitely not geared to the short-term visitor. It is often necessary to pay an expensive membership plus a monthly tariff. Most pools also require you to produce a medical certificate assuring your good health, and have lane-only swimming, so check to see if free swimming (nuoto libero) is possible. The state-owned pools can be slightly cheaper, but you still have to pay an initial membership fee.

The **Shangri-La Hotel** opens its pool to non-residents in the summer months, as does the **Cavalieri Hilton Hotel**, for a higher entrance fee. The best deal is on a Sunday when the sports club and swimming pool **La Margherita** opens to non-members 10am–1pm, for a reasonable entrance charge. **Piscina delle Rose** in EUR is an Olympic-sized pool open from June to September 9am–5.30pm during the week, 9am–7pm at weekends.

HEALTH CLUBS

LIKE THE swimming pools, Roman health clubs usually require both a membership fee and monthly payments. For a short stay in Rome, it is more sensible to try the facilities in your hotel, or, if you are willing to pay, head for one of the private clubs. Use of club facilities may well be negotiable.

The **Roman Sports Centre** welcomes daily members for a reasonable price (€26) and you can use the swimming pools, the gym and the sauna. The facilities are open 9am–10pm. Be sure to wear lycra, as shorts made from other materials are not allowed.

JOGGING AND CYCLING

ROME'S PERFECT climate and stunning scenery attract thousands of well-dressed joggers and cyclists into the city's many parks. Early on weekday mornings or at any time on a Sunday you'll find the more popular locations looking more like a high-speed fashion show than sweat tracks. Each March, however, more serious runners take part in the Rome Marathon.

Villa Doria Pamphilj (see p267) is an extensive park situated above the Janiculum, where you can choose among three tracks, plenty of open spaces and a network of paths. **Villa Borghese** (see p258) is another vast popular place with a running track.

Alternatively, jog under the acacia trees and palms at Villa Torlonia, on the spot-lit track at Villa Glori, or combine sport with culture by running the **Via Appia Antica** (see p265) branching off into Parco Caffarella. Other favourite places are Viale delle Terme di Caracalla, Circo Massimo, Parco degli Aquedotti and Parco di Colle Oppio.

All of the above are also ideal for cyclists, and you can hire bikes from many places including **Collalti** and **Treno e Scooter Rent**.

CHILDREN'S ROME

ITALIANS LOVE HAVING children around, and you can be sure yours will be made welcome wherever they go. But there are few special facilities for children, and the heat, crowds and lack of clean public loos mean that Rome is not an ideal city for a holiday with babies or under-sevens. It does, however, have plenty to offer slightly older children, especially those who are keen on

Renaissance cherub from the Villa Farnesina

history or art. The temptation may be to wear yourself and your children out by packing too many sights into one day. Plan in advance and leave plenty of time to wander around the city: looking at the quirkier fountains and monuments, watching knife-grinders at work in the markets, and spending hours agonizing over the choice of ice-cream flavours and special pizza toppings.

PRACTICAL ADVICE

IF YOU ARE bringing your children to Rome, try to come in early spring or late autumn, when the weather is good, but not too hot. Easter is best avoided, as the city is more crowded than usual, and you're constantly jostled on packed buses and streets. Where you stay is crucial. A hotel near the Villa Borghese park will give your children plenty of chance to relax and let off steam, though you may end up spending a lot of time and money to get to and from the town centre. A hotel in the old centre is ideal, as you can easily pop back during the day for a rest and a clean bathroom. As hygienic toilets and changing facilities are rare within the city, it is really not advisable to bring a baby to Rome unless you are visiting friends or family. As with many historic cities, Rome may not instantly appeal to all children, but there is plenty to inspire their imaginations. Use this book to make the buildings and history come alive. Children might also enjoy learning a few Italian words and phrases so they can order food and buy things by themselves.

Jogging in Villa Borghese

If lingering over drinks on the café terraces is what you enjoy best, bring your offspring something to keep them busy once they have finished with their treat: crayons and paper, a computer game or a Walkman. Alternatively, most other adults are very tolerant of children running around and making a noise while they relax and, if yours are reasonably outgoing, they could join in with the local children playing ball games in early evenings on piazzas like Campo de' Fiori.

If you feel the need for a total break, most hotels will be able to provide a babysitter or help you to contact a qualified childminding agency.

In the event of bad luck, see pages 360–61 for information on what to do and a list of emergency numbers.

Fairground in the Villa Borghese park

GETTING AROUND

BUMPY COBBLES, narrow streets without pavements and overcrowded buses make pushing children around in pushchairs tiring work. Mothers with young children are, however, usually allowed to jump queues. The Metro is often less crowded. Kids under 1 m (3 ft 3 in) tall travel free on public transport.

Although the city is not good for cyclists, families with older children could hire bikes to ride along the Tiber on the cycle tracks to the north of the city, or to take on a regional train into the country. The bikes, tandems and rickshaws for hire in Villa Borghese are good fun, and the bike hire hut in the Pincio gardens has free baby seats.

Anyone over the age of 14 can ride a scooter under 50 cc, although Rome is not the best place for novices *(see p378)*.

A hire bike with free baby seat

Pony-pulled trains in the Villa Borghese park

EATING OUT

CHILDREN ARE normally warmly welcomed in neighbourhood pizzerias and trattorias, and high chairs are often available for toddlers and babies. If there is no high chair, be prepared for the waiters to improvise for you with armloads of cushions or telephone directories. Most places are perfectly happy to serve half portions, or to let children share meals.

In trattorias it can sometimes be difficult to be exactly sure what a certain dish contains (especially when there is no menu and the dishes of the day are reeled off, usually at top speed, by the waiter), so faddy eaters are likely to be happier in pizzerias *(see pp318–21)*. Here they can choose their own topping (remember that *prosciutto,* which is usually translated in menus as ham, is cured). The most entertaining pizzerias for kids are the old-fashioned ones where they can watch the chefs pound, stretch and flip the pizza dough. The best places get busy from around 8.30pm, so it is wise to go early to avoid having to queue. If all else fails, there are many branches of McDonald's.

PICNICS

PICNICS IN THE parks are ideal, and shopping for the food is often half the fun. There is no problem finding small cartons of fruit juice and branded canned drinks, but these are expensive unless you go to a supermarket – the branch of Oviesse on Viale Trastevere is the most convenient. Water from the drinking fountains is potable, so it is worth carrying plastic cups around.

As well as picnic food from bakeries and markets, there are lots of scrumptious takeaway foods. Many of them are appealingly messy, so it is wise to take paper tissues. Try deep-fried fruit and vegetables from Cose Fritte on Via di Ripetta and *supplì al telefono,* rice croquettes with a gooey string of mozzarella inside, from *pizza al taglio* or *pizza rustica* outlets. A *tramezzino* comes quite close to an English sandwich and if your kids are miserable without Marmite, you can find it (and other foreign foods) at Castroni on Via Cola di Rienzo.

Feeding pigeons on Piazza Navona

ICE CREAM

ROME, OF COURSE, is famous for ice cream; you and your children are likely to be tempted at every turn. Real ice-cream fans may even want to plan their day's sightseeing round one of the best *gelaterie (see pp319–21).* It is far cheaper to buy either a cone or tub of ice cream to eat in the street, but in some of the more traditional places it is worth paying to sit down. At Fassi, they have an old-fashioned ice cream-making machine on display and at Giolitti, you can enjoy gargantuan sundaes in the elegant parlour *(see p109).*

Investigating some of the hundreds of Italian ice-cream flavours

Sightseeing with Children

Entrance to the Villa Borghese Zoo

GENERAL TIPS

ROME DOES NOT have many museums with the sort of hands-on exhibits that many other cities lay on for children. However, Bernini's marble elephant *(see p108)* and the fat *facchino*, or porter *(p107)*, appeal to kids. The Capuchin cemetery at Santa Maria della Concezione *(p254)*, the catacombs *(pp264–6)* and the Mamertine Prison *(p91)* will grab the more ghoulish imaginations, and children will enjoy putting their hands into the Bocca della Verità *(p202)*.

Look for details like the dirty toenails on figures in Caravaggio's paintings, the Etruscan votives, which were offered to the gods, at the Villa Giulia *(pp262–3)*, and the illusory collapsing ceiling in the Chiesa Nuova as well as the fake dome of Sant' Ignazio di Loyola *(see p106)*.

Museums your children will enjoy include **Museo Explora**, the city's new museum for children, full of interesting hands-on exhibits, and the Museo delle Mura, which explores the length of the Aurelian Wall *(p196)*. Among the churches, St Peter's *(see p230)* and San Clemente *(see pp186–7)* are most fun.

At the Vatican children will like the animal statues and mosaics in the Animal Gallery and also the Sistine Ceiling *(p246)*, especially if they get to know that Michelangelo had to paint it hunched up on a scaffolding platform.

Museo Explora

Via Flamino 80. **Map** 1 C5.
📞 06-361 3776 *(booking necessary)*.
🌐 www.mdbr.it

ANCIENT RUINS

THE ANCIENT RUINS best appreciated by children are the Colosseum *(see pp92–5)*, and Trajan's Markets *(see pp 88–9)*. You can still make out what both these buildings looked like from their remains. The scant ruins of the Forum and Palatine, on the other hand, may not appeal so strongly. Ostia Antica, where the remains include a theatre, shop and 20-seater public toilet, is much more likely to interest them *(see pp270–71)*.

Mosaic from the Vatican

MOSAICS

THERE ARE SCORES of vivid, sometimes quirky, mosaics in buildings all over Rome. Many of these are particularly appealing to children. Details in the mosaics range from brilliantly coloured flowers, leaves, animals and buildings (in the churches of San Clemente, Santa Prassede and Santa Maria in Trastevere, *see p186, p171 and pp212–13*) to the debris of a banquet (in the Vatican's Museo Gregorio Profano, *see pp234–5*).

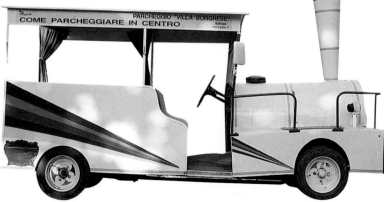

Model trains in Villa Borghese

ENTERTAINMENT

To find out what's on for children in Rome, scour the cinema pages of the newpapers and the listings in *Trovaroma, Roma c'è, Wanted in Rome* and entertainment websites *(see pp340–1)*. For older children, **Time Elevator**, presents 3,000 years of Rome's history in an educational yet entertaining way. Most theatres and cinemas have reduced entry fees for children, but shows are often only in Italian.

There are cartoons shown at Villa Borghese's Cinema dei Piccoli and traditional puppet shows every afternoon, except Wednesday, on Janiculum hill.

An appealing time for children to be in Rome is over Christmas, when Piazza Navona hosts

Stall at the Christmas toy fair on Piazza Navona

Resting on the kerb side

a Christmas toy fair, where stalls sell toys and sweets.

Time Elevator
Via SS Apostoli 20. **Map** 5 A4 & 12 F3. ☎ 06-699 0053.

PARKS

Villa Borghese *(see p258)* has rowing boats to hire; pony-cart rides; bikes to rent; a mini cinema; a small funfair; and a zoo. Villa Celimontana *(see p193)* has bike trails, and open-air theatre performances in the summer. The old-fashioned amusement park LUNEUR at EUR *(see p266)* can be good fun. Also in EUR is the Piscina delle Rose, a swimming pool open in the summer *(see p351)*. The Bomarzo Monster Park, 95 km (60 miles) north of Rome, was built in the 16th century for a mad duke.

Children can clamber over its giant stone monsters.

TOYS

A visit to a Roman toyshop can be a lot of fun. **Città del Sole** sells educational toys and games, while **Al Sogno** is a dream come true for kids who love stuffed animals.

Città del Sole
Via della Scrofa 65. **Map** 4 F3 & 12 D2. ☎ 06-687 5404.

Al Sogno
Piazza Navona 53. **Map** 4 E4 & 11 C3. ☎ 06-686 4198.

CHILDREN'S CLOTHES

Italians adore dressing their children up, and on Sunday afternoons in particular, you are likely to encounter young children dressed as if they had walked straight out of a costume drama: girls in frills and flounces and boys in velvet breeches or knee-length shorts.

Many shops sell beautifully hand-crafted children's shoes and clothes – the downside is that they can often be expensive and impractical: dry-clean-only clothes are common and shoes are not made for mud.

Lavori Artigianali Femminili sells handmade silk and wool clothes for children up to eight. **Baby House** offers *haute couture* for children, including clothes by top designers, and **Benetton** sells smart casuals.

Baby House
Via Cola di Rienzo 117. **Map** 3 C2. ☎ 06-321 4291.

Benetton
Via Cesare Battista 129. **Map** 5 A4 & 12 F3. ☎ 06-6992 4010.

Lavori Artigianali Femminili
Via Capo le Case 6. **Map** 5 A3 & 12 F1. ☎ 06-679 2992.

SURVIVAL GUIDE

PRACTICAL INFORMATION

ROMANS OFTEN SEEM unconcerned by the priceless art treasures and ancient ruins which lie casually among the buildings and workings of their hectic 20th-century city. Visitors nearly always find these wonders very exciting, but it is not always easy to make the most of them. Relaxed local attitudes make for hundreds of variations in opening hours. Many places close for several hours over lunch and reopen in the late afternoon; some museums are open in the mornings only. Bank and shop hours can be just as difficult to pin down. On a more positive note, many of the main sights are within easy walking distance of one another. Start your day early and wear comfortable shoes for the Roman cobblestones. It can be a delightfully informal city to visit, but remember to observe dress rules to cover up in churches, since this is one area where the Italians are very strict.

MUSEUMS AND MONUMENTS

MANY MUSEUMS are now open all day, although most close on Mondays. If you are particularly keen to see a specific monument or museum, make sure it is open before you set out. Many museums don't allow visitors to enter in the last half an hour or so before they close.

Roma c'è, a listings guide to the city

There is usually an admission charge for museums and monuments, although some are free on Sundays. Many museums offer a reduced entrance fee for children under 18, students with the appropriate ID and senior citizens from the European Union. If you don't see any reductions advertised it is always worth asking.

Entrance to all churches is free, and many contain works of art that are worthy of the world's greatest museums. Some of Rome's sights are accessible only on personal application or by written appointment. Examples include Nero's Aqueduct or the gardens at the Vatican.

The *Area by Area* section of this guide gives opening times for each sight and tells you whether there is an admission charge. A useful booklet called *Roma c'è*, gives up-to-date details of current exhibitions at Rome's main museums and galleries.

Typical traffic congestion in Via delle Quattro Fontane

TOURIST INFORMATION

PICK UP details of special tours here at the main tourist office (**APT**). APT will also help with accommodation (*see p289*). Information kiosks run by the Comune di Roma have English-speaking staff providing free maps, leaflets and advice. Or ring the **Rome City Council Tourist Information Call Center** for information in English. Besides the official tourist offices, good travel agents such as **CIT** or the **American Express** office can also be helpful to visitors. For information on Italian cities and areas outside Rome, contact **ENIT** (the National Tourist Board), who have offices in all the main cities.

A word of warning: prices and opening times change often and sights can be closed for what seem to be unbelievably long periods of restoration (*chiuso per restauro*) or because of a strike (*sciopero*).

ENTE NAZIONALE ITALIANO PER IL TURISMO

ENIT logo

An electric minibus: useful for the historic centre

ENTERTAINMENT INFORMATION

THE WEEKLY *Trovaroma*, in the Thursday edition of *La Repubblica*, and *Roma c'è*, published on Wednesdays, are

the main guides to what's on. English listings are also in *Wanted in Rome*. Full entertainment information can be found on page 340.

Trovaroma

GUIDED TOURS

SEVERAL COMPANIES offer tours with English-speaking guides; these include **CIT**, **American Express**, **Green Line Tours**, **Carrani Tours**, **Rome Revealed Tours** and **Through Eternity Tours**. Full-day city tours including lunch cost around €75; half-day tours around €30. Alternatively the No. 110 ATAC bus passes many of the main sights on a 3-hour circuit. The journey costs around €8 and leaves from Termini every 30 minutes between 10am and 6pm. Tour guides can be hired at many of the major sights, such as the Roman Forum *(see pp78–87)*. Employ only the official guides and establish the fee in advance; they charge around €50 for a half-day tour.

ATAC, the Rome bus company

VISITING CHURCHES

MANY OF ITALY'S churches are very dark, but they usually have electric light meters to illuminate chapels and works of art. The meters are coin-operated. Recorded information in several languages is often available at coin-operated machines. Dress codes are firmly upheld in churches; St Peter's *(see pp230–33)* is especially strict – you cannot wear shorts.

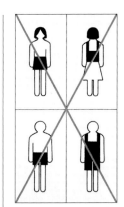

Unacceptable dress in church: both sexes should cover torsos and upper arms

ETIQUETTE

PEOPLE IN ROME are generally courteous and friendly to foreign visitors. Italians are delighted at any effort to speak their language, so it is worth learning a few phrases *(see p431)*. Italians tend to drink only with meals and are unlikely to be seen drunk – obvious drunkenness is frowned upon. Smoking is common in bars, restaurants and on streets, but banned on public transport.

TIPPING

FOREIGNERS ARE expected to tip, although Italians themselves don't always do so. Leave a few coins in bars or cafés; in restaurants where service is not included, leave around 10 per cent. Keep change handy for taxi drivers, sacristans, chambermaids, doormen and porters.

ROME FOR THE DISABLED

ROME IS not particularly well organized to cater for the disabled. Look before crossing at traffic lights and pedestrian crossings – not all vehicles stop when you might expect. The seriously disabled will need help getting around. Ramps, lifts and modified WCs exist in an increasing number of places, including Termini station and the Colosseum. It may be worth asking before entering

restaurants, since some have wheelchair access to the dining area but not to the WC. If you have no escort, consider a specially designed package tour, or contact an organization for disabled travellers before you set off. The Vatican Museums, Sistine Chapel and St Peter's are all accessible by wheelchair. The Vatican Museums recently received an EU award for improving accessibility for the disabled and staff offer help if needed.

WCs

PUBLIC TOILETS are few and far between. There are clean ones by the Colosseum (with facilities for the disabled), at St Peter's and in the Rinascente store *(see p323)*. Most cafés let you use theirs if you ask. Take your own paper.

USEFUL ADDRESSES

American Express
Piazza di Spagna 38. **Map** 5 A2.
[06-676 41.

APT
Via Parigi 5. **Map** 5 C3. **Open** 9am–7pm Mon–Sat. [06-488 991.

Carrani Tours
Via V. E. Orlando 95. **Map** 5 C3.
[06-488 0510.

CIT
Piazza della Repubblica 65.
Map 5 C3. [06-462 0311.
W www.citviaggi.it

ENIT
Via Marghera 2. **Map** 6 E3.
[06-497 11.
W www.italiantourism.com

Green Line Tours
Via Farini 5A. **Map** 6 D4.
[06-481 5764.

Rome City Council Tourist Information Call Center
[06-3600 4399.
W www.romaturismo.it

Rome Revealed Tours
[06-3247 4317.
W www.romerevealed.com

Through Eternity Tours
Via Sinuessa 8. **Map** 9 C3. [06-700 9336. W www.througheternity.com

Banking and Local Currency

MONEY SERVICES are not always fast in Rome. Transactions can involve considerable paperwork and a lot of waiting around. On the whole, bank exchange rates are more favourable than those in travel agents and hotels – the deal just takes longer to complete. Small change is indispensable, since coins are needed for telephones, tips and for illuminating works of art and chapels in churches *(see p359)*.

Eagle sculpture on the Ministry of Finance

CHANGING MONEY

IT IS BEST to have a few euros when you arrive, so you won't have to change money immediately. However, there are increasing numbers of convenient electronic exchange machines at arrival points. There are now several throughout the city too. Multilingual instructions are available. You simply feed in notes of a foreign currency, and should get some euros back. Exchange rates vary from place to place. The Banco di Santo Spirito office at Fiumicino airport offers reasonable rates.

For the best rates, change money at a bank (look for the sign *Cambio*). Hotels tend to give poor rates, even if they charge modest commissions. At the Vatican Museums *(see p235)*, you aren't charged any commission. The American Express office *(see p359)* offers good rates and is open on Saturday mornings. Cardholders may withdraw up to $1,000 (or £500) a week from the cash machine, but you have to pay a fee for this service and need to organize a PIN (personal identification number) linked to your account before you travel.

Automatic exchange machine

CREDIT CARDS

CREDIT CARDS, which used to be regarded with great suspicion in Italy, are now much more widely accepted in hotels, restaurants and shops. All major credit and charge cards (American Express, Access/MasterCard, Visa, Diners Club) are well known. Banks and cash dispensers are more likely to accept Visa cards for cash advances, but Access (MasterCard) is accepted by many retail outlets in Italy. Take both if you have them. Paying for anything in foreign currency will almost always be expensive.

Some restaurants and shops set a minimum expenditure level, below which they will not accept credit card payment. Check you have some cash just in case.

TRAVELLERS' CHEQUES

IF YOU OPT for travellers' cheques, choose a well-known name such as American Express, or take those issued through a major bank. Most issuers charge 1 per cent commission on travellers' cheques. Get some small denominations, so you won't be left with huge amounts of euros at the end of your trip. But don't forget that the minimum commission charged for each transaction (and the amount of time involved) may make changing small amounts of money uneconomical.

Always record the travellers' cheque numbers and refund addresses separately from the cheques themselves in case they are stolen. Some places will charge you for each cheque.

Check the exchange rates before you travel and decide whether euro, dollar or sterling cheques are more appropriate.

OPENING HOURS

BANKS ARE USUALLY open 8.30am–1.20pm and 3–4.30pm Mon–Fri, but opening times vary and banks are closed for public holidays and at weekends.

Bureaux de Change have more generous opening times, similar to shop hours. The exchange offices at Termini station *(see p372)* are also open on Sundays.

USING BANKS

QUEUES IN BANKS can be long and the form-filling involved in changing money can take up a lot of valuable holiday time. You usually have to queue first at the *cambio*, then at the *cassa* to obtain your cash. Take some form of identification with you, such as a passport. Metal objects may set off emergency detectors as you enter.

One of the major Italian banks

Exchange office at one of the Italian national banks

The Bank of Rome, which has branches in other Italian cities

THE EURO

TWELVE COUNTRIES have replaced their traditional currencies, such as the Italian lire, with the euro. Austria, Belgium, Finland, France, Germany, Greece, Ireland, Italy, Luxembourg, Netherlands, Portugal and Spain chose to join the new currency; the UK, Denmark and Sweden stayed out, with an option to review their situation. The euro was introduced on 1 January 1999, but only for banking purposes. Notes and coins came into circulation on 1 January 2002. A transition period allowed both euros and local currencies to be used simultaneously, but all the old currencies were phased out by mid-2002. All euro notes and coins can be used anywhere inside the participating member states.

Bank Notes

Euro bank notes have seven denominations. The €5 note (grey in colour) is the smallest, followed by the €10 note (pink), €20 note (blue), €50 note (orange), €100 note (green), €200 note (yellow) and €500 note (purple). All notes show the stars of the European Union.

5 euros

10 euros

20 euros

50 euros

100 euros

200 euros

500 euros

2 euros

1 euro

50 cents

20 cents

10 cents

Coins

The euro has eight coin denominations: €1 and €2; 50 cents, 20 cents, 10 cents, 5 cents, 2 cents and 1 cent. The €2 and €1 coins are both silver and gold in colour. The 50-, 20- and 10-cent coins are gold. The 5-, 2- and 1-cent coins are bronze.

5 cents

2 cents

1 cent

GETTING TO ROME

MANY NATIONAL AIRLINES, including Italy's Alitalia, fly direct to Rome from most European cities and several in North America and Australia. There are no direct flights from New Zealand, but passengers can catch connections from either Frankfurt or London. Rome's Fiumicino airport expanded considerably in the late 1990s to accommodate the growing number of visitors. Rome also has train and coach links with the rest of Europe. These take a lot longer than flights (about 24 hours from London, compared with about 3 hours by air), but tend to cost about the same, so are only really worthwhile if you want to travel overland. The trains are often crowded in summer.

Alitalia aircraft

Part of the new extension to Fiumicino airport

BY AIR

IF YOU'RE FLYING from the United States, **Delta**, **US Airways**, Continental and **Alitalia** operate regular direct scheduled flights to Rome, with services from New York. Flying time is about 8½ hours. **Air Canada** and **Qantas** flights generally arrive and depart from Milan. The Italian state airline, Alitalia, also flies between Rome and New York, San Francisco, Los Angeles, Atlanta, Chicago, Montreal, Toronto and Sydney, though most of these intercontinental flights involve changing at Milan. It may be considerably cheaper for intercontinental travellers to take a budget flight to London, Paris, Athens, Frankfurt or Amsterdam and continue the journey to Rome from there. **British Airways** and Alitalia operate direct scheduled flights from London Heathrow to Rome (Fiumicino), and you can also fly from Gatwick, Birmingham and Manchester. Among the airlines using Rome as an intercontinental transit point is Ethiopian Airlines: fares are cheaper, but flights are less frequent and are sometimes subject to long delays.

Excursion fares generally offer the best value in scheduled flights, but you must purchase them well in advance. They are subject to penalty clauses if you cancel, so it is advisable to take out insurance as soon as you buy your ticket. If you are based in or travelling via the UK, it is worth looking on the Internet. You can book low-cost tickets direct from airlines **easyJet** and **Ryanair**, which have daily flights from London Stansted to Rome (Ciampino). Hotels and car rental can also be booked via these airlines' websites, and both offer their

Alitalia flight tickets

Check-in area at Fiumicino, Rome's main international airport own privately chartered bus to take travellers from Ciampino airport to Termini.

Regular charter flights for Rome's Ciampino airport run all year round. Most leave from Stansted, Gatwick and Luton, but there are a few flights from Manchester, Glasgow and Birmingham. The price of fares varies, peaking in summer and in Holy Week for the Pope's Easter blessing. In Rome, the **American Express** travel office will also book flights.

Easy-to-follow signs at Ostiense

AIRLINE NUMBERS

Air Canada
■ 06-659 1300.
W www.aircanada.com

Alitalia
■ 06-656 43 (information),
06-656 42 (international),
06-656 41 (domestic).
W www.alitalia.com

American Express
■ 06-676 41.

British Airways
■ 199 712 266
W www.britishairways.com

Delta Air Lines
■ 800 477 999. W www.delta.com

easyJet
W www.easyjet.com

Qantas
■ 06-5248 2725.
W www.quantas.com

Ryanair
W www.ryanair.com

US Airways
■ 8488 13177.
W www.usair.com

PACKAGE HOLIDAYS

PACKAGE HOLIDAYS to Rome can be much better value than travelling independently. For European visitors there are weekend packages and two- or three-centre holidays; Rome is frequently packaged with Florence and Venice.

Those from further afield can visit the city during Europe-wide tours. Most package companies include transfers from the airport to your hotel.

FIUMICINO AIRPORT

ROME HAS TWO international airports. Leonardo da Vinci – often known as Fiumicino – handles most scheduled flights, and is about 30 km (18 miles) southwest of the city. The airport has three terminals: Terminal A for domestic flights, Terminal B for international flights within the European Union, and Terminal C for all other international flights.

From Fiumicino there are two types of train to Rome: one (€5) runs every 15–30 minutes (6.27am–11.27pm) around Rome to Fara Sabina station, stopping at Trastevere, Ostiense, Tuscolana and Tiburtina, but not at Termini. The other, "Leonardo Express", is faster and more expensive (€9.50), running non-stop to Termini every half hour (6.37am–11.37pm). If the ticket office (which also sells Metro tickets) is not open, tackle the automatic ticket machine. Remember to specify which train you want when buying your ticket.

Ostiense is linked with Piramide Metro (Line B) where you can catch an underground train to the city centre from 5.30am until 11.30pm daily (to 12.30am Sat). It can be hard to find a taxi at Ostiense after 9pm, but there are buses (Nos. 95 and 30) to Piazza Venezia.

In addition, car rental is available from offices at the

Ciampino, a more basic airport used by most charter flights

The train linking Fiumicino airport to Stazione Termini

airport (see p379). Efforts have been made at Fiumicino to improve both the airport and the surrounding area. These developments include a raised pedestrian walkway for travelling between car parks, the railway station and various points within the airport, the expansion of Terminal A, and a four-star hotel near to the terminals.

Shuttle bus to car-hire lots at Fiumicino

CIAMPINO AIRPORT

THE OTHER AIRPORT that serves Rome is Ciampino, about 15 km (9 miles) south-east and used by the majority of charter flights. Major car hire firms have a rental office at the airport, though you may find it less harrowing to get into the city centre on public transport or by taxi.

The swiftest way to get to the centre of Rome from Ciampino is by Cotral bus to Anagnina Metro station, then by underground train to Termini. Tickets (€1) should be bought before-hand at the machines near the bus stop. A local bus service links the airport to Ciampino mainline station. If you take a taxi from the airport, be careful and only use official cabs. Make sure that the fare meter is switched on and showing only the minimum charge before you leave the airport.

Arriving in Rome

THIS MAP shows the main bus, rail and Metro links used by travellers arriving in Rome. The connections between Rome's two airports and the city centre are shown, as well as links between Rome and the rest of Italy and international rail routes from neighbouring European countries. Travel information, including details of journey times and service frequency, is listed separately in each box.

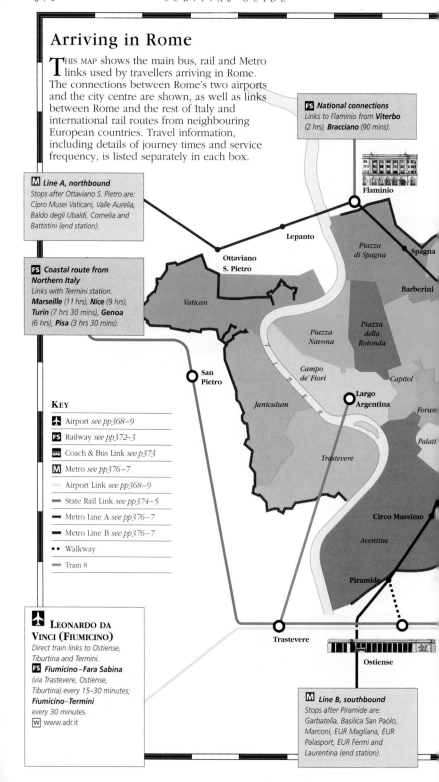

FS *National connections*
Links to Flaminio from **Viterbo**
(2 hrs), **Bracciano** *(90 mins).*

Flaminio

M *Line A, northbound*
Stops after Ottaviano S. Pietro are: Cipro Musei Vaticani, Valle Aurelia, Baldo degli Ubaldi, Cornelia and Battistini (end station).

Lepanto

Piazza di Spagna **Spagna**

Ottaviano S. Pietro

Barberini

FS *Coastal route from Northern Italy*
Links with Termini station.
Marseille *(11 hrs),* **Nice** *(9 hrs),*
Turin *(7 hrs 30 mins),* **Genoa**
(6 hrs), **Pisa** *(3 hrs 30 mins).*

Vatican

Piazza Navona

Piazza della Rotonda

Campo de' Fiori

Capitol

San Pietro

Janiculum

Largo Argentina

Forum

KEY

🛪 Airport *see pp368–9*

FS Railway *see pp372–3*

🚌 Coach & Bus Link *see p373*

M Metro *see pp376–7*

— Airport Link *see pp368–9*

— State Rail Link *see pp374–5*

— Metro Line A *see pp376–7*

— Metro Line B *see pp376–7*

•• Walkway

— Tram 8

Palati

Trastevere

Circo Massimo

Aventine

Piramide

🛪 **LEONARDO DA VINCI (FIUMICINO)**
Direct train links to Ostiense, Tiburtina and Termini.
FS *Fiumicino–Fara Sabina*
(via Trastevere, Ostiense, Tiburtina) every 15–30 minutes;
Fiumicino–Termini
every 30 minutes.
W www.adr.it

Trastevere

Ostiense

M *Line B, southbound*
Stops after Piramide are: Garbatella, Basilica San Paolo, Marconi, EUR Magliana, EUR Palasport, EUR Fermi and Laurentina (end station).

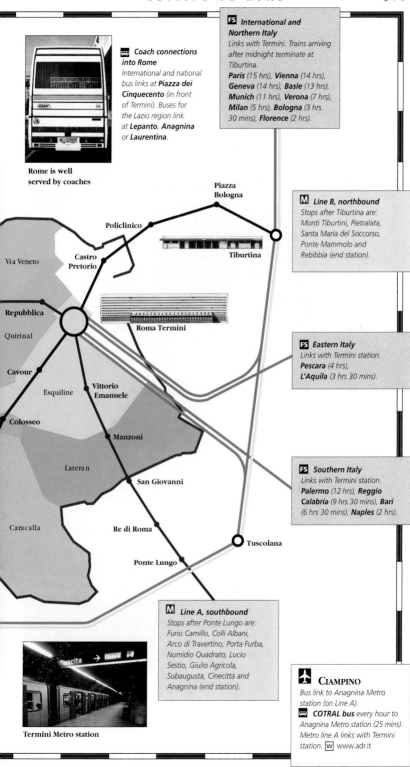

FS *International and Northern Italy*
Links with Termini. Trains arriving after midnight terminate at Tiburtina.
Paris *(15 hrs)*, **Vienna** *(14 hrs)*, **Geneva** *(14 hrs)*, **Basle** *(13 hrs)*, **Munich** *(11 hrs)*, **Verona** *(7 hrs)*, **Milan** *(5 hrs)*, **Bologna** *(3 hrs 30 mins)*, **Florence** *(2 hrs)*.

Coach connections into Rome
International and national bus links at **Piazza dei Cinquecento** *(in front of Termini)*. Buses for the Lazio region link at **Lepanto**, **Anagnina** or **Laurentina**.

Rome is well served by coaches

Piazza Bologna

M *Line B, northbound*
Stops after Tiburtina are: Monti Tiburtini, Pietralata, Santa Maria del Soccorso, Ponte Mammolo and Rebibbia (end station).

Policlinico

Via Veneto

Castro Pretorio

Tiburtina

Repubblica

Quirinal

Roma Termini

Cavour

FS *Eastern Italy*
Links with Termini station.
Pescara *(4 hrs)*, **L'Aquila** *(3 hrs 30 mins)*.

Esquiline

Vittorio Emanuele

Colosseo

Manzoni

Lateran

FS *Southern Italy*
Links with Termini station.
Palermo *(12 hrs)*, **Reggio Calabria** *(9 hrs 30 mins)*, **Bari** *(6 hrs 30 mins)*, **Naples** *(2 hrs)*.

San Giovanni

Caracalla

Re di Roma

Tuscolana

Ponte Lungo

M *Line A, southbound*
Stops after Ponte Lungo are: Furio Camillo, Colli Albani, Arco di Travertino, Porta Furba, Numidio Quadrato, Lucio Sestio, Giulio Agricola, Subaugusta, Cinecittà and Anagnina (end station).

✈ **CIAMPINO**
Bus link to Anagnina Metro station (on Line A).
COTRAL bus every hour to Anagnina Metro station (25 mins). Metro line A links with Termini station. **W** www.adr.it

Termini Metro station

Reaching Rome by Train, Coach or Car

A NY OVERLAND journey to Rome is fastest by train, though there are coach connections to most major European cities. Within Italy, journeys between large cities are usually also best done by train, but when travelling from towns which are not on the main Intercity rail routes, coaches can be quicker. For drivers, the Italian Automobile Club *(see p361)* provides free assistance and excellent maps to members of affiliated automobile clubs from all over the world.

The Eurostar – Italy's fastest train

The concourse at Stazione Termini

STAZIONE TERMINI

S TAZIONE TERMINI, Rome's main train station, is also the hub of the urban transport system. Beneath it is the only interchange between the city's two Metro lines, and outside, on Piazza dei Cinquecento, is the central bus terminus. Though it is one of Rome's most stunning 20th-century buildings, it also has unsavoury aspects, so don't linger longer than necessary at night.

If you do arrive late, aim to leave the neighbourhood as swiftly as you can. There are usually taxis (go to the official queue) even in the small hours, and many of the city's night buses start at Termini.

In summer the station gets very crowded, and you can expect long queues at ticket booths, bureaux de change and at both the transport and tourist information offices. There is a left luggage office, a police station where you should report anything lost or stolen on a train or in the station, and a small Citalia office where you can exchange money as well as get travel information. There is an international telephone office *(see p364)*, a bookshop, a post office and tobacconists (where you can buy bus and Metro tickets). Other facilities at the station include a bar and restaurant on the mezzanine floor with more eateries and shops on the lower, Termini Forum level. The new Multi-Service gallery near platform 1 has desks for car-hire firms as well as reduced train fare companies. Note, however, that there are no waiting rooms.

Of Rome's other stations, four are most likely to be of

FS logo

BINARIO 17
Platform sign

← uscita
Exit sign

interest to tourists. They are Ostiense and Trastevere, for trains to Fiumicino airport and Viterbo *(see p271)*; Tiburtina, for some of the late-night trains on the north-south line through Italy; and Roma Nord for trains to Prima Porta.

TRAVELLING BY TRAIN

I TALIAN STATE RAILWAYS (Ferrovie dello Stato or FS) have several levels of service, from Locale trains which stop at every station, to the Eurostar, a super-fast and extremely luxurious train, which offers first- and second-class service.

The Eurostar runs between Rome and Milan, Turin, Genoa, Bari, Naples and Venice. You have to reserve and you are charged hefty supplements for the privileges of speed, hostess service and free newspapers. You also pay a supplement on Intercity trains. These trains are for fast long-distance journeys and have both first- and second-class carriages. They run from Rome to Venice, Milan, Florence, Naples and other cities. You should book in high season

Termini, the heart of Italy's rail network and Rome's transport system

An international Eurocity train

and at weekends. Booking is obligatory on services that are marked in the timetable by a boxed R on a white background. Tickets for immediate travel can be bought at the station, but allow plenty of time to queue. From Rome you can also take international or Eurocity (EC) trains to destinations all over Europe. A useful website concerning Italian trains is www.trenitalia. com. Here you can check times and buy tickets

Ferrovie dello Stato
[C] 89 20 21.
[W] www.trenitalia.com

MACHINES FOR FS RAIL TICKETS

These machines are easy to use, and most have instructions on screen in a choice of six languages. They accept coins, notes and credit cards.

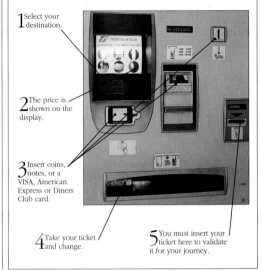

1 Select your destination.

2 The price is shown on the display.

3 Insert coins, notes, or a VISA, American Express or Diners Club card.

4 Take your ticket and change.

5 You must insert your ticket here to validate it for your journey.

COACH TRAVEL

Most regional and long-distance coaches are blue

LONG-DISTANCE coaches terminate at Tiburtina, which is the city's main coach station. Information and tickets for Eurolines coaches to European cities are available from **Lazzi Express**. The **Appian Line** offers regular services within Italy. Its itineraries include Florence, Naples, Capri, Sorrento and Pompei, and, in summer, Venice and Assisi. Local buses, serving villages and towns within the Lazio region, are run **COTRAL**. All bus stations used by COTRAL are linked to Metro

stations. Tickets are bought on the spot and cannot be booked in advance. Some day trips from Rome by bus are described on pages 268–71.

Appian Line
Piazza dell'Esquilino 6–7.
Map 6 D4. [C] 06-48 78 61.

Lazzi Express
Via Tagliamento 27B.
[C] 06-884 08 40.

COTRAL
[C] 800 150 008.

TRAVELLING BY CAR

TO DRIVE YOUR own car in Italy you need an international Green Card (for insurance purposes) and the vehicle registration document. A translation of your driving licence, available at Italian tourist offices abroad, is also

Blue signs showing A roads and green signs showing motorways

useful. Wearing seatbelts is compulsory in Italy. You must also carry a warning triangle in case of breakdown. Main routes to Rome connect with the Grande Raccordo Anulare (GRA), Rome's ring-road.

Tolls are charged on all Italian motorways. You can buy magnetic motorway toll cards from motoring organizations before entering Italy.

Eurolines coach running between Rome and the rest of Europe

GETTING AROUND ROME

ROME'S CENTRE is compact and, even though walking absolutely everywhere would be over-ambitious, it is a city in which you can spend much of your time on foot. As the main streets in the centre are usually clogged with traffic, driving and cycling cannot be recommended, but courageous motorbike or scooter riders can have great fun buzzing

Crash helmets, compulsory on all motorcycles and scooters

around on a rented Vespa. Travelling by bus and tram can be very slow, so use overland public transport only when you have a long way to go. The Metro, designed to connect the suburbs with the centre, has no stops in the historic city centre near the Pantheon or Piazza Navona, though it is certainly the swiftest way of crossing the city.

WALKING

WANDERING through Rome's old centre is one of the most enjoyable aspects of being in the city. You can take in the architectural details, absorb the streetlife, make diversions at will, and peek into any church, shop or bar that catches your interest. And you can easily visit, or at least see, several of the main tourist sights in a few hours. The Colosseum, for example, is only about 2.5 km (1.5 miles) from the Spanish Steps. Your route could pass by the Forum, Piazza Venezia and several churches; other sights, such as the Trevi Fountain, the Galleria Doria Pamphilj and the Pantheon, are just a short detour away.

Explore the city area by area, using public transport when distances are too far.

Directions for walkers

Although some parts of the historic centre are now pedestrianized, a street which is closed to cars may still be used by cyclists and scooter riders. There have been many plans to create more traffic-free zones, and even to ban anything on wheels from some parts of the city – but imposing such measures on a population as insubordinate as Rome's is not easily done.

If you find the summer heat hard to bear, remember that the narrow cobbled streets get little sunlight and remain relatively cool, while walking into an open piazza can be like stepping into a furnace.

During the height of summer, you'll have a more enjoyable time if you follow the example of the Italians. Walk slowly on the shady side of the street; have a long lunch followed by a siesta in the hottest part of the day. You can continue exploring in the late afternoon, when churches and shops reopen and the streets are at their liveliest. Wandering at night is worthwhile, as the streets are cool and many façades floodlit.

Pedestrian crossing: only slightly safer than the open road

CROSSING ROADS

FIRST IMPRESSIONS suggest there can be only two sorts of pedestrian in Rome: the quick and the dead. Even if you cross roads by sets of traffic lights and pedestrian crossings strictly in your favour, there is sure to be some van or Vespa hurtling towards you with apparently homicidal intent. Fortunately, Roman drivers have quick reactions. The pious would attribute this to the protection of Santa Francesca Romana (*see p87*), cynics to the fact that according to Italian insurance law, drivers are responsible for any road accident. Whatever the inspiration, accidents are quite rare. The best tactic is to be as alert and confident

Avanti: go! Pedestrians have right of way

Alt: stop! Traffic has right of way

Pedestrian crossing

Watch out for children

as Romans. The roads are very busy. When crossing, try to leave as large a gap as possible between yourself and oncoming traffic. Step purposefully into the road, facing approaching motorists with a determined glare. The trick now is to keep going steadily: do not hesitate, or change your course, and do not run. As long as a driver can see you, he or she should stop, or at least swerve, albeit at the last moment.

Pedestrians and drivers must both take particular care at night, when the traffic lights are switched to a constantly flashing amber, turning the crossings into free-for-alls.

STREET SIGNS

THEORETICALLY, although it may not always seem to be the case, pedestrians have right of way at crossings when the green *avanti* sign is lit up. The red sign *alt* means you must wait. Underground crossings are indicated by a sign reading *sottopassaggio*.

It is easy to get lost in the maze of streets and piazzas that comprise the historic centre. Until you know your way around you can follow the yellow signs marking routes between the sights and piazzas of particular interest to tourists. Routes leading to general landmarks are indicated by signs on a brown or grey background.

No stopping

continua
No parking

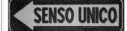
One-way street

strada senza uscita
No through road

DRIVING

DRIVING IN CENTRAL Rome can be an extremely intimidating experience for visitors. The flamboyant aggression of Italian drivers is notorious, pedestrians step out into the roads without warning, and the one-way system operating in much of the centre makes retaining a sense of direction impossible. You'll also find motorists overtaking on the wrong side,

Directions to parking areas

while scooters and Vespas zoom among the lanes of traffic and go the wrong way down one-way streets. One rule to remember is to give way to the right. Unless you are accustomed to driving in Italian cities, leave your car at home – or, failing that, in a guarded car park.

Car thefts are rife in Rome, so never leave anything of value in your car, even out of sight: areas such as Campo de' Fiori are patrolled by gangs on the lookout for anyone leaving cameras, fur coats and other costly items in their boots. You should also remove your car radio – you won't be the only person carrying one into a bar, restaurant or disco.

Take extra care if driving late at night. Not only do traffic lights switch to flashing amber, but many Italians are astonishingly cavalier about driving under the influence of drink or drugs.

PARKING

THE MOST convenient car park is below the Villa Borghese. Much of the city centre is reserved for residents with permits but there are around 2,000 metered parking spaces (from 8am–8pm). If you do find a legal place to park, however, you may return and find that you have been hemmed in by double-parked cars. Locations of some of the most useful car parks are listed on page 379.

PETROL

PETROL IS very expensive. It can be bought from roadside petrol pumps (many of which are self-service, operated by banknotes or credit cards), as well as from regular garages. Check whether your car uses lead-free petrol *(benzina senza piombo* or *benzina verde)* or not. Late-night petrol stations are listed on page 379.

Agip
The state petrol company logo

ILLEGAL PARKING

Rome's traffic police are vigilant. If you've parked illegally, your car may be clamped or (if it's causing an obstruction) towed away, so phone 06-67 691 to check before reporting it stolen. No-parking zones should be clearly marked, but look carefully, in case the sign is hidden by a tree.

zona rimozione fermata consentita per salita e discesa con conducente a bordo
Signpost for a tow away area *(zona rimozione)*

A tow truck at work

Travelling by Bus, Tram and Metro

Rome's public transport system is cheap in comparison with the rest of Europe, and it is as efficient as the busy streets allow. Priests, nuns, tourists, pilgrims, businessmen and pickpockets all pile aboard, transforming the buses and trams into mobile saunas during the summer. The system embraces the entire city, but short distances are better covered on foot, because heavy traffic often blocks the roads. Getting off at the right stop can be difficult, but other passengers will usually help if you ask for directions. Always keep a tight hold on your valuables.

Rome–Gubbio bus

BUSES AND TRAMS

Rome's public bus and tram company is called **ATAC** (Azienda Tramvie e Autobus del Comune di Roma). Scores of buses and several trams cover most parts of the city. They run from early morning until about midnight. There are also a few night buses.

Apart from a few electric minibuses (116, 117, 119), no buses can run through the narrow streets of the historic centre. But there are plenty of bus routes to take you within a short walk of the main sights *(see inside back cover)*.

Bus stops list the details of routes taken by all buses using that stop. Night buses are marked with a blue owl on the bus stop.

FERMATA

Bus stop listing details of routes served

SPECIAL BUS SERVICES

There are two bus services designed especially for tourists; the 110 and the Archeobus service. The 110, a red, open-topped double-

decker, passes many of the city's tourist attractions and leaves from Piazza dei Cinquecento every half-hour between 10am and 6pm. Linking the city centre with the catacombs and the monuments on the Via Appia Antica, the Archeobus leaves Piazza Venezia on the hour between 10am and 4pm.

USING BUSES AND TRAMS

The main terminus is on Piazza dei Cinquecento outside Termini station, but there are other major route hubs throughout the city, most usefully those at Piazza del Risorgimento, Piazza San Silvestro and Piazza Venezia. Information on public transport can be obtained from ATAC kiosks, the customer service office or the ATAC website. Tickets can be purchased from automatic machines at main bus stops and at Metro and train stations, newsagents and tobacconists. Note that you can't buy tickets on the bus itself.

In the day, you should board the bus at the back. There will be an orange machine there to time-stamp your ticket, or a yellow equivalent that automatically cancels the new electronic tickets. Timed tickets, *biglietto integrato a tempo* (BIT), can be used on all means of transport. Free transport maps can be found at the Via Volturno office.

INFORMATION

ATAC
Piazza dei Cinquecento. **Map** 6 D3.
📞 800-43 1784. W www.atac.roma.it
Open 8am–8pm Mon–Sat.

Customer Service
Via Volturno 59. **Map** 6 D3. *Open 9am–1pm Mon–Fri (also 2.30–5pm Tue & Thu).*

TICKETS

Tickets for city buses, trams and Metros have to be bought before you travel and stamped in the appropriate machine as soon as you start your journey. You can buy tickets at bars, news-stands and tobacconists, as well as at Metro stations and bus termini. Look out for places displaying ATAC (for bus, Metro and tram) and FS (train) stickers. There are also automatic ticket machines at main bus stops and train and Metro stations that take coins, though it is wise to have the exact amount of change.

BIT tickets are valid for 75 minutes, during which time you can take one Metro ride and hop on and off as many buses and trams as you like. If you are going to make four or more journeys in one day, it is worth buying a *biglietto*

A modern tram taking passengers through the city

One of Rome's red and grey ATAC buses

integrato giornaliero (BIG) ticket. These give you a day's travel on the buses, trams and the Metro. To travel further afield in Lazio, consider buying a regional BIRG ticket. There are also three-day, seven-day and monthly (calendar month) passes that are valid for the whole transport system, with discounts for students and people over 65. Fare-dodging is common, but incurs a hefty on-the-spot fine.

METROPOLITANA

ROME'S underground system, the Metropolitana, has two lines (A and B) which cross the city in a rough X-shape, converging at Termini station *(see inside back cover and pp370–71).* Line A (red) leads from Battistini in the west to Anagnina in the southeast

Metro logo

of the city, from where buses go to Ciampino airport. Line B (blue) runs from Rebibbia in the northeast, down to EUR in the southwest, where buses leave for the coast. Stations are clearly marked by the Metro logo, a large white M on a red background.

The system was designed to ferry commuters in from the suburbs, so is not very useful within the centre, but the Metro is a fairly speedy way of crossing the city. Among the most useful stations are Colosseo, Spagna, San Giovanni, Ottaviano S. Pietro and Piramide (for trains to Fiumicino). Both metro lines run from 5.30am until 11.30pm every day (to 12.30am Saturday). For more information, visit the official website (www.metroroma.it).

USEFUL BUS AND TRAM ROUTES

This map shows some of the buses that go through interesting parts of Rome with good views of major sights. The 40 Express and 64 are always full of tourists, since they go from Termini to St Peter's and the Vatican. The other routes are likely to be less crowded. The 3 tram follows a long leisurely route around the southeast of the city, while bus 23 goes along the Tiber.

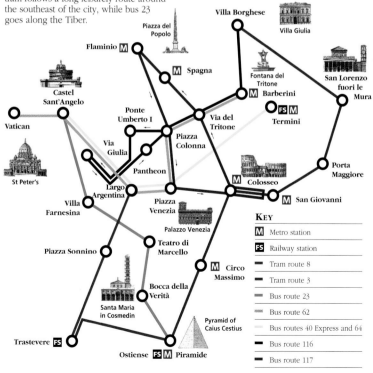

KEY

M	Metro station
FS	Railway station
	Tram route 8
	Tram route 3
	Bus route 23
	Bus route 62
	Bus routes 40 Express and 64
	Bus route 116
	Bus route 117

STREET FINDER

MAP REFERENCES given with sights, restaurants, hotels, shops and entertainment venues refer to the maps in this section *(see* How the Map References Work *opposite)*. A complete index of the street names and places of interest marked on the maps follows on pages 382–91. The key map below shows the area of Rome covered by the *Street Finder*. This includes the sightseeing areas (which are colour-coded) as well as the whole of central Rome with all the districts important for restaurants, hotels and entertainment venues. Because the historic centre is so packed with sights, there is a large-scale map of this area on pages 11 and 12.

HOW THE MAP REFERENCES WORK

The first figure tells you which Street Finder map to turn to.

Trevi Fountain ➐

Fontana di Trevi. **Map** 5 A3 & 12 F2. 🚌 52, 53, 61, 62, 63, 71, 80, 95, 116, 119.

The letter and number are a grid reference. You will find the letters at the top and bottom of the map and the numbers at the sides.

The second reference refers to the large-scale maps of central Rome (11 & 12). It is read in exactly the same way as the first.

The map continues on map 8 of the Street Finder.

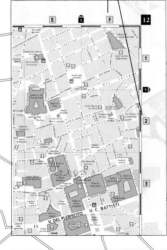

The key to the abbreviations used in the Street Finder is on page 382.

KEY TO STREET FINDER

🟫	Major sight
🟦	Places of interest
🟪	Railway station
M	Metro station
🚌	Bus terminus
🚊	Tram terminus
P	Main car parks
🛈	Tourist information office
✚	Hospital with casualty unit
🚓	Police station
✝	Church
✡	Synagogue
⊠	Post office
═	Railway line
←	One-way street
═	Steps
▬▬	City wall

SCALE OF MAPS 1–10

0 metres	250	
		1:13,000
0 yards	250	

SCALE OF MAPS 11 & 12

0 metres	150	
		1:8,000
0 yards	150	

Street Finder Index

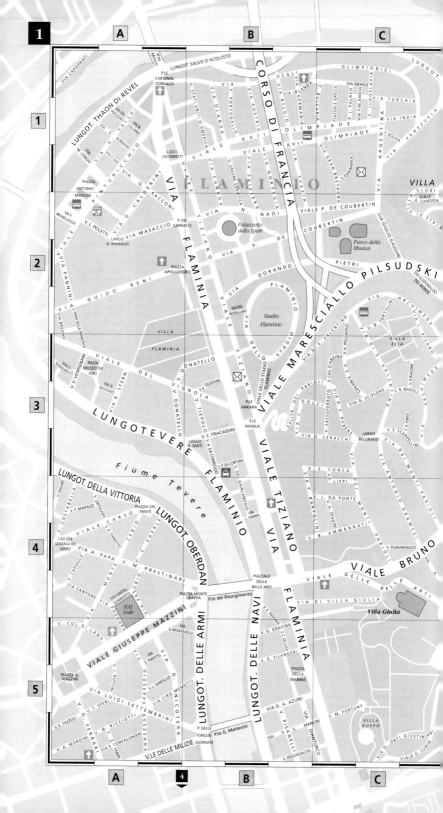

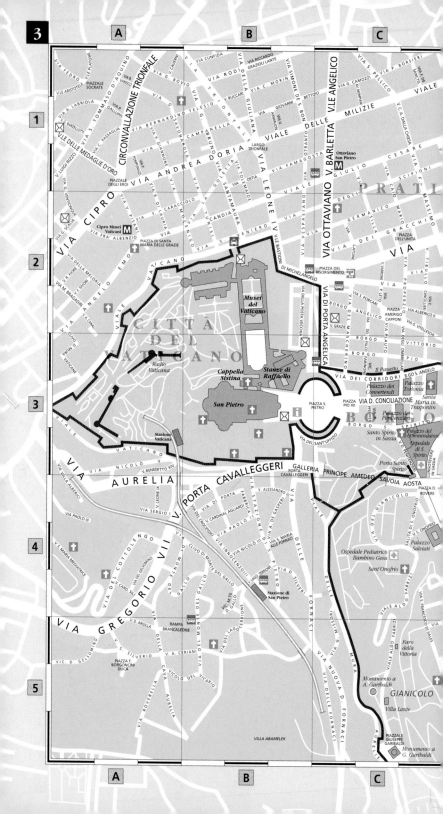

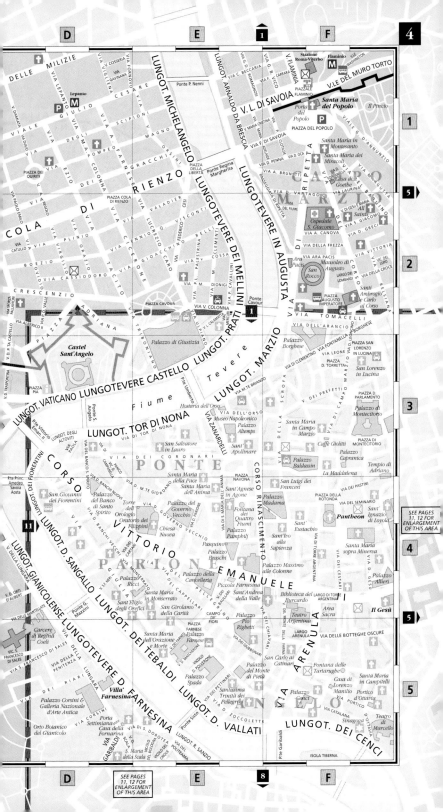

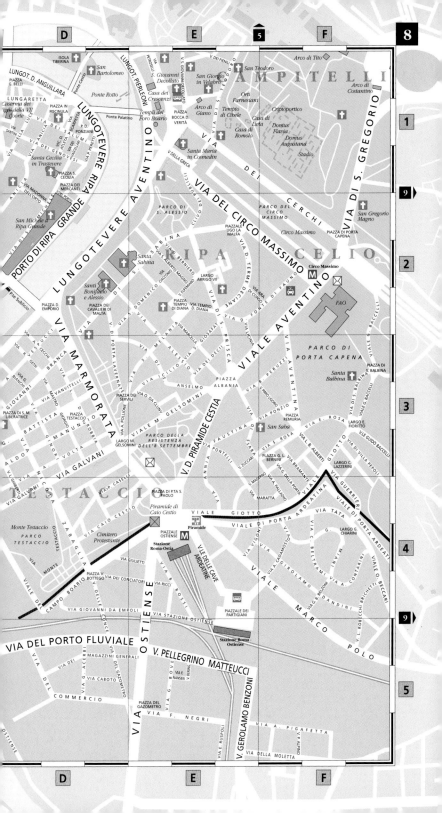

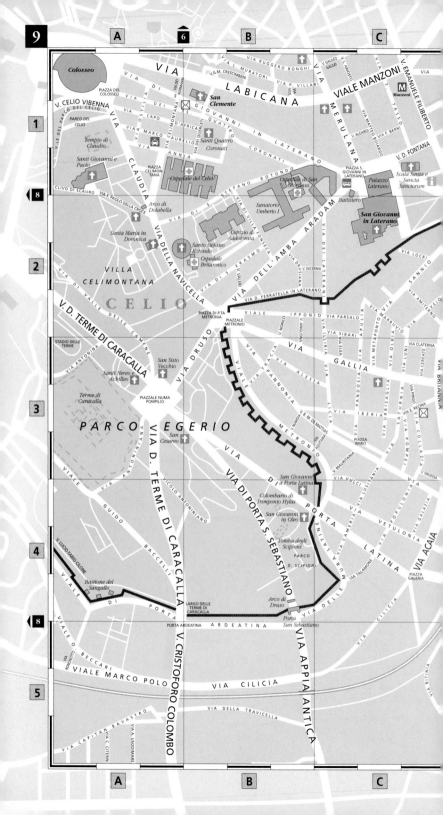

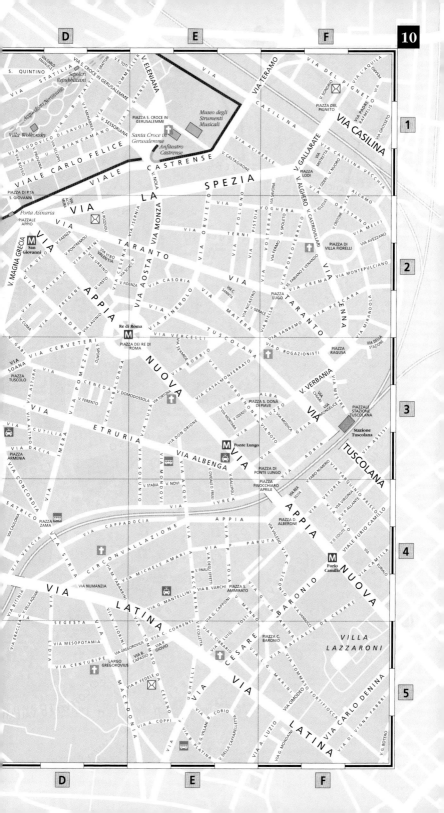

General Index

Acknowledgments

DORLING KINDERSLEY would like to thank the following people whose contributions and assistance have made the preparation of this book possible.

MAIN CONTRIBUTORS

Olivia Ercoli is an art historian and tour guide, who has lived all her life in Rome. Bilingual in English and Italian, she lectures on art history and writes on a range of subjects for English and Italian publications.

Travel writer Ros Belford conceived the idea of the Virago Woman's Guides, of which she is now series editor, and wrote the *Virago Woman's Guide to Rome*. She has travelled widely in Europe and as well as writing guide books contributes to a variety of publications including *The Guardian*.

Roberta Mitchell heads the editorial section of the UN's Publishing Division in Rome, where she has lived for many years. An experienced writer and editor with extensive knowledge of the city, she has contributed to a number of guides to Rome including the *American Express Guide to Rome*.

CONTRIBUTORS

Sam Cole, Mary Jane Cryan Pancani, Daphne Wilson Ercoli, Laura Ercoli, Lindsay Hunt, Adrian James, Christopher McDowall, Davina Palmer, Rodney Palmer, Debra Shipley.

DORLING KINDERSLEY wishes to thank the following editors and researchers at Websters International Publishers: Sandy Carr, Matthew Barrell, Siobhan Bremner, Serena Cross, Valeria Fabbri, Annie Galpin, Gemma Hancock, Celia Woolfrey.

ADDITIONAL PHOTOGRAPHY

Max Alexander, Foto Carfagna + Associati, Demetrio Carrasco, Andy Crawford, Philip Enticknap, Steve Gorton, John Heseltine, Neil Mersh, Poppy, David Sutherland, Martin Woodward.

ADDITIONAL ILLUSTRATIONS

Anne Bowes, Robin Carter, Gillie Newman, Chris D Orr.

ADDITIONAL PICTURE RESEARCH

Sharon Buckley.

CARTOGRAPHY

Advanced Illustration (Cheshire), Contour Publishing (Derby), Euromap Limited (Berkshire). Street Finder maps: ERA Maptec Ltd (Dublin) adapted with permission from original survey and mapping from Shobunsha (Japan).

CARTOGRAPHIC RESEARCH

James Anderson, Donna Rispoli, Joan Russell.

RESEARCH ASSISTANCE

Janet Abbott, Flaminia Allvin, Fabrizio Ardito, Licia Bronzin, Lupus Sabene.

DESIGN AND EDITORIAL ASSISTANCE

Kristin Dolina-Adamczyk, Peter Bently, Hilary Bird, Lucinda Cooke, Michelle Crane, Vanessa Courtier, Claire Edwards, Jon Eldan, Simon Farbrother, Vanessa Hamilton, Marcus Hardy, Sasha Heseltine, Sally Ann Hibbard, Paul Hines, Stephanie Jackson, Steve Knowlden, Mary Lambert, Maite Lantaron, Janette Leung, Jane Middleton, Ian Midson, Fiona Morgan, Helen Partington, Naomi Peck, Carolyn Pyrah, Salim Qurashi, Sands Publishing Solutions, Jane Shaw, Clare Sullivan, Rachel Symons, Andrew Szudek, Daphne Trotter, Karen Villabona, Diana Vowles, Lynda Warrington, Stewart J. Wild.

SPECIAL ASSISTANCE

Dottore Riccardo Baldini, Signor Mario di Bartolomeo of the Soprintendenza dei Beni Artistici e Storici di Roma, Belloni, Dorling Kindersley picture department, Peter Douglas, David Gleave MW, Debbie Harris, Emma Hutton and Cooling Brown Partnership, Marina Tavolato, Dottoressa Todaro and Signora Camimiti at the Ministero dell'Interno, Trestini.

PHOTOGRAPHY PERMISSIONS

DORLING KINDERSLEY would like to thank the following for their kind permission to photograph at their establishments: Bathsheba Abse at the Keats-Shelley Memorial House, Accademia dei Lincei, Accanto, Aeroporti di Roma, Aldrovandi Palace, Alpheus, Banco di Santo Spirito at Palazzo del Monte di Pietà, Rory Bruck at Babington's, Caffè Giolitti, Caffè Latino, Comune di Roma (Ripartizione X), Comunità Ebraica di Roma, Guido Cornini at Monumenti Musei e Gallerie Pontificie, Direzione Sanitaria Ospedale di Santo Spirito, Dottoressa Laura Falsini at the Soprintendenza Archeologica di Etruria Meridionale, Hotel Gregoriana, Hotel

Majestic, Hotel Regina Baglioni, Marco Marchetti at Ente EUR, Dottoressa Mercalli at the Museo Nazionale di Castel Sant'Angelo, Ministero dell'Interno, Plaza Minerva, Ristorante Alberto Ciarla, Ristorante Filetti di Baccalà, Ristorante Romolo, Signor Rulli and Signor Angeli at the Soprintendenza Archeologica di Roma, Soprintendenza Archeologica per il Lazio, Soprintendenza per i Beni Ambientali e Architettonici, Soprintendenza per i Beni Artistici e Storici di Roma, Daniela Tabo at the Musei Capitolini, Villa d'Este, Villa San Pio, Mrs Marjorie Weeke at St Peter's.

PICTURE CREDITS

t = top; tl = top left; tc = top centre;
tr = top right; cla = centre left above;
ca = centre above; cra = centre right above;
cl = centre left; c = centre; cr = centre right;
clb = centre left below; cb = centre below;
crb = centre right below; bl = bottom left;
b = bottom; bc = bottom centre;
br = bottom right.

Every effort has been made to trace the copyright holders and we apologize for any unintentional omissions. We would be pleased to insert the appropriate acknowledgments in any subsequent edition of this publication.

Works of art have been reproduced with the permission of the following copyright holders: © DACS: Città con Cattedrale Gotica, 1925 by Paul Klee 241b.

The publishers are grateful to the following individuals, companies and picture libraries for permission to reproduce their photographs:

ACCADEMIA NAZIONALE DI SAN LUCA, Rome: 160b; AFE: 57b, 61cr; Sandro Battaglia 59c, 61clb, 61br, 324br; Louise Goldman 157t; G La Malfa 251t; AEROPORTI DI ROMA: 368b; AGENZIA SINTESI: Fabio Fiorani 360br, 361t, 361b; Antonella di Girolamo 361c; Marco Marcotulli 360bc; R Venturi 360bl; AGF FOTO: 38–39c; ALDROVANDI PALACE HOTEL: 291b; ALITALIA: 368t, 369cl; ALLSPORT: David Cannon 39br; ANCIENT ART AND ARCHITECTURE: 16bl, 20tl, 21tl, 25bc, 34crb, 35tc, 44cl; ARTOTHEK, Städelsches Kunstinstitut Frankfurt, Goethe in the Roman Campagna by JHW Tischbein 136t.

BIBLIOTECA REALE, Torino: 28–29c; BRIDGEMAN ART LIBRARY, LONDON/NEW YORK: 18br, 37tr;

Agnew & Sons, London 51tr; Antikenmuseum Staatliches Museum, Berlin 19bl; Biblioteca Publica Episcopal, Barcelona/Index 114bl; Bibliothèque da la Sorbonne 28c, British Museum, London 27ctr; Château de Versailles, France/Giraudon 33tr, 54cl; Christie's, London 40, 55tr, 68b, 95t; The Fine Art Society, London 151tr, 279tl; Galleria degli Uffizi, Florence 31bl; Greek Museum, University of Newcastle-upon-Tyne 16br; King Street Galleries, London 33br; Louvre, Paris/Lauros-Giraudon 56br; Louvre, Paris/Giraudon 26br; Roy Miles Gallery, 29 Bruton St, London 228t; Musée des Beaux-Arts, Nantes 53t; Museo e Gallerie Nazionali di Capodimonte, Naples, Detail from the predella of San Ludovico by Simone Martini 26tr; Musée Condé, Chantilly f.71v Très Riches Heures, 26tc; Museum of Fine Arts, Budapest 110bl; Museo Archeologico di Villa Giulia 48cl; Museo Poldi Pezzoli, Milan 54tr; Palazzo Doria Pamphilj, Rome 107b; Piacenza Town Hall, Italy/Index 27br; Private Collection 19br, 22bl, 24br, 27tr, 178b; Pushkin Museum, Moscow 111t; Sotheby's, London 18bl; Vatican Museums & Galleries 41ca, 237tr.

CAPITOLINE MUSEUMS, ROME: 73cra; CEPHAS PICTURE LIBRARY: Mick Rock 306tr; VANESSA COURTIER: 355t.

IL DAGHERROTIPO: 118clb, 145cra,322t, 323bl, 366br, 372cla, 377t; Stefano Chieppa 152cl, 378b; Museo di Roma/Giorgio Oddi 118b; Stephano Occhibelli 12c, 116; Giorgio Oddi 53cl; Paolo Priori 204tr; Giovanni Rinaldi 196tr, 374t; CM DIXON: 17bl, 24c, 268b, 269t, 269b.

ECOLE NATIONALE SUPERIEURE DES BEAUX-ARTS: 21cr, 22–23, 248t, 284–285b; ENTE NAZIONALE ITALIANO PER IL TURISMO: 358cl, cr; ET ARCHIVE: 14, 17tr, 17clb, 18tr, 19tc, 23t, 27cl, 28tl, 31br, 32br, 37br, 48tl, 306tl; MARY EVANS PICTURE LIBRARY: 9, 18cl, 23cl, 24cl, 29br, 30cb, 30b, 31t, 34tl, 34cr, 34bl, 54tl, 56tl, 67bl, 74t, 81b, 91t, 92b, 94bl, 127c, 135t, 213b.

CORALDO FALSINI: 39tl, 340b, 341t, 341c; FERROVIE DELLO STATO: 372clb, 373tr; WERNER FORMAN ARCHIVE: 17cr, 20bl, 22tl, 23cr, 23bl, 23br, 47tr, 155t, 163tr, 175c; FOLKLORE MUSEUM, Rome: 210br.

GARDEN PICTURE LIBRARY: Bob Challinor 172cb; GIRAUDON: 15b, 28br, 36br, 55tl; JACKIE GORDON: 364bl; RONALD GRANT: 52br, 340t.

SONIA HALLIDAY: 19c, 22br, 25cl; Laura Lushington 24bl; ROBERT HARDING PICTURE LIBRARY: 23cra, 32bl, 79cr, 177t, 268c, 353c; Mario Carrieri 35tr; Caffè Greco, Rome by Ludwig Passini 309tr; John G Ross 38tl, 59cl, 341b; Sheila Terry 39cl; G White 59br; MICHAEL HOLFORD: 70b; HULTON DEUTSCH: 36tl, 38bc, 57cr, 63, 175b, 287c, 357c.

KATZ/FSP: 19tr, 25bl, 26bc, 31cl, 54bc, 55tc, 56cl, 57cl, 75cl, 75cr, 78tc, 93b, 112c, 122t, 125tr, 126tl, 132br, 133cr, 136bl, 139bl, 139br, 162tr, 172bl, 172br, 183br, 192bl, 196c, 210c, 220bl, 227cr, 229cr; Alinari 80br, 141bl, 174t, 254b; Anderson 78cr, 138bl, 163tl, 228b.

MAGNUM: Erich Lessing 15t, 17tl, 89br; MARKA: V Arcomano 33cr; Roberto Benzi 325crb; Piranha 325cra; Lorenzo Sechi 224br; MORO ROMA: 36cl, 37cl, 38br, 39tr, 39bl.

NATIONAL PORTRAIT GALLERY, London: 55cr, 55b, 56tr, 57tr; GRAZIA NERI: Vision/Anna Caltabiano 358b; Vision/Giorgio Casulich 112br, 156br, 325crc; Vision/Roberta Krasnig 124tr, 283t; © NIPPON TELEVISION NETWORK CORPORATION, Tokyo 1999: 244b and all pictures on 246-7.

LA REPUBBLICA TROVAROMA: 359tl; REX FEATURES: Steve Wood 39cr.

SCALA GROUP S.P.A: 94t, 125tl, 278cl, Casa di Augusto 97t, Chiesa del Gesù 115t, Galleria Borghese 32cla, 260tr, Galleria Colonna 157b, Galleria Doria Pamphilj 46br, 105cr, Galleria Spada 46cl, Galleria degli Uffizi 16–17, 27bl, Museo d'Arte Orientale 174t, 174br, Musei Capitolini 47bl, Museo della Civiltà Romana 48tr, 48b, Museo delle Terme 21tr, Museo Napoleonico 49cr, Museo Nazionale, Napoli 21cl, Museo Nazionale, Ravenna 22cl, Museo del Risorgimento, Milano 36clb, 36–37c, Museo del Risorgimento, Roma 37tl, Museo di San Marco 54bl, Palazzo Barberini 253bl, Palazzo Ducale 8, 19tr, Palazzo della Farnesina 220ct, Palazzo Madama 20cl, Palazzo Venezia 47cr, 66bl, San Carlo alle Quattro Fontane 33cl, Santa Cecilia in Trastevere 32tl, San Clemente 35bl, Santa Costanza 24–25c, Santa Maria Antiqua 24tl, Santa Maria dell'Anima 121t, Santa Maria Maggiore 43tr, Santa Maria del Popolo 139tr, 139c, Santa Prassede 26bl, 28bl, Santa Sabina 25tc, 29cl, Vatican Museums 19bc, 25t, 25cr, 25cra, 27cr, 29tl, 29cr, 30tl, 30ct, 31cr, 31bc, 32cr, 32clb, 41tr, 46tl, 48cr, 49bl, 224bl, 225cr, 235t, 238tl, 238br, 240t, 240b, 241t, 241c, 241b, 242tl, 242c, 242b, 243t, 243c, 243b, 245 (all 4).

TONY STONE IMAGES: Richard Passmore 1c; TOPHAM PICTURE SOURCE: 38cl.

ZEFA: 2, 230cl, 231br, 356–7, 358t, 372t; Eric Carle 58t; Kohlhas 231t.

Thanks also to Dottoressa Giulia De Marchi of L'ACCADEMIA NAZIONALE DI SAN LUCA, Rome for 160b, Rettore Padre Libianchi of LA CHIESA DI SANT'IGNAZIO DI LOYOLA for 106t, ENTE NAZIONALE PER IL TURISMO, HASSLER HOTEL, Rome for 293tl, GRAND HOTEL, Rome for 293crb and to LA REPUBBLICA TROVAROMA.

JACKET
Front - DK PICTURE LIBRARY: John Heseltine bc, crb; GETTY IMAGES: Glen Allison clb; PICTURES COLOUR LIBRARY: main image. Back - DK PICTURE LIBRARY: t, b. Spine - PICTURES COLOUR LIBRARY.

All other images © Dorling Kindersley.
For further information see: www.dkimages.com

DORLING KINDERSLEY SPECIAL EDITIONS

Dorling Kindersley books can be purchased in bulk quantities at discounted prices for use in promotions or as premiums. We are also able to offer special editions and personalized jackets, corporate imprints, and excerpts from all of our books, tailored specifically to meet your own needs.

To find out more, please contact: (in the United Kingdom) – Sarah.Burgess@dk.com or SPECIAL SALES, DORLING KINDERSLEY LIMITED, 80 STRAND, LONDON WC2R 0RL;

(in the United States) – SPECIAL MARKETS DEPARTMENT, DK PUBLISHING, INC., 375 HUDSON STREET, NEW YORK, NY 10014.

Phrase Book

In Emergency

Help!	**Aiuto!**	*eye-yoo-toh*
Stop!	**Fermate!**	*fair-mah-teh*
Call a doctor	**Chiama un medico**	*kee-ah-mah oon meh-dee-koh*
Call an ambulance	**Chiama un' ambulanza**	*kee-ah-mah oon am-boo-lan-tsa*
Call the police	**Chiama la polizia**	*kee-ah-mah ee pol-ee-tsee-ah*
Call the fire brigade	**Chiama i pompieri**	*kee-ah-mah ee pom-pee-air-ee*
Where is the telephone?	**Dov'è il telefono?**	*dov-eh eel teh-leh-foh-noh?*
The nearest hospital?	**L'ospedale più vicino?**	*loss-peh-dah-leh pee-oovee-chee-noh?*

Communication Essentials

Yes/No	**Sì/No**	*see/noh*
Please	**Per favore**	*pair fah-vor-eh*
Thank you	**Grazie**	*grah-tsee-eh*
Excuse me	**Mi scusi**	*mee skoo-zee*
Hello	**Buon giorno**	*bwon jor-noh*
Good bye	**Arrivederci**	*ah-ree-veh-dair-chee*
Good evening	**Buona sera**	*bwon-ah sair-ah*
morning	**la mattina**	*lah mat-tee-nah*
afternoon	**il pomeriggio**	*eel poh-meh-ree-joh*
evening	**la sera**	*lah sair-ah*
yesterday	**ieri**	*ee-air-ee*
today	**oggi**	*oh-jee*
tomorrow	**domani**	*doh-mah-nee*
here	**qui**	*kwee*
there	**la**	*lah*
What?	**Quale?**	*kwah-leh?*
When?	**Quando?**	*kwan-doh?*
Why?	**Perchè?**	*pair-keh?*
Where?	**Dove?**	*doh-veh*

Useful Phrases

How are you?	**Come sta?**	*koh-meh stah?*
Very well, thank you.	**Molto bene, grazie.**	*moll-toh beh-neh grah-tsee-eh*
Pleased to meet you.	**Piacere di conoscerla.**	*pee-ah-chair-eh dee cob-noh-shair-lah*
See you soon.	**A più tardi.**	*ah pee-oo tar-dee*
That's fine.	**Va bene.**	*va beh-neh*
Where is/are ...?	**Dov'è/Dove sono ...?**	*dov-eh/doveh soh-noh?*
How long does it take to get to ...?	**Quanto tempo ci vuole per andare a ...?**	*kwan-toh tem-poh chee voo-oh-leh pair an-dar-eh ah...?*
How do I get to ...?	**Come faccio per arrivare a ...?**	*koh-meh fah-choh pair arri-var-eh ah...?*
Do you speak English?	**Parla inglese?**	*par-lah een-gleh-zeh?*
I don't understand.	**Non capisco.**	*non ka-pee-skoh*
Could you speak more slowly, please?	**Può parlare più lentamente, per favore?**	*pwoh par-lah-reh pee-oo len-ta-men-teh pair fah-vor-eh?*
I'm sorry.	**Mi dispiace.**	*mee dee-spee-ah-cheh*

Useful Words

big	**grande**	*gran-deh*
small	**piccolo**	*pee-koh-loh*
hot	**caldo**	*kal-doh*
cold	**freddo**	*fred-doh*
good	**buono**	*bwoh-noh*
bad	**cattivo**	*kat-tee-voh*
enough	**basta**	*bas-tah*
well	**bene**	*beh-neh*
open	**aperto**	*ah-pair-toh*
closed	**chiuso**	*kee-oo-zoh*
left	**a sinistra**	*ah see-nee-strah*
right	**a destra**	*ah dess-trah*
straight on	**sempre dritto**	*sem-preh dree-toh*
near	**vicino**	*vee-chee-noh*
far	**lontano**	*lon-tah-noh*
up	**su**	*soo*
down	**giù**	*joo*
early	**presto**	*press-toh*
late	**tardi**	*tar-dee*
entrance	**entrata**	*en-trah-tah*
exit	**uscita**	*oo-shee-ta*
toilet	**il gabinetto**	*eel gah-bee-net-toh*
free, unoccupied	**libero**	*lee-bair-oh*
free, no charge	**gratuito**	*grah-too-ee-toh*

Making a Telephone Call

I'd like to place a long-distance call.	**Vorrei fare una interurbana.**	*vor-ray far-eh oona in-tair-oor-bah-nah*
I'd like to make a reverse-charge call.	**Vorrei fare una telefonata a carico del destinatario.**	*vor-ray far-eh oona teh-leh-fon-ah-tah ah kar-ee-koh dell dess-tee-nah-tar-ree-oh*
I'll try again later.	**Ritelefono più tardi.**	*ree-teh-leh-foh-noh pee-oo tar-dee*
Can I leave a message?	**Posso lasciare un messaggio?**	*poss-oh lash-ah-reh oon mess-sah-joh?*
Hold on	**Un attimo, per favore**	*oon ah-tee-moh, pair fah-vor-eh*
Could you speak up a little please?	**Può parlare più forte, per favore?**	*pwoh par-lah-reh pee-oo for-teh, pair fah-vor-eh?*
local call	**la telefonata locale**	*lah teh-leh-fon-ah-ta loh-kah-leh*

Shopping

How much does this cost?	**Quant'è, per favore?**	*kwan-teh pair fah-vor-eh?*
I would like ...	**Vorrei ...**	*vor-ray*
Do you have ...?	**Avete ...?**	*ah-veh-teh...?*
I'm just looking.	**Sto soltanto guardando.**	*stoh sol-tan-toh gwar-dan-doh*
Do you take credit cards?	**Accettate carte di credito?**	*ah-chet-tah-teh kar-teh dee creh-dee-toh?*
What time do you open/close?	**A che ora apre/ chiude?**	*ah keh or-ah ah-preh/kee-oo-deh?*
this one	**questo**	*kweh-stoh*
that one	**quello**	*kwell-oh*
expensive	**caro**	*kar-oh*
cheap	**a buon prezzo**	*ah buon pret-soh*
size, clothes	**la taglia**	*lah tah-lee-ah*
size, shoes	**il numero**	*eel noo-mair-oh*
white	**bianco**	*bee-ang-koh*
black	**nero**	*neh-roh*
red	**rosso**	*ross-oh*
yellow	**giallo**	*jal-loh*
green	**verde**	*vair-deh*
blue	**blu**	*bloo*
brown	**marrone**	*mar-roh-neh*

Types of Shop

antique dealer	**l'antiquario**	*lan-tee-kwah-ree-oh*
bakery	**la panetteria**	*lah pah-net-tair-ree-ah*
bank	**la banca**	*lah bang-kah*
bookshop	**la libreria**	*lah lee-breh-ree-ah*
butcher's	**la macelleria**	*lah mah-chell-eh-ree-ah*
cake shop	**la pasticceria**	*lah pas-tee-chair-ee-ah*
chemist's	**la farmacia**	*lah far-mah-chee-ah*
department store	**il grande magazzino**	*eel gran-deh mag-gad-zee-noh*
delicatessen	**la salumeria**	*lah sah-loo-meh-ree-ah*
fishmonger's	**la pescheria**	*lah pess-keh-ree-ah*
florist	**il fioraio**	*eel fee-or-eye-oh*
greengrocer	**il fruttivendolo**	*eel froo-tee-ven-doh-loh*
grocery	**alimentari**	*ah-lee-men-tah-ree*
hairdresser	**il parrucchiere**	*eel par-oo-kee-air-eh*
ice cream parlour	**la gelateria**	*lah jel-lah-tair-ree-ah*
market	**il mercato**	*eel mair-kah-toh*
news-stand	**l'edicola**	*leh-dee-koh-lah*
post office	**l'ufficio postale**	*loo-fee-choh pos-tah-leh*
shoe shop	**il negozio di scarpe**	*eel neh-goh-tsioh dee skar-peh*
supermarket	**il supermercato**	*su-pair-mair-kah-toh*
tobacconist	**il tabaccaio**	*eel tah-bak-eye-oh*
travel agency	**l'agenzia di viaggi**	*lah-jen-tsee-ah dee vee-ad-jee*

Sightseeing

art gallery	**la pinacoteca**	*lah peena-koh-teh-kah*
bus stop	**la fermata dell'autobus**	*lah fair-mah-tah dell ow-toh-booss*
church	**la chiesa**	*lah kee-eh-zah*
	la basilica	*lah bah-seel-i-kah*
garden	**il giardino**	*eel jar-dee-no*
library	**la biblioteca**	*lah beeb-lee-oh-teh-kah*
museum	**il museo**	*eel moo-zeh-oh*
railway station	**la stazione**	*lah stat-see-oh-neh*
tourist information	**l'ufficio turistico**	*loo-fee-choh too-ree-stee-koh*
closed for the public holiday	**chiuso per la festa**	*kee-oo-zoh pair lah fess-tah*

STAYING IN A HOTEL

Do you have any vacant rooms?	**Avete camere libere?**	ab-veb-teh kab-mair-eh lee-bair-eh?
double room	**una camera doppia**	oona kab-mair-ab dob-pee-ah
with double bed	**con letto matrimoniale**	kon let-toh mab-tree-moh-nee-ab-leh
twin room	**una camera con due letti**	oona kab-mair-ab kon doo-eh let-tee
single room	**una camera singola**	oona kab-mair-ab sing-gob-lah
room with a bath, shower	**una camera con bagno, con doccia**	oona kab-mair-ab kon ban-yob, kon dot-chah
porter	**il facchino**	eel fab-kee-nob
key	**la chiave**	lah kee-ab-veh
I have a reservation.	**Ho fatto una prenotazione.**	oh fat-toh oona preb-nob-tah-tsee-ob-neh

EATING OUT

Have you got a table for ...?	**Avete una tavola per ... ?**	ab-veb-teh oona tab-vob-lah pair ...?
I'd like to reserve a table.	**Vorrei riservare una tavola.**	vor-ray ree-sair-vab-reb oona tab-vob-lah
breakfast	**colazione**	koh-lab-tsee-ob-neh
lunch	**pranzo**	pran-tsoh
dinner	**cena**	cheb-nab
The bill, please.	**Il conto, per favore.**	eel kon-toh pair fab-vor-eh
I am a vegetarian.	**Sono vegetariano/a.**	soh-nob veb-jeb-tar-ee-ab-nob/nah
waitress	**cameriera**	kab-mair-ee-air-ah
waiter	**cameriere**	kab-mair-ee-air-eb
fixed price menu	**il menù a prezzo fisso**	eel meb-noo ab pret-soh fee-soh
dish of the day	**piatto del giorno**	pee-ab-toh dell jor-no
starter	**antipasto**	an-tee-pass-toh
first course	**il primo**	eel pree-moh
main course	**il secondo**	eel seb-kon-dob
vegetables	**il contorno**	eel kon-tor-nob
dessert	**il dolce**	eel doll-cheb
cover charge	**il coperto**	eel kob-pair-tob
wine list	**la lista dei vini**	lah lee-stab day vee-nee
rare	**al sangue**	al sang-gweb
medium	**al puntino**	al poon-tee-nob
well done	**ben cotto**	ben kot-tob
glass	**il bicchiere**	eel bee-kee-air-eb
bottle	**la bottiglia**	lah bot-teel-yab
knife	**il coltello**	eel kol-tell-ob
fork	**la forchetta**	lah for-ket-tah
spoon	**il cucchiaio**	eel koo-kee-eye-ob

MENU DECODER

apple	**la mela**	lah meb-lah
artichoke	**il carciofo**	eel kar-choff-ob
aubergine	**la melanzana**	lah meb-lan-tsab-nah
baked	**al forno**	al for-nob
beans	**i fagioli**	ee fab-job-lee
beef	**il manzo**	eel man-tsoh
beer	**la birra**	lah beer-rab
boiled	**lesso**	less-ob
bread	**il pane**	eel pab-neh
broth	**il brodo**	eel brob-dob
butter	**il burro**	eel boor-ob
cake	**la torta**	lah tor-tab
cheese	**il formaggio**	eel for-mad-job
chicken	**il pollo**	eel poll-ob
chips	**patatine fritte**	pab-tab-teen-eb free-teh
baby clams	**le vongole**	leb von-gob-leb
coffee	**il caffè**	eel kab-feb
courgettes	**gli zucchini**	lyee dzoo-kee-nee
dry	**secco**	sek-koh
duck	**l'anatra**	lab-nab-trab
egg	**l'uovo**	loo-ob-voh
fish	**il pesce**	eel pesb-eb
fresh fruit	**frutta fresca**	froo-tah fress-kab
garlic	**l'aglio**	labl-yob
grapes	**l'uva**	loo-vah
grilled	**alla griglia**	ab-lah greel-yab
ham	**il prosciutto**	eel pro-sboo-tob
cooked/cured	**cotto/crudo**	kot-toh/kroo-dob
ice cream	**il gelato**	eel jel-lab-toh
lamb	**l'abbacchio**	lab-back-kee-ob
lobster	**l'aragosta**	lah-rah-goss-tab
meat	**la carne**	la kar-neb

milk	**il latte**	eel laht-teb
mineral water fizzy/still	**l'acqua minerale gasata/naturale**	lab-kwab mee-nair-ab-leh gab-zab-tah/nab-too-rab-leb
mushrooms	**i funghi**	ee foon-gee
oil	**l'olio**	loll-yob
olive	**l'oliva**	loh-lee-vab
onion	**la cipolla**	lah chee-poll-ab
orange	**l'arancia**	lah-ran-chab
orange/lemon juice	**succo d'arancia/ di limone**	soo-kob dab-ran-chab/dee lee-mob-neb
peach	**la pesca**	lah pess-kab
pepper	**il pepe**	eel peb-peh
pork	**carne di maiale**	kar-neb dee mah-yab-leh
potatoes	**le patate**	leb pab-tab-teb
prawns	**i gamberi**	ee gam-bair-ee
rice	**il riso**	eel ree-zoh
roast	**arrosto**	ar-ross-tob
roll	**il panino**	eel pab-nee-nob
salad	**l'insalata**	leen-sab-lab-tab
salt	**il sale**	eel sab-leb
sausage	**la salsiccia**	lah sal-see-chab
seafood	**frutti di mare**	froo-tee dee mab-reb
soup	**la zuppa,**	lah tsoo-pab,
	la minestra	lah mee-ness-trab
steak	**la bistecca**	lah bee-stek-kab
strawberries	**le fragole**	leb frab-gob-leb
sugar	**lo zucchero**	lob zoo-kair-ob
tea	**il tè**	eel teb
herb tea	**la tisana**	lah tee-zab-nab
tomato	**il pomodoro**	eel pob-mob-dor-ob
tuna	**il tonno**	ton-nob
veal	**il vitello**	vee-tell-ob
vegetables	**i legumi**	ee leb-goo-mee
vinegar	**l'aceto**	lab-cheb-tob
water	**l'acqua**	lab-kwab
red wine	**vino rosso**	vee-nob ross-ob
white wine	**vino bianco**	vee-nob bee-ang-kob

NUMBERS

1	**uno**	oo-nob
2	**due**	doo-eb
3	**tre**	treb
4	**quattro**	kwat-rob
5	**cinque**	ching-kweb
6	**sei**	say-ee
7	**sette**	set-teb
8	**otto**	ot-tob
9	**nove**	nob-veb
10	**dieci**	dee-eb-chee
11	**undici**	oon-dee-chee
12	**dodici**	dob-dee-chee
13	**tredici**	tray-dee-chee
14	**quattordici**	kwat-tor-dee-chee
15	**quindici**	kwin-dee-chee
16	**sedici**	say-dee-chee
17	**diciassette**	dee-chab-set-teb
18	**diciotto**	dee-chot-tob
19	**diciannove**	dee-chab-nob-veb
20	**venti**	ven-tee
30	**trenta**	tren-tab
40	**quaranta**	kwah-ran-tab
50	**cinquanta**	ching-kwan-tab
60	**sessanta**	sess-an-tab
70	**settanta**	set-tan-tab
80	**ottanta**	ot-tan-tab
90	**novanta**	nob-van-tab
100	**cento**	chen-tob
1,000	**mille**	mee-leb
2,000	**duemila**	doo-eb mee-lab
5,000	**cinquemila**	ching-kweb mee-lab
1,000,000	**un milione**	oon meel-yob-neb

TIME

one minute	**un minuto**	oon mee-noo-tob
one hour	**un'ora**	oon or-ab
half an hour	**mezz'ora**	medz-or-ab
a day	**un giorno**	oon jor-nob
a week	**una settimana**	oona set-tee-mab-nab
Monday	**lunedì**	loo-neb-dee
Tuesday	**martedì**	mar-teb-dee
Wednesday	**mercoledì**	mair-kob-leb-dee
Thursday	**giovedì**	job-veb-dee
Friday	**venerdì**	ven-air-dee
Saturday	**sabato**	sab-bab-tob
Sunday	**domenica**	dob-meb-nee-kab